COMPILATION OF SELECTED
WATER POLLUTION, WASTE CLEANUP, AND WATER RESOURCES LAWS

VOLUME 1 :

FEDERAL WATER POLLUTION CONTROL ACT AND THE OIL POLLUTION ACT OF 1990

As amended through the 118th Congress.

Prepared By M. TWINCHEK

2025

Forward

This Compilation of Selected United States Water Pollution, Waste Cleanup, and Water Resources Laws is a resource for those interested in U.S. laws governing the maintenance, pollution of, and cleanup of the Nation's public waters.

The materials included comes from publicly available, open source information, prepared for the public by the Office of the Legislative Counsel of the U.S. House of Representatives and the Office of the Law Revision Counsel.

Items listed as a Statute Compilation do not appear in the U.S. Code or that have been classified to a title of the U.S. Code that has not been enacted into positive law. Each Statute Compilation incorporates the amendments made to the underlying statute since it was originally enacted and are current as of the date noted.

This compilation is not an official document and should not be cited as evidence of any law. The official version of Federal law is found in the United States Statutes at Large and in the U.S. Code, the legal effect of which is established in sections 112 and 204, respectively, of title 1, United States Code.

A special thanks is extended to the Office of Law Revision Counsel and the House Office of the Legislative Counsel for providing the U.S. Code and statute compilations; and to the Government Publications Office for hosting and making these available for use to the public. An additional thank you is offered to the staff of the House and Senate Committees who were gracious in responding to inquiries and providing background information on the legislation included. Questions and comments may be directed to:

M. Twinchek

Email: mtwinchek@outlook.com

Contents

SELECTED PROVISIONS OF THE FEDERAL WATER POLLUTION CONTROL ACT

CHAPTER 758 OF THE 80TH CONGRESS
AS AMENDED THROUGH PUBLIC LAW 118198

TITLE I—RESEARCH AND RELATED PROGRAMS

FEDERAL WATER POLLUTION CONTROL ACT

[Chapter 758 of the 80th Congress]

[33 U.S.C. 1251 et seq.]

[As Amended Through P.L. 118–198, Enacted December 23, 2024]

AN ACT To provide for water pollution control activities in the Public Health Service of the Federal Security Agency and in the Federal Works Agency, and for other purposes.

Be it enacted by the Senate and House of Representatives of the United States of America in Congress assembled,

TITLE I—RESEARCH AND RELATED PROGRAMS

DECLARATION OF GOALS AND POLICY

SEC. 101. (a) The objective of this Act is to restore and maintain the chemical, physical, and biological integrity of the Nation's waters. In order to achieve this objective it is hereby declared that, consistent with the provisions of this Act—

(1) it is the national goal that the discharge of pollutants into the navigable waters be eliminated by 1985;

(2) it is the national goal that wherever attainable, an interim goal of water quality which provides for the protection and propagation of fish, shellfish, and wildlife and provides for recreation in and on the water be achieved by July 1, 1983;

(3) it is the national policy that the discharge of toxic pollutants in toxic amounts be prohibited;

(4) it is the national policy that Federal financial assistance be provided to construct publicly owned waste treatment works;

(5) it is the national policy that areawide treatment management planning processes be developed and implemented to assure adequate control of sources of pollutants in each State;

(6) it is the national policy that a major research and demonstration effort be made to develop technology necessary to eliminate the discharge of pollutants into the navigable waters, waters of the contiguous zone, and the oceans; and

(7) it is the national policy that programs for the control of nonpoint sources of pollution be developed and implemented in an expeditious manner so as to enable the goals of this Act to be met through the control of both point and nonpoint sources of pollution.

(b) It is the policy of the Congress to recognize, preserve, and protect the primary responsibilities and rights of States to prevent, reduce, and eliminate pollution, to plan the development and use (including restoration, preservation, and enhancement) of land and water resources, and to consult with the Administrator in the exercise of his authority under this Act. It is the policy of Congress that the States manage the construction grant program under this Act and implement the permit programs under sections 402 and 404 of this Act. It is further the policy of the Congress to support and aid research relating to the prevention, reduction, and elimination of pollution, and to provide Federal technical services and financial aid to State and interstate agencies and municipalities in connection with the prevention, reduction, and elimination of pollution.

(c) It is further the policy of Congress that the President, acting through the Secretary of State and such national and international organizations as he determines appropriate, shall take such action as may be necessary to insure that to the fullest extent possible all foreign countries shall take meaningful action for the prevention, reduction, and elimination of pollution in their waters and in international waters and for the achievement of goals regarding the elimination of discharge of pollutants and the improvement of water quality to at least the same extent as the United States does under its laws.

(d) Except as otherwise expressly provided in this Act, the Administrator of the Environmental Protection Agency (hereinafter in this Act called Administrator) shall administer this Act.

(e) Public participation in the development, revision, and enforcement of any regulation, standard, effluent limitation, plan, or program established by the Administrator or any State under this Act shall be provided for, encouraged, and assisted by the Administrator and the States. The Administrator, in cooperation with the States, shall develop and publish regulations specifying minimum guidelines for public participation in such processes.

(f) It is the national policy that to the maximum extent possible the procedures utilized for implementing this Act shall encourage the drastic minimization of paperwork and interagency decision procedures, and the best use of available manpower and funds, so as to prevent needless duplication and unnecessary delays at all levels of government.

(g) It is the policy of Congress that the authority of each State to allocate quantities of water within its jurisdiction shall not be superseded, abrogated or otherwise impaired by this Act. It is the further policy of Congress that nothing in this Act shall be construed to supersede or abrogate rights to quantities of water which have been established by any State. Federal agencies shall co-operate with State and local agencies to develop comprehensive solutions to prevent, reduce and eliminate pollution in concert with programs for managing water resources.

[33 U.S.C. 1251]

COMPREHENSIVE PROGRAMS FOR WATER POLLUTION CONTROL

SEC. 102. (a) The Administrator shall, after careful investigation, and in cooperation with other Federal agencies, State water pollution control agencies, interstate agencies, and the municipalities and industries involved, prepare or develop comprehensive programs for preventing, reducing, or eliminating the pollution of the navigable waters and ground waters and improving the sanitary condition of surface and underground waters. In the development of such comprehensive programs due regard shall be given to the improvements which are necessary to conserve such waters for the protection and propagation of fish and aquatic life and wildlife, recreational purposes, and the withdrawal of such waters for public water supply, agricultural, industrial, and other purposes. For the purpose of this section, the Administrator is authorized to make joint investigations with any such agencies of the condition of any waters in any State or States, and of the discharges of any sewage, industrial wastes, or substance which may adversely affect such waters.

(b)(1) In the survey or planning of any reservoir by the Corps of Engineers, Bureau of Reclamation, or other Federal agency, consideration shall be given to inclusion of storage for regulation of streamflow, except that any such storage and water releases shall not be provided as a substitute for adequate treatment or other methods of controlling waste at the source.

(2) The need for and the value of storage for regulation of streamflow (other than for water quality) including but not limited to navigation, salt water intrusion, recreation, esthetics, and fish and wildlife, shall be determined by the Corps of Engineers, Bureau of Reclamation, or other Federal agencies.

(3) The need for, the value of, and the impact of, storage for water quality control shall be determined by the Administrator, and his views on these matters shall be set forth in any report or presentation to Congress proposing authorization or construction of any reservoir including such storage.

(4) The value of such storage shall be taken into account in determining the economic value of the entire project of which it is a part, and costs shall be allocated to the purpose of regulation of streamflow in a manner which will insure that all project purposes, share equitably in the benefits of multiple-purpose construction.

(5) Costs of regulation of streamflow features incorporated in any Federal reservoir or other impoundment under the provisions of this Act shall be determined and the beneficiaries identified and if the benefits are widespread or national in scope, the costs of such features shall be nonreimbursable.

(6) No license granted by the Federal Power Commission for a hydroelectric power project shall include storage for regulation of streamflow for the purpose of water quality control unless the Administrator shall recommend its inclusion and such reservoir storage capacity shall not exceed such proportion of the total storage required for the water quality control plan as the drainage area of such reservoir bears to the drainage area of the river basin or basins involved in such water quality control plan.

(c)(1) The Administrator shall, at the request of the Governor of a State, or a majority of the Governors when more than one State is involved, make a grant to pay not to exceed 50 per centum of the administrative expenses of a planning agency for a period not to exceed three years, which period shall begin after the date of enactment of the Federal Water Pollution Control Act Amendments of 1972, if such agency provides for adequate representation of appropriate State, interstate, local, or (when appropriate) international interests in the basin or portion thereof involved and is capable of developing an effective, comprehensive water quality control plan for a basin or portion thereof.

(2) Each planning agency receiving a grant under this subsection shall develop a comprehensive pollution control plan for the basin or portion thereof which—

(A) is consistent with any applicable water quality standards, effluent and other limitations, and thermal discharge regulations established pursuant to current law within the basin;

(B) recommends such treatment works as will provide the most effective and economical means of collection, storage, treatment, and elimination of pollutants and recommends means to encourage both municipal and industrial use of such works;

(C) recommends maintenance and improvement of water quality within the basin or portion thereof and recommends methods of adequately financing those facilities as may be necessary to implement the plan; and

(D) as appropriate, is developed in cooperation with, and is consistent with any comprehensive plan prepared by the Water Resources Council, any areawide waste management plans developed pursuant to section 208 of this Act, and any State plan developed pursuant to section 303(e) of this Act.

(3) For the purposes of this subsection the term basin includes, but is not limited to, rivers and their tributaries, streams, coastal waters, sounds, estuaries, bays, lakes, and portions thereof, as well as the lands drained thereby.

(d) [Repealed by section 2021(a) of Public Law 104–66 (109 Stat. 726).]

[33 U.S.C. 1252]

INTERSTATE COOPERATION AND UNIFORM LAWS

SEC. 103. (a) The Administrator shall encourage cooperative activities by the States for the prevention, reduction, and elimination of pollution, encourage the enactment of improved and, so far as practicable, uniform State laws relating to the prevention, reduction, and elimination of pollution; and encourage compacts between States for the prevention and control of pollution.

(b) The consent of the Congress is hereby given to two or more States to negotiate and enter into agreements or compacts, not in conflict with any law or treaty of the United States, for (1) cooperative effort and mutual assistance for the prevention and control of pollution and the enforcement of their respective laws relating thereto, and (2) the establishment of such agencies, joint or otherwise, as they may deem desirable for making effective such agreements and compacts. No such agreement or compact shall be binding or obligatory upon any State a party thereto unless and until it has been approved by the Congress.

[33 U.S.C. 1253]

RESEARCH, INVESTIGATIONS, TRAINING, AND INFORMATION

Sec. 104. (a) The Administrator shall establish national programs for the prevention, reduction, and elimination of pollution and as part of such programs shall—

(1) in cooperation with other Federal, State, and local agencies, conduct and promote the coordination and acceleration of, research, investigations, experiments, training, demonstrations, surveys, and studies relating to the causes, effects, extent, prevention, reduction, and elimination of pollution;

(2) encourage, cooperate with, and render technical services to pollution control agencies and other appropriate public or private agencies, institutions, and organizations, and individuals, including the general public, in the conduct of activities referred to in paragraph (1) of this subsection;

(3) conduct, in cooperation with State water pollution control agencies and other interested agencies, organizations and persons, public investigations concerning the pollution of any navigable waters, and report on the results of such investigations;

(4) establish advisory committees composed of recognized experts in various aspects of pollution and representatives of the public to assist in the examination and evaluation of research progress and proposals and to avoid duplication of research;

(5) in cooperation with the States, and their political subdivisions, and other Federal agencies establish, equip, and maintain a water quality surveillance system for the purpose of monitoring the quality of the navigable waters and ground waters and the contiguous zone and the oceans and the Administrator shall, to the extent practicable, conduct such surveillance by utilizing the resources of the National Aeronautics and Space Administration, the National Oceanic and Atmospheric Administration, the Geological Survey, and the Coast Guard, and shall report on such quality in the report required under subsection (a) of section 516; and

(6) initiate and promote the coordination and acceleration of research designed to develop the most effective practicable tools and techniques for measuring the social and economic costs and benefits of activities which are subject to regulations under this Act; and shall transmit a report on the results of such research to the Congress not later than January 1, 1974.

(b) In carrying out the provisions of subsection (a) of this section the Administrator is authorized to—

(1) collect and make available, through publications and other appropriate means, the results of and other information, including appropriate recommendations by him in connection therewith, pertaining to such research and other activities referred to in paragraph (1) of subsection (a);

(2) cooperate with other Federal departments and agencies, State water pollution control agencies, interstate agencies, other public and private agencies, institutions, organizations, industries involved, and individuals, in the preparation and conduct of such research and other activities referred to in paragraph (1) of subsection (a);

(3) make grants to State water pollution control agencies, interstate agencies, other public or nonprofit private agencies, institutions, organizations, and individuals, for purposes stated in paragraph (1) of subsection (a) of this section;

(4) contract with public or private agencies, institutions, organizations, and individuals, without regard to sections 3648 and 3709 of the Revised Statutes (31 U.S.C. 529; 41 U.S.C. 5), referred to in paragraph (1) of subsection (a);

(5) establish and maintain research fellowships at public or nonprofit private educational institutions or research organizations;

(6) collect and disseminate, in cooperation with other Federal departments and agencies, and with other public or private agencies, institutions, and organizations having related responsibilities, basic data on chemical, physical, and biological effects of varying water quality and other information pertaining to pollution and the prevention, reduction, and elimination thereof;

(7) develop effective and practical processes, methods, and prototype devices for the prevention, reduction, and elimination of pollution; and

(8) make grants to nonprofit organizations—

(A) to provide technical assistance to rural, small, and tribal municipalities for the purpose of assisting, in consultation with the State in which the assistance is provided, such municipalities and tribal governments in the planning, developing, and acquisition of financing for eligible projects and activities described in section 603(c);

(B) to provide technical assistance and training for rural, small, and tribal publicly owned treatment works and decentralized wastewater treatment systems to enable such treatment works and systems to protect water quality and achieve and maintain compliance with the requirements of this Act; and

(C) to disseminate information to rural, small, and tribal municipalities and municipalities that meet the affordability criteria established under section 603(i)(2) by the State in which the municipality is located with respect to planning, design, construction, and operation of publicly owned treatment works and decentralized wastewater treatment systems.

(c) In carrying out the provisions of subsection (a) of this section the Administrator shall conduct research on, and survey the results of other scientific studies on, the harmful effects on the health or welfare of persons caused by pollutants. In order to avoid duplication of effort, the Administrator shall, to the extent practicable, conduct such research in cooperation with and through the facilities of the Secretary of Health, Education, and Welfare.

(d) In carrying out the provisions of this section the Administrator shall develop and demonstrate under varied conditions (including conducting such basic and applied research, studies, and experiments as may be necessary):

(1) Practicable means of treating municipal sewage, and other waterborne wastes to implement the requirements of section 201 of this Act;

(2) Improved methods and procedures to identify and measure the effects of pollutants, including those pollutants created by new technological developments; and

(3) Methods and procedures for evaluating the effects on water quality of augmented streamflows to control pollution not susceptible to other means of

prevention, reduction, or elimination.

(e) The Administrator shall establish, equip, and maintain field laboratory and research facilities, including, but not limited to, one to be located in the northeastern area of the United States, one in the Middle Atlantic area, one in the southeastern area, one in the midwestern area, one in the southwestern area, one in the Pacific Northwest, and one in the State of Alaska, for the conduct of research, investigations, experiments, field demonstrations and studies, and training relating to the prevention, reduction and elimination of pollution. Insofar as practicable, each such facility shall be located near institutions of higher learning in which graduate training in such research might be carried out. In conjunction with the development of criteria under section 403 of this Act, the Administrator shall construct the facilities authorized for the National Marine Water Quality Laboratory established under this subsection.

(f) The Administrator shall conduct research and technical development work, and make studies, with respect to the quality of the waters of the Great Lakes, including an analysis of the present and projected future water quality of the Great Lakes under varying conditions of waste treatment and disposal, an evaluation of the water quality needs of those to be served by such waters, an evaluation of municipal, industrial, and vessel waste treatment and disposal practices with respect to such waters, and a study of alternate means of solving pollution problems (including additional waste treatment measures) with respect to such waters.

(g)(1) For the purpose of providing an adequate supply of trained personnel to operate and maintain existing and future treatment works and related activities, and for the purpose of enhancing substantially the proficiency of those engaged in such activities, the Administrator shall finance pilot programs, in cooperation with State and interstate agencies, municipalities, educational institutions, and other organizations and individuals, of manpower development and training and retraining of persons in, on entering into, the field of operation and maintenance of treatment works and related activities. Such program and any funds expended for such a program shall supplement, not supplant, other manpower and training programs and funds available for the purposes of this paragraph. The Administrator is authorized, under such terms and conditions as he deems appropriate, to enter into agreements with one or more States, acting jointly or severally, or with other public or private agencies or institutions for the development and implementation of such a program.

(2) The Administrator is authorized to enter into agreements with public and private agencies and institutions, and individuals to develop and maintain an effective system for forecasting the supply of, and demand for, various professional and other occupational categories needed for the prevention, reduction, and elimination of pollution in each region, State, or area of the United States and, from time to time, to publish the results of such forecasts.

(3) In furtherance of the purposes of this Act, the Administrator is authorized to—

(A) make grants to public or private agencies and institutions and to individuals for training projects, and provide for the conduct of training by contract with public or private agencies and institutions and with individuals without regard to sections 3648 and 3709 of the Revised Statutes;

(B) establish and maintain research fellowships in the Environmental

Protection Agency with such stipends and allowances, including traveling and subsistence expenses, as he may deem necessary to procure the assistance of the most promising research fellows; and

(C) provide, in addition to the program established under paragraph (1) of this subsection, training in technical matters relating to the causes, prevention, reduction, and elimination of pollution for personnel of public agencies and other persons with suitable qualifications.

(4) The Administrator shall submit, through the President, a report to the Congress not later than December 31, 1973, summarizing the actions taken under this subsection and the effectiveness of such actions, and setting forth the number of persons trained, the occupational categories for which training was provided, the effectiveness of other Federal, State, and local training programs in this field, together with estimates of future needs, recommendations on improving training programs, and such other information and recommendations, including legislative recommendations, as he deems appropriate.

(h) The Administrator is authorized to enter into contracts, with, or make grants to, public or private agencies and organizations and individuals for (A) the purpose of developing and demonstrating new or improved methods for the prevention, removal, reduction, and elimination of pollution in lakes, including the undesirable effects of nutrients and vegetation, and (B) the construction of publicly owned research facilities for such purpose.

(i) The Administrator, in cooperation with the Secretary of the department in which the Coast Guard is operating, shall—

(1) engage in such research, studies, experiments, and demonstrations as he deems appropriate, relative to the removal of oil from any waters and to the prevention, control, and elimination of oil and hazardous substances pollution;

(2) publish from time to time the results of such activities; and

(3) from time to time, develop and publish in the Federal Register specifications and other technical information on the various chemical compounds used in the control of oil and hazardous substances spills.

In carrying out this subsection, the Administrator may enter into contracts with, or make grants to, public or private agencies and organizations and individuals.

(j) The Secretary of the department in which the Coast Guard is operating shall engage in such research, studies, experiments, and demonstrations as he deems appropriate relative to equipment which is to be installed on board a vessel and is designed to receive, retain, treat, or discharge human body wastes and the wastes from toilets and other receptacles intended to receive or retain body wastes with particular emphasis on equipment to be installed on small recreational vessels. The Secretary of the department in which the Coast Guard is operating shall report to Congress the results of such research, studies, experiments, and demonstrations prior to the effective date of any regulations established under section 312 of this Act. In carrying out this subsection the Secretary of the department in which the Coast Guard is operating may enter into contracts with, or make grants to, public or private organizations and individuals.

(k) In carrying out the provisions of this section relating to the conduct by the Administrator of demonstration projects and the development of field laboratories and research facilities, the Administrator may acquire land and interests therein by purchase, with appropriated or donated funds, by donation, or by exchange for acquired or public lands under his jurisdiction which he classifies as suitable for disposition. The values of the properties so exchanged either shall be approximately equal, or if they are not approximately equal, the values shall be equalized by the payment of cash to the grantor or to the Administrator as the circumstances require.

(l)(1) The Administrator shall, after consultation with appropriate local, State, and Federal agencies, public and private organizations, and interested individuals, as soon as practicable but not later than January 1, 1973, develop and issue to the States for the purpose of carrying out this Act the latest scientific knowledge available in indicating the kind and extent of effects on health and welfare which may be expected from the presence of pesticides in the water in varying quantities. He shall revise and add to such information whenever necessary to reflect developing scientific knowledge.

(2) The President shall, in consultation with appropriate local, State, and Federal agencies, public and private organizations, and interested individuals, conduct studies and investigations of methods to control the release of pesticides into the environment which study shall include examination of the persistency of pesticides in the water environment and alternatives thereto. The President shall submit reports, from time to time, on such investigations to Congress together with his recommendations for any necessary legislation.

(m)(1) The Administrator shall, in an effort to prevent degradation of the environment from the disposal of waste oil, conduct a study of (A) the generation of used engine, machine, cooling, and similar waste oil, including quantities generated, the nature and quality of such oil, present collecting methods and disposal practices, and alternate uses of such oil; (B) the long-term, chronic biological effects of the disposal of such waste oil; and (C) the potential market for such oils, including the economic and legal factors relating to the sale of products made from such oils, the level of subsidy, if any, needed to encourage the purchase by public and private nonprofit agencies of products from such oil, and the practicability of Federal procurement, on a priority basis, of products made from such oil. In conducting such study, the Administrator shall consult with affected industries and other persons.

(2) The Administrator shall report the preliminary results of such study to Congress within six months after the date of enactment of the Federal Water Pollution Control Act Amendments of 1972, and shall submit a final report to Congress within 18 months after such date of enactment.

(n)(1) The Administrator shall, in cooperation with the Secretary of the Army, the Secretary of Agriculture, the Water Resources Council, and with other appropriate Federal, State, interstate, or local public bodies and private organizations, institutions, and individuals, conduct and promote, encourage contributions to, continuing comprehensive studies of the effects of pollution, including sedimentation, in the estuaries and estuarine zones of the United States on fish and wildlife, on sport and commercial fishing, on recreation, on water supply and water power, and on other beneficial purposes. Such studies shall also consider the effect of demographic trends, the exploitation of mineral resources and fossil fuels, land and industrial development, navigation, flood and erosion control, and other uses of estuaries and estuarine zones upon the pollution of the waters therein.

(2) In conducting such studies, the Administrator shall assemble, coordinate, and organize all existing pertinent information on the Nation's estuaries and estuarine zones; carry out a program of investigations and surveys to supplement existing information in representative estuaries and estuarine zones; and identify the problems and areas where further research and study are required.

(3) The Administrator shall submit to Congress, from time to time, reports of the studies authorized by this subsection but at least one such report during any six-year period. Copies of each such report shall be made available to all interested parties, public and private.

(4) For the purpose of this subsection, the term estuarine zones means an environmental system consisting of an estuary and those transitional areas which are consistently influenced or affected by water from an estuary such as, but not limited to, salt marshes, coastal and intertidal areas, bays, harbors, lagoons, inshore waters, and channels, and the term estuary means all or part of the mouth of a river or stream or other body of water having unimpaired natural connection with open sea and within which the sea water is measurably diluted with fresh water derived from land drainage.

(o)(1) The Administrator shall conduct research and investigations on devices, systems, incentives, pricing policy, and other methods of reducing the total flow of sewage, including, but not limited to, unnecessary water consumption in order to reduce the requirements for, and the costs of, sewage and waste treatment services. Such research and investigations shall be directed to develop devices, systems, policies, and methods capable of achieving the maximum reduction of unnecessary water consumption.

(2) The Administrator shall report the preliminary results of such studies and investigations to the Congress within one year after the date of enactment of the Federal Water Pollution Control Act Amendments of 1972, and annually thereafter in the report required under subsection (a) of section 516. Such report shall include recommendations for any legislation that may be required to provide for the adoption and use of devices, systems, policies, or other methods of reducing water consumption and reducing the total flow of sewage. Such report shall include an estimate of the benefits to be derived from adoption and use of such devices, systems, policies, or other methods and also shall reflect estimates of any increase in private, public, or other cost that would be occasioned thereby.

(p) In carrying out the provisions of subsection (a) of this section the Administrator shall, in cooperation with the Secretary of Agriculture, other Federal agencies, and the States, carry out a comprehensive study and research program to determine new and improved methods and the better application of existing methods of preventing, reducing, and eliminating pollution from agriculture, including the legal, economic, and other implications of the use of such methods.

(q)(1) The Administrator shall conduct a comprehensive program of research and investigation and pilot project implementation into new and improved methods of preventing, reducing, storing, collecting, treating, or otherwise eliminating pollution from sewage in rural and other areas where collection of sewage in conventional, community-wide sewage collection systems is impractical, uneconomical, or otherwise infeasible, or where soil conditions or other factors preclude the use of septic tank and drainage field systems.

(2) The Administrator shall conduct a comprehensive program of research and investigation and pilot project implementation into new and improved methods for the collection and treatment of sewage and other liquid wastes combined with the treatment and disposal of solid wastes.

(3) The Administrator shall establish, either within the Environmental Protection Agency, or through contract with an appropriate public or private non-profit organization, a national clearinghouse which shall (A) receive reports and information resulting from research, demonstrations, and other projects funded under this Act related to paragraph (1) of this subsection and to subsection (e)(2) of section 105; (B) coordinate and disseminate such reports and information for use by Federal and State agencies, municipalities, institutions, and persons in developing new and improved methods pursuant to this subsection; and (C) provide for the collection and dissemination of reports and information relevant to this subsection from other Federal and State agencies, institutions, universities, and persons.

(4) SMALL FLOWS CLEARINGHOUSE.— Notwithstanding section 205(d) of this Act, from amounts that are set aside for a fiscal year under section 205(i) of this Act and are not obligated by the end of the 24-month period of availability for such amounts under section 205(d), the Administrator shall make available $1,000,000 or such unobligated amount, whichever is less, to support a national clearinghouse within the Environmental Protection Agency to collect and disseminate information on small flows of sewage and innovative or alternative wastewater treatment processes and techniques, consistent with paragraph (3). This paragraph shall apply with respect to amounts set aside under section 205(i) for which the 24-month period of availability referred to in the preceding sentence ends on or after September 30, 1986.

(r) The Administrator is authorized to make grants to colleges and universities to conduct basic research into the structure and function of fresh water aquatic ecosystems, and to improve understanding of the ecological characteristics necessary to the maintenance of the chemical, physical, and biological integrity of freshwater aquatic ecosystems.

(s) The Administrator is authorized to make grants to one or more institutions of higher education (regionally located and to be designated as River Study Centers) for the purpose of conducting and reporting on interdisciplinary studies on the nature of river systems, including hydrology, biology, ecology, economics, the relationship between river uses and land uses, and the effects of development within river basins on river systems and on the value of water resources and water related activities. No such grant in any fiscal year shall exceed $1,000,000.

(t) The Administrator shall, in cooperation with State and Federal agencies and public and private organizations, conduct continuing comprehensive studies of the effects and methods of control of thermal discharges. In evaluating alternative methods of control the studies shall consider (1) such data as are available on the latest available technology, economic feasibility including cost-effectiveness analysis, and (2) the total impact on the environment, considering not only water quality but also air quality, land use, and effective utilization and conservation of fresh water and other natural resources. Such studies shall consider methods of minimizing adverse effects and maximizing beneficial effects of thermal discharges. The results of these studies shall be reported by the Administrator as soon as practicable, but not later than 270 days after enactment of this subsection, and shall be made available to the public and the States, and considered as they become available by the Administrator in carrying out section 316 of this Act and by the State in proposing thermal water quality standards.

(u) There is authorized to be appropriated (1) not to exceed $100,000,000 per fiscal year for the fiscal year ending June 30, 1973, the fiscal year ending June 30, 1974, and the fiscal year ending June 30, 1975, not to exceed $14,039,000 for the fiscal year ending September 30, 1980, not to exceed $20,697,000 for the fiscal year ending September 30, 1981, not to exceed $22,770,000 for the fiscal year ending September 30, 1982, such sums as may be necessary for fiscal years 1983 through 1985, and not to exceed $22,770,000 per fiscal year for each of the fiscal years 1986 through 1990, for carrying out the provisions of this section, other than subsections (g)(1) and (2), (p), (r), and (t), except that such authorizations are not for any research, development, or demonstration activity pursuant to such provisions; (2) not to exceed $7,500,000 for fiscal years 1973, 1974, and 1975, $2,000,000 for fiscal year 1977, $3,000,000 for fiscal year 1978, $3,000,000 for fiscal year 1979, $3,000,000 for fiscal year 1980, $3,000,000 for fiscal year 1981, $3,000,000 for fiscal year 1982, such sums as may be necessary for fiscal years 1983 through 1985, and $3,000,000 per fiscal year for each of the fiscal years 1986 through 1990, for carrying out the provisions of subsection (g)(1); (3) not to exceed $2,500,000 for fiscal years 1973, 1974, and 1975, $1,000,000 for fiscal year 1977, $1,500,000 for fiscal year 1978, $1,500,000 for fiscal year 1979, $1,500,000 for fiscal year 1980, $1,500,000 for fiscal year 1981, $1,500,000 for fiscal year 1982, such sums as may be necessary for fiscal years 1983 through 1985, and $1,500,000 per fiscal year for each of the fiscal years 1986 through 1990, for carrying out the provisions of subsection (g)(2); (4) not to exceed $10,000,000 for each of the fiscal years ending June 30, 1973, June 30, 1974, and June 30, 1975, for carrying out the provisions of subsection (p); (5) not to exceed $15,000,000 per fiscal year for the fiscal years ending June 30, 1973, June 30, 1974, and June 30, 1975, for carrying out the provisions of subsection (r); (6) not to exceed $10,000,000 per fiscal year for the fiscal years ending June 30, 1973, June 30, 1974, and June 30, 1975, for carrying out the provisions of subsection (t); (7) not to exceed $25,000,000 for each of fiscal years 2019 through 2021 for carrying out subsections (b)(3), (b)(8), and (g); and (8) not to exceed $75,000,000 for each of fiscal years 2022 through 2026 for carrying out subsections (b)(3), (b)(8), and (g), of which not less than $50,000,000 each fiscal year shall be used to carry out subsection (b)(8).

(v) Studies Concerning Pathogen Indicators in Coastal Recreation Waters.—Not later than 18 months after the date of the enactment of this subsection, after consultation and in cooperation with appropriate Federal, State, tribal, and local officials (including local health officials), the Administrator shall initiate, and, not later than 3 years after the date of the enactment of this subsection, shall complete, in cooperation with the heads of other Federal agencies, studies to provide additional information for use in developing—

(1) an assessment of potential human health risks resulting from exposure to pathogens in coastal recreation waters, including nongastrointestinal effects;

(2) appropriate and effective indicators for improving detection in a timely manner in coastal recreation waters of the presence of pathogens that are harmful to

human health;

(3) appropriate, accurate, expeditious, and cost-effective methods (including predictive models) for detecting in a timely manner in coastal recreation waters the presence of pathogens that are harmful to human health; and

(4) guidance for State application of the criteria for pathogens and pathogen indicators to be published under section 304(a)(9) to account for the diversity of geographic and aquatic conditions.

(w) Nonprofit Organization.— For purposes of subsection (b)(8), the term nonprofit organization means a nonprofit organization that the Administrator determines, after consultation with the States regarding what small publicly owned treatment works in the State find to be most beneficial and effective, is qualified and experienced in providing on-site training and technical assistance to small publicly owned treatment works.

[33 U.S.C. 1254]

GRANTS FOR RESEARCH AND DEVELOPMENT

Sec. 105. (a) The Administrator is authorized to conduct in the Environmental Protection Agency, and to make grants to any State, municipality, or intermunicipal or interstate agency for the purpose of assisting in the development of—

(1) any project which will demonstrate a new or improved method of preventing, reducing, and eliminating the discharge into any waters of pollutants from sewers which carry storm water or both storm water and pollutants; or

(2) any project which will demonstrate advanced waste treatment and water purification methods (including the temporary use of new or improved chemical additives which provide substantial immediate improvement to existing treatment processes), or new or improved methods of joint treatment systems for municipal and industrial wastes;

and to include in such grants such amounts as are necessary for the purpose of reports, plans, and specifications in connection therewith.

(b) The Administrator is authorized to make grants to any State or States or interstate agency to demonstrate, in river basins or portions thereof, advanced treatment and environmental enhancement techniques to control pollution from all sources, within such basins or portions thereof, including nonpoint sources, together with in stream water quality improvement techniques.

(c) In order to carry out the purposes of section 301 of this Act, the Administrator is authorized to (1) conduct in the Environmental Protection Agency, (2) make grants to persons, and (3) enter into contracts with persons, for research and demonstration projects for prevention of pollution of any waters by industry including, but not limited to, the prevention, reduction, and elimination of the discharge of pollutants. No grant shall be made for any project under this subsection unless the Administrator determines that such project will develop or demonstrate a new or improved method of treating industrial wastes or otherwise prevent pollution by industry, which method shall have industrywide application.

(d) In carrying out the provisions of this section, the Administrator shall conduct, on a priority basis, an accelerated effort to develop, refine, and achieve practical application of:

(1) waste management methods applicable to point and nonpoint sources of pollutants to eliminate the discharge of pollutants, including, but not limited to, elimination of runoff of pollutants and the effects of pollutants from inplace or accumulated sources;

(2) advanced waste treatment methods applicable to point and nonpoint sources, including inplace or accumulated sources of pollutants, and methods for reclaiming and recycling water and confining pollutants so they will not migrate to cause water or other environmental pollution; and

(3) improved methods and procedures to identify and measure the effects of pollutants on the chemical, physical, and biological integrity of water, including those pollutants created by new technological developments.

(e)(1) The Administrator is authorized to (A) make, in consultation with the Secretary of Agriculture, grants to persons for research and demonstration projects with respect to new and improved methods of preventing, reducing, and eliminating pollution from agriculture, and (B) disseminate, in cooperation with the Secretary of Agriculture, such information obtained under this subsection, section 104(p), and section 304 as will encourage and enable the adoption of such methods in the agricultural industry.

(2) The Administrator is authorized, (A) in consultation with other interested Federal agencies, to make grants for demonstration projects with respect to new and improved methods of preventing, reducing, storing, collecting, treating, or otherwise eliminating pollution from sewage in rural and other areas where collection of sewage in conventional, community-wide sewage collection systems is impractical, uneconomical, or otherwise infeasible, or where soil conditions or other factors preclude the use of septic tank and drainage field systems, and (B) in cooperation with other interested Federal and State agencies, to disseminate such information obtained under this subsection as will encourage and enable the adoption of new and improved methods developed pursuant to this subsection.

(f) Federal grants under subsection (a) of this section shall be subject to the following limitations:

(1) No grant shall be made for any project unless such project shall have been approved by the appropriate State water pollution control agency or agencies and by the Administrator;

(2) No grant shall be made for any project in an amount exceeding 75 per centum of cost thereof as determined by the Administrator; and

(3) No grant shall be made for any project unless the Administrator determines that such project will serve as a useful demonstration for the purpose set forth in clause (1) or (2) of subsection (a).

(g) Federal grants under subsections (c) and (d) of this section shall not exceed 75 per centum of the cost of the project.

(h) For the purpose of this section there is authorized to be appropriated $75,000,000 per fiscal year for the fiscal year ending June 30, 1973, the fiscal year ending June 30, 1974, and the fiscal year ending June 30, 1975, and from such appropriations at least 10 per centum of the funds actually appropriated in each fiscal year shall be available only for the purposes of subsection (e).

(i) The Administrator is authorized to make grants to a municipality to assist in the costs of operating and maintaining a project which received a grant under this section, section 104, or section 113 of this Act prior to the date of enactment of this subsection so as to reduce the operation and maintenance costs borne by the recipients of services from such project to costs comparable to those for projects assisted under title II of this Act.

(j) The Administrator is authorized to make a grant to any grantee who received an increased grant pursuant to section 202(a)(2) of this Act. Such grant may pay up to 100 per centum of the costs of technical evaluation of the operation of the treatment works, costs of training of persons (other than employees of the grantee), and costs of disseminating technical information on the operation of the treatment works.

[33 U.S.C. 1255]

GRANTS FOR POLLUTION CONTROL PROGRAMS

SEC. 106. (a) There are hereby authorized to be appropriated the following sums, to remain available until expended, to carry out the purposes of this section—

(1) $60,000,000 for the fiscal year ending June 30, 1973; and

(2) $75,000,000 for the fiscal year ending June 30, 1974, and the fiscal year ending June 30, 1975, $100,000,000 per fiscal year for the fiscal years 1977, 1978, 1979, and 1980, $75,000,000 per fiscal year for the fiscal years 1981 and 1982, such sums as may be necessary for fiscal years 1983 through 1985, and $75,000,000 per fiscal year for each of the fiscal years 1986 through 1990;

for grants to States and to interstate agencies to assist them in administering programs for the prevention, reduction, and elimination of pollution, including enforcement directly or through appropriate State law enforcement officers or agencies.

(b) From the sums appropriated in any fiscal year, the Administrator shall make allotments to the several States and interstate agencies in accordance with regulations promulgated by him on the basis of the extent of the pollution problem in the respective States.

(c) The Administrator is authorized to pay to each State and interstate agency each fiscal year either—

(1) the allotment of such State or agency for such fiscal year under subsection (b), or

(2) the reasonable costs as determined by the Administrator of developing and carrying out a pollution program by such State or agency during such fiscal year,

which ever amount is the lesser.

(d) No grant shall be made under this section to any State or interstate agency for any fiscal year when the expenditure of non-Federal funds by such State or interstate agency during such fiscal year for the recurrent expenses of carrying out its pollution control program are less than the expenditure by such State or interstate agency of non-Federal funds for such recurrent program expenses during the fiscal year ending June 30, 1971.

(e) Beginning in fiscal year 1974 the Administrator shall not make any grant under this section to any State which has not provided or is not carrying out as a part of its program—

(1) the establishment and operation of appropriate devices, methods, systems, and procedures necessary to monitor, and to compile and analyze data on (including classification according to eutrophic condition), the quality of navigable waters and to the extent practicable, ground waters including biological monitoring; and provision for annually updating such data and including it in the report required under section 305 of this Act;

(2) authority comparable to that in section 504 of this Act and adequate contingency plans to implement such authority.

(f) Grants shall be made under this section on condition that—

(1) Such State (or interstate agency) filed with the Administrator within one hundred and twenty days after the date of enactment of this section:

(A) a summary report of the current status of the State pollution control program, including the criteria used by the State in determining priority of treatment works; and

(B) such additional information, data, and reports as the Administrator may require.

(2) No federally assumed enforcement as defined in section 309(a)(2) is in effect with respect to such State or interstate agency.

(3) Such State (or interstate agency) submits within one hundred and twenty days after the date of enactment of this section and before October 1 of each year thereafter for the Administrator's approval of its program for the prevention, reduction, and elimination of pollution in accordance with purposes and provisions of this Act in such form and content as the Administrator may prescribe.

(g) Any sums allotted under subsection (b) in any fiscal year which are not paid shall be reallotted by the Administrator in accordance with regulations promulgated by him.

[33 U.S.C. 1256]

MINE WATER POLLUTION CONTROL DEMONSTRATIONS

SEC. 107. (a) The Administrator in cooperation with the Appalachian Regional Commission and other Federal agencies is authorized to conduct, to make grants for, or to contract for, projects to demonstrate comprehensive approaches to the elimination or control of acid or other mine water pollution resulting from active or abandoned mining operations and other environmental pollution affecting water quality within all or part of a watershed or river basin, including siltation from surface mining. Such projects shall demonstrate the engineering and economic feasibility and practicality of various abatement techniques which will contribute substantially to effective and practical methods of acid or other mine water pollution elimination or control, and other pollution affecting water quality, including techniques that demonstrate the engineering and economic feasibility and practicality of using sewage sludge materials and other municipal wastes to diminish or prevent pollution affecting water quality from acid, sedimentation, or other pollutants and in such projects to restore affected lands to usefulness for forestry, agriculture, recreation, or other beneficial purposes.

(b) Prior to undertaking any demonstration project under this section in the Appalachian region (as defined in section 403 of the Appalachian Regional Development Act of 1965, as amended), the Appalachian Regional Commission shall determine that such demonstration project is consistent with the objectives of the Appalachian Regional Development Act of 1965, as amended.

(c) The Administrator, in selecting watersheds for the purposes of this section, shall be satisfied that the project area will not be affected adversely by the influx of acid or other mine water pollution from nearby sources.

(d) Federal participation in such projects shall be subject to the conditions—

(1) that the State shall acquire any land or interests therein necessary for such project; and

(2) that the State shall provide legal and practical protection to the project area to insure against any activities which will cause future acid or other mine water pollution.

(e) There is authorized to be appropriated $30,000,000 to carry out the provisions of this section, which sum shall be available until expended.

[33 U.S.C. 1257]

POLLUTION CONTROL IN GREAT LAKES

Sec. 108. (a) The Administrator, in cooperation with other Federal departments, agencies, and instrumentalities is authorized to enter into agreements with any State, political subdivision, interstate agency, or other public agency, or combination thereof, to carry out one or more projects to demonstrate new methods and techniques and to develop preliminary plans for the elimination or control of pollution, within all or any part of the watersheds of the Great Lakes. Such projects shall demonstrate the engineering and economic feasibility and practicality of removal of pollutants and prevention of any polluting matter from entering into the Great Lakes in the future and other reduction and remedial techniques which will contribute substantially to effective and practical methods of pollution prevention, reduction, or elimination.

(b) Federal participation in such projects shall be subject to the condition that the State, political subdivision, interstate agency, or other public agency, or combination thereof, shall pay not less than 25 per centum of the actual project costs, which payment may be in any form, including, but not limited to, land or interests therein that is needed for the project, and personal property or services the value of which shall be determined by the Administrator.

(c) There is authorized to be appropriated $20,000,000 to carry out the provisions of subsections (a) and (b) of this section, which sum shall be available until expended.

(d)(1) In recognition of the serious conditions which exist in Lake Erie, the Secretary of the Army, acting through the Chief of Engineers, is directed to design and develop a demonstration waste water management program for the rehabilitation and environmental repair of Lake Erie. Prior to the initiation of detailed engineering and design, the program, along with the specific recommendations of the Chief of Engineers and recommendations for its financing, shall be submitted to the Congress for statutory approval. This authority is in addition to, and not in lieu of, other waste water studies aimed at eliminating pollution emanating from select sources around Lake Erie.

(2) This program is to be developed in cooperation with the Environmental Protection Agency, other interested departments, agencies, and instrumentalities of the Federal Government, and the States and their political subdivisions. This program shall set forth alternative systems for managing waste water on a regional basis and shall provide local and State governments with a range of choice as to the type of system to be used for the treatment of waste water. These alternative systems shall include both advanced waste treatment technology and land disposal systems including aerated treatment-spray irrigation technology and will also include provisions for the disposal of solid wastes, including sludge. Such program should include measures to control point sources of pollution, area sources of pollution, including acid-mine drainage, urban runoff and rural runoff, and in place sources of pollution, including bottom loads, sludge banks, and polluted harbor dredgings.

(e) There is authorized to be appropriated $5,000,000 to carry out the provisions of subsection (d) of this section, which sum shall be available until expended.

[33 U.S.C. 1258]

TRAINING GRANTS AND CONTRACTS

Sec. 109. (a) The Administrator is authorized to make grants to or contracts with institutions of higher education, or combinations of such institutions, to assist them in planning, developing, strengthening, improving, or carrying out programs or projects for the preparation of undergraduate students to enter an occupation which involves the design, operation, and maintenance of treatment works, and other facilities whose purpose is water quality control. Such grants or contracts may include payment of all or part of the cost of programs or projects such as—

(A) planning for the development or expansion of programs or projects for training persons in the operation and maintenance of treatment works;

(B) training and retraining of faculty members;

(C) conduct of short-term or regular session institutes for study by persons engaged in, or preparing to engage in, the preparation of students preparing to enter an occupation involving the operation and maintenance of treatment works;

(D) carrying out innovative and experimental programs of cooperative education involving alternate periods of full-time or part-time academic study at the institution and periods of full-time or part-time employment involving the operation and maintenance of treatment works; and

(E) research into, and development of, methods of training students or faculty, including the preparation of teaching materials and the planning of curriculum.

(b)(1) The Administrator may pay 100 per centum of any additional cost of construction of treatment works required for a facility to train and upgrade waste treatment works operation and maintenance personnel and for the costs of other State treatment works operator training programs, including mobile training units, classroom rental, specialized instructors, and instructional material.

(2) The Administrator shall make no more than one grant for such additional construction in any State (to serve a group of States, where, in his judgment, efficient training programs require multi-State programs), and shall make such grant after consultation with and approval by the State or States on the basis of (A) the suitability of such facility for training operation and maintenance personnel for treatment works throughout such State or States; and (B) a commitment by the State agency or agencies to carry out at such facility a program of training approved by the Administrator. In any case where a grant is made to serve two or more States, the Administrator is authorized to make an additional grant for a supplemental facility in each such State.

(3) The Administrator may make such grant out of the sums allocated to a State under section 205 of this Act, except that in no event shall the Federal cost of any such training facilities exceed $500,000.

(4) The Administrator may exempt a grant under this section from any requirement under section 204(a)(3) of this Act. Any grantee who received a grant under this section prior to enactment of the Clean Water Act of 1977 shall be eligible to have its grant increased by funds made available under such Act.

[33 U.S.C. 1259]

APPLICATION FOR TRAINING GRANT OR CONTRACT; ALLOCATION OF GRANTS OR CONTRACTS

Sec. 110. (1) A grant or contract authorized by section 109 may be made only upon application to the Administrator at such time or times and containing such information as he may prescribe, except that no such application shall be approved unless it—

(A) sets forth programs, activities, research, or development for which a grant is authorized under section 109 and describes the relation to any program set forth by the applicant in an application, if any, submitted pursuant to section 111;

(B) provides such fiscal control and fund accounting procedures as may be necessary to assure proper disbursement of and accounting for Federal funds paid to the applicant under this section; and

(C) provides for making such reports, in such form and containing such information, as the Administrator may require to carry out his functions under this section, and for keeping such records and for affording such access thereto as the Administrator may find necessary to assure the correctness and verification of such reports.

(2) The Administrator shall allocate grants or contracts under section 109 in such manner as will most nearly provide an equitable distribution of the grants or contracts throughout the United States among institutions of higher education which show promise of being able to use funds effectively for the purpose of this section.

(3)(A) Payments under this section may be used in accordance with regulations of the Administrator, and subject to the terms and conditions set forth in an application approved under paragraph (1), to pay part of the compensation of students employed in connection with the operation and maintenance of treatment works, other than as an employee in connection with the operation and maintenance of treatment works or as an employee in any branch of the Government of the United States, as part of a program for which a grant has been approved pursuant to this section.

(B) Departments and agencies of the United States are encouraged, to the extent consistent with efficient administration, to enter into arrangements with institutions of higher education for the full-time, part-time, or temporary employment, whether in the competitive or excepted service, of students enrolled in programs set forth in applications approved under paragraph (1).

[33 U.S.C. 1260]

AWARD OF SCHOLARSHIPS

SEC. 111. (1) The Administrator is authorized to award scholarships in accordance with the provisions of this section for undergraduate study by persons who plan to enter an occupation involving the operation and maintenance of treatment works. Such scholarships shall be awarded for such periods as the Administrator may determine but not to exceed four academic years.

(2) The Administrator shall allocate scholarships under this section among institutions of higher education with programs approved under the provisions of this section for the use of individuals accepted into such programs, in such manner and accordance to such plan as will insofar as practicable—

(A) provide an equitable distribution of such scholarships throughout the United States; and

(B) attract recent graduates of secondary schools to enter an occupation involving the operation and maintenance of treatment works.

(3) The Administrator shall approve a program of any institution of higher education for the purposes of this section only upon application by the institution and only upon his finding—

(A) that such program has as a principal objective the education and training of persons in the operation and maintenance of treatment works;

(B) that such program is in effect and of high quality, or can be readily put into effect and may reasonably be expected to be of high quality;

(C) that the application describes the relation of such program to any program, activity, research, or development set forth by the applicant in an application, if any, submitted pursuant to section 110 of this Act; and

(D) that the application contains satisfactory assurances that (i) the institution will recommend to the Administrator for the award of scholarships under this section, for study in such program, only persons who have demonstrated to the satisfaction of the institution a serious intent, upon completing the program, to enter an occupation involving the operation and maintenance of treatment works, and (ii) the institution will make reasonable continuing efforts to encourage recipients of scholarships under this section, enrolled in such program, to enter occupations involving the operation and maintenance of treatment works upon completing the program.

(4)(A) The Administrator shall pay to persons awarded scholarships under this section such stipends (including such allowances for subsistence and other expenses for such persons and their dependents) as he may determine to be consistent with prevailing practices under comparable federally supported programs.

(B) The Administrator shall (in addition to the stipends paid to persons under paragraph (1)) pay to the institution of higher education at which such person is pursuing his course of study such amount as he may determine to be consistent with prevailing practices under comparable federally supported programs.

(5) A person awarded a scholarship under the provisions of this section shall continue to receive the payments provided in this section only during such periods as the Administrator finds that he is maintaining satisfactory proficiency and devoting full time to study or research in the field in which such scholarship was awarded in an institution of higher education, and is not engaging in gainful employment other than employment approved by the Administrator by or pursuant to regulation.

(6) The Administrator shall by regulation provide that any person awarded a scholarship under this section shall agree in writing to enter and remain in an occupation involving the design, operation, or maintenance of treatment works for such period after completion of his course of studies as the Administrator determines appropriate.

[33 U.S.C. 1261]

DEFINITIONS AND AUTHORIZATIONS

SEC. 112. (a) As used in sections 109 through 112 of this Act—

(1) The term institution of higher education means an educational institution described in the first sentence of section 101 of the Higher Education Act of 1965 (other than an institution of any agency of the United States) which is accredited by a nationally recognized accrediting agency or association approved by the Administrator for this purpose. For purposes of this subsection, the Administrator shall publish a list of nationally recognized accrediting agencies or associations which he determines to be reliable authority as to the quality of training offered.

(2) The term academic year means an academic year or its equivalent, as determined by the Administrator.

(b) The Administrator shall annually report his activities under sections 109 through 112 of this Act, including recommendations for needed revisions in the provisions thereof.

(c) There are authorized to be appropriated $25,000,000 per fiscal year for fiscal years ending June 30, 1973, June 30, 1974, and June 30, 1975, $6,000,000 for the fiscal year ending September 30, 1977, $7,000,000 for the fiscal year ending September 30, 1978, $7,000,000 for the fiscal year ending September 30, 1979, $7,000,000 for the fiscal year ending September 30, 1980, $7,000,000 for the fiscal year ending September 30, 1981, $7,000,000 for the fiscal year ending September 30, 1982, such sums as may be necessary for fiscal years 1983 through 1985, and $7,000,000 per fiscal year for each of the fiscal years 1986 through 1990, to carry out sections 109 through 112 of this Act.

[33 U.S.C. 1262]

ALASKA VILLAGE DEMONSTRATION PROJECTS

SEC. 113. (a) The Administrator is authorized to enter into agreements with the State of Alaska to carry out one or more projects to demonstrate methods to provide for central community facilities for safe water and elimination or control of pollution in those native villages of Alaska without such facilities. Such project shall include provisions for community safe water supply systems, toilets, bathing and laundry facilities, sewage disposal facilities, and other similar facilities, and educational and informational facilities and programs relating to health and hygiene. Such demonstration projects shall be for the further purpose of developing preliminary plans for providing such safe water and such elimination or control of pollution for all native villages in such State.

(b) In carrying out this section the Administrator shall cooperate with the Secretary of Health, Education, and Welfare for the purpose of utilizing such of the personnel and facilities of that Department as may be appropriate.

(c) The Administrator shall report to Congress not later than July 1, 1973, the results of the demonstration projects authorized by this section together with his recommendations, including and necessary legislation, relating to the establishment of a statewide program.

(d) There is authorized to be appropriated not to exceed $2,000,000 to carry out this section. In addition, there is authorized to be appropriated to carry out this section not to exceed $200,000 for the fiscal year ending September 30, 1978, and $220,000 for the fiscal year ending September 30, 1979.

(e) The Administrator is authorized to coordinate with the Secretary of the Department of Health, Education, and Welfare, the Secretary of the Department of Housing and Urban Development, the Secretary of the Department of the Interior, the Secretary of the Department of Agriculture, and the heads of any other departments or agencies he may deem appropriate to conduct a joint study with representatives of the State of Alaska and the appropriate Native organizations (as defined in Public Law 92–203) to develop a comprehensive program for achieving adequate sanitation services in Alaska villages. This study shall be coordinated with the programs and projects authorized by sections 104(q) and 105(e)(2) of this Act. The Administrator shall submit a report of the results of the study, together with appropriate supporting data and such recommendations as he deems desirable, to the Committee on Environment and Public Works of the Senate and to the Committee on Public Works and Transportation of the House of Representatives not later than December 31, 1979. The Administrator shall also submit recommended administrative actions, procedures, and any proposed legislation necessary to implement the recommendations of the study no later than June 30, 1980.

(f) The Administrator is authorized to provide technical, financial and management assistance for operation and maintenance of the demonstration projects constructed under this section, until such time as the recommendations of subsection (e) are implemented.

(g) For the purpose of this section, the term village shall mean an incorporated or unincorporated community with a population of ten to six hundred people living within a two-mile radius. The term sanitation services shall mean water supply, sewage disposal, solid waste disposal and other services necessary to maintain generally accepted standards of personal hygiene and public health.

[33 U.S.C. 1263]

LAKE TAHOE STUDY

SEC. 114. (a) The Administrator, in consultation with the Tahoe Regional Planning Agency, the Secretary of Agriculture, other Federal agencies, representatives of State and local governments, and members of the public, shall conduct a thorough and complete study on the adequacy of and need for extending Federal oversight and control in order to preserve the fragile ecology of Lake Tahoe.

(b) Such study shall include an examination of the interrelationships and responsibilities of the various agencies of the Federal Government and State and local governments with a view to establishing the necessity for redefinition of legal and other arrangements between these various governments, and making specific legislative recommendations to Congress. Such study shall consider the effect of various actions in terms of their environmental impact on the Tahoe Basin, treated as an ecosystem.

(c) The Administrator shall report on such study to Congress not later than one year after the date of enactment of this subsection.

(d) There is authorized to be appropriated to carry out this section not to exceed $500,000.

[33 U.S.C. 1264]

IN-PLACE TOXIC POLLUTANTS

SEC. 115. The Administrator is directed to identify the location of in-place pollutants with emphasis on toxic pollutants in harbors and navigable waterways and is authorized, acting through the Secretary of the Army, to make contracts for the removal and appropriate disposal of such materials from critical port and harbor areas. There is authorized to be appropriated $15,000,000 to carry out the provisions of this section, which sum shall be available until expended.

[33 U.S.C. 1265]

HUDSON RIVER PCB RECLAMATION DEMONSTRATION PROJECT

SEC. 116. (a) The Administrator is authorized to enter into contracts and other agreements with the State of New York to carry out a project to demonstrate methods for the selective removal of polychlorinated biphenyls contaminating bottom sediments of the Hudson River, treating such sediments as required, burying such sediments in secure landfills, and installing monitoring systems for such landfills. Such demonstration project shall be for the purpose of determining the feasibility of indefinite storage in secure landfills of toxic substances and of ascertaining the improvement of the rate of recovery of a toxic contaminated national waterway. No pollutants removed pursuant to this paragraph shall be placed in any landfill unless the Administrator first determines that disposal of the pollutants in such landfill would provide a higher standard of protection of the public health, safety, and welfare than disposal of such pollutants by any other method including, but not limited to, incineration or a chemical destruction process.

(b) The Administrator is authorized to make grants to the State of New York to carry out this section from funds allotted to such State under section 205(a) of this Act, except that the amount of any such grant shall be equal to 75 per centum of the cost of the project and such grant shall be made on condition that non-Federal sources provide the remainder of the cost of such project. The authority of this section shall be available until September 30, 1983. Funds allotted to the State of New York under section 205(a) shall be available under this subsection only to the extent that funds are not available, as determined by the Administrator, to the State of New York for the work authorized by this section under section 115 or 311 of this Act or a comprehensive hazardous substance response and clean up fund. Any funds used under the authority of this subsection shall be deducted from any estimate of the needs of the State of New York prepared under section 616(b). The Administrator may not obligate or expend more than $20,000,000 to carry out this section.

[33 U.S.C. 1266]

SEC. 117. CHESAPEAKE BAY.

(a) Definitions.—In this section, the following definitions apply:

(1) Administrative cost.— The term administrative cost means the cost of salaries and fringe benefits incurred in administering a grant under this section.

(2) Chesapeake bay agreement.— The term Chesapeake Bay Agreement means the formal, voluntary agreements executed to achieve the goal of restoring and protecting the Chesapeake Bay ecosystem and the living resources of the Chesapeake Bay ecosystem and signed by the Chesapeake Executive Council.

(3) Chesapeake bay ecosystem.— The term Chesapeake Bay ecosystem means the ecosystem of the Chesapeake Bay and its watershed.

(4) Chesapeake bay program.— The term Chesapeake Bay Program means the program directed by the Chesapeake Executive Council in accordance with the Chesapeake Bay Agreement.

(5) Chesapeake executive council.— The term Chesapeake Executive Council means the signatories to the Chesapeake Bay Agreement.

(6) Signatory jurisdiction.— The term signatory jurisdiction means a jurisdiction of a signatory to the Chesapeake Bay Agreement.

(b) Continuation of Chesapeake Bay Program.—

(1) In general.— In cooperation with the Chesapeake Executive Council (and as a member of the Council), the Administrator shall continue the Chesapeake Bay Program.

(2) Program office.—

(A) In general.— The Administrator shall maintain in the Environmental Protection Agency a Chesapeake Bay Program Office.

(B) Function.—The Chesapeake Bay Program Office shall provide support to the Chesapeake Executive Council by—

(i) implementing and coordinating science, research, modeling, support services, monitoring, data collection, and other activities that support the Chesapeake Bay Program;

(ii) developing and making available, through publications, technical assistance, and other appropriate means, information pertaining to the environmental quality and living resources of the Chesapeake Bay ecosystem;

(iii) in cooperation with appropriate Federal, State, and local authorities, assisting the signatories to the Chesapeake Bay Agreement in developing and implementing specific action plans to carry out the responsibilities of the signatories to the Chesapeake Bay Agreement;

(iv) coordinating the actions of the Environmental Protection Agency with the actions of the appropriate officials of other Federal agencies and State and local authorities in developing strategies to—

(I) improve the water quality and living resources in the Chesapeake Bay ecosystem; and

(II) obtain the support of the appropriate officials of the agencies and authorities in achieving the objectives of the Chesapeake Bay Agreement; and

(v) implementing outreach programs for public information, education, and participation to foster stewardship of the resources of the Chesapeake Bay.

(c) Interagency Agreements.— The Administrator may enter into an interagency agreement with a Federal agency to carry out this section.

(d) Technical Assistance and Assistance Grants.—

(1) In general.— In cooperation with the Chesapeake Executive Council, the Administrator may provide technical assistance, and assistance grants, to nonprofit organizations, State and local governments, colleges, universities, and interstate agencies to carry out this section, subject to such terms and conditions as the Administrator considers appropriate.

(2) Federal share.—

(A) In general.— Except as provided in subparagraph (B), the Federal share of an assistance grant provided under paragraph (1) shall be determined by the Administrator in accordance with guidance issued by the Administrator.

(B) Small watershed grants program.— The Federal share of an assistance grant provided under paragraph (1) to carry out an implementing activity under subsection (g)(2) shall not exceed 75 percent of eligible project costs, as determined by the Administrator.

(3) Non-federal share.— An assistance grant under paragraph (1) shall be provided on the condition that non-Federal sources provide the remainder of eligible project costs, as determined by the Administrator.

(4) Administrative costs.— Administrative costs shall not exceed 10 percent of the annual grant award.

(e) Implementation and Monitoring Grants.—

(1) In general.—If a signatory jurisdiction has approved and committed to

implement all or substantially all aspects of the Chesapeake Bay Agreement, on the request of the chief executive of the jurisdiction, the Administrator—

(A) shall make a grant to the jurisdiction for the purpose of implementing the management mechanisms established under the Chesapeake Bay Agreement, subject to such terms and conditions as the Administrator considers appropriate; and

(B) may make a grant to a signatory jurisdiction for the purpose of monitoring the Chesapeake Bay ecosystem.

(2) PROPOSALS.—

(A) IN GENERAL.— A signatory jurisdiction described in paragraph (1) may apply for a grant under this subsection for a fiscal year by submitting to the Administrator a comprehensive proposal to implement management mechanisms established under the Chesapeake Bay Agreement.

(B) CONTENTS.—A proposal under subparagraph (A) shall include—

(i) a description of proposed management mechanisms that the jurisdiction commits to take within a specified time period, such as reducing or preventing pollution in the Chesapeake Bay and its watershed or meeting applicable water quality standards or established goals and objectives under the Chesapeake Bay Agreement; and

(ii) the estimated cost of the actions proposed to be taken during the fiscal year.

(3) APPROVAL.— If the Administrator finds that the proposal is consistent with the Chesapeake Bay Agreement and the national goals established under section 101(a), the Administrator may approve the proposal for an award.

(4) FEDERAL SHARE.— The Federal share of a grant under this subsection shall not exceed 50 percent of the cost of implementing the management mechanisms during the fiscal year.

(5) NON-FEDERAL SHARE.— A grant under this subsection shall be made on the condition that non-Federal sources provide the remainder of the costs of implementing the management mechanisms during the fiscal year.

(6) ADMINISTRATIVE COSTS.— Administrative costs shall not exceed 10 percent of the annual grant award.

(7) REPORTING.—On or before October 1 of each fiscal year, the Administrator shall make available to the public a document that lists and describes, in the greatest practicable degree of detail—

(A) all projects and activities funded for the fiscal year;

(B) the goals and objectives of projects funded for the previous fiscal year; and

(C) the net benefits of projects funded for previous fiscal years.

(f) FEDERAL FACILITIES AND BUDGET COORDINATION.—

(1) SUBWATERSHED PLANNING AND RESTORATION.— A Federal agency that owns

or operates a facility (as defined by the Administrator) within the Chesapeake Bay watershed shall participate in regional and subwatershed planning and restoration programs.

(2) COMPLIANCE WITH AGREEMENT.— The head of each Federal agency that owns or occupies real property in the Chesapeake Bay watershed shall ensure that the property, and actions taken by the agency with respect to the property, comply with the Chesapeake Bay Agreement, the Federal Agencies Chesapeake Ecosystem Unified Plan, and any subsequent agreements and plans.

(3) BUDGET COORDINATION.—

(A) IN GENERAL.— As part of the annual budget submission of each Federal agency with projects or grants related to restoration, planning, monitoring, or scientific investigation of the Chesapeake Bay ecosystem, the head of the agency shall submit to the President a report that describes plans for the expenditure of the funds under this section.

(B) DISCLOSURE TO THE COUNCIL.— The head of each agency referred to in subparagraph (A) shall disclose the report under that subparagraph with the Chesapeake Executive Council as appropriate.

(g) CHESAPEAKE BAY PROGRAM.—

(1) MANAGEMENT STRATEGIES.—The Administrator, in coordination with other members of the Chesapeake Executive Council, shall ensure that management plans are developed and implementation is begun by signatories to the Chesapeake Bay Agreement to achieve and maintain—

(A) the nutrient goals of the Chesapeake Bay Agreement for the quantity of nitrogen and phosphorus entering the Chesapeake Bay and its watershed;

(B) the water quality requirements necessary to restore living resources in the Chesapeake Bay ecosystem;

(C) the Chesapeake Bay Basinwide Toxins Reduction and Prevention Strategy goal of reducing or eliminating the input of chemical contaminants from all controllable sources to levels that result in no toxic or bioaccumulative impact on the living resources of the Chesapeake Bay ecosystem or on human health;

(D) habitat restoration, protection, creation, and enhancement goals established by Chesapeake Bay Agreement signatories for wetlands, riparian forests, and other types of habitat associated with the Chesapeake Bay ecosystem; and

(E) the restoration, protection, creation, and enhancement goals established by the Chesapeake Bay Agreement signatories for living resources associated with the Chesapeake Bay ecosystem.

(2) SMALL WATERSHED GRANTS PROGRAM.—The Administrator, in cooperation with the Chesapeake Executive Council, shall—

(A) establish a small watershed grants program as part of the Chesapeake Bay Program; and

(B) offer technical assistance and assistance grants under subsection (d) to local governments and nonprofit organizations and individuals in the Chesapeake Bay region to implement—

(i) cooperative tributary basin strategies that address the water quality and living resource needs in the Chesapeake Bay ecosystem; and

(ii) locally based protection and restoration programs or projects within a watershed that complement the tributary basin strategies, including the creation, restoration, protection, or enhancement of habitat associated with the Chesapeake Bay ecosystem.

(h) STUDY OF CHESAPEAKE BAY PROGRAM.—

(1) IN GENERAL.— Not later than April 22, 2003, and every 5 years thereafter, the Administrator, in coordination with the Chesapeake Executive Council, shall complete a study and submit to Congress a comprehensive report on the results of the study.

(2) REQUIREMENTS.—The study and report shall—

(A) assess the state of the Chesapeake Bay ecosystem;

(B) compare the current state of the Chesapeake Bay ecosystem with its state in 1975, 1985, and 1995;

(C) assess the effectiveness of management strategies being implemented on the date of enactment of this section and the extent to which the priority needs are being met;

(D) make recommendations for the improved management of the Chesapeake Bay Program either by strengthening strategies being implemented on the date of enactment of this section or by adopting new strategies; and

(E) be presented in such a format as to be readily transferable to and usable by other watershed restoration programs.

(i) SPECIAL STUDY OF LIVING RESOURCE RESPONSE.—

(1) IN GENERAL.— Not later than 180 days after the date of enactment of this section, the Administrator shall commence a 5-year special study with full participation of the scientific community of the Chesapeake Bay to establish and expand understanding of the response of the living resources of the Chesapeake Bay ecosystem to improvements in water quality that have resulted from investments made through the Chesapeake Bay Program.

(2) REQUIREMENTS.—The study shall—

(A) determine the current status and trends of living resources, including grasses, benthos, phytoplankton, zooplankton, fish, and shellfish;

(B) establish to the extent practicable the rates of recovery of the living resources in response to improved water quality condition;

(C) evaluate and assess interactions of species, with particular attention to the impact of changes within and among trophic levels; and

(D) recommend management actions to optimize the return of a healthy and balanced ecosystem in response to improvements in the quality and character of the waters of the Chesapeake Bay.

(3) ANNUAL SURVEY.— The Administrator shall carry out an annual survey of sea grasses in the Chesapeake Bay.

(j) AUTHORIZATION OF APPROPRIATIONS.—There are authorized to be appropriated to carry out this section—

(1) for fiscal year 2021, $90,000,000;

(2) for fiscal year 2022, $90,500,000;

(3) for fiscal year 2023, $91,000,000;

(4) for fiscal year 2024, $91,500,000;

(5) for fiscal year 2025, $92,000,000; and

(6) for each of fiscal years 2026 through 2030, $92,000,000.

[33 U.S.C. 1267]

SEC. 118. GREAT LAKES.

(a) FINDINGS, PURPOSE, AND DEFINITIONS.—

(1) FINDINGS.—The Congress finds that—

(A) the Great Lakes are a valuable national resource, continuously serving the people of the United States and other nations as an important source of food, fresh water, recreation, beauty, and enjoyment;

(B) the United States should seek to attain the goals embodied in the Great Lakes Water Quality Agreement of 1978, as amended by the Water Quality Agreement of 1987 and any other agreements and amendments, with particular emphasis on goals related to toxic pollutants; and

(C) the Environmental Protection Agency should take the lead in the effort to meet those goals, working with other Federal agencies and State and local authorities.

(2) PURPOSE.— It is the purpose of this section to achieve the goals embodied in the Great Lakes Water Quality Agreement of 1978, as amended by the Water Quality Agreement of 1987 and any other agreements and amendments, through improved organization and definition of mission on the part of the Agency, funding of State grants for pollution control in the Great Lakes area, and improved accountability for implementation of such agreement.

(3) DEFINITIONS.—For purposes of this section, the term—

(A) Agency means the Environmental Protection Agency;

(B) Great Lakes means Lake Ontario, Lake Erie, Lake Huron (including Lake St. Clair), Lake Michigan, and Lake Superior, and the connecting channels (Saint Mary's River, Saint Clair River, Detroit River, Niagara River, and Saint Lawrence River to the Canadian Border);

(C) Great Lakes System means all the streams, rivers, lakes, and other bodies of water within the drainage basin of the Great Lakes;

(D) Program Office means the Great Lakes National Program Office established by this section;

(E) Research Office means the Great Lakes Research Office established by subsection (d);

(F) area of concern means a geographic area located within the Great Lakes, in which beneficial uses are impaired and which has been officially designated as such under Annex 2 of the Great Lakes Water Quality Agreement;

(G) Great Lakes States means the States of Illinois, Indiana, Michigan, Minnesota, New York, Ohio, Pennsylvania, and Wisconsin;

(H) Great Lakes Water Quality Agreement means the bilateral agreement, between the United States and Canada which was signed in 1978 and amended by the Protocol of 1987;

(I) Lakewide Management Plan means a written document which embodies a systematic and comprehensive ecosystem approach to restoring and protecting the beneficial uses of the open waters of each of the Great Lakes, in accordance with article VI and Annex 2 of the Great Lakes Water Quality Agreement;

(J) Remedial Action Plan means a written document which embodies a systematic and comprehensive ecosystem approach to restoring and protecting the beneficial uses of areas of concern, in accordance with article VI and Annex 2 of the Great Lakes Water Quality Agreement;

(K) site characterization means a process for monitoring and evaluating the nature and extent of sediment contamination in accordance with the Environmental Protection Agency's guidance for the assessment of contaminated sediment in an area of concern located wholly or partially within the United States; and

(L) potentially responsible party means an individual or entity that may be liable under any Federal or State authority that is being used or may be used to facilitate the cleanup and protection of the Great Lakes.

(b) GREAT LAKES NATIONAL PROGRAM OFFICE.— The Great Lakes National Program Office (previously established by the Administrator) is hereby established within the Agency. The Program Office shall be headed by a Director who, by reason of management experience and technical expertise relating to the Great Lakes, is highly qualified to direct the development of programs and plans on a variety of Great Lakes issues. The Great Lakes National Program Office shall be located in a Great Lakes State.

(c) GREAT LAKES MANAGEMENT.—

(1) FUNCTIONS.—The Program Office shall—

(A) in cooperation with appropriate Federal, State, tribal, and international agencies, and in accordance with section 101(e) of this Act, develop and implement specific action plans to carry out the responsibilities of the United States under the Great Lakes Water Quality Agreement of 1978, as amended by the Water Quality Agreement of 1987 and any other agreements and amendments,;[1]

[1] See P.L. 100–688, section 1008.

(B) establish a Great Lakes system-wide surveillance network to monitor the water quality of the Great Lakes, with specific emphasis on the monitoring of toxic pollutants;

(C) serve as the liaison with, and provide information to, the Canadian members of the International Joint Commission and the Canadian counterpart to the Agency;

(D) coordinate actions of the Agency (including actions by headquarters and regional offices thereof) aimed at improving Great Lakes water quality; and

(E) coordinate actions of the Agency with the actions of other Federal agencies and State and local authorities, so as to ensure the input of those agencies and authorities in developing water quality strategies and obtain the support of those agencies and authorities in achieving the objectives of such agreement.

(2) GREAT LAKES WATER QUALITY GUIDANCE.—

(A) By June 30, 1991, the Administrator, after consultation with the Program Office, shall publish in the Federal Register for public notice and comment proposed water quality guidance for the Great Lakes System. Such guidance shall conform with the objectives and provisions of the Great Lakes Water Quality Agreement, shall be no less restrictive than the provisions of this Act and national water quality criteria and guidance, shall specify numerical limits on pollutants in ambient Great Lakes waters to protect human health, aquatic life, and wildlife, and shall provide guidance to the Great Lakes States on minimum water quality standards, antidegradation policies, and implementation procedures for the Great Lakes System.

(B) By June 30, 1992, the Administrator, in consultation with the Program Office, shall publish in the Federal Register, pursuant to this section and the Administrator's authority under this chapter, final water quality guidance for the Great Lakes System.

(C) Within two years after such Great Lakes guidance is published, the Great Lakes States shall adopt water quality standards, antidegradation policies, and implementation procedures for waters within the Great Lakes System which are consistent with such guidance. If a Great Lakes State fails to adopt such standards, policies, and procedures, the Administrator shall promulgate them not later than the end of such two-year period. When reviewing any Great Lakes State's water quality plan, the agency shall consider the extent to which the State has complied with the Great Lakes guidance issued pursuant to this section.

(3) REMEDIAL ACTION PLANS.—

(A) For each area of concern for which the United States has agreed to draft a Remedial Action Plan, the Program Office shall ensure that the Great Lakes State in which such area of concern is located—

(i) submits a Remedial Action Plan to the Program Office by June 30, 1991;

(ii) submits such Remedial Action Plan to the International Joint Commission by January 1, 1992; and

(iii) includes such Remedial Action Plans within the State's water quality plan by January 1, 1993.

(B) For each area of concern for which Canada has agreed to draft a Remedial Action Plan, the Program Office shall, pursuant to subparagraph (c)(1)(C) of this section, work with Canada to assure the submission of such Remedial Action Plans to the International Joint Commission by June 30, 1991, and to finalize such Remedial Action Plans by January 1, 1993.

(C) For any area of concern designated as such subsequent to the enactment of this Act, the Program Office shall (i) if the United States has agreed to draft the Remedial Action Plan, ensure that the Great Lakes State in which such area of concern is located submits such Plan to the Program Office within two years of the area's designation, submits it to the International Joint Commission no later than six months after submitting it to the Program Office, and includes such Plan in the State's water quality plan no later than one year after submitting it to the Commission; and (ii) if Canada has agreed to draft the Remedial Action Plan, work with Canada, pursuant to subparagraph (c)(1)(C) of this section, to ensure the submission of such Plan to the International Joint Commission within two years of the area's designation and the finalization of such Plan no later than eighteen months after submitting it to such Commission.

(D) The Program Office shall compile formal comments on individual Remedial Action Plans made by the International Joint Commission pursuant to section 4(d) of Annex 2 of the Great Lakes Water Quality Agreement and, upon request by a member of the public, shall make such comments available for inspection and copying. The Program Office shall also make available, upon request, formal comments made by the Environmental Protection Agency on individual Remedial Action Plans.

(E) REPORT.—Not later than 1 year after the date of enactment of this subparagraph, the Administrator shall submit to Congress a report on such actions, time periods, and resources as are necessary to fulfill the duties of the Agency relating to oversight of Remedial Action Plans under—

(i) this paragraph; and

(ii) the Great Lakes Water Quality Agreement.

(4) LAKEWIDE MANAGEMENT PLANS.—The Administrator, in consultation with the Program Office shall—

(A) by January 1, 1992, publish in the Federal Register a proposed Lakewide Management Plan for Lake Michigan and solicit public comments;

(B) by January 1, 1993, submit a proposed Lakewide Management Plan for Lake Michigan to the International Joint Commission for review; and

(C) by January 1, 1994, publish in the Federal Register a final Lakewide Management Plan for Lake Michigan and begin implementation.

Nothing in this subparagraph shall preclude the simultaneous development of Lakewide

Management Plans for the other Great Lakes.

(5) SPILLS OF OIL AND HAZARDOUS MATERIALS.— The Program Office, in consultation with the Coast Guard, shall identify areas within the Great Lakes which are likely to experience numerous or voluminous spills of oil or other hazardous materials from land based facilities, vessels, or other sources and, in consultation with the Great Lakes States, shall identify weaknesses in Federal and State programs and systems to prevent and respond to such spills. This information shall be included on at least a biennial basis in the report required by this section.

(6) 5-YEAR PLAN AND PROGRAM.— The Program Office shall develop, in consultation with the States, a five-year plan and program for reducing the amount of nutrients introduced into the Great Lakes. Such program shall incorporate any management program for reducing nutrient runoff from nonpoint sources established under section 319 of this Act and shall include a program for monitoring nutrient runoff into, and ambient levels in, the Great Lakes.

(7) GREAT LAKES RESTORATION INITIATIVE.—

(A) ESTABLISHMENT.— There is established in the Agency a Great Lakes Restoration Initiative (referred to in this paragraph as the Initiative) to carry out programs and projects for Great Lakes protection and restoration.

(B) FOCUS AREAS.—In carrying out the Initiative, the Administrator shall prioritize programs and projects, to be carried out in coordination with non-Federal partners, that address the priority areas described in the Initiative Action Plan, including—

(i) the remediation of toxic substances and areas of concern;

(ii) the prevention and control of invasive species and the impacts of invasive species;

(iii) the protection and restoration of nearshore health and the prevention and mitigation of nonpoint source pollution;

(iv) habitat and wildlife protection and restoration, including wetlands restoration and preservation; and

(v) accountability, monitoring, evaluation, communication, and partnership activities.

(C) PROJECTS.—

(i) IN GENERAL.—In carrying out the Initiative, the Administrator shall collaborate with other Federal partners, including the Great Lakes Interagency Task Force established by Executive Order No. 13340 (69 Fed. Reg. 29043), to select the best combination of programs and projects for Great Lakes protection and restoration using appropriate principles and criteria, including whether a program or project provides—

(I) the ability to achieve strategic and measurable environmental outcomes that implement the Initiative Action Plan and the Great Lakes Water Quality Agreement;

(II) the feasibility of—

(aa) prompt implementation;

(bb) timely achievement of results; and

(cc) resource leveraging; and

(III) the opportunity to improve interagency, intergovernmental, and interorganizational coordination and collaboration to reduce duplication and streamline efforts.

(ii) OUTREACH.— In selecting the best combination of programs and projects for Great Lakes protection and restoration under clause (i), the Administrator shall consult with the Great Lakes States and Indian tribes and solicit input from other non-Federal stakeholders.

(iii) HARMFUL ALGAL BLOOM COORDINATOR.— The Administrator shall designate a point person from an appropriate Federal partner to coordinate, with Federal partners and Great Lakes States, Indian tribes, and other non-Federal stakeholders, projects and activities under the Initiative involving harmful algal blooms in the Great Lakes.

(D) IMPLEMENTATION OF PROJECTS.—

(i) IN GENERAL.—Subject to subparagraph (J)(ii), funds made available to carry out the Initiative shall be used to strategically implement—

(I) Federal projects;

(II) projects carried out in coordination with States, Indian tribes, municipalities, institutions of higher education, and other organizations; and

(III) operations and activities of the Program Office, including remediation of sediment contamination in areas of concern.

(ii) TRANSFER OF FUNDS.—With amounts made available for the Initiative each fiscal year, the Administrator may—

(I) transfer not more than the total amount appropriated under subparagraph (J)(i) for the fiscal year to the head of any Federal department or agency, with the concurrence of the department or agency head, to carry out activities to support the Initiative and the Great Lakes Water Quality Agreement; and

(II) enter into an interagency agreement with the head of any Federal department or agency to carry out activities described in subclause (I).

(iii) AGREEMENTS WITH NON-FEDERAL ENTITIES.—

(I) IN GENERAL.— The Administrator, or the head of any other Federal department or agency receiving funds under clause (ii)(I), may make a grant to, or otherwise enter into an agreement with, a qualified non-Federal entity, as determined by the Administrator or the applicable head of the other Federal department or agency receiving funds, for planning, research, monitoring, outreach, or implementation of a project selected under subparagraph (C), to support the Initiative Action Plan or the Great Lakes Water Quality Agreement.

(II) Qualified non-federal entity.— For purposes of this clause, a qualified non-Federal entity may include a governmental entity, nonprofit organization, institution, or individual.

(E) Scope.—

(i) In general.—Projects may be carried out under the Initiative on multiple levels, including—

(I) locally;

(II) Great Lakes-wide; or

(III) Great Lakes basin-wide.

(ii) Limitation.—No funds made available to carry out the Initiative may be used for any water infrastructure activity (other than a green infrastructure project that improves habitat and other ecosystem functions in the Great Lakes) for which financial assistance is received—

(I) from a State water pollution control revolving fund established under title VI;

(II) from a State drinking water revolving loan fund established under section 1452 of the Safe Drinking Water Act (42 U.S.C. 300j–12); or

(III) pursuant to the Water Infrastructure Finance and Innovation Act of 2014 (33 U.S.C. 3901 et seq.).

(F) Activities by other federal agencies.—Each relevant Federal department or agency shall, to the maximum extent practicable—

(i) maintain the base level of funding for the Great Lakes activities of that department or agency without regard to funding under the Initiative; and

(ii) identify new activities and projects to support the environmental goals of the Initiative.

(G) Revision of initiative action plan.—

(i) In general.— Not less often than once every 5 years, the Administrator, in conjunction with the Great Lakes Interagency Task Force, shall review, and revise as appropriate, the Initiative Action Plan to guide the activities of the Initiative in addressing the restoration and protection of the Great Lakes system.

(ii) Outreach.— In reviewing and revising the Initiative Action Plan under clause (i), the Administrator shall consult with the Great Lakes States and Indian tribes and solicit input from other non-Federal stakeholders.

(H) Monitoring and reporting.—The Administrator shall—

(i) establish and maintain a process for monitoring and periodically reporting to the public on the progress made in implementing the Initiative Action Plan;

(ii) make information about each project carried out under the Initiative

Action Plan available on a public website; and

(iii) provide to the Committee on Transportation and Infrastructure of the House of Representatives and the Committee on Environment and Public Works of the Senate a yearly detailed description of the progress of the Initiative and amounts transferred to participating Federal departments and agencies under subparagraph (D)(ii).

(I) INITIATIVE ACTION PLAN DEFINED.— In this paragraph, the term Initiative Action Plan means the comprehensive, multiyear action plan for the restoration of the Great Lakes, first developed pursuant to the Joint Explanatory Statement of the Conference Report accompanying the Department of the Interior, Environment, and Related Agencies Appropriations Act, 2010 (Public Law 111–88).

(J) FUNDING.—

(i) IN GENERAL.—There are authorized to be appropriated to carry out this paragraph—

(I) $300,000,000 for each of fiscal years 2017 through 2021;

(II) $375,000,000 for fiscal year 2022;

(III) $400,000,000 for fiscal year 2023;

(IV) $425,000,000 for fiscal year 2024;

(V) $450,000,000 for fiscal year 2025; and

(VI) $475,000,000 for fiscal year 2026.

(ii) LIMITATION.—Nothing in this paragraph creates, expands, or amends the authority of the Administrator to implement programs or projects under—

(I) this section;

(II) the Initiative Action Plan; or

(III) the Great Lakes Water Quality Agreement.

(8) ADMINISTRATOR'S RESPONSIBILITY.—The Administrator shall ensure that the Program Office enters into agreements with the various organizational elements of the Agency involved in Great Lakes activities and the appropriate State agencies specifically delineating—

(A) the duties and responsibilities of each such element in the Agency with respect to the Great Lakes;

(B) the time periods for carrying out such duties and responsibilities; and

(C) the resources to be committed to such duties and responsibilities.

(9) BUDGET ITEM.— The Administrator shall, in the Agency's annual budget submission to Congress, include a funding request for the Program Office as a separate budget line item.

(10) CONFINED DISPOSAL FACILITIES.—(A) The Administrator, in consultation with the Assistant Secretary of the Army for Civil Works, shall develop and

implement, within one year of the date of enactment of this paragraph, management plans for every Great Lakes confined disposal facility.

(B) The plan shall provide for monitoring of such facilities, including—

(i) water quality at the site and in the area of the site;

(ii) sediment quality at the site and in the area of the site;

(iii) the diversity, productivity, and stability of aquatic organisms at the site and in the area of the site; and

(iv) such other conditions as the Administrator deems appropriate.

(C) The plan shall identify the anticipated use and management of the site over the following twenty-year period including the expected termination of dumping at the site, the anticipated need for site management, including pollution control, following the termination of the use of the site.

(D) The plan shall identify a schedule for review and revision of the plan which shall not be less frequent than five years after adoption of the plan and every five years thereafter.

(11) REMEDIATION OF SEDIMENT CONTAMINATION IN AREAS OF CONCERN.—

(A) IN GENERAL.— In accordance with this paragraph, the Administrator, acting through the Program Office, may carry out projects that meet the requirements of subparagraph (B).

(B) ELIGIBLE PROJECTS.—A project meets the requirements of this subparagraph if the project is to be carried out in an area of concern located wholly or partially in the United States and the project—

(i) monitors or evaluates contaminated sediment;

(ii) subject to subparagraph (D), implements a plan to remediate contaminated sediment, including activities to restore aquatic habitat that are carried out in conjunction with a project for the remediation of contaminated sediment; or

(iii) prevents further or renewed contamination of sediment.

(C) PRIORITY.—In selecting projects to carry out under this paragraph, the Administrator shall give priority to a project that—

(i) constitutes remedial action for contaminated sediment;

(ii)(I) has been identified in a Remedial Action Plan submitted under paragraph (3); and

(II) is ready to be implemented;

(iii) will use an innovative approach, technology, or technique that may provide greater environmental benefits, or equivalent environmental benefits at a reduced cost; or

(iv) includes remediation to be commenced not later than 1 year after the date of receipt of funds for the project.

(D) LIMITATIONS.—The Administrator may not carry out a project under this paragraph for remediation of contaminated sediments located in an area of concern—

(i) if an evaluation of remedial alternatives for the area of concern has not been conducted, including a review of the short-term and long-term effects of the alternatives on human health and the environment;

(ii) if the Administrator determines that the area of concern is likely to suffer significant further or renewed contamination from existing sources of pollutants causing sediment contamination following completion of the project;

(iii) unless each non-Federal sponsor for the project has entered into a written project agreement with the Administrator under which the party agrees to carry out its responsibilities and requirements for the project; or

(iv) unless the Administrator provides assurance that the Agency has conducted a reasonable inquiry to identify potentially responsible parties connected with the site.

(E) NON-FEDERAL SHARE.—

(i) IN GENERAL.— The non-Federal share of the cost of a project carried out under this paragraph shall be at least 35 percent.

(ii) IN-KIND CONTRIBUTIONS.—

(I) IN GENERAL.— The non-Federal share of the cost of a project carried out under this paragraph may include the value of an in-kind contribution provided by a non-Federal sponsor.

(II) CREDIT.— A project agreement described in subparagraph (D)(iii) may provide, with respect to a project, that the Administrator shall credit toward the non-Federal share of the cost of the project the value of an in-kind contribution made by the non-Federal sponsor, if the Administrator determines that the material or service provided as the in-kind contribution is integral to the project.

(III) WORK PERFORMED BEFORE PROJECT AGREEMENT.— In any case in which a non-Federal sponsor is to receive credit under subclause (II) for the cost of work carried out by the non-Federal sponsor and such work has not been carried out by the non-Federal sponsor as of the date of enactment of this subclause, the Administrator and the non-Federal sponsor shall enter into an agreement under which the non-Federal sponsor shall carry out such work, and only work carried out following the execution of the agreement shall be eligible for credit.

(IV) LIMITATION.—Credit authorized under this clause for a project carried out under this paragraph—

(aa) shall not exceed the non-Federal share of the cost of the project; and

(bb) shall not exceed the actual and reasonable costs of the materials and services provided by the non-Federal sponsor, as determined by the Administrator.

(V) Inclusion of certain contributions.— In this subparagraph, the term in-kind contribution may include the costs of planning (including data collection), design, construction, and materials that are provided by the non-Federal sponsor for implementation of a project under this paragraph.

(iii) Treatment of credit between projects.— Any credit provided under this subparagraph towards the non-Federal share of the cost of a project carried out under this paragraph may be applied towards the non-Federal share of the cost of any other project carried out under this paragraph by the same non-Federal sponsor for a site within the same area of concern.

(iv) Non-federal share.—The non-Federal share of the cost of a project carried out under this paragraph—

(I) may include monies paid pursuant to, or the value of any in-kind contribution performed under, an administrative order on consent or judicial consent decree; but

(II) may not include any funds paid pursuant to, or the value of any in-kind contribution performed under, a unilateral administrative order or court order.

(v) Operation and maintenance.— The non-Federal share of the cost of the operation and maintenance of a project carried out under this paragraph shall be 100 percent.

(F) Site characterization.—

(i) In general.— The Administrator, in consultation with any affected State or unit of local government, shall carry out at Federal expense the site characterization of a project under this paragraph for the remediation of contaminated sediment.

(ii) Limitation.— For purposes of clause (i), the Administrator may carry out one site assessment per discrete site within a project at Federal expense.

(G) Coordination.— In carrying out projects under this paragraph, the Administrator shall coordinate with the Secretary of the Army, and with the Governors of States in which the projects are located, to ensure that Federal and State assistance for remediation in areas of concern is used as efficiently as practicable.

(H) Authorization of appropriations.—

(i) In general.— In addition to other amounts authorized under this section, there is authorized to be appropriated to carry out this paragraph $50,000,000 for each of fiscal years 2004 through 2010.

(ii) Availability.— Funds made available under clause (i) shall remain available until expended.

(iii) Allocation of funds.— Not more than 20 percent of the funds appropriated pursuant to clause (i) for a fiscal year may be used to carry out subparagraph (F).

(12) PUBLIC INFORMATION PROGRAM.—

(A) IN GENERAL.— The Administrator, acting through the Program Office and in coordination with States, Indian tribes, local governments, and other entities, may carry out a public information program to provide information relating to the remediation of contaminated sediment to the public in areas of concern that are located wholly or partially in the United States.

(B) AUTHORIZATION OF APPROPRIATIONS.— There is authorized to be appropriated to carry out this paragraph $1,000,000 for each of fiscal years 2004 through 2010.

(d) GREAT LAKES RESEARCH.—

(1) ESTABLISHMENT OF RESEARCH OFFICE.— There is established within the National Oceanic and Atmospheric Administration the Great Lakes Research Office.

(2) IDENTIFICATION OF ISSUES.— The Research Office shall identify issues relating to the Great Lakes resources on which research is needed. The Research Office shall submit a report to Congress on such issues before the end of each fiscal year which shall identify any changes in the Great Lakes system with respect to such issues.

(3) INVENTORY.— The Research Office shall identify and inventory, Federal, State, university, and tribal environmental research programs (and, to the extent feasible, those of private organizations and other nations) relating to the Great Lakes system, and shall update that inventory every four years.

(4) RESEARCH EXCHANGE.— The Research Office shall establish a Great Lakes research exchange for the purpose of facilitating the rapid identification, acquisition, retrieval, dissemination, and use of information concerning research projects which are ongoing or completed and which affect the Great Lakes System.

(5) RESEARCH PROGRAM.— The Research Office shall develop, in cooperation with the Coordination Office, a comprehensive environmental research program and data base for the Great Lakes system[2]. The data base shall include, but not be limited to, data relating to water quality, fisheries, and biota.

[2] Probably should read Great Lakes System.

(6) MONITORING.— The Research Office shall conduct, through the Great Lakes Environmental Research Laboratory, the National Sea Grant College program, other Federal laboratories, and the private sector, appropriate research and monitoring activities which address priority issues and current needs relating to the Great Lakes.

(7) LOCATION.— The Research Office shall be located in a Great Lakes State.

(e) RESEARCH AND MANAGEMENT COORDINATION.—

(1) JOINT PLAN.— Before October 1 of each year, the Program Office and the Research Office shall prepare a joint research plan for the fiscal year which begins in the following calendar year.

(2) CONTENTS OF PLAN.—Each plan prepared under paragraph (1) shall—

(A) identify all proposed research dedicated to activities conducted under the Great Lakes Water Quality Agreement of 1978;

(B) include the Agency's assessment of priorities for research needed to fulfill the terms of such Agreement; and

(C) identify all proposed research that may be used to develop a comprehensive environmental data base for the Great Lakes System and establish priorities for development of such data base.

(3) Health research report.—(A) Not later than September 30, 1994, the Program Office, in consultation with the Research Office, the Agency for Toxic Substances and Disease Registry, and Great Lakes States shall submit to the Congress a report assessing the adverse effects of water pollutants in the Great Lakes System on the health of persons in Great Lakes States and the health of fish, shellfish, and wildlife in the Great Lakes System. In conducting research in support of this report, the Administrator may, where appropriate, provide for research to be conducted under cooperative agreements with Great Lakes States.

(B) There is authorized to be appropriated to the Administrator to carry out this section not to exceed $3,000,000 for each of fiscal years 1992, 1993, and 1994.

(f) Interagency Cooperation.— The head of each department, agency, or other instrumentality of the Federal Government which is engaged in, is concerned with, or has authority over programs relating to research, monitoring, and planning to maintain, enhance, preserve, or rehabilitate the environmental quality and natural resources of the Great Lakes, including the Chief of Engineers of the Army, the Chief of the Soil Conservation Service, the Commandant of the Coast Guard, the Director of the Fish and Wildlife Service, and the Administrator of the National Oceanic and Atmospheric Administration, shall submit an annual report to the Administrator with respect to the activities of that agency or office affecting compliance with the Great Lakes Water Quality Agreement of 1978.

(g) Relationship to Existing Federal and State Laws and International Treaties.—Nothing in this section shall be construed—

(1) to affect the jurisdiction, powers, or prerogatives of any department, agency, or officer of the Federal Government or of any State government, or of any tribe, nor any powers, jurisdiction, or prerogatives of any international body created by treaty with authority relating to the Great Lakes; or

(2) to affect any other Federal or State authority that is being used or may be used to facilitate the cleanup and protection of the Great Lakes.

(h) Authorizations of Great Lakes Appropriations.—There are authorized to be appropriated to the Administrator to carry out this section not to exceed—

(1) $11,000,000 per fiscal year for the fiscal years 1987, 1988, 1989, and 1990, and $25,000,000 for fiscal year 1991;

(2) such sums as are necessary for each of fiscal years 1992 through 2003; and

(3) $25,000,000 for each of fiscal years 2004 through 2008.

[33 U.S.C. 1268]

SEC. 119. **LONG ISLAND SOUND.**—(a) The Administrator shall continue the Management Conference of the Long Island Sound Study (hereinafter referred to as the Conference) as established pursuant to section 320 of this Act, and shall establish an office (hereinafter referred to as the Office) to be located on or near Long Island Sound.

(b) ADMINISTRATION AND STAFFING OF OFFICE.— The Office shall be headed by a Director, who shall be detailed by the Administrator, following consultation with the Administrators of EPA regions I and II, from among the employees of the Agency who are in civil service. The Administrator shall delegate to the Director such authority and detail such additional staff as may be necessary to carry out the duties of the Director under this section.

(c) DUTIES OF THE OFFICE.—The Office shall assist the conference study in carrying out its goals. Specifically, the Office shall—

(1) assist and support the implementation of the Comprehensive Conservation and Management Plan for Long Island Sound developed pursuant to section 320 of this Act, including efforts to establish, within the process for granting watershed general permits, a system for promoting innovative methodologies and technologies that are cost-effective and consistent with the goals of the Plan;

(2) conduct or commission studies deemed necessary for strengthened implementation of the Comprehensive Conservation and Management Plan including, but not limited to—

(A) population growth and the adequacy of wastewater treatment facilities;

(B) the use of biological methods for nutrient removal in sewage treatment plants;

(C) contaminated sediments, and dredging activities;

(D) nonpoint source pollution abatement and land use activities in the Long Island Sound watershed;

(E) wetland protection and restoration;

(F) atmospheric deposition of acidic and other pollutants into Long Island Sound;

(G) water quality requirements to sustain fish, shellfish, and wildlife populations, and the use of indicator species to assess environmental quality;

(H) State water quality programs, for their adequacy pursuant to implementation of the Comprehensive Conservation and Management Plan;

(I) options for long-term financing of wastewater treatment projects and water pollution control programs;[3]

[3] So in law. The word and probably should appear at the end of subparagraph (I) and not at the end of Subparagraph (J).

(J) environmental vulnerabilities of the Long Island Sound watershed, including—

(i) the identification and assessment of such vulnerabilities in the watershed;

(ii) the development and implementation of adaptation strategies to reduce such vulnerabilities; and

(iii) the identification and assessment of the effects of sea level rise on water quality, habitat, and infrastructure; and[3]

(3) coordinate the grant, research and planning programs authorized under this section;

(4) develop and implement strategies to increase public education and awareness with respect to the ecological health and water quality conditions of Long Island Sound;

(5) provide administrative and technical support to the conference study;

(6) collect and make available to the public (including on a publicly accessible website) publications, and other forms of information the conference study determines to be appropriate, relating to the environmental quality of Long Island Sound;

(7) monitor the progress made toward meeting the identified goals, actions, and schedules of the Comprehensive Conservation and Management Plan, including through the implementation and support of a monitoring system for the ecological health and water quality conditions of Long Island Sound; and

(8) convene conferences and meetings for legislators from State governments and political subdivisions thereof for the purpose of making recommendations for coordinating legislative efforts to facilitate the environmental restoration of Long Island Sound and the implementation of the Comprehensive Conservation and Management Plan.

(d) GRANTS.—(1) The Administrator is authorized to make grants for projects and studies which will help implement the Long Island Sound Comprehensive Conservation and Management Plan. Special emphasis shall be given to implementation, research and planning, enforcement, and citizen involvement and education.

(2) State, interstate, and regional water pollution control agencies, and other public or nonprofit private agencies, institutions, and organizations held to be eligible for grants pursuant to this subsection.

(3) Citizen involvement and citizen education grants under this subsection shall not exceed 95 per centum of the costs of such work. All other grants under this subsection shall not exceed 60 percent of the research, studies, or work. All grants shall be made on the condition that the non-Federal share of such costs are provided from non-Federal sources.

(e) ASSISTANCE TO DISTRESSED COMMUNITIES.—

(1) ELIGIBLE COMMUNITIES.— For the purposes of this subsection, a distressed community is any community that meets affordability criteria established by the State in which the community is located, if such criteria are developed after public review and comment.

(2) PRIORITY.— In making assistance available under this section for the upgrading of wastewater treatment facilities, the Administrator may give priority to a distressed community.

(f) REPORT.—

(1) IN GENERAL.—Not later than 2 years after the date of enactment of this Act, and biennially thereafter, the Director of the Office, in consultation with the Governor of each Long Island Sound State, shall submit to Congress a report that—

(A) summarizes and assesses the progress made by the Office and the Long Island Sound States in implementing the Long Island Sound Comprehensive Conservation and Management Plan, including an assessment of the progress made toward meeting the performance goals and milestones contained in the Plan;

(B) assesses the key ecological attributes that reflect the health of the ecosystem of the Long Island Sound watershed;

(C) describes any substantive modifications to the Long Island Sound Comprehensive Conservation and Management Plan made during the 2-year period preceding the date of submission of the report;

(D) provides specific recommendations to improve progress in restoring and protecting the Long Island Sound watershed, including, as appropriate, proposed modifications to the Long Island Sound Comprehensive Conservation and Management Plan;

(E) identifies priority actions for implementation of the Long Island Sound Comprehensive Conservation and Management Plan for the 2-year period following the date of submission of the report; and

(F) describes the means by which Federal funding and actions will be coordinated with the actions of the Long Island Sound States and other entities.

(2) PUBLIC AVAILABILITY.— The Administrator shall make the report described in paragraph (1) available to the public, including on a publicly accessible website.

(g) FEDERAL ENTITIES.—

(1) COORDINATION.— The Administrator shall coordinate the actions of all Federal departments and agencies that affect water quality in the Long Island Sound watershed in order to improve the water quality and living resources of the watershed.

(2) METHODS.—In carrying out this section, the Administrator, acting through the Director of the Office, may—

(A) enter into interagency agreements; and

(B) make intergovernmental personnel appointments.

(4)[4] CONSISTENCY WITH COMPREHENSIVE CONSERVATION AND MANAGEMENT PLAN.— To the maximum extent practicable, the head of each Federal department or agency that owns or occupies real property, or carries out activities, within the Long Island Sound watershed shall ensure that the property and all activities carried out by the department or agency are consistent with the Long Island Sound Comprehensive Conservation and Management Plan (including any related subsequent agreements and plans).

[4] So in law. Subsection (g), as added by section 4104(a)(4) of Public Law 115–270, does not include a paragraph (3) before paragraph (4).

(h) AUTHORIZATION OF APPROPRIATIONS.— There is authorized to be appropriated to the Administrator to carry out this section $40,000,000 for each of fiscal years 2019 through 2023.

[33 U.S.C. 1269]

SEC. 120. PATRICK LEAHY LAKE CHAMPLAIN BASIN PROGRAM.

(a) ESTABLISHMENT.—

(1) IN GENERAL.— There is established a Lake Champlain Management Conference to develop a comprehensive pollution prevention, control, and restoration plan for Lake Champlain. The Administrator shall convene the management conference within ninety days of the date of enactment of this section.

(2) IMPLEMENTATION.—The Administrator—

(A) may provide support to the State of Vermont, the State of New York, and the New England Interstate Water Pollution Control Commission for the implementation of the Patrick Leahy Lake Champlain Basin Program; and

(B) shall coordinate actions of the Environmental Protection Agency under subparagraph (A) with the actions of other appropriate Federal agencies.

(b) MEMBERSHIP.—The Members of the Management Conference shall be comprised of—

(1) the Governors of the States of Vermont and New York;

(2) each interested Federal agency, not to exceed a total of five members;

(3) the Vermont and New York Chairpersons of the Vermont, New York, Quebec Citizens Advisory Committee for the Environmental Management of Lake Champlain;

(4) four representatives of the State legislature of Vermont;

(5) four representatives of the State legislature of New York;

(6) six persons representing local governments having jurisdiction over any land or water within the Lake Champlain basin, as determined appropriate by the Governors; and

(7) eight persons representing affected industries, nongovernmental organizations, public and private educational institutions, and the general public, as determined appropriate by the trigovernmental Citizens Advisory Committee for the Environmental Management of Lake Champlain, but not to be current members of the Citizens Advisory Committee.

(c) TECHNICAL ADVISORY COMMITTEE.—(1) The Management Conference shall, not later than one hundred and twenty days after the date of enactment of this section, appoint a Technical Advisory Committee.

(2) Such Technical Advisory Committee shall consist of officials of: appropriate departments and agencies of the Federal Government; the State governments of New

York and Vermont; and governments of political subdivisions of such States; and public and private research institutions.

(d) RESEARCH PROGRAM.— The Management Conference shall establish a multi-disciplinary environmental research program for Lake Champlain. Such research program shall be planned and conducted jointly with the Lake Champlain Research Consortium.

(e) POLLUTION PREVENTION, CONTROL, AND RESTORATION PLAN.—(1) Not later than three years after the date of the enactment of this section, the Management Conference shall publish a pollution prevention, control, and restoration plan for Lake Champlain.

(2) The Plan developed pursuant to this section shall—

(A) identify corrective actions and compliance schedules addressing point and nonpoint sources of pollution necessary to restore and maintain the chemical, physical, and biological integrity of water quality, a balanced, indigenous population of shellfish, fish and wildlife, recreational, and economic activities in and on the lake;

(B) incorporate environmental management concepts and programs established in State and Federal plans and programs in effect at the time of the development of such plan;

(C) clarify the duties of Federal and State agencies in pollution prevention and control activities, and to the extent allowable by law, suggest a timetable for adoption by the appropriate Federal and State agencies to accomplish such duties within a reasonable period of time;

(D) describe the methods and schedules for funding of programs, activities, and projects identified in the Plan, including the use of Federal funds and other sources of funds;

(E) include a strategy for pollution prevention and control that includes the promotion of pollution prevention and management practices to reduce the amount of pollution generated in the Lake Champlain basin; and

(F) be reviewed and revised, as necessary, at least once every 5 years, in consultation with the Administrator and other appropriate Federal agencies.

(3) The Administrator, in cooperation with the Management Conference, shall provide for public review and comment on the draft Plan. At a minimum, the Management Conference shall conduct one public meeting to hear comments on the draft plan in the State of New York and one such meeting in the State of Vermont.

(4) Not less than one hundred and twenty days after the publication of the Plan required pursuant to this section, the Administrator shall approve such plan if the plan meets the requirements of this section and the Governors of the States of New York and Vermont concur.

(5) Upon approval of the plan, such plan shall be deemed to be an approved management program for the purposes of section 319(h) of this Act and such plan shall be deemed to be an approved comprehensive conservation and management plan pursuant to section 320 of this Act.

(f) GRANT ASSISTANCE.—(1) The Administrator may, in consultation with participants in the Patrick Leahy Lake Champlain Basin Program, make grants to State, interstate, and regional water pollution control agencies, and public or nonprofit agencies, institutions, and organizations.

(2) Grants under this subsection shall be made for assisting research, surveys, studies, and modeling and technical and supporting work necessary for the development and implementation of the Plan.

(3) The amount of grants to any person under this subsection for a fiscal year shall not exceed 75 per centum of the costs of such research, survey, study and work and shall be made available on the condition that non-Federal share of such costs are provided from non-Federal sources.

(4) The Administrator may establish such requirements for the administration of grants as he determines to be appropriate.

(g) DEFINITIONS.—In this section:

(1) PATRICK LEAHY LAKE CHAMPLAIN BASIN PROGRAM.— The term Patrick Leahy Lake Champlain Basin Program means the coordinated efforts among the Federal Government, State governments, and local governments to implement the Plan.

(2) LAKE CHAMPLAIN DRAINAGE BASIN.— The term Lake Champlain drainage basin means all or part of Clinton, Franklin, Warren, Essex, and Washington counties in the State of New York and all or part of Franklin, Hamilton, Grand Isle, Chittenden, Addison, Rutland, Bennington, Lamoille, Orange, Washington, Orleans, and Caledonia counties in Vermont, that contain all of the streams, rivers, lakes, and other bodies of water, including wetlands, that drain into Lake Champlain.

(3) PLAN.— The term Plan means the plan developed under subsection (e).

(h) NO EFFECT ON CERTAIN AUTHORITY.—Nothing in this section—

(1) affects the jurisdiction or powers of—

(A) any department or agency of the Federal Government or any State government; or

(B) any international organization or entity related to Lake Champlain created by treaty or memorandum to which the United States is a signatory;

(2) provides new regulatory authority for the Environmental Protection Agency; or

(3) affects section 304 of the Great Lakes Critical Programs Act of 1990 (Public Law 101–596; 33 U.S.C. 1270 note).

(i) AUTHORIZATION OF APPROPRIATIONS.— There is authorized to be appropriated to the Administrator to carry out this section $35,000,000 for each of fiscal years 2023 through 2027, to remain available until expended.

[33 U.S.C. 1270]

SEC. 121. LAKE PONTCHARTRAIN BASIN.

(a) ESTABLISHMENT OF RESTORATION PROGRAM.— The Administrator shall establish within the Environmental Protection Agency the Lake Pontchartrain Basin Restoration Program.

(b) PURPOSE.— The purpose of the program shall be to restore the ecological health of the Basin by developing and funding restoration projects and related scientific and public education projects.

(c) DUTIES.—In carrying out the program, the Administrator shall—

(1) provide administrative and technical assistance to a management conference convened for the Basin under section 320;

(2) assist and support the activities of the management conference, including the implementation of recommendations of the management conference;

(3) support environmental monitoring of the Basin and research to provide necessary technical and scientific information;

(4) develop a comprehensive research plan to address the technical needs of the program;

(5) coordinate the grant, research, and planning programs authorized under this section;

(6) collect and make available to the public publications, and other forms of information the management conference determines to be appropriate, relating to the environmental quality of the Basin; and

(7) ensure that the comprehensive conservation and management plan approved for the Basin under section 320 is reviewed and revised in accordance with section 320 not less often than once every 5 years, beginning on the date of enactment of this paragraph.

(d) GRANTS.—The Administrator may make grants to pay not more than 75 percent of the costs—

(1) for restoration projects and studies identified in the comprehensive conservation and management plan approved for the Basin under section 320; and

(2) for public education projects recommended by the management conference.

(e) DEFINITIONS.—In this section, the following definitions apply:

(1) BASIN.— The term Basin means the Lake Pontchartrain Basin, a 10,000 square mile watershed encompassing 16 parishes in the State of Louisiana and 4 counties in the State of Mississippi.

(2) PROGRAM.— The term program means the Lake Pontchartrain Basin Restoration Program established under subsection (a).

(f) AUTHORIZATION OF APPROPRIATIONS.—

(1) IN GENERAL.— There is authorized to be appropriated to carry out this section $20,000,000 for each of fiscal years 2001 through 2012 and the amount appropriated for fiscal year 2009 for each of fiscal years 2013 through 2017. Such sums shall remain available until expended.

(2) PUBLIC EDUCATION PROJECTS.— Not more than 15 percent of the amount appropriated pursuant to paragraph (1) in a fiscal year may be expended on grants for public education projects under subsection (d)(2).

(3) ADMINISTRATIVE EXPENSES.— Not more than 5 percent of the amounts appropriated to carry out this section may be used for administrative expenses.

[33 U.S.C. 1273]

SEC. 122. WATERSHED PILOT PROJECTS.

(a) IN GENERAL.—The Administrator, in coordination with the States, may provide technical assistance and grants to a municipality or municipal entity to carry out pilot projects relating to the following areas:

(1) WATERSHED MANAGEMENT OF WET WEATHER DISCHARGES.— The management of municipal combined sewer overflows, sanitary sewer overflows, and stormwater discharges, on an integrated watershed or subwatershed basis for the purpose of demonstrating the effectiveness of a unified wet weather approach.

(2) STORMWATER BEST MANAGEMENT PRACTICES.— The control of pollutants from municipal separate storm sewer systems for the purpose of demonstrating and determining controls that are cost-effective and that use innovative technologies to manage, reduce, treat, recapture, or reuse municipal stormwater, including techniques that utilize infiltration, evapotranspiration, and reuse of stormwater onsite.

(3) WATERSHED PARTNERSHIPS.— Efforts of municipalities and property owners to demonstrate cooperative ways to address nonpoint sources of pollution to reduce adverse impacts on water quality.

(4) INTEGRATED WATER RESOURCE PLAN.— The development of an integrated water resource plan for the coordinated management and protection of surface water, ground water, and stormwater resources on a watershed or subwatershed basis to meet the objectives, goals, and policies of this Act.

(5) MUNICIPALITY-WIDE STORMWATER MANAGEMENT PLANNING.— The development of a municipality-wide plan that identifies the most effective placement of stormwater technologies and management approaches, to reduce water quality impairments from stormwater on a municipality-wide basis.

(6) INCREASED RESILIENCE OF TREATMENT WORKS.— Efforts to assess future risks and vulnerabilities of publicly owned treatment works to manmade or natural disasters, including extreme weather events and sea-level rise, and to carry out measures, on a systemwide or area-wide basis, to increase the resiliency of publicly owned treatment works.

(b) ADMINISTRATION.— The Administrator, in coordination with the States, shall provide municipalities participating in a pilot project under this section the ability to engage in innovative practices, including the ability to unify separate wet weather control efforts under a single permit.

(c) REPORT TO CONGRESS.— Not later than October 1, 2015, the Administrator shall transmit to Congress a report on the results of the pilot projects conducted under this section and their possible application nationwide.

[33 U.S.C. 1274]

SEC. 123. COLUMBIA RIVER BASIN RESTORATION.

(a) DEFINITIONS.—In this section, the following definitions apply:

(1) COLUMBIA RIVER BASIN.— The term Columbia River Basin means the entire United States portion of the Columbia River watershed.

(2) ESTUARY PARTNERSHIP.— The term Estuary Partnership means the Lower Columbia Estuary Partnership, an entity created by the States of Oregon and Washington and the Environmental Protection Agency under section 320.

(3) ESTUARY PLAN.—

(A) IN GENERAL.— The term Estuary Plan means the Estuary Partnership Comprehensive Conservation and Management Plan adopted by the Environmental Protection Agency and the Governors of Oregon and Washington on October 20, 1999, under section 320.

(B) INCLUSION.— The term Estuary Plan includes any amendments to the plan.

(4) LOWER COLUMBIA RIVER ESTUARY.— The term Lower Columbia River Estuary means the mainstem Columbia River from the Bonneville Dam to the Pacific Ocean and tidally influenced portions of tributaries to the Columbia River in that region.

(5) MIDDLE AND UPPER COLUMBIA RIVER BASIN.— The term Middle and Upper Columbia River Basin means the region consisting of the United States portion of the Columbia River Basin above Bonneville Dam.

(6) PROGRAM.— The term Program means the Columbia River Basin Restoration Program established under subsection (b)(1)(A).

(b) COLUMBIA RIVER BASIN RESTORATION PROGRAM.—

(1) ESTABLISHMENT.—

(A) IN GENERAL.— The Administrator shall establish within the Environmental Protection Agency a Columbia River Basin Restoration Program.

(B) EFFECT.—

(i) The establishment of the Program does not modify any legal or regulatory authority or program in effect as of the date of enactment of this section, including the roles of Federal agencies in the Columbia River Basin.

(ii) This section does not create any new regulatory authority.

(2) SCOPE OF PROGRAM.— The Program shall consist of a collaborative stakeholder-based program for environmental protection and restoration activities throughout the Columbia River Basin.

(3) DUTIES.—The Administrator shall—

(A) assess trends in water quality, including trends that affect uses of the water of the Columbia River Basin;

(B) collect, characterize, and assess data on water quality to identify possible causes of environmental problems; and

(C) provide grants in accordance with subsection (d) for projects that assist in—

(i) eliminating or reducing pollution;

(ii) cleaning up contaminated sites;

(iii) improving water quality;

(iv) monitoring to evaluate trends;

(v) reducing runoff;

(vi) protecting habitat; or

(vii) promoting citizen engagement or knowledge.

(c) STAKEHOLDER WORKING GROUP.—

(1) ESTABLISHMENT.— The Administrator shall establish a Columbia River Basin Restoration Working Group (referred to in this subsection as the Working Group).

(2) MEMBERSHIP.—

(A) IN GENERAL.— Membership in the Working Group shall be on a voluntary basis and any person invited by the Administrator under this subsection may decline membership.

(B) INVITED REPRESENTATIVES.—The Administrator shall invite, at a minimum, representatives of—

(i) each State located in whole or in part in the Columbia River Basin;

(ii) the Governors of each State located in whole or in part in the Columbia River Basin;

(iii) each federally recognized Indian tribe in the Columbia River Basin;

(iv) local governments in the Columbia River Basin;

(v) industries operating in the Columbia River Basin that affect or could affect water quality;

(vi) electric, water, and wastewater utilities operating in the Columba River Basin;

(vii) private landowners in the Columbia River Basin;

(viii) soil and water conservation districts in the Columbia River Basin;

(ix) nongovernmental organizations that have a presence in the Columbia River Basin;

(x) the general public in the Columbia River Basin; and

(xi) the Estuary Partnership.

(3) GEOGRAPHIC REPRESENTATION.—The Working Group shall include representatives from—

(A) each State located in whole or in part in the Columbia River Basin; and

(B) each of the lower, middle, and upper basins of the Columbia River.

(4) DUTIES AND RESPONSIBILITIES.—The Working Group shall—

(A) recommend and prioritize projects and actions; and

(B) review the progress and effectiveness of projects and actions implemented.

(5) LOWER COLUMBIA RIVER ESTUARY.—

(A) ESTUARY PARTNERSHIP.— The Estuary Partnership shall perform the duties and fulfill the responsibilities of the Working Group described in paragraph (4) as those duties and responsibilities relate to the Lower Columbia River Estuary for such time as the Estuary Partnership is the management conference for the Lower Columbia River National Estuary Program under section 320.

(B) DESIGNATION.— If the Estuary Partnership ceases to be the management conference for the Lower Columbia River National Estuary Program under section 320, the Administrator may designate the new management conference to assume the duties and responsibilities of the Working Group described in paragraph (4) as those duties and responsibilities relate to the Lower Columbia River Estuary.

(C) INCORPORATION.— If the Estuary Partnership is removed from the National Estuary Program, the duties and responsibilities for the lower 146 miles of the Columbia River pursuant to this section shall be incorporated into the duties of the Working Group.

(d) GRANTS.—

(1) IN GENERAL.— The Administrator shall establish a voluntary, competitive Columbia River Basin program to provide grants to State governments, tribal governments, regional water pollution control agencies and entities, local government entities, nongovernmental entities, or soil and water conservation districts to develop or implement projects authorized under this section for the purpose of environmental protection and restoration activities throughout the Columbia River Basin.

(2) FEDERAL SHARE.—

(A) IN GENERAL.—Except as provided in subparagraph (B), the Federal share of the cost of any project or activity carried out using funds from a grant provided to any person (including a State, tribal, or local government or interstate or regional agency) under this subsection for a fiscal year—

(i) shall not exceed 75 percent of the total cost of the project or activity; and

(ii) shall be made on condition that the non-Federal share of such total cost shall be provided from non-Federal sources.

(B) EXCEPTIONS.—With respect to cost-sharing for a grant provided under this subsection—

(i) a tribal government may use Federal funds for the non-Federal share; and

(ii) the Administrator may increase the Federal share under such circumstances as the Administrator determines to be appropriate.

(3) ALLOCATION.—In making grants using funds appropriated to carry out this section, the Administrator shall—

(A) provide not less than 25 percent of the funds to make grants for projects, programs, and studies in the Lower Columbia River Estuary;

(B) provide not less than 25 percent of the funds to make grants for projects, programs, and studies in the Middle and Upper Columbia River Basin, including the Snake River Basin; and

(C) retain not more than 5 percent of the funds for the Environmental Protection Agency for purposes of implementing this section.

(4) REPORTING.—

(A) IN GENERAL.— Each grant recipient under this subsection shall submit to the Administrator reports on progress being made in achieving the purposes of this section.

(B) REQUIREMENTS.— The Administrator shall establish requirements and timelines for recipients of grants under this subsection to report on progress made in achieving the purposes of this section.

(5) RELATIONSHIP TO OTHER FUNDING.—

(A) IN GENERAL.— Nothing in this subsection limits the eligibility of the Estuary Partnership to receive funding under section 320(g).

(B) LIMITATION.— None of the funds made available under this subsection may be used for the administration of a management conference under section 320.

(6) AUTHORIZATION OF APPROPRIATIONS.— There is authorized to be appropriated to carry out this subsection $30,000,000 for each of fiscal years 2020 and 2021.

(e) ANNUAL BUDGET PLAN.—The President, as part of the annual budget submission of the President to Congress under section 1105(a) of title 31, United States Code, shall submit information regarding each Federal agency involved in protection and restoration of the Columbia River Basin, including an interagency crosscut budget that displays for each Federal agency—

(1) the amounts obligated for the preceding fiscal year for protection and restoration projects, programs, and studies relating to the Columbia River Basin;

(2) the estimated budget for the current fiscal year for protection and restoration projects, programs, and studies relating to the Columbia River Basin; and

(3) the proposed budget for protection and restoration projects, programs, and studies relating to the Columbia River Basin.

[33 U.S.C. 1275]

SEC. 124. ENHANCED AQUIFER USE AND RECHARGE.

(a) IN GENERAL.—Subject to the availability of appropriations, the Administrator shall provide funding to carry out groundwater research on enhanced aquifer use and recharge in support of sole-source aquifers, of which—

(1) not less than 50 percent shall be used to provide 1 grant to a State, unit of local government, or Indian Tribe to carry out activities that would directly support that research; and

(2) the remainder shall be provided to 1 appropriate research center.

(b) COORDINATION.— As a condition of accepting funds under subsection (a), the State, unit of local government, or Indian Tribe and the appropriate research center that receive funds under that subsection shall establish a formal research relationship for the purpose of coordinating efforts under this section.

(c) AUTHORIZATION OF APPROPRIATIONS.— There is authorized to be appropriated to the Administrator to carry out this section $5,000,000 for each of fiscal years 2022 through 2026.

[33 U.S.C. 1276]

SEC. 125. SAN FRANCISCO BAY RESTORATION GRANT PROGRAM.

(a) DEFINITIONS.—In this section:

(1) ESTUARY PARTNERSHIP.— The term Estuary Partnership means the San Francisco Estuary Partnership, designated as the management conference for the San Francisco Bay under section 320.

(2) SAN FRANCISCO BAY PLAN.—The term San Francisco Bay Plan means—

(A) until the date of the completion of the plan developed by the Director under subsection (d), the comprehensive conservation and management plan approved under section 320 for the San Francisco Bay estuary; and

(B) on and after the date of the completion of the plan developed by the Director under subsection (d), the plan developed by the Director under subsection (d).

(b) PROGRAM OFFICE.—

(1) ESTABLISHMENT.— The Administrator shall establish in the Environmental Protection Agency a San Francisco Bay Program Office. The Office shall be located at the headquarters of Region 9 of the Environmental Protection Agency.

(2) APPOINTMENT OF DIRECTOR.— The Administrator shall appoint a Director of the Office, who shall have management experience and technical expertise relating to the San Francisco Bay and be highly qualified to direct the development and implementation of projects, activities, and studies necessary to implement the San Francisco Bay Plan.

(3) DELEGATION OF AUTHORITY; STAFFING.— The Administrator shall delegate to the Director such authority and provide such staff as may be necessary to carry out this section.

(c) ANNUAL PRIORITY LIST.—

(1) IN GENERAL.— After providing public notice, the Director shall annually compile a priority list, consistent with the San Francisco Bay Plan, identifying and prioritizing the projects, activities, and studies to be carried out with amounts made available under subsection (e).

(2) Inclusions.—The annual priority list compiled under paragraph (1) shall include the following:

(A) Projects, activities, and studies, including restoration projects and habitat improvement for fish, waterfowl, and wildlife, that advance the goals and objectives of the San Francisco Bay Plan, for—

(i) water quality improvement, including the reduction of marine litter;

(ii) wetland, riverine, and estuary restoration and protection;

(iii) nearshore and endangered species recovery; and

(iv) adaptation to climate change.

(B) Information on the projects, activities, and studies specified under subparagraph (A), including—

(i) the identity of each entity receiving assistance pursuant to subsection (e); and

(ii) a description of the communities to be served.

(C) The criteria and methods established by the Director for identification of projects, activities, and studies to be included on the annual priority list.

(3) Consultation.—In compiling the annual priority list under paragraph (1), the Director shall consult with, and consider the recommendations of—

(A) the Estuary Partnership;

(B) the State of California and affected local governments in the San Francisco Bay estuary watershed;

(C) the San Francisco Bay Restoration Authority; and

(D) any other relevant stakeholder involved with the protection and restoration of the San Francisco Bay estuary that the Director determines to be appropriate.

(d) San Francisco Bay Plan.—

(1) In general.— Not later than 5 years after the date of enactment of this section, the Director, in conjunction with the Estuary Partnership, shall review and revise the comprehensive conservation and management plan approved under section 320 for the San Francisco Bay estuary to develop a plan to guide the projects, activities, and studies of the Office to address the restoration and protection of the San Francisco Bay.

(2) Revision of san francisco bay plan.— Not less often than once every 5 years after the date of the completion of the plan described in paragraph (1), the Director shall review, and revise as appropriate, the San Francisco Bay Plan.

(3) Outreach.— In carrying out this subsection, the Director shall consult with the Estuary Partnership and Indian tribes and solicit input from other non-Federal stakeholders.

(e) Grant Program.—

(1) In general.— The Director may provide funding through cooperative

agreements, grants, or other means to State and local agencies, special districts, and public or nonprofit agencies, institutions, and organizations, including the Estuary Partnership, for projects, activities, and studies identified on the annual priority list compiled under subsection (c).

(2) MAXIMUM AMOUNT OF GRANTS; NON-FEDERAL SHARE.—

(A) MAXIMUM AMOUNT OF GRANTS.— Amounts provided to any entity under this section for a fiscal year shall not exceed an amount equal to 75 percent of the total cost of any projects, activities, and studies that are to be carried out using those amounts.

(B) NON-FEDERAL SHARE.— Not less than 25 percent of the cost of any project, activity, or study carried out using amounts provided under this section shall be provided from non-Federal sources.

(f) FUNDING.—

(1) ADMINISTRATIVE EXPENSES.— Of the amount made available to carry out this section for a fiscal year, the Director may not use more than 5 percent to pay administrative expenses incurred in carrying out this section.

(2) PROHIBITION.— No amounts made available under this section may be used for the administration of a management conference under section 320.

[33 U.S.C. 1276a]

SEC. 126. PUGET SOUND.

(a) DEFINITIONS.—In this section:

(1) COASTAL NONPOINT POLLUTION CONTROL PROGRAM.— The term Coastal Nonpoint Pollution Control Program means the State of Washington's Coastal Nonpoint Pollution Control Program approved under section 6217 of the Coastal Zone Act Reauthorization Amendments of 1990.

(2) DIRECTOR.— The term Director means the Director of the Program Office.

(3) FEDERAL ACTION PLAN.— The term Federal Action Plan means the plan developed under subsection (c)(3)(B).

(4) INTERNATIONAL JOINT COMMISSION.— The term International Joint Commission means the International Joint Commission established by the Treaty relating to the boundary waters and questions arising along the boundary between the United States and Canada, signed at Washington January 11, 1909, and entered into force May 5, 1910 (36 Stat. 2448; TS 548; 12 Bevans 319).

(5) PACIFIC SALMON COMMISSION.— The term Pacific Salmon Commission means the Pacific Salmon Commission established by the United States and Canada under the Treaty concerning Pacific salmon, with annexes and memorandum of understanding, signed at Ottawa January 28, 1985, and entered into force March 18, 1985 (TIAS 11091; 1469 UNTS 357) (commonly known as the Pacific Salmon Treaty).

(6) PROGRAM OFFICE.— The term Program Office means the Puget Sound Recovery National Program Office established by subsection (b).

(7) PUGET SOUND ACTION AGENDA; ACTION AGENDA.— The term Puget Sound

Action Agenda or Action Agenda means the most recent plan developed by the Puget Sound National Estuary Program Management Conference, in consultation with the Puget Sound Tribal Management Conference, and approved by the Administrator as the comprehensive conservation and management plan for the Puget Sound under section 320.

(8) PUGET SOUND FEDERAL LEADERSHIP TASK FORCE.— The term Puget Sound Federal Leadership Task Force means the Puget Sound Federal Leadership Task Force established under subsection (c).

(9) PUGET SOUND FEDERAL TASK FORCE.— The term Puget Sound Federal Task Force means the Puget Sound Federal Task Force established in 2016 under a memorandum of understanding among 9 Federal agencies.

(10) PUGET SOUND NATIONAL ESTUARY PROGRAM MANAGEMENT CONFERENCE.— The term Puget Sound National Estuary Program Management Conference means the management conference for the Puget Sound convened pursuant to section 320.

(11) PUGET SOUND PARTNERSHIP.— The term Puget Sound Partnership means the State agency created under the laws of the State of Washington (section 90.71.210 of the Revised Code of Washington), or its successor agency that has been designated by the Administrator as the lead entity to support the Puget Sound National Estuary Program Management Conference.

(12) PUGET SOUND REGION.—

(A) IN GENERAL.— The term Puget Sound region means the land and waters in the northwest corner of the State of Washington from the Canadian border to the north to the Pacific Ocean on the west, including Hood Canal and the Strait of Juan de Fuca.

(B) INCLUSION.— The term Puget Sound region includes all watersheds that drain into the Puget Sound.

(13) PUGET SOUND TRIBAL MANAGEMENT CONFERENCE.— The term Puget Sound Tribal Management Conference means the 20 treaty Indian tribes of western Washington and the Northwest Indian Fisheries Commission.

(14) SALISH SEA.— The term Salish Sea means the network of coastal waterways on the west coast of North America that includes the Puget Sound, the Strait of Georgia, and the Strait of Juan de Fuca.

(15) SALMON RECOVERY PLANS.— The term Salmon Recovery Plans means the recovery plans for salmon and steelhead species approved by the Secretary of the Interior under section 4(f) of the Endangered Species Act of 1973 that are applicable to the Puget Sound region.

(16) STATE ADVISORY COMMITTEE.— The term State Advisory Committee means the advisory committee established by subsection (d).

(17) TREATY RIGHTS AT RISK INITIATIVE.— The term Treaty Rights at Risk Initiative means the report from the treaty Indian tribes of western Washington entitled Treaty Rights At Risk: Ongoing Habitat Loss, the Decline of the Salmon Resource, and Recommendations for Change and dated July 14, 2011, or its

successor report that outlines issues and offers solutions for the protection of Tribal treaty rights, recovery of salmon habitat, and management of sustainable treaty and nontreaty salmon fisheries, including through Tribal salmon hatchery programs.

(b) PUGET SOUND RECOVERY NATIONAL PROGRAM OFFICE.—

(1) ESTABLISHMENT.— There is established in the Environmental Protection Agency a Puget Sound Recovery National Program Office, to be located in the State of Washington.

(2) DIRECTOR.—

(A) IN GENERAL.—There shall be a Director of the Program Office, who shall have leadership and project management experience and shall be highly qualified to—

(i) direct the integration of multiple project planning efforts and programs from different agencies and jurisdictions; and

(ii) align numerous, and possibly competing, priorities to accomplish visible and measurable outcomes under the Action Agenda.

(B) POSITION.— The position of Director of the Program Office shall be a career reserved position, as such term is defined in section 3132 of title 5, United States Code.

(3) DELEGATION OF AUTHORITY; STAFFING.— Using amounts made available to carry out this section, the Administrator shall delegate to the Director such authority and provide such staff as may be necessary to carry out this section.

(4) DUTIES.—The Director shall—

(A) coordinate and manage the timely execution of the requirements of this section, including the formation and meetings of the Puget Sound Federal Leadership Task Force;

(B) coordinate activities related to the restoration and protection of the Puget Sound across the Environmental Protection Agency;

(C) coordinate and align the activities of the Administrator with the Action Agenda, Salmon Recovery Plans, the Treaty Rights at Risk Initiative, and the Coastal Nonpoint Pollution Control Program;

(D) promote the efficient use of Environmental Protection Agency resources in pursuit of the restoration and protection of the Puget Sound;

(E) serve on the Puget Sound Federal Leadership Task Force and collaborate with, help coordinate, and implement activities with other Federal agencies that have responsibilities involving the restoration and protection of the Puget Sound;

(F) provide or procure such other advice, technical assistance, research, assessments, monitoring, or other support as is determined by the Director to be necessary or prudent to most efficiently and effectively fulfill the objectives and priorities of the Action Agenda, the Salmon Recovery Plans, the Treaty Rights at Risk Initiative, and the Coastal Nonpoint Pollution Control Program, consistent with the best available science, to ensure the health of the Puget Sound ecosystem;

(G) track the progress of the Environmental Protection Agency toward meeting the agency's specified objectives and priorities within the Action Agenda and the Federal Action Plan;

(H) implement the recommendations of the Comptroller General set forth in the report entitled Puget Sound Restoration: Additional Actions Could Improve Assessments of Progress and dated July 19, 2018;

(I) serve as liaison and coordinate activities for the restoration and protection of the Salish Sea with Canadian authorities, the Pacific Salmon Commission, and the International Joint Commission; and

(J) carry out such additional duties as the Director determines necessary and appropriate.

(c) PUGET SOUND FEDERAL LEADERSHIP TASK FORCE.—

(1) ESTABLISHMENT.— There is established a Puget Sound Federal Leadership Task Force.

(2) MEMBERSHIP.—

(A) COMPOSITION.—The Puget Sound Federal Leadership Task Force shall be composed of the following members:

(i) The following individuals appointed by the Secretary of Agriculture:

(I) A representative of the National Forest Service.

(II) A representative of the Natural Resources Conservation Service.

(ii) A representative of the National Oceanic and Atmospheric Administration appointed by the Secretary of Commerce.

(iii) The following individuals appointed by the Secretary of Defense:

(I) A representative of the Corps of Engineers.

(II) A representative of the Joint Base Lewis-McChord.

(III) A representative of the Commander, Navy Region Northwest.

(iv) The Director of the Program Office.

(v) The following individuals appointed by the Secretary of Homeland Security:

(I) A representative of the Coast Guard.

(II) A representative of the Federal Emergency Management Agency.

(vi) The following individuals appointed by the Secretary of the Interior:

(I) A representative of the Bureau of Indian Affairs.

(II) A representative of the United States Fish and Wildlife Service.

(III) A representative of the United States Geological Survey.

(IV) A representative of the National Park Service.

(vii) The following individuals appointed by the Secretary of Transportation:

(I) A representative of the Federal Highway Administration.

(II) A representative of the Federal Transit Administration.

(viii) Representatives of such other Federal agencies, programs, and initiatives as the other members of the Puget Sound Federal Leadership Task Force determines necessary.

(B) QUALIFICATIONS.— Members appointed under this paragraph shall have experience and expertise in matters of restoration and protection of large watersheds and bodies of water, or related experience that will benefit the restoration and protection of the Puget Sound.

(C) CO-CHAIRS.—

(i) IN GENERAL.—The following members of the Puget Sound Federal Leadership Task Force shall serve as Co-Chairs of the Puget Sound Federal Leadership Task Force:

(I) The representative of the National Oceanic and Atmospheric Administration.

(II) The Director of the Program Office.

(III) The representative of the Corps of Engineers.

(ii) LEADERSHIP.— The Co-Chairs shall ensure the Puget Sound Federal Leadership Task Force completes its duties through robust discussion of all relevant issues. The Co-Chairs shall share leadership responsibilities equally.

(3) DUTIES.—

(A) GENERAL DUTIES.—The Puget Sound Federal Leadership Task Force shall—

(i) uphold Federal trust responsibilities to restore and protect resources crucial to Tribal treaty rights, including by carrying out government-to-government consultation with Indian tribes when requested by such tribes;

(ii) provide a venue for dialogue and coordination across all Federal agencies represented by a member of the Puget Sound Federal Leadership Task Force to align Federal resources for the purposes of carrying out the requirements of this section and all other Federal laws that contribute to the restoration and protection of the Puget Sound, including by—

(I) enabling and encouraging such agencies to act consistently with the objectives and priorities of the Action Agenda, the Salmon Recovery Plans, the Treaty Rights at Risk Initiative, and the Coastal Nonpoint Pollution Control Program;

(II) facilitating the coordination of Federal activities that impact such restoration and protection;

(III) facilitating the delivery of feedback given by such agencies to the Puget Sound Partnership during the development of the Action Agenda;

(IV) facilitating the resolution of interagency conflicts associated with such restoration and protection among such agencies;

(V) providing a forum for exchanging information among such agencies regarding activities being conducted, including obstacles or efficiencies found, during restoration and protection activities; and

(VI) promoting the efficient use of government resources in pursuit of such restoration and protection through coordination and collaboration, including by ensuring that the Federal efforts relating to the science necessary for such restoration and protection are consistent, and not duplicative, across the Federal Government;

(iii) catalyze public leaders at all levels to work together toward shared goals by demonstrating interagency best practices coming from such agencies;

(iv) provide advice and support on scientific and technical issues and act as a forum for the exchange of scientific information about the Puget Sound;

(v) identify and inventory Federal environmental research and monitoring programs related to the Puget Sound, and provide such inventory to the Puget Sound National Estuary Program Management Conference;

(vi) ensure that Puget Sound restoration and protection activities are as consistent as practicable with ongoing restoration and protection and related efforts in the Salish Sea that are being conducted by Canadian authorities, the Pacific Salmon Commission, and the International Joint Commission;

(vii) ensure that Puget Sound restoration and protection activities are consistent with national security interests;

(viii) establish any working groups or committees necessary to assist the Puget Sound Federal Leadership Task Force in its duties, including relating to public policy and scientific issues; and

(ix) raise national awareness of the significance of the Puget Sound.

(B) PUGET SOUND FEDERAL ACTION PLAN.—

(i) IN GENERAL.— Not later than 5 years after the date of enactment of this section, the Puget Sound Federal Leadership Task Force shall develop and approve a Federal Action Plan that leverages Federal programs across agencies and serves to coordinate diverse programs and priorities for the restoration and protection of the Puget Sound.

(ii) REVISION OF PUGET SOUND FEDERAL ACTION PLAN.— Not less often than once every 5 years after the date of approval of the Federal Action Plan under clause (i), the Puget Sound Federal Leadership Task Force shall review, and revise as appropriate, the Federal Action Plan.

(C) FEEDBACK BY FEDERAL AGENCIES.—In facilitating feedback under subparagraph (A)(ii)(III), the Puget Sound Federal Leadership Task Force shall request Federal agencies to consider, at a minimum, possible Federal actions within the Puget Sound region designed to—

(i) further the goals, targets, and actions of the Action Agenda, the Salmon Recovery Plans, the Treaty Rights at Risk Initiative, and the Coastal Nonpoint Pollution Control Program;

(ii) as applicable, implement and enforce this Act, the Endangered Species Act of 1973, and all other Federal laws that contribute to the restoration and protection of the Puget Sound, including those that protect Tribal treaty rights;

(iii) prevent the introduction and spread of invasive species;

(iv) protect marine and wildlife habitats;

(v) protect, restore, and conserve forests, wetlands, riparian zones, and nearshore waters;

(vi) promote resilience to climate change and ocean acidification effects;

(vii) restore fisheries so that they are sustainable and productive;

(viii) preserve biodiversity;

(ix) restore and protect ecosystem services that provide clean water, filter toxic chemicals, and increase ecosystem resilience; and

(x) improve water quality, including by preventing and managing stormwater runoff, incorporating erosion control techniques and trash capture devices, using sustainable stormwater practices, and mitigating and minimizing nonpoint source pollution, including marine litter.

(4) PARTICIPATION OF STATE ADVISORY COMMITTEE AND PUGET SOUND TRIBAL MANAGEMENT CONFERENCE.— The Puget Sound Federal Leadership Task Force shall carry out its duties with input from, and in collaboration with, the State Advisory Committee and the Puget Sound Tribal Management Conference, including by seeking advice and recommendations on the actions, progress, and issues pertaining to the restoration and protection of the Puget Sound.

(5) MEETINGS.—

(A) INITIAL MEETING.—The Puget Sound Federal Leadership Task Force shall meet not later than 180 days after the date of enactment of this section—

(i) to determine if all Federal agencies are properly represented;

(ii) to establish the bylaws of the Puget Sound Federal Leadership Task Force;

(iii) to establish necessary working groups or committees; and

(iv) to determine subsequent meeting times, dates, and logistics.

(B) SUBSEQUENT MEETINGS.— After the initial meeting, the Puget Sound Federal Leadership Task Force shall meet, at a minimum, twice per year to carry out the duties of the Puget Sound Federal Leadership Task Force.

(C) WORKING GROUP MEETINGS.— A meeting of any established working group or committee of the Puget Sound Federal Leadership Task Force shall not be considered a biannual meeting for purposes of subparagraph (B).

(D) JOINT MEETINGS.—The Puget Sound Federal Leadership Task Force—

(i) shall offer to meet jointly with the Puget Sound National Estuary Program Management Conference and the Puget Sound Tribal Management Conference, at a minimum, once per year; and

(ii) may consider such a joint meeting to be a biannual meeting of the Puget Sound Federal Leadership Task Force for purposes of subparagraph (B).

(E) QUORUM.— A simple majority of the members of the Puget Sound Federal Leadership Task Force shall constitute a quorum.

(F) VOTING.— For the Puget Sound Federal Leadership Task Force to take an official action, a quorum shall be present, and at least a two-thirds majority of the members present shall vote in the affirmative.

(6) PUGET SOUND FEDERAL LEADERSHIP TASK FORCE PROCEDURES AND ADVICE.—

(A) ADVISORS.— The Puget Sound Federal Leadership Task Force may seek advice and input from any interested, knowledgeable, or affected party as the Puget Sound Federal Leadership Task Force determines necessary to perform its duties.

(B) COMPENSATION.— A member of the Puget Sound Federal Leadership Task Force shall receive no additional compensation for service as a member on the Puget Sound Federal Leadership Task Force.

(C) TRAVEL EXPENSES.— Travel expenses incurred by a member of the Puget Sound Federal Leadership Task Force in the performance of service on the Puget Sound Federal Leadership Task Force may be paid by the agency that the member represents.

(7) PUGET SOUND FEDERAL TASK FORCE.—

(A) IN GENERAL.— On the date of enactment of this section, the 2016 memorandum of understanding establishing the Puget Sound Federal Task Force shall cease to be effective.

(B) USE OF PREVIOUS WORK.— The Puget Sound Federal Leadership Task Force shall, to the extent practicable, use the work product produced, relied upon, and analyzed by the Puget Sound Federal Task Force in order to avoid duplicating the efforts of the Puget Sound Federal Task Force.

(d) STATE ADVISORY COMMITTEE.—

(1) ESTABLISHMENT.— There is established a State Advisory Committee.

(2) MEMBERSHIP.— The State Advisory Committee shall consist of up to seven members designated by the governing body of the Puget Sound Partnership, in consultation with the Governor of Washington, who will represent Washington State agencies that have significant roles and responsibilities related to the restoration and

protection of the Puget Sound.

(e) Puget Sound Federal Leadership Task Force Biennial Report on Puget Sound Restoration and Protection Activities.—

(1) In general.— Not later than 1 year after the date of enactment of this section, and biennially thereafter, the Puget Sound Federal Leadership Task Force, in collaboration with the Puget Sound Tribal Management Conference and the State Advisory Committee, shall submit to the President, Congress, the Governor of Washington, and the governing body of the Puget Sound Partnership a report that summarizes the progress, challenges, and milestones of the Puget Sound Federal Leadership Task Force relating to the restoration and protection of the Puget Sound.

(2) Contents.—The report submitted under paragraph (1) shall include a description of the following:

(A) The roles and progress of each State, local government entity, and Federal agency that has jurisdiction in the Puget Sound region relating to meeting the identified objectives and priorities of the Action Agenda, the Salmon Recovery Plans, the Treaty Rights at Risk Initiative, and the Coastal Nonpoint Pollution Control Program.

(B) If available, the roles and progress of Tribal governments that have jurisdiction in the Puget Sound region relating to meeting the identified objectives and priorities of the Action Agenda, the Salmon Recovery Plans, the Treaty Rights at Risk Initiative, and the Coastal Nonpoint Pollution Control Program.

(C) A summary of specific recommendations concerning implementation of the Action Agenda and the Federal Action Plan, including challenges, barriers, and anticipated milestones, targets, and timelines.

(D) A summary of progress made by Federal agencies toward the priorities identified in the Federal Action Plan.

(f) Tribal Rights and Consultation.—

(1) Preservation of tribal treaty rights.— Nothing in this section affects, or is intended to affect, any right reserved by treaty between the United States and one or more Indian tribes.

(2) Consultation.— Nothing in this section affects any authorization or obligation of a Federal agency to consult with an Indian tribe under any other provision of law.

(g) Consistency.—

(1) In general.—Actions authorized or implemented under this section shall be consistent with—

(A) the Salmon Recovery Plans;

(B) the Coastal Nonpoint Pollution Control Program; and

(C) the water quality standards of the State of Washington approved by the Administrator under section 303.

(2) FEDERAL ACTIONS.—All Federal agencies represented on the Puget Sound Federal Leadership Task Force shall act consistently with the protection of Tribal, treaty-reserved rights and, to the greatest extent practicable given such agencies' existing obligations under Federal law, act consistently with the objectives and priorities of the Action Agenda, the Salmon Recovery Plans, the Treaty Rights at Risk Initiative, and the Coastal Nonpoint Pollution Control Program, when—

(A) conducting Federal agency activities within or outside the Puget Sound that affect any land or water use or natural resources of the Puget Sound region, including activities performed by a contractor for the benefit of a Federal agency;

(B) interpreting and enforcing regulations that impact the restoration and protection of the Puget Sound;

(C) issuing Federal licenses or permits that impact the restoration and protection of the Puget Sound; and

(D) granting Federal assistance to State, local, and Tribal governments for activities related to the restoration and protection of the Puget Sound.

[33 U.S.C. 1276b]

TITLE II—GRANTS FOR CONSTRUCTION OF TREATMENT WORKS

TITLE II—GRANTS FOR CONSTRUCTION OF TREATMENT WORKS

PURPOSE

SEC. 201. (a) It is the purpose of this title to require and to assist the development and implementation of waste treatment management plans and practices which will achieve the goals of this Act.

(b) Waste treatment management plans and practices shall provide for the application of the best practicable waste treatment technology before any discharge into receiving waters, including reclaiming and recycling of water, and confined disposal of pollutants so they will not migrate to cause water or other environmental pollution and shall provide for consideration of advanced waste treatment techniques.

(c) To the extent practicable, waste treatment management shall be on an areawide basis and provide control or treatment of all point and nonpoint sources of pollution, including in place or accumulated pollution sources.

(d) The Administrator shall encourage waste treatment management which results in the construction of revenue producing facilities providing for—

(1) the recycling of potential sewage pollutants through the production of agriculture, silviculture, or aquaculture products, or any combination thereof;

(2) the confined and contained disposal of pollutants not recycled;

(3) the reclamation of wastewater; and

(4) the ultimate disposal of sludge in a manner that will not result in environmental hazards.

(e) The Administrator shall encourage waste treatment management which results in integrating facilities for sewage treatment and recycling with facilities to treat, dispose of, or utilize other industrial and municipal wastes, including but not limited to solid waste and waste heat and thermal discharges. Such integrated facilities shall be designed and operated to produce revenues in excess of capital and operation and maintenance costs and such revenues shall be used by the designated regional management agency to aid in financing other environmental improvement programs.

(f) The Administrator shall encourage waste treatment management which combines open space and recreational considerations with such management.

(g)(1) The Administrator is authorized to make grants to any State, municipality, or intermunicipal or interstate agency for the construction of publicly owned treatment works. On and after October 1, 1984, grants under this title shall be made only for projects for secondary treatment or more stringent treatment, or any cost effective alternative thereto, new interceptors and appurtenances, and infiltration-in-flow correction. Notwithstanding the preceding sentences, the Administrator may make grants on and after October 1, 1984, for (A) any project within the definition set forth in section 212(2) of this Act, other than for a project referred to in the preceding sentence, and (B) any purpose for which a grant may be made under sections[5] 319 (h) and (i) of this Act (including any innovative and alternative approaches for the control of nonpoint sources of pollution), except that not more than 20 per centum (as determined by the Governor of the State) of the amount allotted to a State under section 205 of this Act for any fiscal year shall be obligated in such State under authority of this sentence.

[5] So in original. Probably should be section.

(2) The Administrator shall not make grants from funds authorized for any fiscal year beginning after June 30, 1974, to any State, municipality, or intermunicipal or interstate agency for the erection, building, acquisition, alteration, remodeling, improvement, or extension of treatment works unless the grant applicant has satisfactorily demonstrated to the Administrator that—

(A) alternative waste management techniques have been studied and evaluated and the works proposed for grant assistance will provide for the application of the best practicable waste treatment technology over the life of the works consistent with the purposes of this title; and

(B) as appropriate, the works proposed for grant assistance will take into account and allow to the extent practicable the application of technology at a later date which will provide for the reclaiming or recycling of water or otherwise eliminate the discharge of pollutants.

(3) The Administrator shall not approve any grant after July 1, 1973, for treatment works under this section unless the applicant shows to the satisfaction of the Administrator that each sewer collection system discharging into such treatment works is not subject to excessive infiltration.

(4) The Administrator is authorized to make grants to applicants for treatment works grants under this section for such sewer system evaluation studies as may be necessary to carry out the requirements of paragraph (3) of this subsection. Such grants shall be made in accordance with rules and regulations promulgated by the Administrator. Initial rules and regulations shall be promulgated under this paragraph not later than 120 days after the date of enactment of the Federal Water Pollution Control Act Amendments of 1972.

(5) The Administrator shall not make grants from funds authorized for any fiscal year beginning after September 30, 1978, to any State, municipality, or intermunicipal or interstate agency for the erection, building, acquisition, alteration, remodeling, improvement, or extension of treatment works unless the grant applicant has satisfactorily demonstrated to the Administrator that innovative and alternative wastewater treatment processes and techniques which provide for the reclaiming and reuse of water, otherwise eliminate the discharge of pollutants, and utilize recycling techniques, land treatment, new or improved methods of waste treatment management for municipal and industrial waste (discharged into municipal systems) and the confined disposal of pollutants, so that pollutants will not migrate to cause water or other environmental pollution, have been fully studied and evaluated by the applicant taking into account section 201(d) of this Act and taking into account and allowing to the extent practicable the more efficient use of energy and resources.

(6) The Administrator shall not make grants from funds authorized for any

fiscal year beginning after September 30, 1978, to any State, municipality, or intermunicipal or interstate agency for the erection, building, acquisition, alteration, remodeling, improvement, or extension of treatment works unless the grant applicant has satisfactorily demonstrated to the Administrator that the applicant has analyzed the potential recreation and open space opportunities in the planning of the proposed treatment works.

(h) A grant may be made under this section to construct a privately owned treatment works serving one or more principal residences or small commercial establishments constructed prior to, and inhabited on, the date of enactment of this subsection where the Administrator finds that—

(1) a public body otherwise eligible for a grant under subsection (g) of this section has applied on behalf of a number of such units and certified that public ownership of such works is not feasible;

(2) such public body has entered into an agreement with the Administrator which guarantees that such treatment works will be properly operated and maintained and will comply with all other requirements of section 204 of this Act and includes a system of charges to assure that each recipient of waste treatment services under such a grant will pay its proportionate share of the cost of operation and maintenance (including replacement); and

(3) the total cost and environmental impact of providing waste treatment services to such residences or commercial establishments will be less than the cost of providing a system of collection and central treatment of such wastes.

(i) The Administrator shall encourage waste treatment management methods, processes, and techniques which will reduce total energy requirements.

(j) The Administrator is authorized to make a grant for any treatment works utilizing processes and techniques meeting the guidelines promulgated under section 304(d)(3) of this Act, if the Administrator determines it is in the public interest and if in the cost effectiveness study made of the construction grant application for the purpose of evaluating alternative treatment works, the life cycle cost of the treatment works for which the grant is to be made does not exceed the life cycle cost of the most cost effective alternative by more than 15 per centum.

(k) No grant made after November 15, 1981, for a publicly owned treatment works, other than for facility planning and the preparation of construction plans and specifications, shall be used to treat, store, or convey the flow of any industrial user into such treatment works in excess of a flow per day equivalent to fifty thousand gallons per day of sanitary waste. This subsection shall not apply to any project proposed by a grantee which is carrying out an approved project to prepare construction plans and specifications for a facility to treat wastewater, which received its grant approval before May 15, 1980. This subsection shall not be in effect after November 15, 1981.

(l)(1) After the date of enactment of this subsection, Federal grants shall not be made for the purpose of providing assistance solely for facility plans, or plans, specifications, and estimates for any proposed project for the construction of treatment works. In the event that the proposed project receives a grant under this section for construction, the Administrator shall make an allowance in such grant for non-Federal funds expended during the facility planning and advanced engineering and design phase at the prevailing

Federal share under section 202(a) of this Act, based on the percentage of total project costs which the Administrator determines is the general experience for such projects.

(2)(A) Each State shall use a portion of the funds allotted to such State each fiscal year, but not to exceed 10 per centum of such funds, to advance to potential grant applicants under this title the costs of facility planning or the preparation of plans, specifications, and estimates.

(B) Such an advance shall be limited to the allowance for such costs which the Administrator establishes under paragraph (1) of this subsection, and shall be provided only to a potential grant applicant which is a small community and which in the judgment of the State would otherwise be unable to prepare a request for a grant for construction costs under this section.

(C) In the event a grant for construction costs is made under this section for a project for which an advance has been made under this paragraph, the Administrator shall reduce the amount of such grant by the allowance established under paragraph (1) of this subsection. In the event no such grant is made, the State is authorized to seek repayment of such advance on such terms and conditions as it may determine.

(m)(1) Notwithstanding any other provisions of this title, the Administrator is authorized to make a grant from any funds otherwise allotted to the State of California under section 205 of this Act to the project (and in the amount) specified in Order WQG 81–1 of the California State Water Resources Control Board.

(2) Notwithstanding any other provision of this Act, the Administrator shall make a grant from any funds otherwise allotted to the State of California to the city of Eureka, California, in connection with project numbered C–06–2772, for the purchase of one hundred and thirty-nine acres of property as environmental mitigation for siting of the proposed treatment plant.

(3) Notwithstanding any other provision of this Act, the Administrator shall make a grant from any funds otherwise allotted to the State of California to the city of San Diego, California, in connection with that city's aquaculture sewage process (total resources recovery system) as an innovative and alternative waste treatment process.

(n)(1) On and after October 1, 1984, upon the request of the Governor of an affected State, the Administrator is authorized to use funds available to such State under section 205 to address water quality problems due to the impacts of discharges from combined storm water and sanitary sewer overflows, which are not otherwise eligible under this subsection, where correction of such discharges is a major priority for such State.

(2) Beginning fiscal year 1983, the Administrator shall have available $200,000,000 per fiscal year in addition to those funds authorized in section 207 of this Act to be utilized to address water quality problems of marine bays and estuaries subject to lower levels of water quality due to the impacts of discharges from combined storm water and sanitary sewer overflows from adjacent urban complexes, not otherwise eligible under this subsection. Such sums may be used as deemed appropriate by the Administrator as provided in paragraphs (1) and (2) of this subsection, upon the request of and demonstration of water quality benefits by the Governor of an affected State.

(o) The Administrator shall encourage and assist applicants for grant assistance under this title to develop and file with the Administrator a capital financing plan which, at a minimum—

(1) projects the future requirements for waste treatment services within the applicant's jurisdiction for a period of no less than ten years;

(2) projects the nature, extent, timing, and costs of future expansion and reconstruction of treatment works which will be necessary to satisfy the applicant's projected future requirements for waste treatment services; and

(3) sets forth with specificity the manner in which the applicant intends to finance such future expansion and reconstruction.

(p) Time Limit on Resolving Certain Disputes.— In any case in which a dispute arises with respect to the awarding of a contract for construction of treatment works by a grantee of funds under this title and a party to such dispute files an appeal with the Administrator under this title for resolution of such dispute, the Administrator shall make a final decision on such appeal within 90 days of the filing of such appeal.

[33 U.S.C. 1281]

FEDERAL SHARE

Sec. 202. (a)(1) The amount of any grant for treatment works made under this Act from funds authorized for any fiscal year beginning after June 30, 1971, and ending before October 1, 1984, shall be 75 per centum of the cost of construction thereof (as approved by the Administrator), and for any fiscal year beginning on or after October 1, 1984, shall be 55 per centum of the cost of construction thereof (as approved by the Administrator), unless modified to a lower percentage rate uniform throughout a State by the Governor of that State with the concurrence of the Administrator. Within ninety days after the enactment of this sentence the Administrator shall issue guidelines for concurrence in any such modification, which shall provide for the consideration of the unobligated balance of sums allocated to the State under section 205 of this Act, the need for assistance under this title in such State, and the availability of State grant assistance to replace the Federal share reduced by such modification. The payment of any such reduced Federal share shall not constitute an obligation on the part of the United States or a claim on the part of any State or grantee to reimbursement for the portion of the Federal share reduced in any such State. Any grant (other than for reimbursement) made prior to the date of enactment of the Federal Water Pollution Control Act Amendments of 1972 from any funds authorized for any fiscal year beginning after June 30, 1971, shall, upon the request of the applicant, be increased to the applicable percentage under this section. Notwithstanding the first sentence of this paragraph, in any case where a primary, secondary, or advanced waste treatment facility or its related interceptors or a project for infiltration-in-flow correction has received a grant for erection, building, acquisition, alteration, remodeling, improvement, extension, or correction before October 1, 1984, all segments and phases of such facility, interceptors, and project for infiltration-in-flow correction shall be eligible for grants at 75 per centum of the cost of construction thereof for any grant made pursuant to a State obligation which obligation occurred before October 1, 1990. Notwithstanding the first sentence of this paragraph, in the case of a project for which an application for a grant under this title has been made to the Administrator before October 1, 1984, and which project is under judicial injunction on such date prohibiting its construction, such project shall be eligible for grants at 75 percent of the cost of construction thereof. Notwithstanding the first sentence of this paragraph, in the case of the Wyoming Valley Sanitary Authority project mandated by judicial order under a proceeding begun prior to October 1, 1984, and a project for wastewater treatment for Altoona, Pennsylvania, such projects shall be eligible for grants at 75 percent of the cost of construction thereof.

(2) The amount of any grant made after September 30, 1978, and before October 1, 1981, for any eligible treatment works or significant portion thereof utilizing innovative or alternative wastewater treatment processes and techniques referred to in section 201(g)(5) shall be 85 per centum of the cost of construction thereof, unless modified by the Governor of the State with the concurrence of the Administrator to a percentage rate no less than 15 per centum greater than the modified uniform percentage rate in which the Administrator has concurred pursuant to paragraph (1) of this subsection. The amount of any grant made after September 30, 1981, for any eligible treatment works or unit processes and techniques thereof utilizing innovative or alternative wastewater treatment processes and techniques referred to in section 201(g)(5) shall be a percentage of the cost of construction thereof equal to 20 per centum greater than the percentage in effect under paragraph (1) of this subsection for such works or unit processes and techniques, but in no event greater than 85 per centum of the cost of construction thereof. No grant shall be made under this paragraph for construction of a treatment works in any State unless the proportion of the State contribution to the non-Federal share of construction costs for all treatment works in such State receiving a grant under this paragraph is the same as or greater than the proportion of the State contribution (if any) to the non-Federal share of construction costs for all treatment works receiving grants in such State under paragraph (1) of this subsection.

(3) In addition to any grant made pursuant to paragraph (2) of this subsection, the Administrator is authorized to make a grant to fund all of the costs of the modification or replacement of any facilities constructed with a grant made pursuant to paragraph (2) if the Administrator finds that such facilities have not met design performance specifications unless such failure is attributable to negligence on the part of any person and if such failure has significantly increased capital or operating and maintenance expenditures. In addition, the Administrator is authorized to make a grant to fund all of the costs of the modification or replacement of biodisc equipment (rotating biological contactors) in any publicly owned treatment works if the Administrator finds that such equipment has failed to meet design performance specifications, unless such failure is attributable to negligence on the part of any person, and if such failure has significantly increased capital or operating and maintenance expenditures.

(4) For the purposes of this section, the term eligible treatment works means those treatment works in each State which meet the requirements of section 201(g)(5) of this Act and which can be fully funded from funds available for such purpose in such State.

(b) The amount of the grant for any project approved by the Administrator after January 1, 1971, and before July 1, 1971, for the construction of treatment works, the actual erection, building or acquisition of which was not commenced prior to July 1,

1971, shall, upon the request of the applicant, be increased to the applicable percentage under subsection (a) of this section for grants for treatment works from funds for fiscal years beginning after June 30, 1971, with respect to the cost of such actual erection, building, or acquisition. Such increased amount shall be paid from any funds allocated to the State in which the treatment works is located without regard to the fiscal year for which such funds were authorized. Such increased amount shall be paid for such project only if—

(1) a sewage collection system that is a part of the same total waste treatment system as the treatment works for which such grant was approved is under construction or is to be constructed for use in conjunction with such treatment works, and if the cost of such sewage collection system exceeds the cost of such treatment works, and

(2) the State water pollution control agency or other appropriate State authority certifies that the quantity of available ground water will be insufficient, inadequate, or unsuitable for public use, including the ecological preservation and recreational use of surface water bodies, unless effluents from publicly-owned treatment works after adequate treatment are returned to the ground water consistent with acceptable technological standards.

(c) Notwithstanding any other provision of law, sums allotted to the Commonwealth of Puerto Rico under section 205 of this Act for fiscal year 1981 shall remain available for obligation for the fiscal year for which authorized and for the period of the next succeeding twenty-four months. Such sums and any unobligated funds available to Puerto Rico from allotments for fiscal years ending prior to October 1, 1981, shall be available for obligation by the Administrator of the Environmental Protection Agency only to fund the following systems: Aguadilla, Arecibo, Mayaguez, Carolina, and Camuy Hatillo. These funds may be used by the Commonwealth of Puerto Rico to fund the non-Federal share of the costs of such projects. To the extent that these funds are used to pay the non-Federal share, the Commonwealth of Puerto Rico shall repay to the Environmental Protection Agency such amounts on terms and conditions developed and approved by the Administrator in consultation with the Governor of the Commonwealth of Puerto Rico. Agreement on such terms and conditions, including the payment of interest to be determined by the Secretary of the Treasury, shall be reached prior to the use of these funds for the Commonwealth's non-Federal share. No Federal funds awarded under this provision shall be used to replace local governments funds previously expended on these projects.

[33 U.S.C. 1282]

PLANS, SPECIFICATIONS, ESTIMATES, AND PAYMENTS

SEC. 203. (a)(1) Each applicant for a grant shall submit to the Administrator for his approval, plans, specifications, and estimates for each proposed project for the construction of treatment works for which a grant is applied for under section 201(g)(1) from funds allotted to the State under section 205 and which otherwise meets the requirements of this Act. The Administrator shall act upon such plans, specifications, and estimates as soon as practicable after the same have been submitted, and his approval of any such plans, specifications, and estimates shall be deemed a contractual obligation of the United States for the payment of its proportional contribution to such project.

(2) AGREEMENT ON ELIGIBLE COSTS.—

(A) LIMITATION ON MODIFICATIONS.— Before taking final action on any plans, specifications, and estimates submitted under this subsection after the 60th day following the date of the enactment of the Water Quality Act of 1987, the Administrator shall enter into a written agreement with the applicant which establishes and specifies which items of the proposed project are eligible for Federal payments under this section. The Administrator may not later modify such eligibility determinations unless they are found to have been made in violation of applicable Federal statutes and regulations.

(B) LIMITATION ON EFFECT.— Eligibility determinations under this paragraph shall not preclude the Administrator from auditing a project pursuant to section 501 of this Act, or other authority, or from withholding or recovering Federal funds for costs which are found to be unreasonable, unsupported by adequate documentation, or otherwise unallowable under applicable Federal costs principles, or which are incurred on a project which fails to meet the design specifications or effluent limitations contained in the grant agreement and permit pursuant to section 402 of this Act for such project.

(3) In the case of a treatment works that has an estimated total cost of $8,000,000 of less (as determined by the Administrator), and the population of the applicant municipality is twenty-five thousand or less (according to the most recent United States census), upon completion of an approved facility plan, a single grant may be awarded for the combined Federal share of the cost of preparing construction plans and specifications, and the building and erection of the treatment works.

(b) The Administrator shall, from time to time as the work progresses, make payments to the recipient of a grant for costs of construction incurred on a project. These payments shall at no time exceed the Federal share of the cost of construction incurred to the date of the voucher covering such payment plus the Federal share of the value of the materials which have been stockpiled in the vicinity of such construction in conformity to plans and specifications for the project.

(c) After completion of a project and approval of the final voucher by the Administrator, he shall pay out of the appropriate sums the unpaid balance of the Federal share payable on account of such project.

(d) Nothing in this Act shall be construed to require, or to authorize the Administrator to require, that grants under this Act for construction of treatment works be made only for projects which are operable units usable for sewage collection, transportation, storage, waste treatment, or for similar purposes without additional construction.

(e) At the request of a grantee under this title, the Administrator is authorized to provide technical and legal assistance in the administration and enforcement of any contract in connection with treatment works assisted under this title, and to intervene in any civil action involving the enforcement of such a contract.

(f) DESIGN/BUILD PROJECTS.—

(1) AGREEMENT.— Consistent with State law, an applicant who proposes to

construct waste water treatment works may enter into an agreement with the Administrator under this subsection providing for the preparation of construction plans and specifications and the erection of such treatment works, in lieu of proceeding under the other provisions of this section.

(2) LIMITATION ON PROJECTS.—Agreements under this subsection shall be limited to projects under an approved facility plan which projects are—

(A) treatment works that have an estimated total cost of $8,000,000 or less; and

(B) any of the following types of waste water treatment systems: aerated lagoons, trickling filters, stabilization ponds, land application systems, sand filters, and subsurface disposal systems.

(3) REQUIRED TERMS.—An agreement entered into under this subsection shall—

(A) set forth an amount agreed to as the maximum Federal contribution to the project, based upon a competitively bid document of basic design data and applicable standard construction specifications and a determination of the federally eligible costs of the project at the applicable Federal share under section 202 of this Act;

(B) set forth dates for the start and completion of construction of the treatment works by the applicant and a schedule of payments of the Federal contribution to the project;

(C) contain assurances by the applicant that (i) engineering and management assistance will be provided to manage the project; (ii) the proposed treatment works will be an operable unit and will meet all the requirements of this title; and (iii) not later than 1 year after the date specified as the date of completion of construction of the treatment works, the treatment works will be operating so as to meet the requirements of any applicable permit for such treatment works under section 402 of this Act;

(D) require the applicant to obtain a bond from the contractor in an amount determined necessary by the Administrator to protect the Federal interest in the project; and

(E) contain such other terms and conditions as are necessary to assure compliance with this title (except as provided in paragraph (4) of this subsection).

(4) LIMITATION ON APPLICATION.— Subsections (a), (b), and (c) of this section shall not apply to grants made pursuant to this subsection.

(5) RESERVATION TO ASSURE COMPLIANCE.— The Administrator shall reserve a portion of the grant to assure contract compliance until final project approval as defined by the Administrator. If the amount agreed to under paragraph (3)(A) exceeds the cost of designing and constructing the treatment works, the Administrator shall reallot the amount of the excess to the State in which such treatment works are located for the fiscal year in which such audit is completed.

(6) LIMITATION ON OBLIGATIONS.— The Administrator shall not obligate more than 20 percent of the amount allotted to a State for a fiscal year under section 205

of this Act for grants pursuant to this subsection.

(7) Allowance.— The Administrator shall determine an allowance for facilities planning for projects constructed under this subsection in accordance with section 201(l).

(8) Limitation on federal contributions.— In no event shall the Federal contribution for the cost of preparing construction plans and specifications and the building and erection of treatment works pursuant to this subsection exceed the amount agreed upon under paragraph (3).

(9) Recovery action.— In any case in which the recipient of a grant made pursuant to this subsection does not comply with the terms of the agreement entered into under paragraph (3), the Administrator is authorized to take such action as may be necessary to recover the amount of the Federal contribution to the project.

(10) Prevention of double benefits.— A recipient of a grant made pursuant to this subsection shall not be eligible for any other grants under this title for the same project.

[33 U.S.C. 1283]

LIMITATIONS AND CONDITIONS

Sec. 204. (a) Before approving grants for any project for any treatment works under section 201(g)(1) the Administrator shall determine—

(1) that any required areawide waste treatment management plan under section 208 of this Act (A) is being implemented for such area and the proposed treatment works are included in such plan, or (B) is being developed for such area and reasonable progress is being made toward its implementation and the proposed treatment works will be included in such plan;

(2) that (A) the State in which the project is to be located (i) is implementing any required plan under section 303(e) of this Act and the proposed treatment works are in conformity with such plan, or (ii) is developing such a plan and the proposed treatment works will be in conformity with such plan, and (B) such State is in compliance with section 305(b) of this Act;

(3) that such works have been certified by the appropriate State water pollution control agency as entitled to priority over such other works in the State in accordance with any applicable State plan under section 303(e) of this Act, except that any priority list developed pursuant to section 303(e)(3)(H) may be modified by such State in accordance with regulations promulgated by the Administrator to give higher priority for grants for the Federal share of the cost of preparing construction drawings and specifications for any treatment works utilizing processes and techniques meeting the guidelines promulgated under section 304(d)(3) of this Act for grants for the combined Federal share of the cost of preparing construction drawings and specifications and the building and erection of any treatment works meeting the requirements of the next to the last sentence of section 203(a) of this Act which utilizes processes and techniques meeting the guidelines promulgated under section 304(d)(3) of this Act.[6]

[6] So in law. The period should be a semicolon.

(4) that the applicant proposing to construct such works agrees to pay the non-Federal costs of such works and has made adequate provisions satisfactory to the Administrator for assuring proper and efficient operation, including the employment of trained management and operations personnel, and the maintenance of such works in accordance with a plan of operation approved by the state water pollution control agency or, as appropriate, the interstate agency, after construction thereof;

(5) that the size and capacity of such works relate directly to the needs to be served by such works, including sufficient reserve capacity. The amount of reserve capacity provided shall be approved by the Administrator on the basis of a comparison of the cost of constructing such reserves as a part of the works to be funded and the anticipated cost of providing expanded capacity at a date when such capacity will be required, after taking into account, in accordance with regulations promulgated by the Administrator, efforts to reduce total flow of sewage and unnecessary water consumption. The amount of reserve capacity eligible for a grant under this title shall be determined by the Administrator taking into account the projected population and associated commercial and industrial establishments within the jurisdiction of the applicant to be served by such treatment works as identified in an approved facilities plan, an areawide plan under section 208, or an applicable municipal master plan of development. For the purpose of this paragraph, section 208, and any such plan, projected population shall be determined on the basis of the latest information available from the United States Department of Commerce or from the States as the Administrator, by regulation, determines appropriate. Beginning October 1, 1984, no grants shall be made under this title to construct that portion of any treatment works providing reserve capacity in excess of existing needs (including existing needs of residential, commercial, industrial, and other users) on the date of approval of a grant for the erection, building, acquisition, alteration, remodeling, improvement, or extension of a project for secondary treatment or more stringent treatment or new interceptors and appurtenances, except that in no event shall reserve capacity of a facility and its related interceptors to which this subsection applies be in excess of existing needs on October 1, 1990. In any case in which an applicant proposes to provide reserve capacity greater than that eligible for Federal financial assistance under this title, the incremental costs of the additional reserve capacity shall be paid by the applicant;

(6) that no specification for bids in connection with such works shall be written in such a manner as to contain proprietary, exclusionary, or discriminatory requirements other than those based upon performance, unless such requirements are necessary to test or demonstrate a specific thing or to provide for necessary interchangeability of parts and equipment. When in the judgment of the grantee, it is impractical or uneconomical to make a clear and accurate description of the technical requirements, a brand name or equal description may be used as a means to define the performance or other salient requirements of a procurement, and in doing so the grantee need not establish the existence of any source other than the brand or source so named.

(b)(1) Notwithstanding any other provision of this title, the Administrator shall not approve any grant for any treatment works under section 201(g)(1) after March 1, 1973, unless he shall first have determined that the applicant (A) has adopted or will adopt a system of charges to assure that each recipient of waste treatment services within the applicant's jurisdiction, as determined by the Administrator, will pay its proportionate share (except as otherwise provided in this paragraph) of the costs of operation and maintenance (including replacement) of any waste treatment services provided by the applicant; and (B) has legal, institutional, managerial, and financial capability to insure adequate construction, operation, and maintenance of treatment works throughout the applicant's jurisdiction, as determined by the Administrator. In any case where an applicant which, as of the date of enactment of this sentence, uses a system of dedicated ad valorem taxes and the Administrator determines that the applicant has a system of charges which results in the distribution of operation and maintenance costs for treatment works within the applicant's jurisdiction, to each user class, in proportion to the contribution to the total cost of operation and maintenance of such works by each user class (taking into account total waste water loading of such works, the constituent elements of the waste, and other appropriate factors), and such applicant is otherwise in compliance with clause (A) of this paragraph with respect to each industrial user, then such dedicated ad valorem tax system shall be deemed to be the user charge system meeting the requirements of clause (A) of this paragraph for the residential user class and such small non-residential user classes as defined by the Administrator. In defining small non-residential users, the Administrator shall consider the volume of wastes discharged into the treatment works by such users and the constituent elements of such wastes as well as such other factors as he deems appropriate. A system of user charges which imposes a lower charge for low-income residential users (as defined by the Administrator) shall be deemed to be a user charge system meeting the requirements of clause (A) of this paragraph if the Administrator determines that such system was adopted after public notice and hearing.

(2) The Administrator shall, within one hundred and eighty days after the date of enactment of the Federal Water Pollution Control Act Amendments of 1972, and after consultation with appropriate State, interstate, municipal and intermunicipal agencies, issue guidelines applicable to payment of waste treatment costs by industrial and nonindustrial receipts of waste treatment services which shall establish (A) classes of users of such services, including categories of industrial users; (B) criteria against which to determine the adequacy of charges imposed on classes and categories of users reflecting all factors that influence the cost of waste treatment, including strength, volume, and delivery flow rate characteristics of waste; and (C) model systems and rates of user charges typical of various treatment works serving municipal-industrial communities.

(3) Approval by the Administrator of a grant to an interstate agency established by interstate compact for any treatment works shall satisfy any other requirement that such works be authorized by Act of Congress.

(4) A system of charges which meets the requirement of clause (A) of paragraph (1) of this subsection may be based on something other than metering the sewage or water supply flow of residential recipients of waste treatment services, including ad valorem taxes. If the system of charges is based on something other than metering the Administrator shall require (A) the applicant to establish a system by which the

necessary funds will be available for the proper operation and maintenance of the treatment works; and (B) the applicant to establish a procedure under which the residential user will be notified as to that portion of his total payment which will be allocated to the costs of the waste treatment services.

(c) The next to the last sentence of paragraph (5) of subsection (a) of this section shall not apply in any case where a primary, secondary, or advanced waste treatment facility or its related interceptors has received a grant for erection, building, acquisition, alteration, remodeling, improvement, or extension before October 1, 1984, and all segments and phases of such facility and interceptors shall be funded based on a 20-year reserve capacity in the case of such facility and a 20-year reserve capacity in the case of such interceptors, except that, if a grant for such interceptors has been approved prior to the date of enactment of the Municipal Wastewater Treatment Construction Grant Amendments of 1981, such interceptors shall be funded based on the approved reserve capacity not to exceed 40 years.

(d)(1) A grant for the construction of treatment works under this title shall provide that the engineer or engineering firm supervising construction or providing architect engineering services during construction shall continue its relationship to the grant applicant for a period of one year after the completion of construction and initial operation of such treatment works. During such period such engineer or engineering firm shall supervise operation of the treatment works, train operating personnel, and prepare curricula and training material for operating personnel. Costs associated with the implementation of this paragraph shall be eligible for Federal assistance in accordance with this title.

(2) On the date one year after the completion of construction and initial operation of such treatment works, the owner and operator of such treatment works shall certify to the Administrator whether or not such treatment works meet the design specifications and effluent limitations contained in the grant agreement and permit pursuant to section 402 of the Act for such works. If the owner and operator of such treatment works cannot certify that such treatment works meet such design specifications and effluent limitations, any failure to meet such design specifications and effluent limitations shall be corrected in a timely manner, to allow such affirmative certification, at other than Federal expense.

(3) Nothing in this section shall be construed to prohibit a grantee under this title from requiring more assurances, guarantees, or indemnity or other contractual requirements from any party to a contract pertaining to a project assisted under this title, than those provided under this subsection.

[33 U.S.C. 1284]

ALLOTMENT

SEC. 205. (a) Sums authorized to be appropriated pursuant to section 207 for each fiscal year beginning after June 30, 1972, before September 30, 1977, shall be allotted by the Administrator not later than the January 1st immediately preceding the beginning of the fiscal year for which authorized, except that the allotment for fiscal year 1973 shall be made not later than 30 days after the date of enactment of the Federal Water Pollution Control Act Amendments of 1972. Such sums shall be allotted among the States by the Administrator in accordance with regulations promulgated by him, in the ratio that the estimated cost of constructing all needed publicly owned treatment works in each State bears to the estimated cost of construction of all needed publicly owned treatment works in all of the States. For the fiscal years ending June 30, 1973, and June 30, 1974, such ratio shall be determined on the basis of table III of House Public Works Committee Print No. 92–50. For the fiscal year ending June 30, 1975, such ratio shall be determined one-half on the basis of table I of House Public Works Committee Print Numbered 93–28 and one-half on the basis of table II of such print, except that no State shall receive an allotment less than that which it received for the fiscal year ending June 30, 1972, as set forth in table III of such print. Allotments for fiscal years which begin after the fiscal year ending June 30, 1975, shall be made only in accordance with a revised cost estimate made and submitted to Congress in accordance with section 516(b) of this Act and only after such revised cost estimate shall have been approved by law specifically enacted hereafter.

(b)(1) Any sums allotted to a State under subsection (a) shall be available for obligation under section 203 on and after the date of such allotment. Such sums shall continue available for obligation in such State for a period of one year after the close of the fiscal year for which such sums are authorized. Any amounts so allotted which are not obligated by the end of such one-year period shall be immediately reallotted by the Administrator, in accordance with regulations promulgated by him, generally on the basis of the ratio used in making the last allotment of sums under this section. Such reallotted sums shall be added to the last allotments made to the States. Any sum made available to a State by reallotment under this subsection shall be in addition to any funds otherwise allotted to such State for grants under this title during any fiscal year.

(2) Any sums which have been obligated under section 203 and which are released by the payment of the final voucher for the project shall be immediately credited to the State to which such sums were last allotted. Such released sums shall be added to the amounts last allotted to such State and shall be immediately available for obligation in the same manner and to the same extent as such last allotment.

(c)(1) Sums authorized to be appropriated pursuant to section 207 for the fiscal years during the period beginning October 1, 1977, and ending September 30, 1981, shall be allotted for each such year by the Administrator not later than the tenth day which begins after the date of enactment of the Clean Water Act of 1977. Notwithstanding any other provision of law, sums authorized for the fiscal years ending September 30, 1978, September 30, 1979, September 30, 1980, and September 30, 1981, shall be allotted in accordance with table 3 of Committee Print Numbered 95–30 of the Committee on Public Works and Transportation of the House of Representatives.

(2) Sums authorized to be appropriated pursuant to section 207 for the fiscal years 1982, 1983, 1984, and 1985 shall be allotted for each such year by the Administrator not later than the tenth day which begins after the date of enactment of the Municipal Wastewater Treatment Construction Grant Amendments of 1981. Notwithstanding any other provision of law, sums authorized for the fiscal year ending September 30, 1982, shall be allotted in accordance with table 3 of Committee Print Numbered 95–30 of the Committee on Public Works and Transportation of the House of Representatives. Sums authorized for the fiscal years ending September 30, 1983, September 30, 1984, September 30, 1985, and September 30, 1986, shall be allotted in accordance with the following table:

States:	Fiscal years 1983 through 19851
Alabama	.011398
Alaska	.006101
Arizona	.006885
Arkansas	.006668
California	.072901
Colorado	.008154
Connecticut	.012487
Delaware	.004965
District of Columbia	.004965
Florida	.034407
Georgia	.017234
Hawaii	.007895
Idaho	.004965
Illinois	.046101
Indiana	.024566
Iowa	.013796
Kansas	.009201
Kentucky	.012973
Louisiana	.011205
Maine	.007788
Maryland	.024653
Massachusetts	.034608
Michigan	.043829
Minnesota	.018735
Mississippi	.009184
Missouri	.028257
Montana	.004965
Nebraska	.005214
Nevada	.004965
New Hampshire	.010186
New Jersey	.041654
New Mexico	.004965
New York	.113097
North Carolina	.018396
North Dakota	.004965
Ohio	.057383
Oklahoma	.008235
Oregon	.011515
Pennsylvania	.040377
Rhode Island	.006750
South Carolina	.010442
South Dakota	.004965
Tennessee	.014807
Texas	.038726
Utah	.005371
Vermont	.004965
Virginia	.020861
Washington	.017726
West Virginia	.015890
Wisconsin	.027557
Wyoming	.004965
Samoa	.000915
Guam	.000662
Northern Marianas	.000425

States:	*Fiscal years 1983 through 1985*1
Puerto Rico	.013295
Pacific Trust Territories	.001305
Virgin Islands	.000531
United States totals	.999996
1So in original. Probably should be 1986.	

(3) FISCAL YEARS 1987–1990.— Sums authorized to be appropriated pursuant to section 207 for the fiscal years 1987, 1988, 1989, and 1990 shall be allotted for each such year by the Administrator not later than the 10th day which begins after the date of the enactment of this paragraph. Sums authorized for such fiscal years shall be allotted in accordance with the following table:

States:	
Alabama	.011309
Alaska	.006053
Arizona	.006831
Arkansas	.006616
California	.072333
Colorado	.008090
Connecticut	.012390
Delaware	.004965
District of Columbia	.004965
Florida	.034139
Georgia	.017100
Hawaii	.007833
Idaho	.004965
Illinois	.045741
Indiana	.024374
Iowa	.013688
Kansas	.009129
Kentucky	.012872
Louisiana	.011118
Maine	.007829
Maryland	.024461
Massachusetts	.034338
Michigan	.043487
Minnesota	.018589
Mississippi	.009112
Missouri	.028037
Montana	.004965
Nebraska	.005173
Nevada	.004965
New Hampshire	.010107
New Jersey	.041329
New Mexico	.004965
New York	.111632
North Carolina	.018253
North Dakota	.004965
Ohio	.056936
Oklahoma	.008171
Oregon	.011425

States:

Pennsylvania	.040062
Rhode Island	.006791
South Carolina	.010361
South Dakota	.004965
Tennessee	.014692
Texas	.046226
Utah	.005329
Vermont	.004965
Virginia	.020698
Washington	.017588
West Virginia	.015766
Wisconsin	.027342
Wyoming	.004965
American Samoa	.000908
Guam	.000657
Northern Marianas	.000422
Puerto Rico	.013191
Pacific Trust Territories	.001295
Virgin Islands	.000527

(d) Sums allotted to the States for a fiscal year shall remain available for obligation for the fiscal year for which authorized and for the period of the next succeeding twelve months. The amount of any allotment not obligated by the end of such twenty-four-month period shall be immediately reallotted by the Administrator on the basis of the same ratio as applicable to sums allotted for the then current fiscal year, except that none of the funds reallotted by the Administrator for fiscal year 1978 and for fiscal years thereafter shall be allotted to any State which failed to obligate any of the funds being reallotted. Any sum made available to a State by reallotment under this subsection shall be in addition to any funds otherwise allotted to such State for grants under this title during any fiscal year.

(e) For the fiscal years 1978, 1979, 1980, 1981, 1982, 1983, 1984, 1985, 1986, 1987, 1988, 1989, and 1990, no State shall receive less than one-half of 1 per centum of the total allotment under subsection (c) of this section, except that in the case of Guam, Virgin Islands, American Samoa, and the Trust Territories not more than thirty-three one-hundredths of 1 per centum in the aggregate shall be allotted to all four for these jurisdictions. For the purpose of carrying out this subsection there are authorized to be appropriated, subject to such amounts as are provided in appropriation Acts, not to exceed $75,000,000 for each fiscal years 1978, 1979, 1980, 1981, 1982, 1983, 1984, 1985, 1986, 1987, 1988, 1989, and 1990. If for any fiscal year the amount appropriated under authority of this subsection is less than the amount necessary to carry out this subsection, the amount each State receives under this subsection for such year shall be the same ratio for the amount such State would have received under this subsection in such year if the amount necessary to carry it out had been appropriated as the amount appropriated for such year bears to the amount necessary to carry out this subsection for such year.

(f) Notwithstanding any other provision of this section, sums made available between January 1, 1975, and March 1, 1975, by the Administrator for obligation shall be available for obligation until September 30, 1978.

(g)(1) The Administrator is authorized to reserve each fiscal year not to exceed 2 per centum of the amount authorized under section 207 of this title for purposes of the allotment made to each State under this section on or after October 1, 1977, except in the case of any fiscal year beginning on or after October 1, 1981, and ending before October 1, 1994, in which case the percentage authorized to be reserved shall not exceed 4 per centum.[7] or $400,000 whichever amount is the greater. Sums so reserved shall be available for making grants to such State under paragraph (2) of this subsection for the same period as sums are available from such allotment under subsection (d) of this section, and any such grant shall be available for obligation only during such period. Any grant made from sums reserved under this subsection which has not been obligated by the end of the period for which available shall be added to the amount last allotted to such State under this section and shall be immediately available for obligation in the same manner and to the same extent as such last allotment. Sums authorized to be reserved by this paragraph shall be in addition to and not in lieu of any other funds which may be authorized to carry out this subsection.

[7] P.L. 97–117 added this phrase with a period at the end; probably should be a comma.

(2) The Administrator is authorized to grant to any State from amounts reserved to such State under this subsection, the reasonable costs of administering any aspects of sections 201, 203, 204, and 212 of this Act the responsibility for administration of which the Administrator has delegated to such State. The Administrator may increase such grant to take into account the reasonable costs of administering an approved program under section 402 or 404, administering a statewide waste treatment management planning program under section 208(b)(4), and managing waste treatment construction grants for small communities.

(h) The Administrator shall set aside from funds authorized for each fiscal year beginning on or after October 1, 1978, a total (as determined by the Governor of the State) of not less than 4 percent nor more than 7½ percent of the sums allotted to any State with a rural population of 25 per centum or more of the total population of such State, as determined by the Bureau of the Census. The Administrator may set aside no more than 7½ percent of the sums allotted to any other State for which the Governor requests such action. Such sums shall be available only for alternatives to conventional sewage treatment works for municipalities having a population of three thousand five hundred or less, or for the highly dispersed sections of larger municipalities, as defined by the Administrator.

(i) Set-Aside for Innovative and Alternative Projects.— Not less than ½ of 1 percent of funds allotted to a State for each of the fiscal years ending September 30, 1979, through September 30, 1990, under subsection (c) of this section shall be expended only for increasing the Federal share of grants for construction of treatment works utilizing innovative processes and techniques pursuant to section 202(a)(2) of this Act. Including the expenditures authorized by the preceding sentence, a total of 2 percent of the funds allotted to a State for each of the fiscal years ending September 30, 1979, and September 30, 1980, and 3 percent of the funds allotted to a State for the fiscal year ending September 30, 1981, under subsection (c) of this section shall be expended only for increasing grants for construction of treatment works pursuant to section 202(a)(2) of this Act. Including the expenditures authorized by the first sentence of this subsection, a total (as determined by the Governor of the State) of not less than

4 percent nor more than 7½ percent of the funds allotted to such State under subsection (c) of this section for each of the fiscal years ending September 30, 1982, through September 30, 1990, shall be expended only for increasing the Federal share of grants for construction of treatment works pursuant to section 202(a)(2) of this Act.

(j)(1) The Administrator shall reserve each fiscal year not to exceed 1 per centum of the sums allotted and available for obligation to each State under this section for each fiscal year beginning on or after October 1, 1981, or $100,000, whichever amount is the greater.

(2) Such sums shall be used by the Administrator to make grants to the States to carry out water quality management planning, including, but not limited to—

(A) identifying most cost effective and locally acceptable facility and non-point measures to meet and maintain water quality standards;

(B) developing an implementation plan to obtain State and local financial and regulatory commitments to implement measures developed under subparagraph (A);

(C) determining the nature, extent, and causes of water quality problems in various areas of the State and interstate region, and reporting on these annually; and

(D) determining those publicly owned treatment works which should be constructed with assistance under this title, in which areas and in what sequence, taking into account the relative degree of effluent reduction attained, the relative contributions to water quality of other point or nonpoint sources, and the consideration of alternatives to such construction, and implementing section 303(e) of this Act.

(3) In carrying out planning with grants made under paragraph (2) of this subsection, a State shall develop jointly with local, regional, and interstate entities, a plan for carrying out the program and give funding priority to such entities and designated or undesignated public comprehensive planning organizations to carry out the purposes of this subsection. In giving such priority, the State shall allocate at least 40 percent of the amount granted to such State for a fiscal year under paragraph (2) of this subsection to regional public comprehensive planning organizations in such State and appropriate interstate organizations for the development and implementation of the plan described in this paragraph. In any fiscal year for which the Governor, in consultation with such organizations and with the approval of the Administrator, determines that allocation of at least 40 percent of such amount to such organizations will not result in significant participation by such organizations in water quality management planning and not significantly assist in development and implementation of the plan described in this paragraph and achieving the goals of this Act, the allocation to such organization may be less than 40 percent of such amount.

(4) All activities undertaken under this subsection shall be in coordination with other related provisions of this Act.

(5) Nonpoint source reservation.— In addition to the sums reserved under paragraph (1), the Administrator shall reserve each fiscal year for each State 1

percent of the sums allotted and available for obligation to such State under this section for each fiscal year beginning on or after October 1, 1986, or $100,000, whichever is greater, for the purpose of carrying out section 319 of this Act. Sums so reserved in a State in any fiscal year for which such State does not request the use of such sums, to the extent such sums exceed $100,000, may be used by such State for other purposes under this title.

(k) The Administrator shall allot to the State of New York from sums authorized to be appropriated for the fiscal year ending September 30, 1982, an amount necessary to pay the entire cost of conveying sewage from the Convention Center of the City of New York to the Newtown sewage treatment plant, Brooklyn-Queens area, New York. The amount allotted under this subsection shall be in addition to and not in lieu of any other amounts authorized to be allotted to such State under this Act.

(l) Marine Estuary Reservation.—

(1) Reservation of funds.—

(A) General rule.— Prior to making allotments among the States under subsection (c) of this section, the Administrator shall reserve funds from sums appropriated pursuant to section 207 for each fiscal year beginning after September 30, 1986.

(B) Fiscal years 1987 and 1988.— For each of fiscal years 1987 and 1988 the reservation shall be 1 percent of the sums appropriated pursuant to section 207 for such fiscal year.

(C) Fiscal years 1989 and 1990.— For each of fiscal years 1989 and 1990 the reservation shall be 1½ percent of the funds appropriated pursuant to section 207 for such fiscal year.

(2) Use of funds.— Of the sums reserved under this subsection, two-thirds shall be available to address water quality problems of marine bays and estuaries subject to lower levels of water quality due to the impacts of discharges from combined storm water and sanitary sewer overflows from adjacent urban complexes, and one-third shall be available for the implementation of section 320 of this Act, relating to the national estuary program.

(3) Period of availability.— Sums reserved under this subsection shall be subject to the period of availability for obligation established by subsection (d) of this section.

(4) Treatment of certain body of water.— For purposes of this section and section 201(n), Newark Bay, New Jersey, and the portion of the Passaic River up to Little Falls, in the vicinity of Beatties Dam, shall be treated as a marine bay and estuary.

(m) Discretionary Deposits Into State Water Pollution Control Revolving Funds.—

(1) From construction grant allotments.— In addition to any amounts deposited in a water pollution control revolving fund established by a State under title VI, upon request of the Governor of such State, the Administrator shall make available to the State for deposit, as capitalization grants, in such fund in any fiscal year beginning after September 30, 1986, such portion of the amounts allotted

to such State under this section for such fiscal year as the Governor considers appropriate; except that (A) in fiscal year 1987, such deposit may not exceed 50 percent of the amounts allotted to such State under this section for such fiscal year, and (B) in fiscal year 1988, such deposit may not exceed 75 percent of the amounts allotted to such State under this section for this[8] fiscal year.

[8] So in original. Probably should be such.

(2) NOTICE REQUIREMENT.—The Governor of a State may make a request under paragraph (1) for a deposit into the water pollution control revolving fund of such State—

(A) in fiscal year 1987 only if no later than 90 days after the date of the enactment of this subsection, and

(B) in each fiscal year thereafter only if 90 days before the first day of such fiscal year,

the State provides notice of its intent to make such deposit.

(3) EXCEPTION.— Sums reserved under section 205(j) of this Act shall not be available for obligation under this subsection.

[33 U.S.C. 1285]

REIMBURSEMENT AND ADVANCED CONSTRUCTION

SEC. 206. (a) Any publicly owned treatment works in a State on which construction was initiated after June 30, 1966, but before July 1, 1973, which was approved by the appropriate State water pollution control agency and which the Administrator finds meets the requirements of section 8 of this Act in effect at the time of the initiation of construction shall be reimbursed a total amount equal to the difference between the amount of Federal financial assistance, if any, received under such section 8 for such project and 50 per centum of the cost of such project, or 55 per centum of the project cost where the Administrator also determines that such treatment works was constructed in conformity with a comprehensive metropolitan treatment plan as described in section 8(f) of the Federal Water Pollution Control Act as in effect immediately prior to the date of enactment of the Federal Water Pollution Control Act Amendments of 1972. Nothing in this subsection shall result in any such works receiving Federal grants from all sources in excess of 80 per centum of the cost of such project.

(b) Any publicly owned treatment works constructed with or eligible for Federal financial assistance under this Act in a State between June 30, 1956, and June 30, 1966, which was approved by the State water pollution control agency and which the Administrator finds meets the requirements of section 8 of this Act prior to the date of enactment of the Federal Water Pollution Control Act Amendments of 1972 but which was constructed without assistance under such section 8 or which received such assistance in an amount less than 30 per centum of the cost of such project shall qualify for payments and reimbursement of State or local funds used for such project from sums allocated to such State under this section in an amount which shall not exceed the difference between the amount of such assistance, if any, received for such project and 30 per centum of the cost of such project.

(c) No publicly owned treatment works shall receive any payment or reimbursement under subsection (a) or (b) of this section unless an application for such assistance is filed with the Administrator within the one year period which begins on the date of enactment of the Federal Water Pollution Control Act Amendments of 1972. Any application filed within such one year period may be revised from time to time, as may be necessary.

(d) The Administrator shall allocate to each qualified project under subsection (a) of this section each fiscal year for which funds are appropriated under subsection (e) of this section an amount which bears the same ratio to the unpaid balance of the reimbursement due such project as the total of such funds for such year bears to the total unpaid balance of reimbursement due all such approved projects on the date of enactment of such appropriation. The Administrator shall allocate to each qualified project under subsection (b) of this section each fiscal year for which funds are appropriated under subsection (e) of this section an amount which bears the same ratio to the unpaid balance of the reimbursement due such project as the total of such funds for such year bears to the total unpaid balance of reimbursement due all such approved projects on the date of enactment of such appropriation.

(e) There is authorized to be appropriated to carry out subsection (a) of this section not to exceed $2,600,000,000 and, to carry out subsection (b) of this section, not to exceed $750,000,000. The authorizations contained in this subsection shall be the sole source of funds for reimbursements authorized by this section.

(f)(1) In any case where a substantial portion of the funds allotted to a State for the current fiscal year under this title have been obligated under section 201(g), or will be so obligated in a timely manner (as determined by the Administrator), and there is construction of any treatment works project without the aid of Federal funds and in accordance with all procedures and all requirements applicable to treatment works projects, except those procedures and requirements which limit construction of projects to those constructed with the aid of previously allotted Federal funds, the Administrator, upon his approval of an application made under this subsection therefore, is authorized to pay the Federal share of the cost of construction of such project when additional funds are allotted to the State under this title if prior to the construction of the project the Administrator approves plans, specifications, and estimates therefor in the same manner as other treatment works projects. The Administrator may not approve an application under this subsection unless an authorization is in effect for the first fiscal year in the period for which the application requests payment and such requested payment for that fiscal year does not exceed the State's expected allotment from such authorization. The Administrator shall not be required to make such requested payment for any fiscal year—

(A) to the extent that such payment would exceed such State's allotment of the amount appropriated for such fiscal year; and

(B) unless such payment is for a project which, on the basis of an approved funding priority list of such State, is eligible to receive such payment based on the allotment and appropriation for such fiscal year.

To the extent that sufficient funds are not appropriated to pay the full Federal share with respect to a project for which obligations under the provisions of this subsection have been made, the Administrator shall reduce the Federal share to such amount less than 75 per centum as such appropriations do provide.

(2) In determining the allotment for any fiscal year under this title, any treatment works project constructed in accordance with this section and without the aid of Federal funds shall not be considered completed until an application under the provisions of this subsection with respect to such project has been approved by the Administrator, or the availability of funds from which this project is eligible for reimbursement has expired, whichever first occurs.

[33 U.S.C. 1286]

AUTHORIZATION

SEC. 207. There is authorized to be appropriated to carry out this title, other than sections 206(e), 208 and 209, for the fiscal year ending June 30, 1973, not to exceed $5,000,000,000, for the fiscal year ending June 30, 1974, not to exceed $6,000,000,000, and for the fiscal year ending June 30, 1975, not to exceed $7,000,000,000, and subject to such amounts as are provided in appropriation Acts, for the fiscal year ending September 30, 1977, $1,000,000,000 for the fiscal year ending September 30, 1978, $4,500,000,000 and for the fiscal years ending September 30, 1979, September 30, 1980, not to exceed $5,000,000,000; for the fiscal year ending September 30, 1981, not to exceed $2,548,837,000; and for the fiscal years ending September 30, 1982, September 30, 1983, September 30, 1984, and September 30, 1985, not to exceed $2,400,000,000 per fiscal year; and for each of the fiscal years ending September 30, 1986, September 30, 1987, and September 30, 1988, not to exceed $2,400,000,000; and for each of the fiscal years ending September 30, 1989, and September 30, 1990, not to exceed $1,200,000,000.

[33 U.S.C. 1287]

AREAWIDE WASTE TREATMENT MANAGEMENT

SEC. 208. (a) For the purpose of encouraging and facilitating the development and implementation of areawide waste treatment management plans—

(1) The Administrator, within ninety days after the date of enactment of this Act and after consultation with appropriate Federal, State, and local authorities, shall by regulation publish guidelines for the identification of those areas which, as a result of urban-industrial concentrations or other factors, have substantial water quality control problems.

(2) The Governor of each State, within sixty days after publication of the guidelines issued pursuant to paragraph (1) of this subsection, shall identify each area within the State which, as a result of urban-industrial concentrations or other factors, has substantial water quality control problems. Not later than one hundred and twenty days following such identification and after consultation with appropriate elected and other officials of local governments having jurisdiction in such areas, the Governor shall designate (A) the boundaries of each such area, and (B) a single representative organization, including elected officials from local governments or their designees, capable of developing effective areawide waste treatment management plans for such an area. The Governor may in the same manner at any later time identify any additional area (or modify an existing area) for which he determines areawide waste treatment management to be appropriate, designate the boundaries of such area, and designate an organization capable of

developing effective areawide waste treatment management plans for such area.

(3) With respect to any area which, pursuant to the guidelines published under paragraph (1) of this subsection, is located in two or more States, the Governors of the respective States shall consult and cooperate in carrying out the provisions of paragraph (2), with a view toward designating the boundaries of the interstate area having common water quality control problems and for which areawide waste treatment management plans would be most effective, and toward designating, within one hundred and eighty days after publication of guidelines issued pursuant to paragraph (1) of this subsection, of a single representative organization capable of developing effective areawide waste treatment management plans for such area.

(4) If a Governor does not act, either by designating or determining not to make a designation under paragraph (2) of this subsection, within the time required by such paragraph, or if, in the case of an interstate area, the Governors of the States involved do not designate a planning organization within the time required by paragraph (3) of this subsection, the chief elected officials of local governments within an area may by agreement designate (A) the boundaries for such an area, and (B) a single representative organization including elected officials from such local governments, or their designees, capable of developing an areawide waste treatment management plan for such area.

(5) Existing regional agencies may be designated under paragraphs (2), (3), and (4) of this subsection.

(6) The State shall act as a planning agency for all portions of such State which are not designated under paragraphs (2), (3), or (4) of this subsection.

(7) Designations under this subsection shall be subject to the approval of the Administrator.

(b)(1)(A) Not later than one year after the date of designation of any organization under subsection (a) of this section such organization shall have in operation a continuing areawide waste treatment management planning process consistent with section 201 of this Act. Plans prepared in accordance with this process shall contain alternatives for waste treatment management, and be applicable to all wastes generated within the area involved. The initial plan prepared in accordance with such process shall be certified by the Governor and submitted to the Administrator not later than two years after the planning process is in operation.

(B) For any agency designated after 1975 under subsection (a) of this section and for all portions of a State for which the State is required to act as the planning agency in accordance with subsection (a)(6), the initial plan prepared in accordance with such process shall be certified by the Governor and submitted to the Administrator not later than three years after the receipt of the initial grant award authorized under subsection (f) of this section.

(2) Any plan prepared under such process shall include, but not be limited to—

(A) the identification of treatment works necessary to meet the anticipated municipal and industrial waste treatment needs of the area over a twenty-year period, annually updated (including an analysis of alternative waste treatment systems), including any requirements for the acquisition of land for treatment purposes; the necessary waste water collection and urban storm water runoff systems; and a program to provide the necessary financial arrangements for the development of such treatment works, and an identification of open space and recreation opportunities that can be expected to result from improved water quality, including consideration of potential use of lands associated with treatment works and increased access to water-based recreation;

(B) the establishment of construction priorities for such treatment works and time schedules for the initiation and completion of all treatment works;

(C) the establishment of a regulatory program to—

(i) implement the waste treatment management requirements of section 201(c),

(ii) regulate the location, modification, and construction of any facilities within such area which may result in any discharge in such area, and

(iii) assure that any industrial or commercial waste discharged into any treatment works in such area meet applicable pretreatment requirements;

(D) the identification of those agencies necessary to construct, operate, and maintain all facilities required by the plan and otherwise to carry out the plan;

(E) the identification of the measures necessary to carry out the plan (including financing), the period of time necessary to carry out the plan, the costs of carrying out the plan within such time, and the economic, social, and environmental impact of carrying out the plan within such time;

(F) a process to (i) identify, if appropriate, agriculturally and silviculturally related nonpoint sources of pollution, including return flows from irrigated agriculture, and their cumulative effects, runoff from manure disposal areas, and from land used for livestock and crop production, and (ii) set forth procedures and methods (including land use requirements) to control to the extent feasible such sources;

(G) a process of (i) identify, if appropriate, mine-related sources of pollution including new, current, and abandoned surface and underground mine runoff, and (ii) set forth procedures and methods (including land use requirements) to control to the extent feasible such sources;

(H) a process to (i) identify construction activity related sources of pollution, and (ii) set forth procedures and methods (including land use requirements) to control to the extent feasible such sources;

(I) a process to (i) identify, if appropriate, salt water intrusion into rivers, lakes, and estuaries resulting from reduction of fresh water flow from any cause, including irrigation, obstruction, ground water extraction, and diversion, and (ii) set forth procedures and methods to control such intrusion to the extent feasible where such procedures and methods are otherwise a part of the waste treatment management plan;

(J) a process to control the disposition of all residual waste generated in such area which could affect water quality; and

(K) a process to control the disposal of pollutants on land or in subsurface excavations within such area to protect ground and surface water quality.

(3) Areawide waste treatment management plans shall be certified annually by the Governor or his designee (or Governors or their designees, where more than one State is involved) as being consistent with applicable basin plans and such areawide waste treatment management plans shall be submitted to the Administrator for his approval.

(4)(A) Whenever the Governor of any State determines (and notifies the Administrator) that consistency with a statewide regulatory program under section 303 so requires, the requirements of clauses (F) through (K) of paragraph (2) of this subsection shall be developed and submitted by the Governor to the Administrator for approval for application to a class or category of activity throughout such State.

(B) Any program submitted under subparagraph (A) of this paragraph which, in whole or in part, is to control the discharge or other placement of dredged or fill material into the navigable waters shall include the following:

(i) A consultation process which includes the State agency with primary jurisdiction over fish and wildlife resources.

(ii) A process to identify and manage the discharge or other placement of dredged or fill material which adversely affects navigable waters, which shall complement and be coordinated with a State program under section 404 conducted pursuant to this Act.

(iii) A process to assure that any activity conducted pursuant to a best management practice will comply with the guidelines established under section 404(b)(1), and sections 307 and 403 of this Act.

(iv) A process to assure that any activity conducted pursuant to a best management practice can be terminated or modified for cause including, but not limited to, the following:

(I) violation of any condition of the best management practice;

(II) change in any activity that requires either a temporary or permanent reduction or elimination of the discharge pursuant to the best management practice.

(v) A process to assure continued coordination with Federal and Federal-State water-related planning and reviewing processes, including the National Wetlands Inventory.

(C) If the Governor of a State obtains approval from the Administrator of a statewide regulatory program which meets the requirements of subparagraph (B) of this paragraph and if such State is administering a permit program under section 404 of this Act, no person shall be required to obtain an individual permit pursuant to such section, or to comply with a general permit issued pursuant to such section, with respect to any appropriate activity within such State for which a best management practice has been approved by the Administrator under the program approved by the Administrator pursuant to this paragraph.

(D)(i) Whenever the Administrator determines after public hearing that a State is not administering a program approved under this section in accordance with the requirements of this section, the Administrator shall so notify the State, and if appropriate corrective action is not taken within a reasonable time, not to exceed ninety days, the Administrator shall withdraw approval of such program. The Administrator shall not withdraw approval of any such program unless he shall first have notified the State, and made public, in writing, the reasons for such withdrawal.

(ii) In the case of a State with a program submitted and approved under this paragraph, the Administrator shall withdraw approval of such program under this subparagraph only for a substantial failure of the State to administer its program in accordance with the requirements of this paragraph.

(c)(1) The Governor of each State, in consultation with the planning agency designated under subsection (a) of this section, at the time a plan is submitted to the Administrator, shall designate one or more waste treatment management agencies (which may be an existing or newly created local, regional or State agency or political subdivision) for each area designated under subsection (a) of this section and submit such designations to the Administrator.

(2) The Administrator shall accept any such designation, unless, within 120 days of such designation, he finds that the designated management agency (or agencies) does not have adequate authority—

(A) to carry out appropriate portions of an areawide waste treatment management plan developed under subsection (b) of this section;

(B) to manage effectively waste treatment works and related facilities serving such area in conformance with any plan required by subsection (b) of this section;

(C) directly or by contract, to design and construct new works, and to operate and maintain new and existing works as required by any plan developed pursuant to subsection (b) of this section;

(D) to accept and utilize grants, or other funds from any source, for waste treatment management purposes;

(E) to raise revenues, including the assessment of waste treatment charges;

(F) to incur short- and long-term indebtedness;

(G) to assure in implementation of an areawide waste treatment management plan that each participating community pays its proportionate share of treatment costs;

(H) to refuse to receive any wastes from any municipality or subdivision thereof, which does not comply with any provisions of an approved plan under this section applicable to such area; and

(I) to accept for treatment industrial wastes.

(d) After a waste treatment management agency having the authority required by subsection (c) has been designated under such subsection for an area and a plan for such area has been approved under subsection (b) of this section, the Administrator shall not make any grant for construction of a publicly owned treatment works under section 201(g)(1) within such area except to such designated agency and for works in conformity with such plan.

(e) No permit under section 402 of this Act shall be issued for any point source which is in conflict with a plan approved pursuant to subsection (b) of this section.

(f)(1) The Administrator shall make grants to any agency designated under subsection (a) of this section for payment of the reasonable costs of developing and operating a continuing areawide waste treatment management planning process under subsection (b) of this section.

(2) For the two-year period beginning on the date of the first grant is made under paragraph (1) of this subsection to an agency, if such first grant is made before October 1, 1977, the amount of each such grant to such agency shall be 100 per centum of the costs of developing and operating a continuing areawide waste treatment management planning process under subsection (b) of this section, and thereafter the amount granted to such agency shall not exceed 75 per centum of such costs in each succeeding one-year period. In the case of any other grant made to an agency under such paragraph (1) of this subsection, the amount of such grant shall not exceed 75 per centum of the costs of developing and operating a continuing areawide waste treatment management planning process in any year.

(3) Each applicant for a grant under this subsection shall submit to the Administrator for his approval each proposal for which a grant is applied for under this subsection. The Administrator shall act upon such proposal as soon as practicable after it has been submitted, and his approval of that proposal shall be deemed a contractual obligation of the United States for the payment of its contribution to such proposal, subject to such amounts as are provided in appropriation Acts. There is authorized to be appropriated to carry out this subsection not to exceed $50,000,000 for the fiscal year ending June 30, 1973, not to exceed $100,000,000 for the fiscal year ending June 30, 1974, not to exceed $150,000,000 per fiscal year for the fiscal years ending June 30, 1975, September 30, 1977, September 30, 1978, September 30, 1979, and September 30, 1980, not to exceed $100,000,000 per fiscal year for the fiscal years ending September 30, 1981, and September 30, 1982, and such sums as may be necessary for fiscal years 1983 through 1990.

(g) The Administrator is authorized, upon request of the Governor or the designated planning agency, and without reimbursement, to consult with, and provide technical assistance to, any agency designated under subsection (a) of this section in the development of areawide waste treatment management plans under subsection (b) of this section.

(h)(1) The Secretary of the Army, acting through the Chief of Engineers, in cooperation with the Administrator is authorized and directed, upon request of the Governor or the designated planning organization, to consult with, and provide technical assistance to, any agency designed[9] under subsection (a) of this section in developing and operating a continuing areawide waste treatment management planning process under subsection (b) of this section.

[9] So in original. Probably should be designated.

(2) There is authorized to be appropriated to the Secretary of the Army, to carry out this subsection, not to exceed $50,000,000 per fiscal year for the fiscal years ending June 30, 1973, and June 30, 1974.

(i)(1) The Secretary of the Interior, acting through the Director of the United States Fish and Wildlife Service, shall, upon request of the Governor of a State, and without reimbursement, provide technical assistance to such State in developing a statewide program for submission to the Administrator under subsection (b)(4)(B) of this section and in implementing such program after its approval.

(2) There is authorized to be appropriated to the Secretary of the Interior $6,000,000 to complete the National Wetlands Inventory of the United States, by December 31, 1981, and to provide information from such Inventory to States as it becomes available to assist such States in the development and operation of programs under this Act.

(j)(1) The Secretary of Agriculture, with the concurrence of the Administrator, and acting through the Soil Conservation Service and such other agencies of the Department of Agriculture as the Secretary may designate, is authorized and directed to establish and administer a program to enter into contracts, subject to such amounts as are provided in advance by appropriation acts, of not less than five years nor more than ten years with owners and operators having control of rural land for the purpose of installing and maintaining measures incorporating best management practices to control nonpoint source pollution for improved water quality in those States or areas for which the Administrator has approved a plan under subsection (b) of this section where the practices to which the contracts apply are certified by the management agency designated under subsection (c)(1) of this section to be consistent with such plans and will result in improved water quality. Such contracts may be entered into during the period ending not later than September 31[10], 1988. Under such contracts the land owners or operator shall agree—

[10] So in original.

(i) to effectuate a plan approved by a soil conservation district, where one exists, under this section for his farm, ranch, or other land substantially in accordance with the schedule outlined therein unless any requirement thereof is waived or modified by the Secretary;

(ii) to forfeit all rights to further payments or grants under the contract and refund to the United States all payments and grants received thereunder, with interest, upon his violation of the contract at any stage during the time he has control of the land if the Secretary, after considering the recommendations of the soil conservation district, where one exists, and the Administrator, determines that such violation is of such a nature as to warrant termination of the contract, or to make refunds or accept such payment adjustments as the Secretary may deem appropriate if he determines that the violation by the owner or operator does not warrant termination of the contract;

(iii) upon transfer of his right and interest in the farm, ranch, or other land during the contract period to forfeit all rights to further payments or grants under the contract and refund to the United States all payments or grants received thereunder, with interest, unless the transferee of any such land agrees with the Secretary to assume all obligations of the contract;

(iv) not to adopt any practice specified by the Secretary on the advice of the Administrator in the contract as a practice which would tend to defeat the purposes of the contract;

(v) to such additional provisions as the Secretary determines are desirable and includes in the contract to effectuate the purposes of the program or to facilitate the practical administration of the program.

(2) In return for such agreement by the landowner or operator the Secretary shall agree to provide technical assistance and share the cost of carrying out those conservation practices and measures set forth in the contract for which he determines that cost sharing is appropriate and in the public interest and which are approved for cost sharing by the agency designated to implement the plan developed under subsection (b) of this section. The portion of such cost (including labor) to be shared shall be that part which the Secretary determines is necessary and appropriate to effectuate the installation of the water quality management practices and measures under the contract, but not to exceed 50 per centum of the total cost of the measures set forth in the contract; except the Secretary may increase the matching cost share where he determines that (1) the main benefits to be derived from the measures are related to improving offsite water quality, and (2) the matching share requirement would place a burden on the landowner which would probably prevent him from participating in the program.

(3) The Secretary may terminate any contract with a landowner or operator by mutual agreement with the owner or operator if the Secretary determines that such termination would be in the public interest, and may agree to such modification of contracts previously entered into as he may determine to be desirable to carry out the purposes of the program or facilitate the practical administration thereof or to accomplish equitable treatment with respect to other conservation, land use, or water quality programs.

(4) In providing assistance under this subsection the Secretary will give priority to those areas and sources that have the most significant effect upon water quality. Additional investigations or plans may be made, where necessary, to supplement approved water quality management plans, in order to determine priorities.

(5) The Secretary shall, where practicable, enter into agreements with soil conservation districts, State soil and water conservation agencies, or State water quality agencies to administer all or part of the program established in this subsection under regulations developed by the Secretary. Such agreements shall provide for the submission of such reports as the Secretary deems necessary, and for payment by the United States of such portion of the costs incurred in the administration of the program as the Secretary may deem appropriate.

(6) The contracts under this subsection shall be entered into only in areas where the management agency designated under subsection (c)(1) of this section assures an adequate level of participation by owners and operators having control of rural land in such areas. Within such areas the local soil conservation district, where one exists, together with the Secretary of Agriculture, will determine the priority of assistance

among individual land owners and operators to assure that the most critical water quality problems are addressed.

(7) The Secretary, in consultation with the Administrator and subject to section 304(k) of this Act, shall, not later than September 30, 1978, promulgate regulations for carrying out this subsection and for support and cooperation with other Federal and non-Federal agencies for implementation of this subsection.

(8) This program shall not be used to authorize or finance projects that would otherwise be eligible for assistance under the terms of Public Law 83–566.

(9) There are hereby authorized to be appropriated to the Secretary of Agriculture $200,000,000 for fiscal year 1979, $400,000,000 for fiscal year 1980, $100,000,000 for fiscal year 1981, $100,000,000 for fiscal year 1982, and such sums as may be necessary for fiscal years 1983 through 1990, to carry out this subsection. The program authorized under this subsection shall be in addition to, and not in substitution of, other programs in such area authorized by this or any other public law.

[33 U.S.C. 1288]

BASIN PLANNING

SEC. 209. (a) The President, acting through the Water Resources Council, shall, as soon as practicable, prepare a Level B plan under the Water Resources Planning Act for all basins in the United States. All such plans shall be completed not later than January 1, 1980, except that priority in the preparation of such plans shall be given to those basins and portions thereof which are within those areas designated under paragraphs (2), (3), and (4) of subsection (a) of section 208 of this Act.

(b) The President, acting through the Water Resources Council, shall report annually to Congress on progress being made in carrying out this section. The first such report shall be submitted not later than January 31, 1973.

(c) There is authorized to be appropriated to carry out this section not to exceed $200,000,000.

[33 U.S.C. 1289]

ANNUAL SURVEY

SEC. 210. The Administrator shall annually make a survey to determine the efficiency of the operation and maintenance of treatment works constructed with grants made under this Act, as compared to the efficiency planned at the time the grant was made. The results of such annual survey shall be included in the report required under section 516(a) of this Act.

[33 U.S.C. 1290]

SEWAGE COLLECTION SYSTEMS

SEC. 211. (a) No grant shall be made for a sewage collection system under this title unless such grant (1) is for replacement or major rehabilitation of an existing collection system and is necessary to the total integrity and performance of the waste treatment works servicing such community, or (2) is for a new collection system in an existing community with sufficient existing or planned capacity adequately to treat such collected sewage and is consistent with section 201 of this Act.

(b) If the Administrator uses population density as a test for determining the eligibility of a collector sewer for assistance it shall be only for the purpose of evaluating alternatives and determining the needs for such system in relation to ground or surface water quality impact.

(c) No grant shall be made under this title from funds authorized for any fiscal year during the period beginning October 1, 1977, and ending September 30, 1990, for treatment works for control of pollutant discharges from separate storm sewer systems. [33 U.S.C. 1291]

DEFINITIONS

Sec. 212. As used in this title—

(1) The term construction means any one or more of the following: preliminary planning to determine the feasibility of treatment works, engineering, architectural, legal, fiscal, or economic investigations or studies, surveys, designs, plans, working drawings, specifications, procedures, field testing of innovative or alternative waste water treatment processes and techniques meeting guidelines promulgated under section 304(d)(3) of this Act, or other necessary actions, erection, building, acquisition, alteration, remodeling, improvement, or extension of treatment works, or the inspection or supervision of any of the foregoing items.

(2)(A) The term treatment works means any devices and systems used in the storage, treatment, recycling, and reclamation of municipal sewage or industrial wastes of a liquid nature to implement section 201 of this Act, or necessary to recycle or reuse water at the most economical cost over the estimated life of the works, including intercepting sewers, outfall sewers, sewage collection systems, pumping, power, and other equipment, and their appurtenances; extensions, improvements, remodeling, additions, and alterations thereof; elements essential to provide a reliable recycled supply such as standby treatment units and clear well facilities; and acquisition of the land that will be an integral part of the treatment process (including land use for the storage of treated wastewater in land treatment systems prior to land application) or will be used for ultimate disposal of residues resulting from such treatment and acquisition of other land, and interests in land, that are necessary for construction.

(B) In addition to the definition contained in subparagraph (A) of this paragraph, treatment works means any other method or system for preventing, abating, reducing, storing, treating, separating, or disposing of municipal waste, including storm water runoff, or industrial waste, including waste in combined storm water and sanitary sewer systems. Any application for construction grants which includes wholly or in part such methods or systems shall, in accordance with guidelines published by the Administrator pursuant to subparagraph (C) of this paragraph, contain adequate data and analysis demonstrating such proposal to be, over the life of such works, the most cost efficient alternative to comply with sections 301 or 302 of this Act, or the requirements of section 201 of this Act.

(C) For the purposes of subparagraph (B) of this paragraph, the Administrator shall, within one hundred and eighty days after the date of enactment of this title, publish and thereafter revise no less often than annually, guidelines for the evaluation of methods, including cost-effective analysis, described in subparagraph (B) of this paragraph.

(3) The term replacement as used in this title means those expenditures for obtaining and installing equipment, accessories, or appurtenances during the useful life of the treatment works necessary to maintain the capacity and performance for which such works are designed and constructed.

[33 U.S.C. 1292]

LOAN GUARANTEES FOR CONSTRUCTION OF TREATMENT WORKS

SEC. 213. (a) Subject to the conditions of this section and to such terms and conditions as the Administrator determines to be necessary to carry out the purposes of this title, the Administrator is authorized to guarantee, and to make commitments to guarantee, the principal and interest (including interest accruing between the date of default and the date of the payment in full of the guarantee) of any loan, obligation, or participation therein of any State, municipality, or intermunicipal or interstate agency issued directly and exclusively to the Federal Financing Bank to finance that part of the cost of any grant-eligible project for the construction of publicly owned treatment works not paid for with Federal financial assistance under this title (other than this section), which project the Administrator has determined to be eligible for such financial assistance under this title, including, but not limited to, projects eligible for reimbursement under section 206 of this title.

(b) No guarantee, or commitment to make a guarantee, may be made pursuant to this section—

(1) unless the Administrator certifies that the issuing body is unable to obtain on reasonable terms sufficient credit to finance its actual needs without such guarantee; and

(2) unless the Administrator determines that there is a reasonable assurance or repayment of the loan, obligation, or participation therein.

A determination of whether financing is available at reasonable rates shall be made by the Secretary of the Treasury with relationship to the current average yield on outstanding marketable obligations of municipalities of comparable maturity.

(c) The Administrator is authorized to charge reasonable fees for the investigation of an application for a guarantee and for the issuance of a commitment to make a guarantee.

(d) The Administrator, in determining whether there is a reasonable assurance of repayment, may require a commitment which would apply to such repayment. Such commitment may include, but not be limited to, any funds received by such grantee from the amounts appropriated under section 206 of this Act.

[33 U.S.C. 1293]

PUBLIC INFORMATION

SEC. 214. The Administrator shall develop and operate within one year of the date of enactment of this section, a continuing program of public information and education

on recycling and reuse of wastewater (including sludge), the use of land treatment, and methods for the reduction of wastewater volume.
[33 U.S.C. 1294]

REQUIREMENTS FOR AMERICAN MATERIALS

SEC. 215. Notwithstanding any other provision of law, no grant for which application is made after February 1, 1978, shall be made under this title for any treatment works unless only such unmanufactured articles, materials, and supplies as have been mined or produced in the United States, and only such manufactured articles, materials, and supplies as have been manufactured in the United States, substantially all from articles, materials, or supplies mined, produced, or manufactured, as the case may be, in the United States will be used in such treatment works. This section shall not apply in any case where the Administrator determines, based upon those factors the Administrator deems relevant, including the available resources of the agency, it to be inconsistent with the public interest (including multilateral government procurement agreements) or the cost to be unreasonable, or if articles, materials, or supplies of the class or kind to be used or the articles, materials, or supplies from which they are manufactured are not mined, produced, or manufactured, as the case may be, in the United States in sufficient and reasonably available commercial quantities and of a satisfactory quality.
[33 U.S.C. 1295]

DETERMINATION OF PRIORITY

SEC. 216. Notwithstanding any other provision of this Act, the determination of the priority to be given each category of projects for construction of publicly owned treatment works within each State shall be made solely by that State, except that if the Administrator, after a public hearing, determines that a specific project will not result in compliance with the enforceable requirements of this Act, such project shall be removed from the State's priority list and such State shall submit a revised priority list. These categories shall include, but not be limited to (A) secondary treatment, (B) more stringent treatment, (C) infiltration-in-flow correction, (D) major sewer system rehabilitation, (E) new collector sewers and appurtenances, (F) new interceptors and appurtenances, and (G) correction of combined sewer overflows. Not less than 25 per centum of funds allocated to a State in any fiscal year under this title for construction of publicly owned treatment works in such State shall be obligated for those types of projects referred to in clauses (D), (E), (F), and (G) of this section, if such projects are on such State's priority list for that year and are otherwise eligible for funding in that fiscal year. It is the policy of Congress that projects for wastewater treatment and management undertaken with Federal financial assistance under this Act by any State, municipality, or intermunicipal or interstate agency shall be projects which, in the estimation of the State, are designed to achieve optimum water quality management, consistent with the public health and water quality goals and requirements of the Act.
[33 U.S.C. 1296]

COST-EFFECTIVENESS GUIDELINES

SEC. 217. Any guidelines for cost-effectiveness analysis published by the Administrator under this title shall provide for the identification and selection of cost effective alternatives to comply with the objective and goals of this Act and sections

201(b), 201(d), 201(g)(2)(A), and 301(b)(2)(B) of this Act.
[33 U.S.C. 1297]

COST EFFECTIVENESS

SEC. 218. (a) It is the policy of Congress that a project for waste treatment and management undertaken with Federal financial assistance under this Act by any State, municipality, or intermunicipal or interstate agency shall be considered as an overall waste treatment system for waste treatment and management, and shall be that system which constitutes the most economical and cost-effective combination of devices and systems used in the storage, treatment, recycling, and reclamation of municipal sewage or industrial wastes of a liquid nature to implement section 201 of this Act, or necessary to recycle or reuse water at the most economical cost over the estimated life of the works, including intercepting sewers, outfall sewers, sewage collection systems, pumping power, and other equipment, and their appurtenances; extension, improvements, remodeling, additions, and alterations thereof; elements essential to provide a reliable recycled supply such as standby treatment units and clear well facilities; and any works, including site acquisition of the land that will be an integral part of the treatment process (including land use for the storage of treated wastewater in land treatment systems prior to land application) or which is used for ultimate disposal of residues resulting from such treatment; water efficiency measures and devices; and any other method or system for preventing, abating, reducing, storing, treating, separating, or disposing of municipal waste, including storm water runoff, or industrial waste, including waste in combined storm water and sanitary sewer systems; to meet the requirements of this Act.

(b) In accordance with the policy set forth in subsection (a) of this section, before the Administrator approves any grant to any State, municipality, or intermunicipal or interstate agency for the erection, building, acquisition, alteration, remodeling, improvement, or extension of any treatment works the Administrator shall determine that the facilities plan of which such treatment works are a part constitutes the most economical and cost-effective combination of treatment works over the life of the project to meet the requirements of this Act, including, but not limited to, consideration of construction costs, operation, maintenance, and replacement costs.

(c) In furtherance of the policy set forth in subsection (a) of this section, the Administrator shall require value engineering review in connection with any treatment works, prior to approval of any grant for the erection, building, acquisition, alteration, remodeling, improvement, or extension of such treatment works, in any case in which the cost of such erection, building, acquisition, alteration, remodeling, improvement, or extension is projected to be in excess of $10,000,000. For purposes of this subsection, the term value engineering review means a specialized cost control technique which uses a systematic and creative approach to identify and to focus on unnecessarily high cost in a project in order to arrive at a cost saving without sacrificing the reliability or efficiency of the project.

(d) This section applies to projects for waste treatment and management for which no treatment works including a facilities plan for such project have received Federal financial assistance for the preparation of construction plans and specifications under this Act before the date of enactment of this section.

[33 U.S.C. 1298]

STATE CERTIFICATION OF PROJECTS

SEC. 219. Whenever the Governor of a State which has been delegated sufficient authority to administer the construction grant program under this title in that State certifies to the Administrator that a grant application meets applicable requirements of Federal and State law for assistance under this title, the Administrator shall approve or disapprove such application within 45 days of the date of receipt of such application. If the Administrator does not approve or disapprove such application within 45 days of receipt, the application shall be deemed approved. If the Administrator disapproves such application the Administrator shall state in writing the reasons for such disapproval. Any grant approved or deemed approved under this section shall be subject to amounts provided in appropriation Acts.

[33 U.S.C. 1299]

SEC. 220. PILOT PROGRAM FOR ALTERNATIVE WATER SOURCE PROJECTS.

(a) POLICY.— Nothing in this section shall be construed to affect the application of section 101(g) of this Act and all of the provisions of this section shall be carried out in accordance with the provisions of section 101(g).

(b) DEFINITIONS.—In this section:

(1) ALTERNATIVE WATER SOURCE PROJECT.— The term alternative water source project means a project designed to provide municipal, industrial, and agricultural water supplies in an environmentally sustainable manner by conserving, managing, reclaiming, or reusing water, wastewater, or stormwater or by treating wastewater or stormwater for groundwater recharge, potable reuse, or other purposes. Such term does not include water treatment or distribution facilities.

(2) CRITICAL WATER SUPPLY NEEDS.— The term critical water supply needs means existing or reasonably anticipated future water supply needs that cannot be met by existing water supplies, as identified in a comprehensive statewide or regional water supply plan or assessment projected over a planning period of at least 20 years.

(c) ESTABLISHMENT.— The Administrator may establish a pilot program to make grants to State, interstate, and intrastate water resource development agencies (including water management districts and water supply authorities), local government agencies, private utilities, and nonprofit entities for alternative water source projects to meet critical water supply needs.

(d) ELIGIBLE ENTITY.— The Administrator may make grants under this section to an entity only if the entity has authority under State law to develop or provide water for municipal, industrial, and agricultural uses in an area of the State that is experiencing critical water supply needs.

(e) SELECTION OF PROJECTS.—

(1) LIMITATION.— A project that has received construction funds under the reclamation and reuse program conducted under the Reclamation Projects Authorization and Adjustment Act of 1992 (43 U.S.C. 390h et seq.) shall not be eligible for grant assistance under this section.

(2) GEOGRAPHICAL DISTRIBUTION.— Alternative water source projects selected

by the Administrator under this section shall reflect a variety of geographical and environmental conditions.

(f) Uses of Grants.— Amounts from grants received under this section may be used for engineering, design, construction, and final testing of alternative water source projects designed to meet critical water supply needs. Such amounts may not be used for planning, feasibility studies or for operation, maintenance, replacement, repair, or rehabilitation.

(g) Cost Sharing.— The Federal share of the eligible costs of an alternative water source project carried out using assistance made available under this section shall not exceed 50 percent.

(h) Reports.— On or before September 30, 2004, the Administrator shall transmit to Congress a report on the results of the pilot program established under this section, including progress made toward meeting the critical water supply needs of the participants in the pilot program.

(i) Authorization of Appropriations.—

(1) In general.— There is authorized to be appropriated to carry out this section $25,000,000 for each of fiscal years 2022 through 2026, to remain available until expended.

(2) Limitation on use of funds.— Of the amounts made available for grants under paragraph (1), not more than 2 percent may be used to pay the administrative costs of the Administrator.

[33 U.S.C. 1300]

SEC. 221. SEWER OVERFLOW AND STORMWATER REUSE MUNICIPAL GRANTS.

(a) In General.—

(1) Grants to states.—The Administrator may make grants to States for the purpose of providing grants to a municipality or municipal entity for planning, design, and construction of—

(A) treatment works to intercept, transport, control, treat, or reuse municipal combined sewer overflows, sanitary sewer overflows, or stormwater;

(B) notification systems to inform the public of combined sewer or sanitary overflows that result in sewage being released into rivers and other waters; and

(C) any other measures to manage, reduce, treat, or recapture stormwater or subsurface drainage water eligible for assistance under section 603(c).

(2) Direct municipal grants.— Subject to subsection (g), the Administrator may make a direct grant to a municipality or municipal entity for the purposes described in paragraph (1).

(b) Prioritization.—In selecting from among municipalities applying for grants under subsection (a), a State or the Administrator shall give priority to an applicant that—

(1) is a municipality that is a financially distressed community under subsection (c);

(2) has implemented or is complying with an implementation schedule for the

nine minimum controls specified in the CSO control policy referred to in section 402(q)(1) and has begun implementing a long-term municipal combined sewer overflow control plan or a separate sanitary sewer overflow control plan;

(3) is requesting a grant for a project that is on a State's intended use plan pursuant to section 606(c); or

(4) is an Alaska Native Village.

(c) FINANCIALLY DISTRESSED COMMUNITY.—

(1) DEFINITION.— In subsection (b), the term financially distressed community means a community that meets affordability criteria established by the State in which the community is located, if such criteria are developed after public review and comment.

(2) CONSIDERATION OF IMPACT ON WATER AND SEWER RATES.— In determining if a community is a distressed community for the purposes of subsection (b), the State shall consider, among other factors, the extent to which the rate of growth of a community's tax base has been historically slow such that implementing a plan described in subsection (b)(2) would result in a significant increase in any water or sewer rate charged by the community's publicly owned wastewater treatment facility.

(3) INFORMATION TO ASSIST STATES.— The Administrator may publish information to assist States in establishing affordability criteria under paragraph (1).

(d) COST-SHARING.—

(1) IN GENERAL.— The Federal share of the cost of activities carried out using amounts from a grant made under subsection (a) shall be not less than 55 percent of the cost.

(2) RURAL AND FINANCIALLY DISTRESSED COMMUNITIES.— To the maximum extent practicable, the Administrator shall work with States to prevent the non-Federal share requirements under this subsection from being passed on to rural communities and financially distressed communities (as those terms are defined in subsection (f)(2)(B)(i)).

(3) TYPES OF NON-FEDERAL SHARE.— The applicable non-Federal share of the cost under this subsection may include, in any amount, public and private funds and in-kind services, and may include, notwithstanding section 603(h), financial assistance, including loans, from a State water pollution control revolving fund.

(e) ADMINISTRATIVE REQUIREMENTS.— A project that receives assistance under this section shall be carried out subject to the same requirements as a project that receives assistance from a State water pollution control revolving fund under title VI, except to the extent that the Governor of the State in which the project is located determines that a requirement of title VI is inconsistent with the purposes of this section. For the purposes of this subsection, a Governor may not determine that the requirements of title VI relating to the application of section 513 are inconsistent with the purposes of this section.

(f) AUTHORIZATION OF APPROPRIATIONS.—

(1) IN GENERAL.— There is authorized to be appropriated to carry out this section

$280,000,000 for each of fiscal years 2022 through 2026.

(2) MINIMUM ALLOCATIONS.—

(A) GREEN PROJECTS.— To the extent there are sufficient eligible project applications, the Administrator shall ensure that a State uses not less than 20 percent of the amount of the grants made to the State under subsection (a) in a fiscal year to carry out projects to intercept, transport, control, treat, or reuse municipal combined sewer overflows, sanitary sewer overflows, or stormwater through the use of green infrastructure, water and energy efficiency improvements, and other environmentally innovative activities.

(B) RURAL OR FINANCIALLY DISTRESSED COMMUNITY ALLOCATION.—

(i) DEFINITIONS.—In this subparagraph:

(I) FINANCIALLY DISTRESSED COMMUNITY.— The term financially distressed community has the meaning given the term in subsection (c)(1).

(II) RURAL COMMUNITY.— The term rural community means a city, town, or unincorporated area that has a population of not more than 10,000 inhabitants.

(ii) ALLOCATION.—

(I) IN GENERAL.—To the extent there are sufficient eligible project applications, the Administrator shall ensure that a State uses not less than 25 percent of the amount of the grants made to the State under subsection (a) in a fiscal year to carry out projects in rural communities or financially distressed communities for the purpose of planning, design, and construction of—

(aa) treatment works to intercept, transport, control, treat, or reuse municipal sewer overflows, sanitary sewer overflows, or stormwater; or

(bb) any other measures to manage, reduce, treat, or recapture stormwater or subsurface drainage water eligible for assistance under section 603(c).

(II) RURAL COMMUNITIES.— Of the funds allocated under subclause (I) for the purposes described in that subclause, to the extent there are sufficient eligible project applications, the Administrator shall ensure that a State uses not less than 60 percent to carry out projects in rural communities.

(g) ALLOCATION OF FUNDS.—

(1) FISCAL YEAR 2019.— Subject to subsection (h), the Administrator shall use the amounts appropriated to carry out this section for fiscal year 2019 for making grants to municipalities and municipal entities under subsection (a)(2) in accordance with the criteria set forth in subsection (b).

(2) FISCAL YEAR 2020 AND THEREAFTER.— Subject to subsection (h), the Administrator shall use the amounts appropriated to carry out this section for fiscal

year 2020 and each fiscal year thereafter for making grants to States under subsection (a)(1) in accordance with a formula to be established by the Administrator, after providing notice and an opportunity for public comment, that allocates to each State a proportional share of such amounts based on the total needs of the State for municipal combined sewer overflow controls, sanitary sewer overflow controls, and stormwater identified in the most recent detailed estimate and comprehensive study submitted pursuant to section 516 and any other information the Administrator considers appropriate.

(h) ADMINISTRATIVE EXPENSES.—Of the amounts appropriated to carry out this section for each fiscal year—

(1) the Administrator may retain an amount not to exceed 1 percent for the reasonable and necessary costs of administering this section; and

(2) the Administrator, or a State, may retain an amount not to exceed 4 percent of any grant made to a municipality or municipal entity under subsection (a), for the reasonable and necessary costs of administering the grant.

(i) REPORTS.—

(1) PERIODIC REPORTS.—

(A) IN GENERAL.—Not later than December 31, 2003, and periodically thereafter, the Administrator shall transmit to Congress a report containing—

(i) recommended funding levels for grants under this section; and

(ii) a description of the extent to which States pass costs associated with the non-Federal share requirements under subsection (d) to local communities, with a focus on rural communities and financially distressed communities (as those terms are defined in subsection (f)(2)(B)(i)).

(B) REQUIREMENT.— The funding levels recommended under subparagraph (A)(i) shall be sufficient to ensure the continued expeditious implementation of municipal combined sewer overflow and sanitary sewer overflow controls nationwide.

(2) USE OF FUNDS.— Not later than 2 years after the date of enactment of this paragraph, the Administrator shall submit to the Committee on Environment and Public Works of the Senate and the Committee on Transportation and Infrastructure of the House of Representatives a report that describes the implementation of the grant program under this section, which shall include a description of the grant recipients, sources of funds for non-Federal share requirements under subsection (d), and grant amounts made available under the program.

[33 U.S.C. 1301]

SEC. 222. WASTEWATER EFFICIENCY GRANT PILOT PROGRAM.

(a) ESTABLISHMENT.— Subject to the availability of appropriations, the Administrator shall establish a wastewater efficiency grant pilot program (referred to in this section as the pilot program) to award grants to owners or operators of publicly owned treatment works to carry out projects that create or improve waste-to-energy systems.

(b) SELECTION.—

(1) APPLICATIONS.— To be eligible to receive a grant under the pilot program, an owner or operator of a treatment works shall submit to the Administrator an application at such time, in such manner, and containing such information as the Administrator may require.

(2) NUMBER OF RECIPIENTS.— The Administrator shall select not more than 15 recipients of grants under the pilot program from applications submitted under paragraph (1).

(c) USE OF FUNDS.—

(1) IN GENERAL.—Subject to paragraph (2), a recipient of a grant under the pilot program may use grant funds for—

(A) sludge collection;

(B) installation of anaerobic digesters;

(C) methane capture;

(D) methane transfer;

(E) facility upgrades and retrofits necessary to create or improve waste-to-energy systems; and

(F) other new and emerging, but proven, technologies that transform waste to energy.

(2) LIMITATION.— A grant to a recipient under the pilot program shall be not more than $4,000,000.

(d) REPORTS.—

(1) REPORT TO THE ADMINISTRATOR.— Not later than 2 years after receiving a grant under the pilot program and each year thereafter for which amounts are made available for the pilot program under subsection (e), the recipient of the grant shall submit to the Administrator a report describing the impact of that project on the communities within 3 miles of the treatment works.

(2) REPORT TO CONGRESS.—Not later than 1 year after first awarding grants under the pilot program and each year thereafter for which amounts are made available for the pilot program under subsection (e), the Administrator shall submit to Congress a report describing—

(A) the applications received by the Administrator for grants under the pilot program; and

(B) the projects for which grants were awarded under the pilot program.

(e) AUTHORIZATION OF APPROPRIATIONS.—

(1) IN GENERAL.— There is authorized to be appropriated to carry out the pilot program $20,000,000 for each of fiscal years 2022 through 2026, to remain available until expended.

(2) LIMITATION ON USE OF FUNDS.— Of the amounts made available for grants under paragraph (1), not more than 2 percent may be used to pay the administrative costs of the Administrator.

[33 U.S.C. 1302]

SEC. 223. CLEAN WATER INFRASTRUCTURE RESILIENCY AND SUSTAINABILITY PROGRAM.

(a) DEFINITIONS.—In this section:

(1) ELIGIBLE ENTITY.—The term eligible entity means—

(A) a municipality; or

(B) an intermunicipal, interstate, or State agency.

(2) NATURAL HAZARD.— The term natural hazard means a hazard caused by natural forces, including extreme weather events, sea-level rise, and extreme drought conditions.

(3) PROGRAM.— The term program means the clean water infrastructure resilience and sustainability program established under subsection (b).

(b) ESTABLISHMENT.— Subject to the availability of appropriations, the Administrator shall establish a clean water infrastructure resilience and sustainability program under which the Administrator shall award grants to eligible entities for the purpose of increasing the resilience of publicly owned treatment works to a natural hazard or cybersecurity vulnerabilities.

(c) USE OF FUNDS.—An eligible entity that receives a grant under the program shall use the grant funds for planning, designing, or constructing projects (on a system-wide or area-wide basis) that increase the resilience of a publicly owned treatment works to a natural hazard or cybersecurity vulnerabilities through—

(1) the conservation of water;

(2) the enhancement of water use efficiency;

(3) the enhancement of wastewater and stormwater management by increasing watershed preservation and protection, including through the use of—

(A) natural and engineered green infrastructure; and

(B) reclamation and reuse of wastewater and stormwater, such as aquifer recharge zones;

(4) the modification or relocation of an existing publicly owned treatment works, conveyance, or discharge system component that is at risk of being significantly impaired or damaged by a natural hazard;

(5) the development and implementation of projects to increase the resilience of publicly owned treatment works to a natural hazard or cybersecurity vulnerabilities, as applicable; or

(6) the enhancement of energy efficiency or the use and generation of recovered or renewable energy in the management, treatment, or conveyance of wastewater or stormwater.

(d) APPLICATION.—To be eligible to receive a grant under the program, an eligible entity shall submit to the Administrator an application at such time, in such manner, and containing such information as the Administrator may require, including—

(1) a proposal of the project to be planned, designed, or constructed using funds under the program;

(2) an identification of the natural hazard risk of the area where the proposed project is to be located or potential cybersecurity vulnerability, as applicable, to be addressed by the proposed project;

(3) documentation prepared by a Federal, State, regional, or local government agency of the natural hazard risk of the area where the proposed project is to be located or potential cybersecurity vulnerability, as applicable, of the area where the proposed project is to be located;

(4) a description of any recent natural hazard risk of the area where the proposed project is to be located or potential cybersecurity vulnerabilities that have affected the publicly owned treatment works;

(5) a description of how the proposed project would improve the performance of the publicly owned treatment works under an anticipated natural hazard or natural hazard risk of the area where the proposed project is to be located or a potential cybersecurity vulnerability, as applicable; and

(6) an explanation of how the proposed project is expected to enhance the resilience of the publicly owned treatment works to a natural hazard risk of the area where the proposed project is to be located or a potential cybersecurity vulnerability, as applicable.

(e) GRANT AMOUNT AND OTHER FEDERAL REQUIREMENTS.—

(1) COST SHARE.— Except as provided in paragraph (2), a grant under the program shall not exceed 75 percent of the total cost of the proposed project.

(2) EXCEPTION.—

(A) IN GENERAL.—Except as provided in subparagraph (B), a grant under the program shall not exceed 90 percent of the total cost of the proposed project if the project serves a community that—

(i) has a population of fewer than 10,000 individuals; or

(ii) meets the affordability criteria established by the State in which the community is located under section 603(i)(2).

(B) WAIVER.— At the discretion of the Administrator, a grant for a project described in subparagraph (A) may cover 100 percent of the total cost of the proposed project.

(3) REQUIREMENTS.— The requirements of section 608 shall apply to a project funded with a grant under the program.

(f) REPORT.— Not later than 2 years after the date of enactment of this section, the Administrator shall submit to Congress a report that describes the implementation of the program, which shall include an accounting of all grants awarded under the program, including a description of each grant recipient and each project funded using a grant under the program.

(g) AUTHORIZATION OF APPROPRIATIONS.—

(1) IN GENERAL.— There is authorized to be appropriated to carry out this section $25,000,000 for each of fiscal years 2022 through 2026.

(2) LIMITATION ON USE OF FUNDS.— Of the amounts made available for grants

under paragraph (1), not more than 2 percent may be used to pay the administrative costs of the Administrator.

[33 U.S.C. 1302a]

SEC. 224. SMALL AND MEDIUM PUBLICLY OWNED TREATMENT WORKS CIRCUIT RIDER PROGRAM.

(a) Establishment.— Subject to the availability of appropriations, not later than 180 days after the date of enactment of this section, the Administrator shall establish a circuit rider program (referred to in this section as the circuit rider program) under which the Administrator shall award grants to qualified nonprofit entities, as determined by the Administrator, to provide assistance to owners and operators of small and medium publicly owned treatment works to carry out the activities described in section 602(b)(13).

(b) Limitation.— A grant provided under the circuit rider program shall be in an amount that is not more than $75,000.

(c) Prioritization.—In selecting recipients of grants under the circuit rider program, the Administrator shall give priority to qualified nonprofit entities, as determined by the Administrator, that would serve a community that—

(1) has a history, for not less than the 10 years prior to the award of the grant, of unresolved wastewater issues, stormwater issues, or a combination of wastewater and stormwater issues;

(2) is considered financially distressed;

(3) faces the cumulative burden of stormwater and wastewater overflow issues; or

(4) has previously failed to access Federal technical assistance due to cost-sharing requirements.

(d) Communication.— Each qualified nonprofit entity that receives funding under this section shall, before using that funding to undertake activities to carry out this section, consult with the State in which the assistance is to be expended or otherwise made available.

(e) Report.—Not later than 2 years after the date on which the Administrator establishes the circuit rider program, and every 2 years thereafter, the Administrator shall submit to Congress a report describing—

(1) each recipient of a grant under the circuit rider program; and

(2) a summary of the activities carried out under the circuit rider program.

(f) Authorization of Appropriations.—

(1) In general.— There is authorized to be appropriated to carry out this section $10,000,000 for the period of fiscal years 2022 through 2026.

(2) Limitation on use of funds.— Of the amounts made available for grants under paragraph (1), not more than 2 percent may be used to pay the administrative costs of the Administrator.

[33 U.S.C. 1302b]

SEC. 225. SMALL PUBLICLY OWNED TREATMENT WORKS EFFICIENCY GRANT PROGRAM.

(a) ESTABLISHMENT.— Subject to the availability of appropriations, not later than 180 days after the date of enactment of this section, the Administrator shall establish an efficiency grant program (referred to in this section as the efficiency grant program) under which the Administrator shall award grants to eligible entities for the replacement or repair of equipment that improves water or energy efficiency of small publicly owned treatment works, as identified in an efficiency audit.

(b) ELIGIBLE ENTITIES.—The Administrator may award a grant under the efficiency grant program to—

(1) an owner or operator of a small publicly owned treatment works that serves—

(A) a population of not more than 10,000 people; or

(B) a disadvantaged community; or

(2) a nonprofit organization that seeks to assist a small publicly owned treatment works described in paragraph (1) to carry out the activities described in subsection (a).

(c) REPORT.—Not later than 2 years after the date on which the Administrator establishes the efficiency grant program, and every 2 years thereafter, the Administrator shall submit to Congress a report describing—

(1) each recipient of a grant under the efficiency grant program; and

(2) a summary of the activities carried out under the efficiency grant program.

(d) USE OF FUNDS.—

(1) SMALL SYSTEMS.— Of the amounts made available for grants under this section, to the extent that there are sufficient applications, not less than 15 percent shall be used for grants to publicly owned treatment works that serve fewer than 3,300 people.

(2) LIMITATION ON USE OF FUNDS.— Of the amounts made available for grants under this section, not more than 2 percent may be used to pay the administrative costs of the Administrator.

[33 U.S.C. 1302c]

SEC. 226. GRANTS FOR CONSTRUCTION AND REFURBISHING OF INDIVIDUAL HOUSEHOLD DECENTRALIZED WASTEWATER SYSTEMS FOR INDIVIDUALS WITH LOW OR MODERATE INCOME.

(a) DEFINITION OF ELIGIBLE INDIVIDUAL.— In this section, the term eligible individual means a member of a low-income or moderate-income household, the members of which have a combined income (for the most recent 12-month period for which information is available) equal to not more than 50 percent of the median nonmetropolitan household income for the State or territory in which the household is located, according to the most recent decennial census.

(b) GRANT PROGRAM.—

(1) IN GENERAL.—Subject to the availability of appropriations, the Administrator shall establish a program under which the Administrator shall provide grants to

private nonprofit organizations for the purpose of improving general welfare by providing assistance to eligible individuals—

(A) for the construction, repair, or replacement of an individual household decentralized wastewater treatment system; or

(B) for the installation of a larger decentralized wastewater system designed to provide treatment for 2 or more households in which eligible individuals reside, if—

(i) site conditions at the households are unsuitable for the installation of an individually owned decentralized wastewater system;

(ii) multiple examples of unsuitable site conditions exist in close geographic proximity to each other; and

(iii) a larger decentralized wastewater system could be cost-effectively installed.

(2) Application.— To be eligible to receive a grant under this subsection, a private nonprofit organization shall submit to the Administrator an application at such time, in such manner, and containing such information as the Administrator determines to be appropriate.

(3) Priority.— In awarding grants under this subsection, the Administrator shall give priority to applicants that have substantial expertise and experience in promoting the safe and effective use of individual household decentralized wastewater systems.

(4) Administrative expenses.— A private nonprofit organization may use amounts provided under this subsection to pay the administrative expenses associated with the provision of the services described in paragraph (1), as the Administrator determines to be appropriate.

(c) Grants.—

(1) In general.— Subject to paragraph (2), a private nonprofit organization shall use a grant provided under subsection (b) for the services described in paragraph (1) of that subsection.

(2) Application.— To be eligible to receive the services described in subsection (b)(1), an eligible individual shall submit to the private nonprofit organization serving the area in which the individual household decentralized wastewater system of the eligible individuals is, or is proposed to be, located an application at such time, in such manner, and containing such information as the private nonprofit organization determines to be appropriate.

(3) Priority.— In awarding grants under this subsection, a private nonprofit organization shall give priority to any eligible individual who does not have access to a sanitary sewage disposal system.

(d) Report.— Not later than 2 years after the date of enactment of this section, the Administrator shall submit to the Committee on Environment and Public Works of the Senate and the Committee on Transportation and Infrastructure of the House of Representatives a report describing the recipients of grants under the program under this section and the results of the program under this section.

(e) AUTHORIZATION OF APPROPRIATIONS.—

(1) IN GENERAL.— There is authorized to be appropriated to the Administrator to carry out this section $50,000,000 for each of fiscal years 2022 through 2026.

(2) LIMITATION ON USE OF FUNDS.— Of the amounts made available for grants under paragraph (1), not more than 2 percent may be used to pay the administrative costs of the Administrator.

[33 U.S.C. 1302d]

SEC. 227. CONNECTION TO PUBLICLY OWNED TREATMENT WORKS.

(a) DEFINITIONS.—In this section:

(1) ELIGIBLE ENTITY.—The term eligible entity means—

(A) an owner or operator of a publicly owned treatment works that assists or is seeking to assist low-income or moderate-income individuals with connecting the household of the individual to the publicly owned treatment works; or

(B) a nonprofit entity that assists low-income or moderate-income individuals with the costs associated with connecting the household of the individual to a publicly owned treatment works.

(2) PROGRAM.— The term program means the competitive grant program established under subsection (b).

(3) QUALIFIED INDIVIDUAL.— The term qualified individual has the meaning given the term eligible individual in section 603(j).

(b) ESTABLISHMENT.— Subject to the availability of appropriations, the Administrator shall establish a competitive grant program with the purpose of improving general welfare, under which the Administrator awards grants to eligible entities to provide funds to assist qualified individuals in covering the costs incurred by the qualified individual in connecting the household of the qualified individual to a publicly owned treatment works.

(c) APPLICATION.—

(1) IN GENERAL.— An eligible entity seeking a grant under the program shall submit to the Administrator an application at such time, in such manner, and containing such information as the Administrator may by regulation require.

(2) REQUIREMENT.— Not later than 90 days after the date on which the Administrator receives an application from an eligible entity under paragraph (1), the Administrator shall notify the eligible entity of whether the Administrator will award a grant to the eligible entity under the program.

(d) SELECTION CRITERIA.—In selecting recipients of grants under the program, the Administrator shall use the following criteria:

(1) Whether the eligible entity seeking a grant provides services to, or works directly with, qualified individuals.

(2) Whether the eligible entity seeking a grant—

(A) has an existing program to assist in covering the costs incurred in connecting a household to a publicly owned treatment works; or

(B) seeks to create a program described in subparagraph (A).

(e) REQUIREMENTS.—

(1) VOLUNTARY CONNECTION.—Before providing funds to a qualified individual for the costs described in subsection (b), an eligible entity shall ensure that—

(A) the qualified individual has connected to the publicly owned treatment works voluntarily; and

(B) if the eligible entity is not the owner or operator of the publicly owned treatment works to which the qualified individual has connected, the publicly owned treatment works to which the qualified individual has connected has agreed to the connection.

(2) REIMBURSEMENTS FROM PUBLICLY OWNED TREATMENT WORKS.—An eligible entity that is an owner or operator of a publicly owned treatment works may reimburse a qualified individual that has already incurred the costs described in subsection (b) by—

(A) reducing the amount otherwise owed by the qualified individual to the owner or operator for wastewater or other services provided by the owner or operator; or

(B) providing a direct payment to the qualified individual.

(f) AUTHORIZATION OF APPROPRIATIONS.—

(1) IN GENERAL.— There is authorized to be appropriated to carry out the program $40,000,000 for each of fiscal years 2022 through 2026.

(2) LIMITATIONS ON USE OF FUNDS.—

(A) SMALL SYSTEMS.—Of the amounts made available for grants under paragraph (1), to the extent that there are sufficient applications, not less than 15 percent shall be used to make grants to—

(i) eligible entities described in subsection (a)(1)(A) that are owners and operators of publicly owned treatment works that serve fewer than 3,300 people; and

(ii) eligible entities described in subsection (a)(1)(B) that provide the assistance described in that subsection in areas that are served by publicly owned treatment works that serve fewer than 3,300 people.

(B) ADMINISTRATIVE COSTS.— Of the amounts made available for grants under paragraph (1), not more than 2 percent may be used to pay the administrative costs of the Administrator.

[33 U.S.C. 1302e]

TITLE III—STANDARDS AND ENFORCEMENT

TITLE III—STANDARDS AND ENFORCEMENT

EFFLUENT LIMITATIONS

SEC. 301. (a) Except as in compliance with this section and sections 302, 306, 307, 318, 402, and 404 of this Act, the discharge of any pollutant by any person shall be unlawful.

(b) In order to carry out the objective of this Act there shall be achieved—

(1)(A) not later than July 1, 1977, effluent limitations for point sources, other than publicly owned treatment works, (i) which shall require the application of the best practicable control technology currently available as defined by the Administrator pursuant to section 304(b) of this Act, or (ii) in the case of a discharge into a publicly owned treatment works which meets the requirements of subparagraph (B) of this paragraph, which shall require compliance with any applicable pretreatment requirements and any requirements under section 307 of this Act; and

(B) for publicly owned treatment works in existence on July 1, 1977, or approved pursuant to section 203 of this Act prior to June 30, 1974 (for which construction must be completed within four years of approval), effluent limitations based upon secondary treatment as defined by the Administrator pursuant to section 304(d)(1) of this Act; or,

(C) not later than July 1, 1977, any more stringent limitation, including those necessary to meet water quality standards, treatment standards, or schedules of compliance, established pursuant to any State law or regulations (under authority preserved by section 510) or any other Federal law or regulation, or required to implement any applicable water quality standard established pursuant to this Act.

(2)(A) for pollutants identified in subparagraphs (C), (D), and (F) of this paragraph, effluent limitations for categories and classes of point sources, other than publicly owned treatment works, which (i) shall require application of the best available technology economically achievable for such category or class, which will result in reasonable further progress toward the national goal of eliminating the discharge of all pollutants, as determined in accordance with regulations issued by the Administrator pursuant to section 304(b)(2) of this Act, which such effluent limitations shall require the elimination of discharges of all pollutants if the Administrator finds, on the basis of information available to him (including information developed pursuant to section 315), that such elimination is technologically and economically achievable for a category or class of point sources as determined in accordance with regulations issued by the Administrator pursuant to section 304(b)(2) of this Act, or (ii) in the case of the introduction of a pollutant into a publicly owned treatment works which meets the requirements of subparagraph (B) of this paragraph, shall require compliance with any applicable pretreatment requirements and any other requirement under section 307 of this Act;

[(B) subparagraph (B) repealed by section 21(b) of P.L. 97–117.]

(C) with respect to all toxic pollutants referred to in table 1 of Committee Print Numbered 95–30 of the Committee on Public Works and Transportation of the House of Representatives compliance with effluent limitations in accordance with subparagraph (A) of this paragraph as expeditiously as practicable but in no case later than three years after the date such limitations are promulgated under section 304(b), and in no case later than March 31, 1989;

(D) for all toxic pollutants listed under paragraph (1) of subsection (a) of section 307 of this Act which are not referred to in subparagraph (C) of this paragraph compliance with effluent limitations in accordance with subparagraph (A) of this paragraph as expeditiously as practicable, but in no case later than three years after the date such limitations are promulgated under section 304(b), and in no case later than March 31, 1989;

(E) as expeditiously as practicable but in no case later than three years after the date such limitations are promulgated under section 304(b), and in no case later than March 31, 1989, compliance with effluent limitations for categories and classes of point sources, other than publicly owned treatment works, which in the case of pollutants identified pursuant to section 304(a)(4) of this Act shall require application of the best conventional pollutant control technology as determined in accordance with regulations issued by the Administrator pursuant to section 304(b)(4) of this Act; and

(F) for all pollutants (other than those subject to subparagraphs (C), (D), or (E) of this paragraph) compliance with effluent limitations in accordance with subparagraph (A) of this paragraph as expeditiously as practicable but in no case later than 3 years after the date such limitations are established, and in no case later than March 31, 1989.

(3)(A) for effluent limitations under paragraph (1)(A)(i) of this subsection promulgated after January 1, 1982, and requiring a level of control substantially greater or based on fundamentally different control technology than under permits for an industrial category issued before such date, compliance as expeditiously as practicable but in no case later than three years after the date such limitations are promulgated under section 304(b), and in no case later than March 31, 1989; and

(B) for any effluent limitation in accordance with paragraph (1)(A)(i), (2)(A)(i), or (2)(E) of this subsection established only on the basis of section 402(a)(1) in a permit issued after enactment of the Water Quality Act of 1987, compliance as expeditiously as practicable but in no case later than three years after the date such limitations are established, and in no case later than March 31, 1989.

(c) The Administrator may modify the requirements of subsection (b)(2)(A) of this section with respect to any point source for which a permit application is filed after July 1, 1977, upon a showing by the owner or operator of such point source satisfactory to the Administrator that such modified requirements (1) will represent the maximum use of technology within the economic capability of the owner or operator; and (2) will result in reasonable further progress toward the elimination of the discharge of pollutants.

(d) Any effluent limitation required by paragraph (2) of subsection (b) of this section shall be reviewed at least every five years and, if appropriate, revised pursuant to the procedure established under such paragraph.

(e) Effluent limitations established pursuant to this section or section 302 of this Act shall be applied to all point sources of discharge of pollutants in accordance with the provisions of this Act.

(f) Notwithstanding any other provisions of this Act it shall be unlawful to discharge any radiological, chemical, or biological warfare agent, any high-level radioactive waste, or any medical waste, into the navigable waters.

(g) MODIFICATIONS FOR CERTAIN NONCONVENTIONAL POLLUTANTS.—

(1) GENERAL AUTHORITY.— The Administrator, with the concurrence of the State, may modify the requirements of subsection (b)(2)(A) of this section with respect to the discharge from any point source of ammonia, chlorine, color, iron, and total phenols (4AAP) (when determined by the Administrator to be a pollutant covered by subsection (b)(2)(F)) and any other pollutant which the Administrator lists under paragraph (4) of this subsection.

(2) REQUIREMENTS FOR GRANTING MODIFICATIONS.—A modification under this subsection shall be granted only upon a showing by the owner or operator of a point source satisfactory to the Administrator that—

(A) such modified requirements will result at a minimum in compliance with the requirements of subsection (b)(1)(A) or (C) of this section, whichever is applicable;

(B) such modified requirements will not result in any additional requirements on any other point or nonpoint source; and

(C) such modification will not interfere with the attainment or maintenance of that water quality which shall assure protection of public water supplies, and the protection and propagation of a balanced population of shellfish, fish, and wildlife, and allow recreational activities, in and on the water and such modification will not result in the discharge of pollutants in quantities which may reasonably be anticipated to pose an unacceptable risk to human health or the environment because of bioaccumulation, persistency in the environment, acute toxicity, chronic toxicity (including carcinogenicity, mutagenicity or teratogenicity), or synergistic propensities.

(3) LIMITATION ON AUTHORITY TO APPLY FOR SUBSECTION (C) MODIFICATION.— If an owner or operator of a point source applies for a modification under this subsection with respect to the discharge of any pollutant, such owner or operator shall be eligible to apply for modification under subsection (c) of this section with respect to such pollutant only during the same time period as he is eligible to apply for a modification under this subsection.

(4) PROCEDURES FOR LISTING ADDITIONAL POLLUTANTS.—

(A) GENERAL AUTHORITY.— Upon petition of any person, the Administrator may add any pollutant to the list of pollutants for which modification under this section is authorized (except for pollutants identified pursuant to section 304(a)(4) of this Act, toxic pollutants subject to section 307(a) of this Act, and the thermal component of discharges) in accordance with the provisions of this paragraph.

(B) REQUIREMENTS FOR LISTING.—

(i) SUFFICIENT INFORMATION.— The person petitioning for listing of an additional pollutant under this subsection shall submit to the Administrator sufficient information to make the determinations required by this subparagraph.

(ii) TOXIC CRITERIA DETERMINATION.— The Administrator shall determine whether or not the pollutant meets the criteria for listing as a toxic pollutant under section 307(a) of this Act.

(iii) LISTING AS TOXIC POLLUTANT.— If the Administrator determines that the pollutant meets the criteria for listing as a toxic pollutant under section 307(a), the Administrator shall list the pollutant as a toxic pollutant under section 307(a).

(iv) NONCONVENTIONAL CRITERIA DETERMINATION.— If the Administrator determines that the pollutant does not meet the criteria for listing as a toxic pollutant under such section and determines that adequate test methods and sufficient data are available to make the determinations required by paragraph (2) of this subsection with respect to the pollutant, the Administrator shall add the pollutant to the list of pollutants specified in paragraph (1) of this subsection for which modifications are authorized under this subsection.

(C) REQUIREMENTS FOR FILING OF PETITIONS.—A petition for listing of a pollutant under this paragraph—

(i) must be filed not later than 270 days after the date of promulgation of an applicable effluent guideline under section 304;

(ii) may be filed before promulgation of such guideline; and

(iii) may be filed with an application for a modification under paragraph (1) with respect to the discharge of such pollutant.

(D) DEADLINE FOR APPROVAL OF PETITION.— A decision to add a pollutant to the list of pollutants for which modifications under this subsection are authorized must be made within 270 days after the date of promulgation of an applicable effluent guideline under section 304.

(E) BURDEN OF PROOF.— The burden of proof for making the determinations under subparagraph (B) shall be on the petitioner.

(5) REMOVAL OF POLLUTANTS.— The Administrator may remove any pollutant from the list of pollutants for which modifications are authorized under this subsection if the Administrator determines that adequate test methods and sufficient data are no longer available for determining whether or not modifications may be granted with respect to such pollutant under paragraph (2) of this subsection.

(h) The Administrator, with the concurrence of the State, may issue a permit under section 402 which modifies the requirements of subsection (b)(1)(B) of this section with respect to the discharge of any pollutant from a publicly owned treatment works into marine waters, if the applicant demonstrates to the satisfaction of the Administrator that—

(1) there is an applicable water quality standard specific to the pollutant for which the modification is requested, which has been identified under section 304(a)(6) of this Act;

(2) the discharge of pollutants in accordance with such modified requirements will not interfere, alone or in combination with pollutants from other sources, with the attainment or maintenance of that water quality which assures protection of public water supplies and the protection and propagation of a balanced, indigenous population of shellfish, fish and wildlife, and allows recreational activities, in and on the water;

(3) the applicant has established a system for monitoring the impact of such discharge on a representative sample of aquatic biota, to the extent practicable, and the scope of such monitoring is limited to include only those scientific investigations which are necessary to study the effects of the proposed discharge;

(4) such modified requirements will not result in any additional requirements on any other point or nonpoint source;

(5) all applicable pretreatment requirements for sources introducing waste into such treatment works will be enforced;

(6) in the case of any treatment works serving a population of 50,000 or more, with respect to any toxic pollutant introduced into such works by an industrial discharger for which pollutant there is no applicable pretreatment requirement in effect, sources introducing waste into such works are in compliance with all applicable pretreatment requirements, the applicant will enforce such requirements, and the applicant has in effect a pretreatment program which, in combination with the treatment of discharges from such works, removes the same amount of such pollutant as would be removed if such works were to apply secondary treatment to discharges and if such works had no pretreatment program with respect to such pollutant;

(7) to the extent practicable, the applicant has established a schedule of activities designed to eliminate the entrance of toxic pollutants from nonindustrial sources into such treatment works;

(8) there will be no new or substantially increased discharges from the point source of the pollutant to which the modification applies above that volume of discharge specified in the permit;

(9) the applicant at the time such modification becomes effective will be discharging effluent which has received at least primary or equivalent treatment and which meets the criteria established under section 304(a)(1) of this Act after initial mixing in the waters surrounding or adjacent to the point at which such effluent is discharged.

For the purposes of this subsection the phrase the discharge of any pollutant into marine waters refers to a discharge into deep waters of the territorial sea or the waters of the contiguous zone, or into saline estuarine waters where there is strong tidal movement and other hydrological and geological characteristics which the Administrator determines necessary to allow compliance with paragraph (2) of this subsection, and section 101(a)(2) of this Act. For the purposes of paragraph (9), primary or equivalent treatment means treatment by screening, sedimentation, and skimming adequate to remove at least 30 percent of the biological oxygen demanding material and of the suspended solids in the treatment works influent, and disinfection, where appropriate. A municipality which applies secondary treatment shall be eligible to receive a permit pursuant to this subsection which modifies the requirements of subsection (b)(1)(B) of this section with respect to the discharge of any pollutant from any treatment works owned by such municipality into marine waters. No permit issued under this subsection shall authorize the discharge of sewage sludge into marine waters. In order for a permit to be issued under this subsection for the discharge of a pollutant into marine waters, such marine waters must exhibit characteristics assuring that water providing dilution does not contain significant amounts of previously discharged effluent from such treatment works. No permit issued under this subsection shall authorize the discharge of any pollutant into saline estuarine waters which at the time of application do not support a balanced indigenous population of shellfish, fish and wildlife, or allow recreation in and on the waters or which exhibit ambient water quality below applicable water quality standards adopted for the protection of public water supplies, shellfish, fish and wildlife or recreational activities or such other standards necessary to assure support and protection of such uses. The prohibition contained in the preceding sentence shall apply without regard to the presence or absence of a causal relationship between such characteristics and the applicant's current or proposed discharge. Notwithstanding any other provisions of this subsection, no permit may be issued under this subsection for discharge of a pollutant into the New York Bight Apex consisting of the ocean waters of the Atlantic Ocean westward of 73 degrees 30 minutes west longitude and northward of 40 degrees 10 minutes north latitude.

(i)(1) Where construction is required in order for a planned or existing publicly owned treatment works to achieve limitations under subsection (b)(1)(B) or (b)(1)(C) of this section, but (A) construction cannot be completed within the time required in such subsection, or (B) the United States has failed to make financial assistance under this Act available in time to achieve such limitations by the time specified in such subsection, the owner or operator of such treatment works may request the Administrator (or if appropriate the State) to issue a permit pursuant to section 402 of this Act or to modify a permit issued pursuant to that section to extend such time for compliance. Any such request shall be filed with the Administrator (or if appropriate the State) within 180 days after the date of enactment of the Water Quality Act of 1987. The Administrator (or if appropriate the State) may grant such request and issue or modify such a permit, which shall contain a schedule of compliance for the publicly owned treatment works based on the earliest date by which such financial assistance will be available from the United States and construction can be completed, but in no event later than July 1, 1988, and shall contain such other terms and conditions, including those necessary to carry out subsections (b) through (g) of section 201 of this Act, section 307 of this Act, and such interim effluent limitations applicable to that treatment works as the Administrator determines are necessary to carry out the provisions of this Act.

(2)(A) Where a point source (other than a publicly owned treatment works) will not achieve the requirements of subsections (b)(1)(A) and (b)(1)(C) of this section and—

(i) if a permit issued prior to July 1, 1977, to such point source is based upon a discharge into a publicly owned treatment works; or

(ii) if such point source (other than a publicly owned treatment works) had before July 1, 1977, a contract (enforceable against such point source) to discharge into a publicly owned treatment works; or

(iii) if either an application made before July 1, 1977, for a construction grant under this Act for a publicly owned treatment works, or engineering or architectural plans or working drawings made before July 1, 1977, for a publicly owned treatment works, show that such point source was to discharge into such publicly owned treatment works,

and such publicly owned treatment works is presently unable to accept such discharge without construction, and in the case of a discharge to an existing publicly owned treatment works, such treatment works has an extension pursuant to paragraph (1) of this subsection, the owner or operator of such point source may request the Administrator (or if appropriate the State) to issue or modify such a permit pursuant to such section 402 to extend such time for compliance. Any such request shall be filed with the Administrator (or if appropriate the State) within 180 days after the date of enactment of this subsection or the filing of a request by the appropriate publicly owned treatment works under paragraph (1) of this subsection, whichever is later. If the Administrator (or if appropriate the State) finds that the owner or operator of such point source has acted in good faith, he may grant such request and issue or modify such a permit, which shall contain a schedule of compliance for the point source to achieve the requirements of subsections (b)(1)(A) and (C) of this section and shall contain such other terms and conditions, including pretreatment and interim effluent limitations and water conservation requirements applicable to that point source, as the Administrator determines are necessary to carry out the provisions of this Act.

(B) No time modification granted by the Administrator (or if appropriate the State) pursuant to paragraph (2)(A) of this subsection shall extend beyond the earliest date practicable for compliance or beyond the date of any extension granted to the appropriate publicly owned treatment works pursuant to paragraph (1) of this subsection, but in no event shall it extend beyond July 1, 1988; and no such time modification shall be granted unless (i) the publicly owned treatment works will be in operation and available to the point source before July 1, 1988, and will meet the requirements to subsections (b)(1) (B) and (C) of this section after receiving the discharge from that point source; and (ii) the point source and the publicly owned treatment works have entered into an enforceable contract requiring the point source to discharge into the publicly owned treatment works, the owner or operator of such point source to pay the costs required under section 204 of this Act, and the publicly owned treatment works to accept the discharge from the point source; and (iii) the permit for such point source requires point source to meet all requirements under section 307 (a) and (b) during the period of such time modification.

(j)(1) Any application filed under this section for a modification of the provisions of—

(A) subsection (b)(1)(B) under subsection (h) of this section shall be filed not later that[11] the 365th day which begins after the date of enactment of the

Municipal Wastewater Treatment Construction Grant Amendments of 1981, except that a publicly owned treatment works which prior to December 31, 1982, had a contractual arrangement to use a portion of the capacity of an ocean outfall operated by another publicly owned treatment works which has applied for or received modification under subsection (h), may apply for a modification of subsection (h) in its own right not later than 30 days after the date of the enactment of the Water Quality Act of 1987, and except as provided in paragraph (5);

[11] So in law. Probably should be than.

(B) subsection (b)(2)(A) as it applies to pollutants identified in subsection (b)(2)(F) shall be filed not later than 270 days after the date of promulgation of an applicable effluent guideline under section 304 or not later than 270 days after the date of enactment of the Clean Water Act of 1977, whichever is later.

(2) Subject to paragraph (3) of this section, any application for a modification filed under subsection (g) of this section shall not operate to stay any requirement under this Act, unless in the judgment of the Administrator such a stay or the modification sought will not result in the discharge of pollutants in quantities which may reasonably be anticipated to pose an unacceptable risk to human health or the environment because of bioaccumulation, persistency in the environment, acute toxicity, chronic toxicity (including carcinogenicity, mutagenicity, or teratogenicity), or synergistic propensities, and that there is a substantial likelihood that the applicant will succeed on the merits of such application. In the case of an application filed under subsection (g) of this section, the Administrator may condition any stay granted under this paragraph on requiring the filing of a bond or other appropriate security to assure timely compliance with the requirements from which a modification is sought.

(3) Compliance requirements under subsection (g).—

(A) Effect of filing.— An application for a modification under subsection (g) and a petition for listing of a pollutant as a pollutant for which modifications are authorized under such subsection shall not stay the requirement that the person seeking such modification or listing comply with effluent limitations under this Act for all pollutants not the subject of such application or petition.

(B) Effect of disapproval.— Disapproval of an application for a modification under subsection (g) shall not stay the requirement that the person seeking such modification comply with all applicable effluent limitations under this Act.

(4) Deadline for subsection (g) decision.— An application for a modification with respect to a pollutant filed under subsection (g) must be approved or disapproved not later than 365 days after the date of such filing; except that in any case in which a petition for listing such pollutant as a pollutant for which modifications are authorized under such subsection is approved, such application must be approved or disapproved not later than 365 days after the date of approval of such petition.

(5) Extension of application deadline.—

(A) In general.— In the 180-day period beginning on the date of the enactment of this paragraph, the city of San Diego, California, may apply for a modification pursuant to subsection (h) of the requirements of subsection (b)(1)(B) with respect to biological oxygen demand and total suspended solids in the effluent discharged into marine waters.

(B) Application.—An application under this paragraph shall include a commitment by the applicant to implement a waste water reclamation program that, at a minimum, will—

(i) achieve a system capacity of 45,000,000 gallons of reclaimed waste water per day by January 1, 2010; and

(ii) result in a reduction in the quantity of suspended solids discharged by the applicant into the marine environment during the period of the modification.

(C) Additional conditions.— The Administrator may not grant a modification pursuant to an application submitted under this paragraph unless the Administrator determines that such modification will result in removal of not less than 58 percent of the biological oxygen demand (on an annual average) and not less than 80 percent of total suspended solids (on a monthly average) in the discharge to which the application applies.

(D) Preliminary decision deadline.— The Administrator shall announce a preliminary decision on an application submitted under this paragraph not later than 1 year after the date the application is submitted.

(k) In the case of any facility subject to a permit under section 402 which proposes to comply with the requirements of subsection (b)(2)(A) or (b)(2)(E) of this section by replacing existing production capacity with an innovative production process which will result in an effluent reduction significantly greater than that required by the limitation otherwise applicable to such facility and moves toward the national goal of eliminating the discharge of all pollutants, or with the installation of an innovative control technique that has a substantial likelihood for enabling the facility to comply with the applicable effluent limitation by achieving a significantly greater effluent reduction than that required by the applicable effluent limitation and moves toward the national goal of eliminating the discharge of all pollutants, or by achieving the required reduction with an innovative system that has the potential for significantly lower costs than the systems which have been determined by the Administrator to be economically achievable, the Administrator (or the State with an approved program under section 402, in consultation with the Administrator) may establish a date for compliance under subsection (b)(2)(A) or (b)(2)(E) of this section no later than two years after the date for compliance with such effluent limitation which would otherwise be applicable under such subsection, if it is also determined that such innovative system has the potential for industrywide application.

(l) Other than as provided in subsection (n) of this section, the Administrator may not modify any requirement of this section as it applies to any specific pollutant which is on the toxic pollutant list under section 307(a)(1) of this Act.

(m)(1) The Administrator, with the concurrence of the State, may issue a permit under section 402 which modifies the requirements of subsections (b)(1)(A) and (b)(2)(E) of this section, and of section 403, with respect to effluent limitations to the extent such limitations relate to biochemical oxygen demand and pH from discharges by an industrial discharger in such State into deep waters of the territorial seas, if the applicant demonstrates and the Administrator finds that—

(A) the facility for which modification is sought is covered at the time of the enactment of this subsection by National Pollutant Discharge Elimination System permit number CA0005894 or CA0005282;

(B) the energy and environmental costs of meeting such requirements of subsections (b)(1)(A) and (b)(2)(E) and section 403 exceed by an unreasonable amount the benefits to be obtained, including the objectives of this Act;

(C) the applicant has established a system for monitoring the impact of such discharges on a representative sample of aquatic biota;

(D) such modified requirements will not result in any additional requirements on any other point or nonpoint source;

(E) there will be no new or substantially increased discharges from the point source of the pollutant to which the modification applies above that volume of discharge specified in the permit;

(F) the discharge is into waters where there is strong tidal movement and other hydrological and geological characteristics which are necessary to allow compliance with this subsection and section 101(a)(2) of this Act;

(G) the applicant accepts as a condition to the permit a contractural[12] obligation to use funds in the amount required (but not less than $250,000 per year for ten years) for research and development of water pollution control technology, including but not limited to closed cycle technology;

[12] So in law. Probably should read contractual.

(H) the facts and circumstances present a unique situation which, if relief is granted, will not establish a precedent or the relaxation of the requirements of this Act applicable to similarly situated discharges; and

(I) no owner or operator of a facility comparable to that of the applicant situated in the United States has demonstrated that it would be put at a competitive disadvantage to the applicant (or the parent company or any subsidiary thereof) as a result of the issuance of a permit under this subsection.

(2) The effluent limitations established under a permit issued under paragraph (1) shall be sufficient to implement the applicable State water quality standards, to assure the protection of public water supplies and protection and propagation of a balanced, indigenous population of shellfish, fish, fauna, wildlife, and other aquatic organisms, and to allow recreational activities in and on the water. In setting such limitations, the Administrator shall take into account any seasonal variations and the need for an adequate margin of safety, considering the lack of essential knowledge concerning the relationship between effluent limitations and water quality and the lack of essential knowledge of the effects of discharges on beneficial uses of the receiving waters.

(3) A permit under this subsection may be issued for a period not to exceed five years, and such a permit may be renewed for one additional period not to exceed five years upon a demonstration by the applicant and a finding by the Administrator at the time of application for any such renewal that the provisions of this subsection are met.

(4) The Administrator may terminate a permit issued under this subsection if the Administrator determines that there has been a decline in ambient water quality of the receiving waters during the period of the permit even if a direct cause and effect relationship cannot be shown: *Provided,* That if the effluent from a source with a permit issued under this subsection is contributing to a decline in ambient water quality of the receiving waters, the Administrator shall terminate such permit.

(n) FUNDAMENTALLY DIFFERENT FACTORS.—

(1) GENERAL RULE.—The Administrator, with the concurrence of the State, may establish an alternative requirement under subsection (b)(2) or section 307(b) for a facility that modifies the requirements of national effluent limitation guidelines or categorical pretreatment standards that would otherwise be applicable to such facility, if the owner or operator of such facility demonstrates to the satisfaction of the Administrator that—

(A) the facility is fundamentally different with respect to the factors (other than cost) specified in section 304(b) or 304(g) and considered by the Administrator in establishing such national effluent limitation guidelines or categorical pretreatment standards;

(B) the application—

(i) is based solely on information and supporting data submitted to the Administrator during the rule making for establishment of the applicable national effluent limitation guidelines or categorical pretreatment standard specifically raising the factors that are fundamentally different for such facility; or

(ii) is based on information and supporting data referred to in clause (i) and information and supporting data the applicant did not have a reasonable opportunity to submit during such rulemaking;

(C) the alternative requirement is no less stringent than justified by the fundamental difference; and

(D) the alternative requirement will not result in a non-water quality environmental impact which is markedly more adverse than the impact considered by the Administrator in establishing such national effluent limitation guideline or categorical pretreatment standard.

(2) TIME LIMIT FOR APPLICATIONS.— An application for an alternative requirement which modifies the requirements of an effluent limitation or pretreatment standard under this subsection must be submitted to the Administrator within 180 days after the date on which such limitation or standard is established or revised, as the case may be.

(3) TIME LIMIT FOR DECISION.— The Administrator shall approve or deny by final

agency action an application submitted under this subsection within 180 days after the date such application is filed with the Administrator.

(4) SUBMISSION OF INFORMATION.— The Administrator may allow an applicant under this subsection to submit information and supporting data until the earlier of the date the application is approved or denied or the last day that the Administrator has to approve or deny such application.

(5) TREATMENT OF PENDING APPLICATIONS.— For the purposes of this subsection, an application for an alternative requirement based on fundamentally different factors which is pending on the date of the enactment of this subsection shall be treated as having been submitted to the Administrator on the 180th day following such date of enactment. The applicant may amend the application to take into account the provisions of this subsection.

(6) EFFECT OF SUBMISSION OF APPLICATION.— An application for an alternative requirement under this subsection shall not stay the applicant's obligation to comply with the effluent limitation guideline or categorical pretreatment standard which is the subject of the application.

(7) EFFECT OF DENIAL.— If an application for an alternative requirement which modifies the requirements of an effluent limitation or pretreatment standard under this subsection is denied by the Administrator, the applicant must comply with such limitation or standard as established or revised, as the case may be.

(8) REPORTS.— By January 1, 1997, and January 1 of every odd-numbered year thereafter, the Administrator shall submit to the Committee on Environment and Public Works of the Senate and the Committee on Transportation and Infrastructure of the House of Representatives a report on the status of applications for alternative requirements which modify the requirements of effluent limitations under section 301 or 304 of this Act or any national categorical pretreatment standard under section 307(b) of this Act filed before, on, or after such date of enactment.

(o) APPLICATION FEES.— The Administrator shall prescribe and collect from each applicant fees reflecting the reasonable administrative costs incurred in reviewing and processing applications for modifications submitted to the Administrator pursuant to subsections (c), (g), (i), (k), (m), and (n) of section 301, section 304(d)(4), and section 316(a) of this Act. All amounts collected by the Administrator under this subsection shall be deposited into a special fund of the Treasury entitled Water Permits and Related Services which shall thereafter be available for appropriation to carry out activities of the Environmental Protection Agency for which such fees were collected.

(p) MODIFIED PERMIT FOR COAL REMINING OPERATIONS.—

(1) IN GENERAL.— Subject to paragraphs (2) through (4) of this subsection, the Administrator, or the State in any case which the State has an approved permit program under section 402(b), may issue a permit under section 402 which modifies the requirements of subsection (b)(2)(A) of this section with respect to the pH level of any pre-existing discharge, and with respect to pre-existing discharges of iron and manganese from the remined area of any coal remining operation or with respect to the pH level or level of iron or manganese in any pre-existing discharge affected by the remining operation. Such modified requirements shall apply the best available technology economically achievable on a case-by-case basis, using best professional

judgment, to set specific numerical effluent limitations in each permit.

(2) Limitations.— The Administrator or the State may only issue a permit pursuant to paragraph (1) if the applicant demonstrates to the satisfaction of the Administrator or the State, as the case may be, that the coal remining operation will result in the potential for improved water quality from the remining operation but in no event shall such a permit allow the pH level of any discharge, and in no event shall such a permit allow the discharges of iron and manganese, to exceed the levels being discharged from the remined area before the coal remining operation begins. No discharge from, or affected by, the remining operation shall exceed State water quality standards established under section 303 of this Act.

(3) Definitions.—For purposes of this subsection—

(A) Coal remining operation.— The term coal remining operation means a coal mining operation which begins after the date of the enactment of this subsection at a site on which coal mining was conducted before the effective date of the Surface Mining Control and Reclamation Act of 1977.

(B) Remined area.— The term remined area means only that area of any coal remining operation on which coal mining was conducted before the effective date of the Surface Mining Control and Reclamation Act of 1977.

(C) Pre-existing discharge.— The term pre-existing discharge means any discharge at the time of permit application under this subsection.

(4) Applicability of strip mining laws.— Nothing in this subsection shall affect the application of the Surface Mining Control and Reclamation Act of 1977 to any coal remining operation, including the application of such Act to suspended solids.

[33 U.S.C. 1311]

WATER QUALITY RELATED EFFLUENT LIMITATIONS

Sec. 302. (a) Whenever, in the judgment of the Administrator or as identified under section 304(l), discharges of pollutants from a point source or group of point sources, with the application of effluent limitations required under section 301(b)(2) of this Act, would interfere with the attainment or maintenance of that water quality in a specific portion of the navigable waters which shall assure protection of public health, public water supplies, agricultural and industrial uses, and the protection and propagation of a balanced population of shellfish, fish and wildlife, and allow recreational activities in and on the water, effluent limitations (including alternative effluent control strategies) for such point source or sources shall be established which can reasonably be expected to contribute to the attainment or maintenance of such water quality.

(b) Modifications of Effluent Limitations.—

(1) Notice and hearing.— Prior to establishment of any effluent limitation pursuant to subsection (a) of this section, the Administrator shall publish such proposed limitation and within 90 days of such publication hold a public hearing.

(2) Permits.—

(A) No reasonable relationship.— The Administrator, with the concurrence of the State, may issue a permit which modifies the effluent limitations required by subsection (a) of this section for pollutants other than toxic pollutants if the applicant demonstrates at such hearing that (whether or not technology or other alternative control strategies are available) there is no reasonable relationship between the economic and social costs and the benefits to be obtained (including attainment of the objective of this Act) from achieving such limitation.

(B) REASONABLE PROGRESS.— The Administrator, with the concurrence of the State, may issue a permit which modifies the effluent limitations required by subsection (a) of this section for toxic pollutants for a single period not to exceed 5 years if the applicant demonstrates to the satisfaction of the Administrator that such modified requirements (i) will represent the maximum degree of control within the economic capability of the owner and operator of the source, and (ii) will result in reasonable further progress beyond the requirements of section 301(b)(2) toward the requirements of subsection (a) of this section.

(c) The establishment of effluent limitations under this section shall not operate to delay the application of any effluent limitation established under section 301 of this Act.

[33 U.S.C. 1312]

WATER QUALITY STANDARDS AND IMPLEMENTATION PLANS

SEC. 303. (a)(1) In order to carry out the purpose of this Act, any water quality standard applicable to interstate waters which was adopted by any State and submitted to, and approved by, or is awaiting approval by, the Administrator pursuant to this Act as in effect immediately prior to the date of enactment of the Federal Water Pollution Control Act Amendments of 1972, shall remain in effect unless the Administrator determined that such standard is not consistent with the applicable requirements of this Act as in effect immediately prior to the date of enactment of the Federal Water Pollution Control Act Amendments of 1972. If the Administrator makes such a determination he shall, within three months after the date of enactment of the Federal Water Pollution Control Act Amendments of 1972, notify the State and specify the changes needed to meet such requirements. If such changes are not adopted by the State within ninety days after the date of such notification, the Administrator shall promulgate such changes in accordance with subsection (b) of this section.

(2) Any State which, before the date of enactment of the Federal Water Pollution Control Act Amendments of 1972, has adopted, pursuant to its own law, water quality standards applicable to intrastate waters shall submit such standards to the Administrator within thirty days after the date of enactment of the Federal Water Pollution Control Act Amendments of 1972. Each such standard shall remain in effect, in the same manner and to the same extent as any other water quality standard established under this Act unless the Administrator determines that such standard is inconsistent with the applicable requirements of this Act as in effect immediately prior to the date of enactment of the Federal Water Pollution Control Act Amendments of 1972. If the Administrator makes such a determination he shall not later than the one hundred and twentieth day after the date of submission of such standards, notify the State and specify the changes needed to meet such

requirements. If such changes are not adopted by the State within ninety days after such notification, the Administrator shall promulgate such changes in accordance with subsection (b) of this section.

(3)(A) Any State which prior to the date of enactment of the Federal Water Pollution Control Act Amendments of 1972 has not adopted pursuant to its own laws water quality standards applicable to intrastate waters shall, not later than one hundred and eighty days after the date of enactment of the Federal Water Pollution Control Act Amendments of 1972, adopt and submit such standards to the Administrator.

(B) If the Administrator determines that any such standards are consistent with the applicable requirements of this Act as in effect immediately prior to the date of enactment of the Federal Water Pollution Control Act Amendments of 1972, he shall approve such standards.

(C) If the Administrator determines that any such standards are not consistent with the applicable requirements of this Act as in effect immediately prior to the date of enactment of the Federal Water Pollution Control Act Amendments of 1972, he shall, not later than the ninetieth day after the date of submission of such standards, notify the State and specify the changes to meet such requirements. If such changes are not adopted by the State within ninety days after the date of notification, the Administrator shall promulgate such standards pursuant to subsection (b) of this section.

(b)(1) The Administrator shall promptly prepare and publish proposed regulations setting forth water quality standards for a State in accordance with the applicable requirements of this Act as in effect immediately prior to the date of enactment of the Federal Water Pollution Control Act Amendments of 1972, if—

(A) the State fails to submit water quality standards within the times prescribed in subsection (a) of this section,

(B) a water quality standard submitted by such State under subsection (a) of this section is determined by the Administrator not to be consistent with the applicable requirements of subsection (a) of this section.

(2) The Administrator shall promulgate any water quality standard published in a proposed regulation not later than one hundred and ninety days after the date he publishes any such proposed standard, unless prior to such promulgation, such State has adopted a water quality standard which the Administrator determines to be in accordance with subsection (a) of this section.

(c)(1) The Governor of a State or the State water pollution control agency of such State shall from time to time (but at least once each three year period beginning with the date of enactment of the Federal Water Pollution Control Act Amendments of 1972) hold public hearings for the purpose of reviewing applicable water quality standards and, as appropriate, modifying and adopting standards. Results of such review shall be made available to the Administrator.

(2)(A) Whenever the State revises or adopts a new standard, such revised or new standard shall be submitted to the Administrator. Such revised or new water quality standard shall consist of the designated uses of the navigable waters involved and the water quality criteria for such waters based upon such uses. Such standards shall be such as to protect the public health or welfare, enhance the quality of water and serve the purposes of this Act. Such standards shall be established taking into consideration their use and value for public water supplies, propagation of fish and wildlife, recreational purposes, and agricultural, industrial, and other purposes, and also taking into consideration their use and value for navigation.

(B) Whenever a State reviews water quality standards pursuant to paragraph (1) of this subsection, or revises or adopts new standards pursuant to this paragraph, such State shall adopt criteria for all toxic pollutants listed pursuant to section 307(a)(1) of this Act for which criteria have been published under section 304(a), the discharge or presence of which in the affected waters could reasonably be expected to interfere with those designated uses adopted by the State, as necessary to support such designated uses. Such criteria shall be specific numerical criteria for such toxic pollutants. Where such numerical criteria are not available, whenever a State reviews water quality standards pursuant to paragraph (1), or revises or adopts new standards pursuant to this paragraph, such State shall adopt criteria based on biological monitoring or assessment methods consistent with information published pursuant to section 304(a)(8). Nothing in this section shall be construed to limit or delay the use of effluent limitations or other permit conditions based on or involving biological monitoring or assessment methods or previously adopted numerical criteria.

(3) If the Administrator, within sixty days after the date of submission of the revised or new standard, determines that such standard meets the requirements of this Act, such standard shall thereafter be the water quality standard for the applicable waters of that State. If the Administrator determines that any such revised or new standard is not consistent with the applicable requirements of this Act, he shall not later than the ninetieth day after the date of submission of such standard notify the State and specify the changes to meet such requirements. If such changes are not adopted by the State within ninety days after the date of notification, the Administrator shall promulgate such standard pursuant to paragraph (4) of this subsection.

(4) The Administrator shall promptly prepare and publish proposed regulations setting forth a revised or new water quality standard for the navigable waters involved—

(A) if a revised or new water quality standard submitted by such State under paragraph (3) of this subsection for such waters is determined by the Administrator not to be consistent with the applicable requirements of this Act, or

(B) in any case where the Administrator determines that a revised or new standard is necessary to meet the requirements of this Act.

The Administrator shall promulgate any revised or new standard under this paragraph not later than ninety days after he publishes such proposed standards, unless prior to such promulgation, such State has adopted a revised or new water quality standard which the Administrator determines to be in accordance with this Act.

(d)(1)(A) Each State shall identify those waters within its boundaries for which the effluent limitations required by section 301(b)(1)(A) and section 301(b)(1)(B) are not stringent enough to implement any water quality standard applicable to such waters. The State shall establish a priority ranking for such waters, taking into account the severity of the pollution and the uses to be made of such waters.

(B) Each State shall identify those waters or parts thereof within its boundaries for which controls on thermal discharges under section 301 are not stringent enough to assure protection and propagation of a balanced indigenous population of shellfish, fish, and wildlife.

(C) Each State shall establish for the waters identified in paragraph (1)(A) of this subsection, and in accordance with the priority ranking, the total maximum daily load, for those pollutants which the Administrator identifies under section 304(a)(2) as suitable for such calculation. Such load shall be established at a level necessary to implement the applicable water quality standards with seasonal variations and a margin of safety which takes into account any lack of knowledge concerning the relationship between effluent limitations and water quality.

(D) Each State shall estimate for the waters identified in paragraph (1)(B) of this subsection the total maximum daily thermal load required to assure protection and propagation of a balanced, indigenous population of shellfish, fish and wildlife. Such estimates shall take into account the normal water temperatures, flow rates, seasonal variations, existing sources of heat input, and the dissipative capacity of the identified waters or parts thereof. Such estimates shall include a calculation of the maximum heat input that can be made into each such part and shall include a margin of safety which takes into account any lack of knowledge concerning the development of thermal water quality criteria for such protection and propagation in the identified waters or parts thereof.

(2) Each State shall submit to the Administrator from time to time, with the first such submission not later than one hundred and eighty days after the date of publication of the first identification of pollutants under section 304(a)(2)(D), for his approval the waters identified and the loads established under paragraphs (1)(A), (1)(B), (1)(C), and (1)(D) of this subsection. The Administrator shall either approve or disapprove such identification and load not later than thirty days after the date of submission. If the Administrator approves such identification and load, such State shall incorporate them into its current plan under subsection (e) of this section. If the Administrator disapproves such identification and load, he shall not later than thirty days after the date of such disapproval identify such waters in such State and establish such loads for such waters as he determines necessary to implement the water quality standards applicable to such waters and upon such identification and establishment the State shall incorporate them into its current plan under subsection (e) of this section.

(3) For the specific purpose of developing information, each State shall identify all waters within its boundaries which it has not identified under paragraph (1)(A) and (1)(B) of this subsection and estimate for such waters the total maximum daily load with seasonal variations and margins of safety, for those pollutants which the Administrator identifies under section 304(a)(2) as suitable for such calculation and for thermal discharges, at a level that would assure protection and propagation of a

balanced indigenous population of fish, shellfish and wildlife.

(4) Limitations on revision of certain effluent limitations.—

(A) Standard not attained.— For waters identified under paragraph (1)(A) where the applicable water quality standard has not yet been attained, any effluent limitation based on a total maximum daily load or other waste load allocation established under this section may be revised only if (i) the cumulative effect of all such revised effluent limitations based on such total maximum daily load or waste load allocation will assure the attainment of such water quality standard, or (ii) the designated use which is not being attained is removed in accordance with regulations established under this section.

(B) Standard attained.— For waters identified under paragraph (1)(A) where the quality of such waters equals or exceeds levels necessary to protect the designated use for such waters or otherwise required by applicable water quality standards, any effluent limitation based on a total maximum daily load or other waste load allocation established under this section, or any water quality standard established under this section, or any other permitting standard may be revised only if such revision is subject to and consistent with the antidegradation policy established under this section.

(e)(1) Each State shall have a continuing planning process approved under paragraph (2) of this subsection which is consistent with this Act.

(2) Each State shall submit not later than 120 days after the date of the enactment of the Water Pollution Control Amendments of 1972 to the Administrator for his approval a proposed continuing planning process which is consistent with this Act. Not later than thirty days after the date of submission of such a process the Administrator shall either approve or disapprove such process. The Administrator shall from time to time review each State's approved planning process for the purpose of insuring that such planning process is at all times consistent with this Act. The Administrator shall not approve any State permit program under title IV of this Act for any State which does not have an approved continuing planning process under this section.

(3) The Administrator shall approve any continuing planning process submitted to him under this section which will result in plans for all navigable waters within such State, which include, but are not limited to, the following:

(A) effluent limitations and schedules of compliance at least as stringent as those required by section 301(b)(1), section 301(b)(2), section 306, and section 307, and at least as stringent as any requirements contained in any applicable water quality standard in effect under authority of this section;

(B) the incorporation of all elements of any applicable areawide waste management plans under section 208, and applicable basin plans under section 209 of this Act;

(C) total maximum daily load for pollutants in accordance with subsection (d) of this section;

(D) procedures for revision;

(E) adequate authority for intergovernmental cooperation;

(F) adequate implementation, including schedules of compliance, for revised or new water quality standards, under subsection (c) of this section;

(G) controls over the disposition of all residual waste from any water treatment processing;

(H) an inventory and ranking, in order of priority, of needs for construction of waste treatment works required to meet the applicable requirements of sections 301 and 302.

(f) Nothing in this section shall be construed to affect any effluent limitation, or schedule of compliance required by any State to be implemented prior to the dates set forth in sections 301(b)(1) and 301(b)(2) nor to preclude any State from requiring compliance with any effluent limitation or schedule of compliance at dates earlier than such dates.

(g) Water quality standards relating to heat shall be consistent with the requirements of section 316 of this Act.

(h) For the purposes of this Act the term water quality standards includes thermal water quality standards.

(i) Coastal Recreation Water Quality Criteria.—

(1) Adoption by states.—

(A) Initial criteria and standards.— Not later than 42 months after the date of the enactment of this subsection, each State having coastal recreation waters shall adopt and submit to the Administrator water quality criteria and standards for the coastal recreation waters of the State for those pathogens and pathogen indicators for which the Administrator has published criteria under section 304(a).

(B) New or revised criteria and standards.— Not later than 36 months after the date of publication by the Administrator of new or revised water quality criteria under section 304(a)(9), each State having coastal recreation waters shall adopt and submit to the Administrator new or revised water quality standards for the coastal recreation waters of the State for all pathogens and pathogen indicators to which the new or revised water quality criteria are applicable.

(2) Failure of states to adopt.—

(A) In general.— If a State fails to adopt water quality criteria and standards in accordance with paragraph (1)(A) that are as protective of human health as the criteria for pathogens and pathogen indicators for coastal recreation waters published by the Administrator, the Administrator shall promptly propose regulations for the State setting forth revised or new water quality standards for pathogens and pathogen indicators described in paragraph (1)(A) for coastal recreation waters of the State.

(B) Exception.— If the Administrator proposes regulations for a State described in subparagraph (A) under subsection (c)(4)(B), the Administrator shall publish any revised or new standard under this subsection not later than 42 months after the date of the enactment of this subsection.

(3) APPLICABILITY.— Except as expressly provided by this subsection, the requirements and procedures of subsection (c) apply to this subsection, including the requirement in subsection (c)(2)(A) that the criteria protect public health and welfare.

[33 U.S.C. 1313]

INFORMATION AND GUIDELINES

SEC. 304. (a)(1) The Administrator, after consultation with appropriate Federal and State agencies and other interested persons, shall develop and publish, within one year after the date of enactment of this title (and from time to time thereafter revise) criteria for water quality accurately reflecting the latest scientific knowledge (A) on the kind and extent of all identifiable effects on health and welfare including, but not limited to, plankton, fish, shellfish, wildlife, plant life, shorelines, beaches, esthetics, and recreation which may be expected from the presence of pollutants in any body of water, including ground water; (B) on the concentration and dispersal of pollutants, or their byproducts, through biological, physical, and chemical processes; and (C) on the effects of pollutants on biological community diversity, productivity, and stability, including information on the factors affecting rates of eutrophication and rates of organic and inorganic sedimentation for varying types of receiving waters.

(2) The Administrator, after consultation with appropriate Federal and State agencies and other interested persons, shall develop and publish, within one year after the date of enactment of this title (and from time to time thereafter revise) information (A) on the factors necessary to restore and maintain the chemical, physical, and biological integrity of all navigable waters, ground waters, waters of the contiguous zone, and the oceans; (B) on the factors necessary for the protection and propagation of shellfish, fish, and wildlife for classes and categories of receiving waters and to allow recreational activities in and on the water; and (C) on the measurement and classification of water quality; and (D) for the purpose of section 303, on and the identification of pollutants suitable for maximum daily load measurement correlated with the achievement of water quality objectives.

(3) Such criteria and information and revisions thereof shall be issued to the States and shall be published in the Federal Register and otherwise made available to the public.

(4) The Administrator shall, within 90 days after the date of enactment of the Clean Water Act of 1977 and from time to time thereafter, publish and revise as appropriate information identifying conventional pollutants, including but not limited to, pollutants classified as biological oxygen demanding, suspended solids, fecal coliform, and pH. The thermal component of any discharge shall not be identified as a conventional pollutant under this paragraph.

(5)(A) The Administrator, to the extent practicable before consideration of any request under section 301(g) of this Act and within six months after the date of enactment of the Clean Water Act of 1977, shall develop and publish information on the factors necessary for the protection of public water supplies, and the protection and propagation of a balanced population of shellfish, fish and wildlife, and to allow recreational activities, in and on the water.

(B) The Administrator, to the extent practicable before consideration of any application under section 301(h) of this Act and within six months after the date of enactment of Clean Water Act of 1977, shall develop and publish information on the factors necessary for the protection of public water supplies, and the protection and propagation of a balanced indigenous population of shellfish, fish and wildlife, and to allow recreational activities, in and on the water.

(6) The Administrator shall, within three months after enactment of the Clean Water Act of 1977 and annually thereafter, for purposes of section 301(h) of this Act publish and revise as appropriate information identifying each water quality standard in effect under this Act or State law, the specific pollutants associated with such water quality standard, and the particular waters to which such water quality standard applies.

(7) GUIDANCE TO STATES.— The Administrator, after consultation with appropriate State agencies and on the basis of criteria and information published under paragraphs (1) and (2) of this subsection, shall develop and publish, within 9 months after the date of the enactment of the Water Quality Act of 1987, guidance to the States on performing the identification required by section 304(l)(1) of this Act.

(8) INFORMATION ON WATER QUALITY CRITERIA.— The Administrator, after consultation with appropriate State agencies and within 2 years after the date of the enactment of the Water Quality Act of 1987, shall develop and publish information on methods for establishing and measuring water quality criteria for toxic pollutants on other bases than pollutant-by-pollutant criteria, including biological monitoring and assessment methods.

(9) REVISED CRITERIA FOR COASTAL RECREATION WATERS.—

(A) IN GENERAL.— Not later than 5 years after the date of the enactment of this paragraph, after consultation and in cooperation with appropriate Federal, State, tribal, and local officials (including local health officials), the Administrator shall publish new or revised water quality criteria for pathogens and pathogen indicators (including a revised list of testing methods, as appropriate), based on the results of the studies conducted under section 104(v), for the purpose of protecting human health in coastal recreation waters.

(B) REVIEWS.— Not later than the date that is 5 years after the date of publication of water quality criteria under this paragraph, and at least once every 5 years thereafter, the Administrator shall review and, as necessary, revise the water quality criteria.

(b) For the purpose of adopting or revising effluent limitations under this Act the Administrator shall, after consultation with appropriate Federal and State agencies and other interested persons, publish within one year of enactment of this title, regulations, providing guidelines for effluent limitations, and, at least annually thereafter, revise, if appropriate, such regulations. Such regulations shall—

(1)(A) identify, in terms of amounts of constituents and chemical, physical, and biological characteristics of pollutants, the degree of effluent reduction attainable through the application of the best practicable control technology currently available for classes and categories of point sources (other than publicly owned treatment works); and

(B) specify factors to be taken into account in determining the control measures and practices to be applicable to point sources (other than publicly owned treatment works) within such categories or classes. Factors relating to the assessment of best practical control technology currently available to comply with subsection (b)(1) of section 301 of this Act shall include consideration of the total cost of application of technology in relation to the effluent reduction benefits to be achieved from such application, and shall also take into account the age of equipment and facilities involved, the process employed, the engineering aspects of the application of various types of control techniques, process changes, non-water quality environmental impact (including energy requirements), and such other factors as the Administrator deems appropriate;

(2)(A) identify, in terms of amounts of constituents and chemical, physical, and biological characteristics of pollutants, the degree of effluent reduction attainable through the application of the best control measures and practices achievable including treatment techniques, process and procedure innovations, operating methods, and other alternatives for classes and categories of point sources (other than publicly owned treatment works); and

(B) specify factors to be taken into account in determining the best measures and practices available to comply with subsection (b)(2) of section 301 of this Act to be applicable to any point source (other than publicly owned treatment works) within such categories or classes. Factors relating to the assessment of best available technology shall take into account the age of equipment and facilities involved, the process employed, the engineering aspects of the application of various types of control techniques, process changes, the cost of achieving such effluent reduction, non-water quality environmental impact (including energy requirements), and such other factors as the Administrator deems appropriate;

(3) identify control measures and practices available to eliminate the discharge of pollutants from categories and classes of point sources, taking into account the cost of achieving such elimination of the discharge of pollutants; and

(4)(A) identify, in terms of amounts of constituents and chemical, physical, and biological characteristics of pollutants, the degree of effluent reduction attainable through the application of the best conventional pollutant control technology (including measures and practices) for classes and categories of point sources (other than publicly owned treatment works); and

(B) specify factors to be taken into account in determining the best conventional pollutant control technology measures and practices to comply with section 301(b)(2)(E) of this Act to be applicable to any point source (other than publicly owned treatment works) within such categories or classes. Factors relating to the assessment of best conventional pollutant control technology (including measures and practices) shall include consideration of the reasonableness of the relationship between the costs of attaining a reduction in effluents and the effluent reduction benefits derived, and the comparison of the cost and level of reduction of such pollutants from the discharge from publicly owned treatment works to the cost and level of reduction of such pollutants from a class or category of industrial sources, and shall take into account the age of equipment and facilities involved, the process employed, the engineering aspects of the application of various types of control techniques, process changes, non-water quality environmental impact (including energy requirements), and such other factors as the Administrator deems appropriate.

(c) The Administrator, after consultation, with appropriate Federal and State agencies and other interested persons, shall issue to the States and appropriate water pollution control agencies within 270 days after enactment of this title (and from time to time thereafter) information on the processes, procedures, or operating methods which result in the elimination or reduction of the discharge of pollutants to implement standards of performance under section 306 of this Act. Such information shall include technical and other data, including costs, as are available on alternative methods of elimination or reduction of the discharge of pollutants. Such information, and revisions thereof, shall be published in the Federal Register and otherwise shall be made available to the public.

(d)(1) The Administrator, after consultation with appropriate Federal and State agencies and other interested persons, shall publish within sixty days after enactment of this title (and from time to time thereafter) information, in terms of amounts of constituents and chemical, physical, and biological characteristics of pollutants, on the degree of effluent reduction attainable through the application of secondary treatment.

(2) The Administrator, after consultation with appropriate Federal and State agencies and other interested persons, shall publish within nine months after the date of enactment of this title (and from time to time thereafter) information on alternative waste treatment management techniques and systems available to implement section 201 of this Act.

(3) The Administrator, after consultation with appropriate Federal and State agencies and other interested persons, shall promulgate within one hundred and eighty days after the date of enactment of this subsection guidelines for identifying and evaluating innovative and alternative wastewater treatment processes and techniques referred to in section 201(g)(5) of this Act.

(4) For the purposes of this subsection, such biological treatment facilities as oxidation ponds, lagoons, and ditches and trickling filters shall be deemed the equivalent of secondary treatment. The Administrator shall provide guidance under paragraph (1) of this subsection on design criteria for such facilities, taking into account pollutant removal efficiencies and, consistent with the objective of the Act, assuring that water quality will not be adversely affected by deeming such facilities as the equivalent of secondary treatment.

(e) The Administrator, after consultation with appropriate Federal and State agencies and other interested persons, may publish regulations, supplemental to any effluent limitations specified under subsections (b) and (c) of this section for a class or category of point sources, for any specific pollutant which the Administrator is charged with a duty to regulate as a toxic or hazardous pollutant under section 307(a)(1) or 311 of this Act, to control plant site runoff, spillage or leaks, sludge or waste disposal, and drainage from raw material storage which the Administrator determines are associated with or ancillary to the industrial manufacturing or treatment process within such class or category of point sources and may contribute significant amounts of such pollutants, to navigable waters. Any applicable controls established under this subsection shall be included as a requirement for the purposes of section 301, 302, 306, 307, or 403, as the case may be, in any permit issued to a point source pursuant to section 402 of this Act.

(f) The Administrator, after consultation with appropriate Federal and State agencies and other interested persons, shall issue to appropriate Federal agencies, the States, water pollution control agencies, and agencies designated under section 208 of this Act, within one year after the effective date of this subsection (and from time to time thereafter) information including (1) guidelines for identifying and evaluating the nature and extent of nonpoint sources of pollutants, and (2) processes, procedures, and methods to control pollution resulting from—

(A) agricultural and silvicultural activities, including runoff from fields and crop and forest lands;

(B) mining activities, including runoff and siltation from new, currently operating, and abandoned surface and underground mines;

(C) all construction activity, including runoff from the facilities resulting from such construction;

(D) the disposal of pollutants in wells or in subsurface excavations;

(E) salt water intrusion resulting from reductions of fresh water flow from any cause, including extraction of ground water, irrigation, obstruction, and diversion; and

(F) changes in the movement, flow, or circulation of any navigable waters or ground waters, including changes caused by the construction of dams, levees, channels, causeways, or flow diversion facilities.

Such information and revisions thereof shall be published in the Federal Register and otherwise made available to the public.

(g)(1) For the purpose of assisting States in carrying out programs under section 402 of this Act, the Administrator shall publish, within one hundred and twenty days after the date of enactment of this title, and review at least annually thereafter and, if appropriate, revise guidelines for pretreatment of pollutants which he determines are not susceptible to treatment by publicly owned treatment works. Guidelines under this subsection shall be established to control and prevent the discharge into the navigable waters, the contiguous zone, or the ocean (either directly or through publicly owned treatment works) of any pollutant which interferes with, passes through, or otherwise is incompatible with such works.

(2) When publishing guidelines under this subsection, the Administrator shall designate the category or categories of treatment works to which the guidelines shall apply.

(h) The Administrator shall, within one hundred and eighty days from the date of enactment of this title, promulgate guidelines establishing test procedures for the analysis of pollutants that shall include the factors which must be provided in any certification pursuant to section 401 of this Act or permit application pursuant to section 402 of this Act.

(i) The Administrator shall (1) within sixty days after the enactment of this title promulgate guidelines for the purpose of establishing uniform application forms and other minimum requirements for the acquisition of information from owners and operators of point-sources of discharge subject to any State program under section 402 of this Act, and (2) within sixty days from the date of enactment of this title promulgate guidelines establishing the minimum procedural and other elements of any State program under section 402 of this Act which shall include:

(A) monitoring requirements;

(B) reporting requirements (including procedures to make information available to the public);

(C) enforcement provisions; and

(D) funding, personnel qualifications, and manpower requirements (including a requirement that no board or body which approves permit applications or portions thereof shall include, as a member, any person who receives, or has during the previous two years received, a significant portion of his income directly or indirectly from permit holders or applicants for a permit).

(j) Lake Restoration Guidance Manual.— The Administrator shall, within 1 year after the date of the enactment of the Water Quality Act of 1987 and biennially thereafter, publish and disseminate a lake restoration guidance manual describing methods, procedures, and processes to guide State and local efforts to improve, restore, and enhance water quality in the Nation's publicly owned lakes.

(k)(1) The Administrator shall enter into agreements with the Secretary of Agriculture, the Secretary of the Army, and the Secretary of the Interior, and the heads of such other departments, agencies, and instrumentalities of the United States as the Administrator determines, to provide for the maximum utilization of other Federal laws and programs for the purpose of achieving and maintaining water quality through appropriate implementation of plans approved under section 208 of this Act and nonpoint source pollution management programs approved under section 319 of this Act.

(2) The Administrator is authorized to transfer to the Secretary of Agriculture, the Secretary of the Army, and the Secretary of the Interior and the heads of such other departments, agencies, and instrumentalities of the United States as the Administrator determines, any funds appropriated under paragraph (3) of this subsection to supplement funds otherwise appropriated to programs authorized pursuant to any agreement under paragraph (1).

(3) There is authorized to be appropriated to carry out the provisions of this subsection, $100,000,000 per fiscal year for the fiscal years 1979 through 1983 and such sums as may be necessary for fiscal years 1984 through 1990.

(l) Individual Control Strategies for Toxic Pollutants.—

(1) State list of navigable waters and development of strategies.—Not later than 2 years after the date of the enactment of this subsection, each State shall submit to the Administrator for review, approval, and implementation under this subsection—

(A) a list of those waters within the State which after the application of effluent limitations required under section 301(b)(2) of this Act cannot reasonably be anticipated to attain or maintain (i) water quality standards for such waters reviewed, revised, or adopted in accordance with section 303(c)(2)(B) of this Act, due to toxic pollutants, or (ii) that water quality which shall assure protection of public health, public water supplies, agricultural and industrial uses, and the protection and propagation of a balanced population of shellfish, fish and wildlife, and allow recreational activities in and on the water;

(B) a list of all navigable waters in such State for which the State does not expect the applicable standard under section 303 of this Act will be achieved after the requirements of sections 301(b), 306, and 307(b) are met, due entirely or substantially to discharges from point sources of any toxic pollutants listed pursuant to section 307(a);

(C) for each segment of the navigable waters included on such lists, a determination of the specific point sources discharging any such toxic pollutant which is believed to be preventing or impairing such water quality and the amount of each toxic pollutant discharged by each such source; and

(D) for each such segment, an individual control strategy which the State determines will produce a reduction in the discharge of toxic pollutants from point sources identified by the State under this paragraph through the establishment of effluent limitations under section 402 of this Act and water quality standards under section 303(c)(2)(B) of this Act, which reduction is sufficient, in combination with existing controls on point and nonpoint sources of pollution, to achieve the applicable water quality standard as soon as possible, but not later than 3 years after the date of the establishment of such strategy.

(2) Approval or disapproval.— Not later than 120 days after the last day of the 2-year period referred to in paragraph (1), the Administrator shall approve or disapprove the control strategies submitted under paragraph (1) by any State.

(3) Administrator's action.— If a State fails to submit control strategies in accordance with paragraph (1) or the Administrator does not approve the control strategies submitted by such State in accordance with paragraph (1), then, not later than 1 year after the last day of the period referred to in paragraph (2), the Administrator, in cooperation with such State and after notice and opportunity for public comment, shall implement the requirements of paragraph (1) in such State. In the implementation of such requirements, the Administrator shall, at a minimum, consider for listing under this subsection any navigable waters for which any person submits a petition to the Administrator for listing not later than 120 days after such last day.

(m) Schedule for Review of Guidelines.—

(1) Publication.—Within 12 months after the date of the enactment of the Water Quality Act of 1987, and biennially thereafter, the Administrator shall publish in the Federal Register a plan which shall—

(A) establish a schedule for the annual review and revision of promulgated effluent guidelines, in accordance with subsection (b) of this section;

(B) identify categories of sources discharging toxic or nonconventional pollutants for which guidelines under subsection (b)(2) of this section and section 306 have not previously been published; and

(C) establish a schedule for promulgation of effluent guidelines for categories identified in subparagraph (B), under which promulgation of such guidelines shall be no later than 4 years after such date of enactment for categories identified in the first published plan or 3 years after the publication of the plan for categories identified in later published plans.

(2) PUBLIC REVIEW.— The Administrator shall provide for public review and comment on the plan prior to final publication.

[33 U.S.C. 1314]

WATER QUALITY INVENTORY

SEC. 305. (a) The Administrator, in cooperation with the States and with the assistance of appropriate Federal agencies, shall prepare a report to be submitted to the Congress on or before January 1, 1974, which shall—

(1) describe the specific quality, during 1973, with appropriate supplemental descriptions as shall be required to take into account seasonal, tidal, and other variations, of all navigable waters and the waters of the contiguous zone;

(2) include an inventory of all point sources of discharge (based on a qualitative and quantitative analysis of discharges) of pollutants, into all navigable waters and the waters of the contiguous zone; and

(3) identify specifically those navigable waters, the quality of which—

(A) is adequate to provide for the protection and propagation of a balanced population of shellfish, fish, and wildlife and allow recreational activities in and on the water;

(B) can reasonably be expected to attain such level by 1977 or 1983; and

(C) can reasonably be expected to attain such level by any later date.

(b)(1) Each State shall prepare and submit to the Administrator by April 1, 1975, and shall bring up to date by April 1, 1976, and biennially thereafter, a report which shall include—

(A) a description of the water quality of all navigable waters in such State during the preceding year, with appropriate supplemental descriptions as shall be required to take into account seasonal, tidal, and other variations, correlated with the quality of water required by the objective of this Act (as identified by the Administrator pursuant to criteria published under section 304(a) of this Act) and the water quality described in subparagraph (B) of this paragraph;

(B) an analysis of the extent to which all navigable waters of such State provide for the protection and propagation of a balanced population of shellfish, fish, and wildlife, and allow recreational activities in and on the water;

(C) an analysis of the extent to which the elimination of the discharge of pollutants and a level of water quality which provides for the protection and propagation of a balanced population of shellfish, fish, and wildlife and allows recreational activities in and on the water, have been or will be achieved by the requirements of this Act, together with recommendations as to additional action necessary to achieve such objectives and for what waters such additional action is necessary;

(D) an estimate of (i) the environmental impact, (ii) the economic and social costs necessary to achieve the objective of this Act in such State, (iii) the economic and social benefits of such achievement, and (iv) an estimate of the date of such achievement; and

(E) a description of the nature and extent of nonpoint sources of pollutants, and recommendations as to the programs which must be undertaken to control each category of such sources, including an estimate of the costs of implementing such programs.

(2) The Administrator shall transmit such State reports, together with an analysis thereof, to Congress on or before October 1, 1975, and October 1, 1976, and biennially thereafter.

[33 U.S.C. 1315]

NATIONAL STANDARDS OF PERFORMANCE

SEC. 306. (a) For purposes of this section:

(1) The term standard of performance means a standard for the control of the discharge of pollutants which reflects the greatest degree of effluent reduction which the Administrator determines to be achievable through application of the best available demonstrated control technology, processes, operating methods, or other alternatives, including, where practicable, a standard permitting no discharge of pollutants.

(2) The term new source means any source, the construction of which is commenced after the publication of proposed regulations prescribing a standard of performance under this section which will be applicable to such source, if such standard is thereafter promulgated in accordance with this section.

(3) The term source means any building, structure, facility, or installation from which there is or may be the discharge of pollutants.

(4) The term owner or operator means any person who owns, leases, operates, controls, or supervises a source.

(5) The term construction means any placement, assembly, or installation of facilities or equipment (including contractual obligations to purchase such facilities or equipment) at the premises where such equipment will be used, including preparation work at such premises.

(b)(1)(A) The Administrator shall, within ninety days after the date of enactment of this title publish (and from time to time thereafter shall revise) a list of categories of sources, which shall, at the minimum, include:

pulp and paper mills;

paperboard, builders paper and board mills;

meat product and rendering processing;

dairy product processing;

grain mills;

canned and preserved fruits and vegetables processing;

canned and preserved seafood processing;

sugar processing;

textile mills;

cement manufacturing;

feedlots;

electroplating;

organic chemicals manufacturing;

inorganic chemicals manufacturing;

plastic and synthetic materials manufacturing;

soap and detergent manufacturing;

fertilizer manufacturing;

petroleum refining;

iron and steel manufacturing;

nonferrous metals manufacturing;

phosphate manufacturing;

steam electric powerplants;

ferroalloy manufacturing;

leather tanning and finishing;

glass and asbestos manufacturing;

rubber processing; and

timber products processing.

(B) As soon as practicable, but in no case more than one year, after a category of sources is included in a list under subparagraph (A) of this paragraph, the Administrator shall propose and publish regulations establishing Federal standards of performance for new sources within such category. The Administrator shall afford interested persons an opportunity for written comment on such proposed regulations. After considering such comments, he shall promulgate, within one hundred and twenty days after publication of such proposed regulations, such standards with such adjustments as he deems appropriate. The Administrator shall, from time to time, as technology and alternatives change, revise such standards following the procedure required by this subsection for promulgation of such standards. Standards of performance, or revisions thereof, shall become effective upon promulgation. In establishing or revising Federal standards of performance for new sources under this section, the Administrator shall take into consideration the cost of achieving such effluent reduction, and any non-water quality environmental impact and energy requirements.

(2) The Administrator may distinguish among classes, types, and sizes within categories of new sources for the purpose of establishing such standards and shall consider the type of process employed (including whether batch or continuous).

(3) The provisions of this section shall apply to any new source owned or operated by the United States.

(c) Each State may develop and submit to the Administrator a procedure under State law for applying and enforcing standards of performance for new sources located in such State. If the Administrator finds that the procedure and the law of any State require the application and enforcement of standards of performance to at least the same extent as required by this section, such State is authorized to apply and enforce such standards of performance (except with respect to new sources owned or operated by the United States).

(d) Notwithstanding any other provision of this Act, any point source the construction of which is commenced after the date of enactment of the Federal Water Pollution Control Act Amendments of 1972 and which is so constructed as to meet all applicable standards of performance shall not be subject to any more stringent standard of performance during a ten-year period beginning on the date of completion of such construction or during the period of depreciation or amortization of such facility for the purposes of section 167 or 169 (or both) of the Internal Revenue Code of 1954, whichever period ends first.

(e) After the effective date of standards of performance promulgated under this section, it shall be unlawful for any owner or operator of any new source to operate such source in violation of any standard of performance applicable to such source.

[33 U.S.C. 1316]

TOXIC AND PRETREATMENT EFFLUENT STANDARDS

SEC. 307. (a)(1) On and after the date of enactment of the Clean Water Act of 1977, the list of toxic pollutants or combination of pollutants subject to this Act shall consist of those toxic pollutants listed in table 1 of Committee Print Numbered 95–30 of the Committee on Public Works and Transportation of the House of Representatives, and the Administrator shall publish, not later than the thirtieth day after the date of enactment of the Clean Water Act of 1977, that list. From time to time thereafter, the Administrator may revise such list and the Administrator is authorized to add to or remove from such list any pollutant. The Administrator in publishing any revised list, including the addition or removal of any pollutant from such list, shall take into account the toxicity of the pollutant, its persistence, degradability, the usual or potential presence of the affected organisms in any waters, the importance of the affected organisms, and the nature and extent of the effect of the toxic pollutant on such organisms. A determination of the Administrator under this paragraph shall be final except that if, on judicial review, such determination was based on arbitrary and capricious action of the Administrator, the Administrator shall make a redetermination.

(2) Each toxic pollutant listed in accordance with paragraph (1) of this subsection shall be subject to effluent limitations resulting from the application of the best available technology economically achievable for the applicable category or class of point sources established in accordance with section 301(b)(2)(A) and 304(b)(2) of this Act. The Administrator, in his discretion, may publish in the

Federal Register a proposed effluent standard (which may include a prohibition) establishing requirements for a toxic pollutant which, if an effluent limitation is applicable to a class or category of point sources, shall be applicable to such category or class only if such standard imposes more stringent requirements. Such published effluent standard (or prohibition) shall take into account the toxicity of the pollutant, its persistence, degradability, the usual or potential presence of the affected organisms in any waters, the importance of the affected organisms and the nature and extent of the effect of the toxic pollutant on such organisms, and the extent to which effective control is being or may be achieved under other regulatory authority. The Administrator shall allow a period of not less than sixty days following publication of any such proposed effluent standard (or prohibition) for written comment by interested persons on such proposed standard. In addition, if within thirty days of publication of any such proposed effluent standard (or prohibition) any interested person so requests, the Administrator shall hold a public hearing in connection therewith. Such a public hearing shall provide an opportunity for oral and written presentations, such cross-examination as the Administrator determines is appropriate on disputed issues of material fact, and the transcription of a verbatim record which shall be available to the public. After consideration of such comments and any information and material presented at any public hearing held on such proposed standard or prohibition, the Administrator shall promulgate such standards (or prohibition) with such modifications as the Administrator finds are justified. Such promulgation by the Administrator shall be made within two hundred and seventy days after publication of proposed standard (or prohibition). Such standard (or prohibition) shall be final except that if, on judicial review, such standard was not based on substantial evidence, the Administrator shall promulgate a revised standard. Effluent limitations shall be established in accordance with sections 301(b)(2)(A) and 304(b)(2) for every toxic pollutant referred to in table 1 of Committee Print Numbered 95–30 of the Committee on Public Works and Transportation of the House of Representatives as soon as practicable after the date of enactment of the Clean Water Act of 1977, but no later than July 1, 1980. Such effluent limitations or effluent standards (or prohibitions) shall be established for every other toxic pollutant listed under paragraph (1) of this subsection as soon as practicable after it is so listed.

(3) Each such effluent standard (or prohibition) shall be reviewed and, if appropriate, revised at least every three years.

(4) Any effluent standard promulgated under this section shall be at that level which the Administrator determines provides an ample margin of safety.

(5) When proposing or promulgating any effluent standard (or prohibition) under this section, the Administrator shall designate the category or categories of sources to which the effluent standard (or prohibition) shall apply. Any disposal of dredged material may be included in such a category of sources after consultation with the Secretary of the Army.

(6) Any effluent standard (or prohibition) established pursuant to this section shall take effect on such date or dates as specified in the order promulgating such standard, but in no case, more than one year from the date of such promulgation. If the Administrator determines that compliance within one year from the date

of promulgation is technologically infeasible for a category of sources, the Administrator may establish the effective date of the effluent standard (or prohibition) for such category at the earliest date upon which compliance can be feasibly attained by sources within such category, but in no event more than three years after the date of such promulgation.

(7) Prior to publishing any regulations pursuant to this section the Administrator shall, to the maximum extent practicable within the time provided, consult with appropriate advisory committees, States, independent experts, and Federal departments and agencies.

(b)(1) The Administrator shall, within one hundred and eighty days after the date of enactment of this title and from time to time thereafter, publish proposed regulations establishing pretreatment standards for introduction of pollutants into treatment works (as defined in section 212 of this Act) which are publicly owned for those pollutants which are determined not to be susceptible to treatment by such treatment works or which would interfere with the operation of such treatment works. Not later than ninety days after such publication, and after opportunity for public hearing, the Administrator shall promulgate such pretreatment standards. Pretreatment standards under this subsection shall specify a time for compliance not to exceed three years from the date of promulgation and shall be established to prevent the discharge of any pollutant through treatment works (as defined in section 212 of this Act) which are publicly owned, which pollutant interferes with, passes through, or otherwise is incompatible with such works. If, in the case of any toxic pollutant under subsection (a) of this section introduced by a source into a publicly owned treatment works, the treatment by such works removes all or any part of such toxic pollutant and the discharge from such works does not violate that effluent limitation or standard which would be applicable to such toxic pollutant if it were discharged by such source other than through a publicly owned treatment works, and does not prevent sludge use or disposal by such works in accordance with section 405 of this Act, then the pretreatment requirements for the sources actually discharging such toxic pollutant into such publicly owned treatment works may be revised by the owner or operator of such works to reflect the removal of such toxic pollutant by such works.

(2) The Administrator shall, from time to time, as control technology, processes, operating methods, or other alternative change, revise such standards following the procedures established by this subsection for promulgation of such standards.

(3) When proposing or promulgating any pretreatment standard under this section, the Administrator shall designate the category or categories of sources to which such standard shall apply.

(4) Nothing in this subsection shall affect any pretreatment requirement established by any State or local law not in conflict with any pretreatment standard established under this subsection.

(c) In order to ensure that any source introducing pollutants into a publicly owned treatment works, which source would be a new source subject to section 306 if it were to discharge pollutants, will not cause a violation of the effluent limitations established for any such treatment works, the Administrator shall promulgate pretreatment standards for the category of such sources simultaneously with the promulgation of standards of performance under section 306 for the equivalent category of new sources. Such pretreatment standards shall prevent the discharge of any pollutant into such treatment works, which pollutant may interfere with, pass through, or otherwise be incompatible with such works.

(d) After the effective date of any effluent standard or prohibition or pretreatment standard promulgated under this section, it shall be unlawful for any owner or operator of any source to operate any source in violation of any such effluent standard or prohibition or pretreatment standard.

(e) Compliance Date Extension for Innovative Pretreatment Systems.—In the case of any existing facility that proposes to comply with the pretreatment standards of subsection (b) of this section by applying an innovative system that meets the requirements of section 301(k) of this Act, the owner or operator of the publicly owned treatment works receiving the treated effluent from such facility may extend the date for compliance with the applicable pretreatment standard established under this section for a period not to exceed 2 years—

(1) if the Administrator determines that the innovative system has the potential for industrywide application, and

(2) if the Administrator (or the State in consultation with the Administrator, in any case in which the State has a pretreatment program approved by the Administrator)—

(A) determines that the proposed extension will not cause the publicly owned treatment works to be in violation of its permit under section 402 or of section 405 or to contribute to such a violation, and

(B) concurs with the proposed extension.

[33 U.S.C. 1317]

INSPECTIONS, MONITORING, AND ENTRY

Sec. 308. (a) Whenever required to carry out the objective of this Act, including but not limited to (1) developing or assisting in the development of any effluent limitation, or other limitation, prohibition, or effluent standard, pretreatment standard, or standard of performance under this Act; (2) determining whether any person is in violation of any such effluent limitation, or other limitation, prohibition or effluent standard, pretreatment standard, or standard of performance; (3) any requirement established under this section; or (4) carrying out sections 305, 311, 402, 404 (relating to State permit programs), 405, and 504 of this Act—

(A) the Administrator shall require the owner or operator of any point source to (i) establish and maintain such records, (ii) make such reports, (iii) install, use, and maintain such monitoring equipment or methods (including where appropriate, biological monitoring methods), (iv) sample such effluents (in accordance with such methods, at such locations, at such intervals, and in such manner as the Administrator shall prescribe), and (v) provide such other information as he may reasonably require; and

(B) the Administrator or his authorized representative (including an authorized contractor acting as a representative of the Administrator), upon presentation of his credentials—

(i) shall have a right of entry to, upon, or through any premises in which an effluent source is located or in which any records required to be maintained under clause (A) of this subsection are located, and

(ii) may at reasonable times have access to and copy any records, inspect any monitoring equipment or method required under clause (A), and sample any effluents which the owner or operator of such source is required to sample under such clause.

(b) Any records, reports, or information obtained under this section (1) shall, in the case of effluent data, be related to any applicable effluent limitations, toxic, pretreatment, or new source performance standards, and (2) shall be available to the public, except that upon a showing satisfactory to the Administrator by any person that records, reports, or information, or particular part thereof (other than effluent data), to which the Administrator has access under this section, if made public would divulge methods or processes entitled to protection as trade secrets of such person, the Administrator shall consider such record, report, or information, or particular portion thereof confidential in accordance with the purposes of section 1905 of title 18 of the United States Code. Any authorized representative of the Administrator (including an authorized contractor acting as a representative of the Administrator) who knowingly or willfully publishes, divulges, discloses, or makes known in any manner or to any extent not authorized by law any information which is required to be considered confidential under this subsection shall be fined not more than $1,000 or imprisoned not more than 1 year, or both. Nothing in this subsection shall prohibit the Administrator or an authorized representative of the Administrator (including any authorized contractor acting as a representative of the Administrator) from disclosing records, reports, or information to other officers, employees, or authorized representatives of the United States concerned with carrying out this Act or when relevant in any proceeding under this Act.

(c) Each State may develop and submit to the Administrator procedures under State law for inspection, monitoring, and entry with respect to point sources located in such State. If the Administrator finds that the procedures and the law of any State relating to inspection, monitoring, and entry are applicable to at least the same extent as those required by this section, such State is authorized to apply and enforce its procedures for inspection, monitoring, and entry with respect to point sources located in such State (except with respect to point sources owned or operated by the United States).

(d) ACCESS BY CONGRESS.— Notwithstanding any limitation contained in this section or any other provision of law, all information reported to or otherwise obtained by the Administrator (or any representative of the Administrator) under this Act shall be made available, upon written request of any duly authorized committee of Congress, to such committee.

[33 U.S.C. 1318]

FEDERAL ENFORCEMENT

SEC. 309. (a)(1) Whenever, on the basis of any information available to him, the Administrator finds that any person is in violation of any condition or limitation which implements section 301, 302, 306, 307, 308, 318, or 405 of this Act in a permit issued by a State under an approved permit program under section 402 or 404 of this Act, he shall proceed under his authority in paragraph (3) of this subsection or he shall notify the person in alleged violation and such State of such finding. If beyond the thirtieth day after the Administrator's notification the State has not commenced appropriate enforcement action, the Administrator shall issue an order requiring such person to comply with such condition or limitation or shall bring a civil action in accordance with subsection (b) of this section.

(2) Whenever, on the basis of information available to him, the Administrator finds that violations of permit conditions or limitations as set forth in paragraph (1) of this subsection are so widespread that such violations appear to result from a failure of the State to enforce such permit conditions or limitations effectively, he shall so notify the State. If the Administrator finds such failure extends beyond the thirtieth day after such notice, he shall give public notice of such finding. During the period beginning with such public notice and ending when such State satisfies the Administrator that it will enforce such conditions and limitations (hereafter referred to in this section as the period of federally assumed enforcement), except where an extension has been granted under paragraph (5)(B) of this subsection, the Administrator shall enforce any permit condition or limitation with respect to any person—

(A) by issuing an order to comply with such condition or limitation, or

(B) by bringing a civil action under subsection (b) of this section.

(3) Whenever on the basis of any information available to him the Administrator finds that any person is in violation of section 301, 302, 306, 307, 308, 312(p), 318, or 405 of this Act, or is in violation of any permit condition or limitation implementing any of such sections in a permit issued under section 402 of this Act by him or by a State or in a permit issued under section 404 of this Act by a State, he shall issue an order requiring such person to comply with such section or requirement, or he shall bring a civil action in accordance with subsection (b) of this section.

(4) A copy of any order issued under this subsection shall be sent immediately by the Administrator to the State in which the violation occurs and other affected States. In any case in which an order under this subsection (or notice to a violator under paragraph (1) of this subsection) is issued to a corporation, a copy of such order (or notice) shall be served on any appropriate corporate officers. An order issued under this subsection relating to a violation of section 308 of this Act shall not take effect until the person to whom it is issued has had an opportunity to confer with the Administrator concerning the alleged violation.

(5)(A) Any order issued under this subsection shall be by personal service, shall state with reasonable specificity the nature of the violation, and shall specify a time for compliance not to exceed thirty days in the case of a violation of an interim compliance schedule or operation and maintenance requirement and not to exceed a time the Administrator determines to be reasonable in the case of a violation of a final deadline, taking into account the seriousness of the violation and any good faith efforts to comply with applicable requirements.

(B) The Administrator may, if he determines (i) that any person who is a violator of, or any person who is otherwise not in compliance with, the time requirements under this Act or in any permit issued under this Act, has acted in good faith, and has made a commitment (in the form of contracts or other securities) of necessary resources to achieve compliance by the earliest possible date after July 1, 1977, but not later than April 1, 1979; (ii) that any extension under this provision will not result in the imposition of any additional controls on any other point or nonpoint source; (iii) that an application for a permit under section 402 of this Act was filed for such person prior to December 31, 1974; and (iv) that the facilities necessary for compliance with such requirements are under construction, grant an extension of the date referred to in section 301(b)(1)(A) to a date which will achieve compliance at the earliest time possible but not later than April 1, 1979.

(6) Whenever, on the basis of information available to him, the Administrator finds (A) that any person is in violation of section 301(b)(1) (A) or (C) of this Act, (B) that such person cannot meet the requirements for a time extension under section 301(i)(2) of this Act, and (C) that the most expeditious and appropriate means of compliance with this Act by such person is to discharge into a publicly owned treatment works, then, upon request of such person, the Administrator may issue an order requiring such person to comply with this Act at the earliest date practicable, but not later than July 1, 1983, by discharging into a publicly owned treatment works if such works concur with such order. Such order shall include a schedule of compliance.

(b) The Administrator is authorized to commence a civil action for appropriate relief, including a permanent or temporary injunction, for any violation for which he is authorized to issue a compliance order under subsection (a) of this section. Any action under this subsection may be brought in the district court of the United States for the district in which the defendant is located or resides or is doing business, and such court shall have jurisdiction to restrain such violation and to require compliance. Notice of the commencement of such action shall be given immediately to the appropriate State.

(c) CRIMINAL PENALTIES.—

(1) NEGLIGENT VIOLATIONS.—Any person who—

(A) negligently violates section 301, 302, 306, 307, 308, 311(b)(3), 312(p), 318, or 405 of this Act, or any permit condition or limitation implementing any of such sections in a permit issued under section 402 of this Act by the Administrator or by a State, or any requirement imposed in a pretreatment program approved under section 402(a)(3) or 402(b)(8) of this Act or in a permit issued under section 404 of this Act by the Secretary of the Army or by a State; or

(B) negligently introduces into a sewer system or into a publicly owned treatment works any pollutant or hazardous substance which such person knew or reasonably should have known could cause personal injury or property damage or, other than in compliance with all applicable Federal, State, or local requirements or permits, which causes such treatment works to violate any effluent limitation or condition in any permit issued to the treatment works under section 402 of this Act by the Administrator or a State;

shall be punished by a fine of not less than $2,500 nor more than $25,000 per day of violation, or by imprisonment for not more than 1 year, or by both. If a conviction of a person is for a violation committed after a first conviction of such person under this paragraph, punishment shall be by a fine of not more than $50,000 per day of violation, or by imprisonment of not more than 2 years, or by both.

(2) KNOWING VIOLATIONS.—Any person who—

(A) knowingly violates section 301, 302, 306, 307, 308, 311(b)(3), 312(p), 318, or 405 of this Act, or any permit condition or limitation implementing any of such sections in a permit issued under section 402 of this Act by the Administrator or by a State, or any requirement imposed in a pretreatment program approved under section 402(a)(3) or 402(b)(8) of this Act or in a permit issued under section 404 of this Act by the Secretary of the Army or by a State; or

(B) knowingly introduces into a sewer system or into a publicly owned treatment works any pollutant or hazardous substance which such person knew or reasonably should have known could cause personal injury or property damage or, other than in compliance with all applicable Federal, State, or local requirements or permits, which causes such treatment works to violate any effluent limitation or condition in a permit issued to the treatment works under section 402 of this Act by the Administrator or a State;

shall be punished by a fine of not less that $5,000 nor more than $50,000 per day of violation, or by imprisonment for not more than 3 years, or by both. If a conviction of a person is for a violation committed after a first conviction of such person under this paragraph, punishment shall be by a fine of not more than $100,000 per day of violation, or imprisonment of not more than 6 years, or by both.

(3) KNOWING ENDANGERMENT.—

(A) GENERAL RULE.— Any person who knowingly violates section 301, 302, 303, 306, 307, 308, 311(b)(3), 312(p), 318, or 405 of this Act, or any permit condition or limitation implementing any of such sections in a permit issued under section 402 of this Act by the Administrator or by a State, or in a permit issued under section 404 of this Act by the Secretary of the Army or by a State, and who knows at that time that he thereby places another person in imminent danger of death or serious bodily injury, shall, upon conviction, be subject to a fine of not more than $250,000 or imprisonment of not more than 15 years, or both. A person which is an organization shall, upon conviction of violating this subparagraph, be subject to a fine of not more than $1,000,000. If a conviction of a person is for a violation committed after a first conviction of such person under this paragraph, the maximum punishment shall be doubled with respect to both fine and imprisonment.

(B) ADDITIONAL PROVISIONS.—For the purpose of subparagraph (A) of this paragraph—

(i) in determining whether a defendant who is an individual knew that his conduct placed another person in imminent danger of death or serious bodily injury—

(I) the person is responsible only for actual awareness or actual belief that he possessed; and

(II) knowledge possessed by a person other than the defendant but not by the defendant himself may not be attributed to the defendant;

except that in proving the defendant's possession of actual knowledge, circumstantial evidence may be used, including evidence that the defendant took affirmative steps to shield himself from relevant information;

(ii) it is an affirmative defense to prosecution that the conduct charged was consented to by the person endangered and that the danger and conduct charged were reasonably foreseeable hazards of—

(I) an occupation, a business, or a profession; or

(II) medical treatment or medical or scientific experimentation conducted by professionally approved methods and such other person had been made aware of the risks involved prior to giving consent;

and such defense may be established under this subparagraph by a preponderance of the evidence;

(iii) the term organization means a legal entity, other than a government, established or organized for any purpose, and such term includes a corporation, company, association, firm, partnership, joint stock company, foundation, institution, trust, society, union, or any other association of persons; and

(iv) the term serious bodily injury means bodily injury which involves a substantial risk of death, unconsciousness, extreme physical pain, protracted and obvious disfigurement, or protracted loss or impairment of the function of a bodily member, organ, or mental faculty.

(4) False statements.— Any person who knowingly makes any false material statement, representation, or certification in any application, record, report, plan, or other document filed or required to be maintained under this Act or who knowingly falsifies, tampers with, or renders inaccurate any monitoring device or method required to be maintained under this Act, shall upon conviction, be punished by a fine of not more than $10,000, or by imprisonment for not more than 2 years, or by both. If a conviction of a person is for a violation committed after a first conviction of such person under this paragraph, punishment shall be by a fine of not more than $20,000 per day of violation, or by imprisonment of not more than 4 years, or by both.

(5) Treatment of single operational upset.— For purposes of this subsection, a single operational upset which leads to simultaneous violations of more than one pollutant parameter shall be treated as a single violation.

(6) Responsible corporate officer as person.—For the purpose of this subsection, the term person means, in addition to the definition contained in section 502(5) of this Act, any responsible corporate officer.

(7) Hazardous substance defined.— For the purpose of this subsection, the term hazardous substance means (A) any substance designated pursuant to section 311(b)(2)(A) of this Act, (B) any element, compound, mixture, solution, or

substance designated pursuant to section 102 of the Comprehensive Environmental Response, Compensation, and Liability Act of 1980, (C) any hazardous waste having the characteristics identified under or listed pursuant to section 3001 of the Solid Waste Disposal Act (but not including any waste the regulation of which under the Solid Waste Disposal Act has been suspended by Act of Congress), (D) any toxic pollutant listed under section 307(a) of this Act, and (E) any imminently hazardous chemical substance or mixture with respect to which the Administrator has taken action pursuant to section 7 of the Toxic Substances Control Act.

(d) Any person who violates section 301, 302, 306, 307, 308, 312(p), 318, or 405 of this Act, or any permit condition or limitation implementing any of such sections in a permit issued under section 402 of this Act by the Administrator, or by a State, or in a permit issued under section 404 of this Act by a State, or any requirement imposed in a pretreatment program approved under section 402(a)(3) or 402(b)(8) of this Act, and any person who violates any order issued by the Administrator under subsection (a) of this section, shall be subject to a civil penalty not to exceed $25,000 per day for each violation. In determining the amount of a civil penalty the court shall consider the seriousness of the violation or violations, the economic benefit (if any) resulting from the violation, any history of such violations, any good-faith efforts to comply with the applicable requirements, the economic impact of the penalty on the violator, and such other matters as justice may require. For purposes of this subsection, a single operational upset which leads to simultaneous violations of more than one pollutant parameter shall be treated as a single violation.

(e) Whenever a municipality is a party to a civil action brought by the United States under this section, the State in which such municipality is located shall be joined as a party. Such State shall be liable for payment of any judgment, or any expenses incurred as a result of complying with any judgment, entered against the municipality in such action to the extent that the laws of that State prevent the municipality from raising revenues needed to comply with such judgment.

(f) Whenever, on the basis of any information available to him, the Administrator finds that an owner or operator of any source is introducing a pollutant into a treatment works in violation of subsection (d) of section 307, the Administrator may notify the owner or operator of such treatment works and the State of such violation. If the owner or operator of the treatment works does not commence appropriate enforcement action within 30 days of the date of such notification, the Administrator may commence a civil action for appropriate relief, including but not limited to, a permanent or temporary injunction, against the owner or operator of such treatment works. In any such civil action the Administrator shall join the owner or operator of such source as a party to the action. Such action shall be brought in the district court of the United States in the district in which the treatment works is located. Such court shall have jurisdiction to restrain such violation and to require the owner or operator of the treatment works and the owner or operator of the source to take such action as may be necessary to come into compliance with this Act. Notice of commencement of any such action shall be given to the State. Nothing in this subsection shall be construed to limit or prohibit any other authority the Administrator may have under this Act.

(g) Administrative Penalties.—

(1) Violations.—Whenever on the basis of any information available—

(A) the Administrator finds that any person has violated section 301, 302, 306, 307, 308, 312(p), 318, or 405 of this Act, or has violated any permit condition or limitation implementing any of such sections in a permit issued under section 402 of this Act by the Administrator or by a State, or in a permit issued under section 404 by a State, or

(B) the Secretary of the Army (hereinafter in this subsection referred to as the Secretary) finds that any person has violated any permit condition or limitation in a permit issued under section 404 of this Act by the Secretary,

the Administrator or Secretary, as the case may be, may, after consultation with the State in which the violation occurs, assess a class I civil penalty or a class II civil penalty under this subsection.

(2) CLASSES OF PENALTIES.—

(A) CLASS I.— The amount of a class I civil penalty under paragraph (1) may not exceed $10,000 per violation, except that the maximum amount of any class I civil penalty under this subparagraph shall not exceed $25,000. Before issuing an order assessing a civil penalty under this subparagraph, the Administrator or the Secretary, as the case may be, shall give to the person to be assessed such penalty written notice of the Administrator's or Secretary's proposal to issue such order and the opportunity to request, within 30 days of the date the notice is received by such person, a hearing on the proposed order. Such hearing shall not be subject to section 554 or 556 of title 5, United States Code, but shall provide a reasonable opportunity to be heard and to represent evidence.

(B) CLASS II.— The amount of a class II civil penalty under paragraph (1) may not exceed $10,000 per day for each day during which the violation continues; except that the maximum amount of any class II civil penalty under this subparagraph shall not exceed $125,000. Except as otherwise provided in this subsection, a class II civil penalty shall be assessed and collected in the same manner, and subject to the same provisions, as in the case of civil penalties assessed and collected after notice and opportunity for a hearing on the record in accordance with section 554 of title 5, United States Code. The Administrator and the Secretary may issue rules for discovery procedures for hearings under this subparagraph.

(3) DETERMINING AMOUNT.— In determining the amount of any penalty assessed under this subsection, the Administrator or the Secretary, as the case may be, shall take into account the nature, circumstances, extent and gravity of the violation, or violations, and, with respect to the violator, ability to pay, any prior history of such violations, the degree of culpability, economic benefit or savings (if any) resulting from the violation, and such other matters as justice may require. For purposes of this subsection, a single operational upset which leads to simultaneous violations of more than one pollutant parameter shall be treated as a single violation.

(4) RIGHTS OF INTERESTED PERSONS.—

(A) PUBLIC NOTICE.— Before issuing an order assessing a civil penalty under this subsection the Administrator or Secretary, as the case may be, shall provide public notice of and reasonable opportunity to comment on the proposed issuance of such order.

(B) Presentation of evidence.— Any person who comments on a proposed assessment of a penalty under this subsection shall be given notice of any hearing held under this subsection and of the order assessing such penalty. In any hearing held under this subsection, such person shall have a reasonable opportunity to be heard and to present evidence.

(C) Rights of interested persons to a hearing.— If no hearing is held under paragraph (2) before issuance of an order assessing a penalty under this subsection, any person who commented on the proposed assessment may petition, within 30 days after the issuance of such order, the Administrator or Secretary, as the case may be, to set aside such order and to provide a hearing on the penalty. If the evidence presented by the petitioner in support of the petition is material and was not considered in the issuance of the order, the Administrator or Secretary shall immediately set aside such order and provide a hearing in accordance with paragraph (2)(A) in the case of a class I civil penalty and paragraph (2)(B) in the case of a class II civil penalty. If the Administrator or Secretary denies a hearing under this subparagraph, the Administrator or Secretary shall provide to the petitioner, and publish in the Federal Register, notice of and the reasons for such denial.

(5) Finality of order.— An order issued under this subsection shall become final 30 days after its issuance unless a petition for judicial review is filed under paragraph (8) or a hearing is requested under paragraph (4)(C). If such a hearing is denied, such order shall become final 30 days after such denial.

(6) Effect of order.—

(A) Limitation on actions under other sections.—Action taken by the Administrator or the Secretary, as the case may be, under this subsection shall not affect or limit the Administrator's or Secretary's authority to enforce any provision of this Act; except that any violation—

(i) with respect to which the Administrator or the Secretary has commenced and is diligently prosecuting an action under this subsection,

(ii) with respect to which a State has commenced and is diligently prosecuting an action under a State law comparable to this subsection, or

(iii) for which the Administrator, the Secretary, or the State has issued a final order not subject to further judicial review and the violator has paid a penalty assessed under this subsection, or such comparable State law, as the case may be,

shall not be the subject of a civil penalty action under subsection (d) of this section or section 311(b) or section 505 of this Act.

(B) Applicability of limitation with respect to citizen suits.—The limitations contained in subparagraph (A) on civil penalty actions under section 505 of this Act shall not apply with respect to any violation for which—

(i) a civil action under section 505(a)(1) of this Act has been filed prior to commencement of an action under this subsection, or

(ii) notice of an alleged violation of section 505(a)(1) of this Act has been given in accordance with section 505(b)(1)(A) prior to commencement of an action under this subsection and an action under section 505(a)(1) with respect to such alleged violation is filed before the 120th day after the date on which such notice is given.

(7) Effect of action on compliance.— No action by the Administrator or the Secretary under this subsection shall affect any person's obligation to comply with any section of this Act or with the terms and conditions of any permit issued pursuant to section 402 or 404 of this Act.

(8) Judicial review.—Any person against whom a civil penalty is assessed under this subsection or who commented on the proposed assessment of such penalty in accordance with paragraph (4) may obtain review of such assessment—

(A) in the case of assessment of a class I civil penalty, in the United States District Court for the District of Columbia or in the district in which the violation is alleged to have occurred, or

(B) in the case of assessment of a class II civil penalty, in United States Court of Appeals for the District of Columbia Circuit or for any other circuit in which such person resides or transacts business,

by filing a notice of appeal in such court within the 30-day period beginning on the date the civil penalty order is issued and by simultaneously sending a copy of such notice by certified mail to the Administrator or the Secretary, as the case may be, and the Attorney General. The Administrator or the Secretary shall promptly file in such court a certified copy of the record on which the order was issued. Such court shall not set aside or remand such order unless there is not substantial evidence in the record, taken as a whole, to support the finding of a violation or unless the Administrator's or Secretary's assessment of the penalty constitutes an abuse of discretion and shall not impose additional civil penalties for the same violation unless the Administrator's or Secretary's assessment of the penalty constitutes an abuse of discretion.

(9) Collection.—If any person fails to pay an assessment of a civil penalty—

(A) after the order making the assessment has become final, or

(B) after a court in an action brought under paragraph (8) has entered a final judgment in favor of the Administrator or the Secretary, as the case may be,

the Administrator or the Secretary shall request the Attorney General to bring a civil action in an appropriate district court to recover the amount assessed (plus interest at currently prevailing rates from the date of the final order or the date of the final judgment, as the case may be). In such an action, the validity, amount, and appropriateness of such penalty shall not be subject to review. Any person who fails to pay on a timely basis the amount of an assessment of a civil penalty as described in the first sentence of this paragraph shall be required to pay, in addition to such amount and interest, attorneys fees and costs for collection proceedings and a quarterly nonpayment penalty for each quarter during which such failure to pay persists. Such nonpayment penalty shall be in an amount equal to 20 percent of the aggregate amount of such person's penalties and nonpayment penalties which are unpaid as of the beginning of such quarter.

(10) Subpoenas.— The Administrator or Secretary, as the case may be, may

issue subpoenas for the attendance and testimony of witnesses and the production of relevant papers, books, or documents in connection with hearings under this subsection. In case of contumacy or refusal to obey a subpoena issued pursuant to this paragraph and served upon any person, the district court of the United States for any district in which such person is found, resides, or transacts business, upon application by the United States and after notice to such person, shall have jurisdiction to issue an order requiring such person to appear and give testimony before the administrative law judge or to appear and produce documents before the administrative law judge, or both, and any failure to obey such order of the court may be punished by such court as a contempt thereof.

(11) PROTECTION OF EXISTING PROCEDURES.— Nothing in this subsection shall change the procedures existing on the day before the date of the enactment of the Water Quality Act of 1987 under other subsections of this section for issuance and enforcement of orders by the Administrator.

(h) IMPLEMENTATION OF INTEGRATED PLANS.—

(1) IN GENERAL.— In conjunction with an enforcement action under subsection (a) or (b) relating to municipal discharges, the Administrator shall inform a municipality of the opportunity to develop an integrated plan, as defined in section 402(s).

(2) MODIFICATION.— Any municipality under an administrative order under subsection (a) or settlement agreement (including a judicial consent decree) under subsection (b) that has developed an integrated plan consistent with section 402(s) may request a modification of the administrative order or settlement agreement based on that integrated plan.

[33 U.S.C. 1319]

INTERNATIONAL POLLUTION ABATEMENT

SEC. 310. (a) Whenever the Administrator, upon receipts of reports, surveys, or studies from any duly constituted international agency, has reason to believe that pollution is occurring which endangers the health or welfare of persons in a foreign country, and the Secretary of State requests him to abate such pollution, he shall give formal notification thereof to the State water pollution control agency of the State or States in which such discharge or discharges originate and to the appropriate interstate agency, if any. He shall also promptly call such a hearing, if he believes that such pollution is occurring in sufficient quantity to warrant such action, and if such foreign country has given the United States essentially the same rights with respect to the prevention and control of pollution occurring in that country as is given that country by this subsection. The Administrator, through the Secretary of State, shall invite the foreign country which may be adversely affected by the pollution to attend and participate in the hearing, and the representative of such country shall, for the purpose of the hearing and any further proceeding resulting from such hearing, have all the rights of a State water pollution control agency. Nothing in this subsection shall be construed to modify, amend, repeal, or otherwise affect the provisions of the 1909 Boundary Waters Treaty between Canada and the United States or the Water Utilization Treaty of 1944 between Mexico and the United States (59 Stat. 1219), relative to the control and abatement of pollution in waters covered by those treaties.

(b) The calling of a hearing under this section shall not be construed by the courts, the Administrator, or any person as limiting, modifying, or otherwise affecting the functions and responsibilities of the Administrator under this section to establish and enforce water quality requirements under this Act.

(c) The Administrator shall publish in the Federal Register a notice of a public hearing before a hearing board of five or more persons appointed by the Administrator. A majority of the members of the board and the chairman who shall be designated by the Administrator shall not be officers or employees of Federal, State, or local governments. On the basis of the evidence presented at such hearing, the board shall within sixty days after completion of the hearing make findings of fact as to whether or not such pollution is occurring and shall thereupon by decision, incorporating its findings therein, make such recommendations to abate the pollution as may be appropriate and shall transmit such decision and the record of the hearings to the Administrator. All such decisions shall be public. Upon receipt of such decision, the Administrator shall promptly implement the board's decision in accordance with the provisions of this Act.

(d) In connection with any hearing called under this subsection, the board is authorized to require any persons whose alleged activities result in discharges causing or contributing to pollution to file with it in such forms as it may prescribe, a report based on existing data, furnishing such information as may reasonably be required as to the character, kind, and quantity of such discharges and the use of facilities or other means to prevent or reduce such discharges by the person filing such a report. Such report shall be made under oath or otherwise, as the board may prescribe, and shall be filed with the board within such reasonable period as it may prescribe, unless additional time is granted by it. Upon a showing satisfactory to the board by the person filing such report that such report or portion thereof (other than effluent data), to which the Administrator has access under this section, if made public would divulge trade secrets or secret processes of such person, the board shall consider such report or portion thereof confidential for the purposes of section 1905 of title 18 of the United States Code. If any person required to file any report under this paragraph shall fail to do so within the time fixed by the board for filing the same, and such failure shall continue for thirty days after notice of such default, such person shall forfeit to the United States the sum of $1,000 for each and every day of the continuance of such failure, which forfeiture shall be payable into the Treasury of the United States, and shall be recoverable in a civil suit in the name of the United States in the district court of the United States where such person has his principal office or in any district in which he does business. The Administrator may upon application therefor remit or mitigate any forfeiture provided for under this subsection.

(e) Board members, other than officers or employees of Federal, State, or local governments, shall be for each day (including traveltime) during which they are performing board business, entitled to receive compensation at a rate fixed by the Administrator but not in excess of the maximum rate of pay for grade GS–18, as provided in the General Schedule under section 5332 of title 5 of the United States Code, and shall, notwithstanding the limitations of sections 5703 and 5704 of title 5 of the United States Code, be fully reimbursed for travel, subsistence, and related expenses.

(f) When any such recommendation adopted by the Administrator involves the institution of enforcement proceedings against any person to obtain the abatement of pollution subject to such recommendation, the Administrator shall institute such proceedings if he believes that the evidence warrants such proceedings. The district court of the United States shall consider and determine de novo all relevant issues, but shall receive in evidence the record of the proceedings before the conference or hearing board. The court shall have jurisdiction to enter such judgment and orders enforcing such judgment as it deems appropriate or to remand such proceedings to the Administrator for such further action as it may direct.

[33 U.S.C. 1320]

OIL AND HAZARDOUS SUBSTANCE LIABILITY

SEC. 311. (a) For the purpose of this section, the term—

(1) oil means oil of any kind or in any form, including, but not limited to, petroleum, fuel oil, sludge, oil refuse, and oil mixed with wastes other than dredged spoil;

(2) discharge includes, but is not limited to, any spilling, leaking, pumping, pouring, emitting, emptying or dumping, but excludes (A) discharges in compliance with a permit under section 402 of this Act, (B) discharges resulting from circumstances identified and reviewed and made a part of the public record with respect to a permit issued or modified under section 402 of this Act, and subject to a condition in such permit, ,(C)[13] continuous or anticipated intermittent discharges from a point source, identified in a permit or permit application under section 402 of this Act, which are caused by events occurring within the scope of relevant operating or treatment systems, and (D) discharges incidental to mechanical removal authorized by the President under subsection (c) of this section;

[13] So in law.

(3) vessel means every description of watercraft or other artificial contrivance used, or capable of being used, as a means of transportation on water other than a public vessel;

(4) public vessel means a vessel owned or bareboat-chartered and operated by the United States, or by a State or political subdivision thereof, or by a foreign nation, except when such vessel is engaged in commerce;

(5) United States means the States, the District of Columbia, the Commonwealth of Puerto Rico, the Commonwealth of the Northern Mariana Islands, Guam, American Samoa, the Virgin Islands, and the Trust Territory of the Pacific Islands;

(6) owner or operator means (A) in the case of a vessel, any person owning, operating, or chartering by demise, such vessel, and (B) in the case of an onshore facility, and an offshore facility, any person owning or operating such onshore facility or offshore facility, and (C) in the case of any abandoned offshore facility, the person who owned or operated such facility immediately prior to such abandonment;

(7) person includes an individual, firm, corporation, association, and a partnership;

(8) remove or removal refers to containment and removal of the oil or hazardous

substances from the water and shorelines or the taking of such other actions as may be necessary to prevent, minimize, or mitigate damage to the public health or welfare, including, but not limited to, fish, shellfish, wildlife, and public and private property, shorelines, and beaches;

(9) contiguous zone means the entire zone established or to be established by the United States under article 24 of the Convention on the Territorial Sea and the Contiguous Zone;

(10) onshore facility means any facility (including, but not limited to, motor vehicles and rolling stock) of any kind located in, on, or under, any land within the United States other than submerged land;

(11) offshore facility means any facility of any kind located in, on, or under, any of the navigable waters of the United States, any facility of any kind which is subject to the jurisdiction of the United States and is located in, on, or under any other waters, other than a vessel or a public vessel, and, for the purposes of applying subsections (b), (c), (e), and (o), any foreign offshore unit (as defined in section 1001 of the Oil Pollution Act) or any other facility located seaward of the exclusive economic zone;

(12) act of God means an act occasioned by an unanticipated grave natural disaster;

(13) barrel means 42 United States gallons at 60 degrees Fahrenheit;

(14) hazardous substance means any substance designated pursuant to subsection (b)(2) of this section;

(15) inland oil barge means a non-self-propelled vessel carrying oil in bulk as cargo and certificated to operate only in the inland waters of the United States, while operating in such waters;

(16) inland waters of the United States means those waters of the United States lying inside the baseline from which the territorial sea is measured and those waters outside such baseline which are a part of the Gulf Intracoastal Waterway;

(17) otherwise subject to the jurisdiction of the United States means subject to the jurisdiction of the United States by virtue of United States citizenship, United States vessel documentation or numbering, or as provided for by international agreement to which the United States is a party;

(18) Area Committee means an Area Committee established under subsection (j);

(19) Area Contingency Plan means an Area Contingency Plan prepared under subsection (j);

(20) Coast Guard District Response Group means a Coast Guard District Response Group established under subsection (j);

(21) Federal On-Scene Coordinator means a Federal On-Scene Coordinator designated in the National Contingency Plan;

(22) National Contingency Plan means the National Contingency Plan prepared and published under subsection (d);

(23) National Response Unit means the National Response Unit established under subsection (j);

(24) worst case discharge means—

(A) in the case of a vessel, a discharge in adverse weather conditions of its entire cargo; and

(B) in the case of an offshore facility or onshore facility, the largest foreseeable discharge in adverse weather conditions;

(25) removal costs means—

(A) the costs of removal of oil or a hazardous substance that are incurred after it is discharged; and

(B) in any case in which there is a substantial threat of a discharge of oil or a hazardous substance, the costs to prevent, minimize, or mitigate that threat;

(26) nontank vessel means a self-propelled vessel that—

(A) is at least 400 gross tons as measured under section 14302 of title 46, United States Code, or, for vessels not measured under that section, as measured under section 14502 of that title;

(B) is not a tank vessel;

(C) carries oil of any kind as fuel for main propulsion; and

(D) operates on the navigable waters of the United States, as defined in section 2101(23) of that title;

(27) the term best available science means science that—

(A) maximizes the quality, objectivity, and integrity of information, including statistical information;

(B) uses peer-reviewed and publicly available data; and

(C) clearly documents and communicates risks and uncertainties in the scientific basis for such projects;

(28) the term Chairperson means the Chairperson of the Council;

(29) the term coastal political subdivision means any local political jurisdiction that is immediately below the State level of government, including a county, parish, or borough, with a coastline that is contiguous with any portion of the United States Gulf of Mexico;

(30) the term Comprehensive Plan means the comprehensive plan developed by the Council pursuant to subsection (t);

(31) the term Council means the Gulf Coast Ecosystem Restoration Council established pursuant to subsection (t);

(32) the term Deepwater Horizon oil spill means the blowout and explosion of the mobile offshore drilling unit *Deepwater Horizon* that occurred on April 20, 2010, and resulting hydrocarbon releases into the environment;

(33) the term Gulf Coast region means—

(A) in the Gulf Coast States, the coastal zones (as that term is defined in section 304 of the Coastal Zone Management Act of 1972 (16 U.S.C. 1453)), except that, in this section, the term coastal zones includes land within the coastal zones that is held in trust by, or the use of which is by law subject solely to the discretion of, the Federal Government or officers or agents of the Federal Government)) that border the Gulf of Mexico;

(B) any adjacent land, water, and watersheds, that are within 25 miles of the coastal zones described in subparagraph (A) of the Gulf Coast States; and

(C) all Federal waters in the Gulf of Mexico;

(34) the term Gulf Coast State means any of the States of Alabama, Florida, Louisiana, Mississippi, and Texas; and

(35) the term Trust Fund means the Gulf Coast Restoration Trust Fund established pursuant to section 1602 of the Resources and Ecosystems Sustainability, Tourist Opportunities, and Revived Economies of the Gulf Coast States Act of 2012.

(b)(1) The Congress hereby declares that it is the policy of the United States that there should be no discharges of oil or hazardous substances into or upon the navigable waters of the United States, adjoining shorelines, or into or upon the waters of the contiguous zone, or in connection with activities under the Outer Continental Shelf Lands Act or the Deepwater Port Act of 1974, or which may affect natural resources belonging to, appertaining to, or under the exclusive management authority of the United States (including resources under the Fishery Conservation and Management Act of 1976).

(2)(A) The Administrator shall develop, promulgate, and revise as may be appropriate, regulations designating as hazardous substances, other than oil as defined in this section, such elements and compounds which, when discharged in any quantity into or upon the navigable waters of the United States or adjoining shorelines or the waters of the contiguous zone or in connection with activities under the Outer Continental Shelf Lands Act or the Deepwater Port Act of 1974, or which may affect natural resources belonging to, appertaining to, or under the exclusive management authority of the United States (including resources under the Fishery Conservation and Management Act of 1976), present an imminent and substantial danger to the public health or welfare, including, but not limited to, fish, shellfish, wildlife, shorelines, and beaches.

(B) The Administrator shall within 18 months after the date of enactment of this paragraph, conduct a study and report to the Congress on methods, mechanisms, and procedures to create incentives to achieve a higher standard of care in all aspects of the management and movement of hazardous substances on the part of owners, operators, or persons in charge of onshore facilities, offshore facilities, or vessels. The Administrator shall include in such study (1) limits of liability, (2) liability for third party damages, (3) penalties and fees, (4) spill prevention plans, (5) current practices in the insurance and banking industries, and (6) whether the penalty enacted in subclause (bb) of clause (iii) of subparagraph (B) of subsection (b)(2) of section 311 of Public Law 92–500 should be enacted.

(3) The discharge of oil or hazardous substances (i) into or upon the navigable waters of the United States, adjoining shorelines, or into or upon the waters of the contiguous zone, or (ii) in connection with activities under the Outer Continental Shelf Lands Act or the Deepwater Port Act of 1974, or which may affect natural resources belonging to, appertaining to, or under the exclusive management authority of the United States (including resources under the Fishery Conservation and Management Act of 1976), in such quantities as may be harmful as determined by the President under paragraph (4) of this subsection, is prohibited, except (A) in the case of such discharges into the waters of the contiguous zone or which may affect natural resources belonging to, appertaining to, or under the exclusive management authority of the United States (including resources under the Fishery Conservation and Management Act of 1976), where permitted under the Protocol of 1978 Relating to the International Convention for the Prevention of Pollution from Ships, 1973, and (B) where permitted in quantities and at times and locations or under such circumstances or conditions as the President may, by regulation, determine not to be harmful. Any regulations issued under this subsection shall be consistent with maritime safety and with marine and navigation laws and regulations and applicable water quality standards.

(4) The President shall by regulation determine for the purposes of this section those quantities of oil and any hazardous substances the discharge of which may be harmful to the public health or welfare or the environment of the United States, including but not limited to fish, shellfish, wildlife, and public and private property, shorelines, and beaches.

(5) Any person in charge of a vessel or of an onshore facility or an offshore facility shall, as soon as he has knowledge of any discharge of oil or a hazardous substance from such vessel or facility in violation of paragraph (3) of this subsection, immediately notify the appropriate agency of the United States Government of such discharge. The Federal agency shall immediately notify the appropriate State agency of any State which is, or may reasonably be expected to be, affected by the discharge of oil or a hazardous substance. Any such person (A) in charge of a vessel from which oil or a hazardous substance is discharged in violation of paragraph (3)(i) of this subsection, or (B) in charge of a vessel from which oil or a hazardous substance is discharged in violation of paragraph (3)(ii) of this subsection and who is otherwise subject to the jurisdiction of the United States at the time of the discharge, or (C) in charge of an onshore facility or an offshore facility, who fails to notify immediately such agency of such discharge shall, upon conviction, be fined in accordance with title 18, United States Code, or imprisoned for not more than 5 years, or both. Notification received pursuant to this paragraph shall not be used against any such natural person in any criminal case, except a prosecution for perjury or for giving a false statement.

(6) Administrative penalties.—

(A) Violations.—Any owner, operator, or person in charge of any vessel, onshore facility, or offshore facility—

(i) from which oil or a hazardous substance is discharged in violation of paragraph (3), or

(ii) who fails or refuses to comply with any regulation issued under subsection (j) to which that owner, operator, or person in charge is subject,

may be assessed a class I or class II civil penalty by the Secretary of the department in which the Coast Guard is operating, the Secretary of Transportation, or the Administrator.

(B) Classes of penalties.—

(i) Class I.— The amount of a class I civil penalty under subparagraph (A) may not exceed $10,000 per violation, except that the maximum amount of any class I civil penalty under this subparagraph shall not exceed $25,000. Before assessing a civil penalty under this clause, the Administrator or Secretary, as the case may be, shall give to the person to be assessed such penalty written notice of the Administrator's or Secretary's proposal to assess the penalty and the opportunity to request, within 30 days of the date the notice is received by such person, a hearing on the proposed penalty. Such hearing shall not be subject to section 554 or 556 of title 5, United States Code, but shall provide a reasonable opportunity to be heard and to present evidence.

(ii) Class II.— The amount of a class II civil penalty under subparagraph (A) may not exceed $10,000 per day for each day during which the violation continues; except that the maximum amount of any class II civil penalty under this subparagraph shall not exceed $125,000. Except as otherwise provided in this subsection, a class II civil penalty shall be assessed and collected in the same manner, and subject to the same provisions, as in the case of civil penalties assessed and collected after notice and opportunity for a hearing on the record in accordance with section 554 of title 5, United States Code. The Administrator and Secretary may issue rules for discovery procedures for hearings under this paragraph.

(C) Rights of interested persons.—

(i) Public notice.— Before issuing an order assessing a class II civil penalty under this paragraph the Administrator or Secretary, as the case may be, shall provide public notice of and reasonable opportunity to comment on the proposed issuance of such order.

(ii) Presentation of evidence.— Any person who comments on a proposed assessment of a class II civil penalty under this paragraph shall be given notice of any hearing held under this paragraph and of the order assessing such penalty. In any hearing held under this paragraph, such person shall have a reasonable opportunity to be heard and to present evidence.

(iii) Rights of interested persons to a hearing.— If no hearing is held under subparagraph (B) before issuance of an order assessing a class II civil penalty under this paragraph, any person who commented on the proposed assessment may petition, within 30 days after the issuance of such order, the Administrator or Secretary, as the case may be, to set aside such order and to provide a hearing on the penalty. If the evidence presented by the petitioner in support of the petition is material and was not considered in the issuance of the order, the Administrator or Secretary shall immediately set aside such order and provide a hearing in accordance with subparagraph (B)(ii). If the Administrator or Secretary denies a hearing under this clause, the Administrator or Secretary shall provide to the petitioner, and publish in the Federal Register, notice of and the reasons for such denial.

(D) FINALITY OF ORDER.— An order assessing a class II civil penalty under this paragraph shall become final 30 days after its issuance unless a petition for judicial review is filed under subparagraph (G) or a hearing is requested under subparagraph (C)(iii). If such a hearing is denied, such order shall become final 30 days after such denial.

(E) EFFECT OF ORDER.—Action taken by the Administrator or Secretary, as the case may be, under this paragraph shall not affect or limit the Administrator's or Secretary's authority to enforce any provision of this Act; except that any violation—

(i) with respect to which the Administrator or Secretary has commenced and is diligently prosecuting an action to assess a class II civil penalty under this paragraph, or

(ii) for which the Administrator or Secretary has issued a final order assessing a class II civil penalty not subject to further judicial review and the violator has paid a penalty assessed under this paragraph,

shall not be the subject of a civil penalty action under section 309(d), 309(g), or 505 of this Act or under paragraph (7).

(F) EFFECT OF ACTION ON COMPLIANCE.— No action by the Administrator or Secretary under this paragraph shall affect any person's obligation to comply with any section of this Act.

(G) JUDICIAL REVIEW.—Any person against whom a civil penalty is assessed under this paragraph or who commented on the proposed assessment of such penalty in accordance with subparagraph (C) may obtain review of such assessment—

(i) in the case of assessment of a class I civil penalty, in the United States District Court for the District of Columbia or in the district in which the violation is alleged to have occurred, or

(ii) in the case of assessment of a class II civil penalty, in United States Court of Appeals for the District of Columbia Circuit or for any other circuit in which such person resides or transacts business,

by filing a notice of appeal in such court within the 30-day period beginning on the date the civil penalty order is issued and by simultaneously sending a copy of such notice by certified mail to the Administrator or Secretary, as the case may be, and the Attorney General. The Administrator or Secretary shall promptly file in such court a certified copy of the record on which the order was issued. Such court shall not set aside or remand such order unless there is not substantial evidence in the record, taken as a whole, to support the finding of a violation or unless the Administrator's or Secretary's assessment of the penalty constitutes an abuse of discretion and shall not impose additional civil penalties for the same violation unless the Administrator's or Secretary's assessment of the penalty constitutes an abuse of discretion.

(H) COLLECTION.—If any person fails to pay an assessment of a civil penalty—

(i) after the assessment has become final, or

(ii) after a court in an action brought under subparagraph (G) has entered a final judgment in favor of the Administrator or Secretary, as the case may be,

the Administrator or Secretary shall request the Attorney General to bring a civil action in an appropriate district court to recover the amount assessed (plus interest at currently prevailing rates from the date of the final order or the date of the final judgment, as the case may be). In such an action, the validity, amount, and appropriateness of such penalty shall not be subject to review. Any person who fails to pay on a timely basis the amount of an assessment of a civil penalty as described in the first sentence of this subparagraph shall be required to pay, in addition to such amount and interest, attorneys fees and costs for collection proceedings and a quarterly nonpayment penalty for each quarter during which such failure to pay persists. Such nonpayment penalty shall be in an amount equal to 20 percent of the aggregate amount of such person's penalties and nonpayment penalties which are unpaid as of the beginning of such quarter.

(I) SUBPOENAS.— The Administrator or Secretary, as the case may be, may issue subpoenas for the attendance and testimony of witnesses and the production of relevant papers, books, or documents in connection with hearings under this paragraph. In case of contumacy or refusal to obey a subpoena issued pursuant to this subparagraph and served upon any person, the district court of the United States for any district in which such person is found, resides, or transacts business, upon application by the United States and after notice to such person, shall have jurisdiction to issue an order requiring such person to appear and give testimony before the administrative law judge or to appear and produce documents before the administrative law judge, or both, and any failure to obey such order of the court may be punished by such court as a contempt thereof.

(7) CIVIL PENALTY ACTION.—

(A) DISCHARGE, GENERALLY.— Any person who is the owner, operator, or person in charge of any vessel, onshore facility, or offshore facility from which oil or a hazardous substance is discharged in violation of paragraph (3), shall be subject to a civil penalty in an amount up to $25,000 per day of violation or an amount up to $1,000 per barrel of oil or unit of reportable quantity of hazardous substances discharged.

(B) FAILURE TO REMOVE OR COMPLY.—Any person described in subparagraph (A) who, without sufficient cause—

(i) fails to properly carry out removal of the discharge under an order of the President pursuant to subsection (c); or

(ii) fails to comply with an order pursuant to subsection (e)(1)(B);

shall be subject to a civil penalty in an amount up to $25,000 per day of violation or an amount up to 3 times the costs incurred by the Oil Spill Liability Trust

Fund as a result of such failure.

(C) FAILURE TO COMPLY WITH REGULATION.— Any person who fails or refuses to comply with any regulation issued under subsection (j) shall be subject to a civil penalty in an amount up to $25,000 per day of violation.

(D) GROSS NEGLIGENCE.— In any case in which a violation of paragraph (3) was the result of gross negligence or willful misconduct of a person described in subparagraph (A), the person shall be subject to a civil penalty of not less than $100,000, and not more than $3,000 per barrel of oil or unit of reportable quantity of hazardous substance discharged.

(E) JURISDICTION.— An action to impose a civil penalty under this paragraph may be brought in the district court of the United States for the district in which the defendant is located, resides, or is doing business, and such court shall have jurisdiction to assess such penalty.

(F) LIMITATION.— A person is not liable for a civil penalty under this paragraph for a discharge if the person has been assessed a civil penalty under paragraph (6) for the discharge.

(8) DETERMINATION OF AMOUNT.— In determining the amount of a civil penalty under paragraphs (6) and (7), the Administrator, Secretary, or the court, as the case may be, shall consider the seriousness of the violation or violations, the economic benefit to the violator, if any, resulting from the violation, the degree of culpability involved, any other penalty for the same incident, any history of prior violations, the nature, extent, and degree of success of any efforts of the violator to minimize or mitigate the effects of the discharge, the economic impact of the penalty on the violator, and any other matters as justice may require.

(9) MITIGATION OF DAMAGE.— In addition to establishing a penalty for the discharge of oil or a hazardous substance, the Administrator or the Secretary of the department in which the Coast Guard is operating may act to mitigate the damage to the public health or welfare caused by such discharge. The cost of such mitigation shall be deemed a cost incurred under subsection (c) of this section for the removal of such substance by the United States Government.

(10) RECOVERY OF REMOVAL COSTS.— Any costs of removal incurred in connection with a discharge excluded by subsection (a)(2)(C) of this section shall be recoverable from the owner or operator of the source of the discharge in an action brought under section 309(b) of this Act.

(11) LIMITATION.— Civil penalties shall not be assessed under both this section and section 309 for the same discharge.

(12)[14] WITHHOLDING CLEARANCE.—If any owner, operator, or person in charge of a vessel is liable for a civil penalty under this subsection, or if reasonable cause exists to believe that the owner, operator, or person in charge may be subject to a civil penalty under this subsection, the Secretary of the Treasury, upon the request of the Secretary of the department in which the Coast Guard is operating or the Administrator, shall with respect to such vessel refuse or revoke—

[14] Indentation so in law.

(A) the clearance required by section 4197 of the Revised Statutes of the United States (46 U.S.C. App. 91);

(B) a permit to proceed under section 4367 of the Revised Statutes of the United States (46 U.S.C. App. 313); and

(C) a permit to depart required under section 443 of the Tariff Act of 1930 (19 U.S.C. 1443);

as applicable. Clearance or a permit refused or revoked under this paragraph may be granted upon the filing of a bond or other surety satisfactory to the Secretary of the department in which the Coast Guard is operating or the Administrator.

(c) FEDERAL REMOVAL AUTHORITY.—

(1) GENERAL REMOVAL REQUIREMENT.—(A) The President shall, in accordance with the National Contingency Plan and any appropriate Area Contingency Plan, ensure effective and immediate removal of a discharge, and mitigation or prevention of a substantial threat of a discharge, of oil or a hazardous substance—

(i) into or on the navigable waters;

(ii) on the adjoining shorelines to the navigable waters;

(iii) into or on the waters of the exclusive economic zone; or

(iv) that may affect natural resources belonging to, appertaining to, or under the exclusive management authority of the United States.

(B) In carrying out this paragraph, the President may—

(i) remove or arrange for the removal of a discharge, and mitigate or prevent a substantial threat of a discharge, at any time;

(ii) direct or monitor all Federal, State, and private actions to remove a discharge; and

(iii) remove and, if necessary, destroy a vessel discharging, or threatening to discharge, by whatever means are available.

(2) DISCHARGE POSING SUBSTANTIAL THREAT TO PUBLIC HEALTH OR WELFARE.—(A) If a discharge, or a substantial threat of a discharge, of oil or a hazardous substance from a vessel, offshore facility, or onshore facility is of such a size or character as to be a substantial threat to the public health or welfare of the United States (including but not limited to fish, shellfish, wildlife, other natural resources, and the public and private beaches and shorelines of the United States), the President shall direct all Federal, State, and private actions to remove the discharge or to mitigate or prevent the threat of the discharge.

(B) In carrying out this paragraph, the President may, without regard to any other provision of law governing contracting procedures or employment of personnel by the Federal Government—

(i) remove or arrange for the removal of the discharge, or mitigate or prevent the substantial threat of the discharge; and

(ii) remove and, if necessary, destroy a vessel discharging, or threatening to discharge, by whatever means are available.

(3) ACTIONS IN ACCORDANCE WITH NATIONAL CONTINGENCY PLAN.—(A) Each Federal agency, State, owner or operator, or other person participating in efforts under this subsection shall act in accordance with the National Contingency Plan or as directed by the President.

(B) An owner or operator participating in efforts under this subsection shall act in accordance with the National Contingency Plan and the applicable response plan required under subsection (j), or as directed by the President, except that the owner or operator may deviate from the applicable response plan if the President or the Federal On-Scene Coordinator determines that deviation from the response plan would provide for a more expeditious or effective response to the spill or mitigation of its environmental effects.

(C) In any case in which the President or the Federal On-Scene Coordinator authorizes a deviation from the salvor as part of a deviation under subparagraph (B) from the applicable response plan required under subsection (j), the Commandant of the Coast Guard shall submit to the Committee on Transportation and Infrastructure of the House of Representatives and the Committee on Commerce, Science, and Transportation of the Senate a report describing the deviation and the reasons for such deviation not less than 3 days after such deviation is authorized.

(4) EXEMPTION FROM LIABILITY.—(A) A person is not liable for removal costs or damages which result from actions taken or omitted to be taken in the course of rendering care, assistance, or advice consistent with the National Contingency Plan or as otherwise directed by the President relating to a discharge or a substantial threat of a discharge of oil or a hazardous substance.

(B) Subparagraph (A) does not apply—

(i) to a responsible party;

(ii) to a response under the Comprehensive Environmental Response, Compensation, and Liability Act of 1980 (42 U.S.C. 9601 et seq.);

(iii) with respect to personal injury or wrongful death; or

(iv) if the person is grossly negligent or engages in willful misconduct.

(C) A responsible party is liable for any removal costs and damages that another person is relieved of under subparagraph (A).

(5) OBLIGATION AND LIABILITY OF OWNER OR OPERATOR NOT AFFECTED.—Nothing in this subsection affects—

(A) the obligation of an owner or operator to respond immediately to a discharge, or the threat of a discharge, of oil; or

(B) the liability of a responsible party under the Oil Pollution Act of 1990.

(6) RESPONSIBLE PARTY DEFINED.— For purposes of this subsection, the term responsible party has the meaning given that term under section 1001 of the Oil Pollution Act of 1990.

(d) NATIONAL CONTINGENCY PLAN.—

(1) PREPARATION BY PRESIDENT.— The President shall prepare and publish a

National Contingency Plan for removal of oil and hazardous substances pursuant to this section.

(2) CONTENTS.—The National Contingency Plan shall provide for efficient, coordinated, and effective action to minimize damage from oil and hazardous substance discharges, including containment, dispersal, and removal of oil and hazardous substances, and shall include, but not be limited to, the following:

(A) Assignment of duties and responsibilities among Federal departments and agencies in coordination with State and local agencies and port authorities including, but not limited to, water pollution control and conservation and trusteeship of natural resources (including conservation of fish and wildlife).

(B) Identification, procurement, maintenance, and storage of equipment and supplies.

(C) Establishment or designation of Coast Guard strike teams, consisting of—

(i) personnel who shall be trained, prepared, and available to provide necessary services to carry out the National Contingency Plan;

(ii) adequate oil and hazardous substance pollution control equipment and material; and

(iii) a detailed oil and hazardous substance pollution and prevention plan, including measures to protect fisheries and wildlife.

(D) A system of surveillance and notice designed to safeguard against as well as ensure earliest possible notice of discharges of oil and hazardous substances and imminent threats of such discharges to the appropriate State and Federal agencies.

(E) Establishment of a national center to provide coordination and direction for operations in carrying out the Plan.

(F) Procedures and techniques to be employed in identifying, containing, dispersing, and removing oil and hazardous substances.

(G) A schedule, prepared in cooperation with the States, identifying—

(i) dispersants, other chemicals, and other spill mitigating devices and substances, if any, that may be used in carrying out the Plan,

(ii) the waters in which such dispersants, other chemicals, and other spill mitigating devices and substances may be used, and

(iii) the quantities of such dispersant, other chemicals, or other spill mitigating device or substance which can be used safely in such waters,

which schedule shall provide in the case of any dispersant, chemical, spill mitigating device or substance, or waters not specifically identified in such schedule that the President, or his delegate, may, on a case-by-case basis, identify the dispersants, other chemicals, and other spill mitigating devices and substances which may be used, the waters in which they may be used, and the quantities which can be used safely in such waters.

(H) A system whereby the State or States affected by a discharge of oil or hazardous substance may act where necessary to remove such discharge and such State or States may be reimbursed in accordance with the Oil Pollution Act of 1990, in the case of any discharge of oil from a vessel or facility, for the reasonable costs incurred for that removal, from the Oil Spill Liability Trust Fund.

(I) Establishment of criteria and procedures to ensure immediate and effective Federal identification of, and response to, a discharge, or the threat of a discharge, that results in a substantial threat to the public health or welfare of the United States, as required under subsection (c)(2).

(J) Establishment of procedures and standards for removing a worst case discharge of oil, and for mitigating or preventing a substantial threat of such a discharge.

(K) Designation of the Federal official who shall be the Federal On-Scene Coordinator for each area for which an Area Contingency Plan is required to be prepared under subsection (j).

(L) Establishment of procedures for the coordination of activities of—

(i) Coast Guard strike teams established under subparagraph (C);

(ii) Federal On-Scene Coordinators designated under subparagraph (K);

(iii) District Response Groups established under subsection (j); and

(iv) Area Committees established under subsection (j).

(M) A fish and wildlife response plan, developed in consultation with the United States Fish and Wildlife Service, the National Oceanic and Atmospheric Administration, and other interested parties (including State fish and wildlife conservation officials), for the immediate and effective protection, rescue, and rehabilitation of, and the minimization of risk of damage to, fish and wildlife resources and their habitat that are harmed or that may be jeopardized by a discharge.

(3) Revisions and amendments.— The President may, from time to time, as the President deems advisable, revise or otherwise amend the National Contingency Plan.

(4) Actions in accordance with national contingency plan.— After publication of the National Contingency Plan, the removal of oil and hazardous substances and actions to minimize damage from oil and hazardous substance discharges shall, to the greatest extent possible, be in accordance with the National Contingency Plan.

(e) Civil Enforcement.—

(1) Orders protecting public health.—In addition to any action taken by a State or local government, when the President determines that there may be an imminent and substantial threat to the public health or welfare of the United States, including fish, shellfish, and wildlife, public and private property, shorelines, beaches, habitat, and other living and nonliving natural resources under the jurisdiction or control of the United States, because of an actual or threatened discharge of oil or a hazardous substance from a vessel or facility in violation of

subsection (b), the President may—

(A) require the Attorney General to secure any relief from any person, including the owner or operator of the vessel or facility, as may be necessary to abate such endangerment; or

(B) after notice to the affected State, take any other action under this section, including issuing administrative orders, that may be necessary to protect the public health and welfare.

(2) Jurisdiction of district courts.— The district courts of the United States shall have jurisdiction to grant any relief under this subsection that the public interest and the equities of the case may require.

(f)(1) Except where an owner or operator can prove that a discharge was caused solely by (A) an act of God, (B) an act of war, (C) negligence on the part of the United States Government, or (D) an act or omission of a third party without regard to whether any such act or omission was or was not negligent, or any combination of the foregoing clauses, such owner or operator of any vessel from which oil or a hazardous substance is discharged in violation of subsection (b)(3) of this section shall, notwithstanding any other provision of law, be liable to the United States Government for the actual costs incurred under subsection (c) for the removal of such oil or substance by the United States Government in an amount not to exceed, in the case of an inland oil barge $125 per gross ton of such barge, or $125,000, whichever is greater, and in the case of any other vessel, $150 per gross ton of such vessel (or, for a vessel carrying oil or hazardous substances as cargo, $250,000), whichever is greater, except that where the United States can show that such discharge was the result of willful negligence or willful misconduct within the privity and knowledge of the owner, such owner or operator shall be liable to the United States Government for the full amount of such costs. Such costs shall constitute a maritime lien on such vessel which may be recovered in an action in rem in the district court of the United States for any district within which any vessel may be found. The United States may also bring an action against the owner or operator of such vessel in any court of competent jurisdiction to recover such costs.

(2) Except where an owner or operator of an onshore facility can prove that a discharge was caused solely by (A) an act of God, (B) an act of war, (C) negligence on the part of the United States Government, or (D) an act or omission of a third party without regard to whether any such act or omission was or was not negligent, or any combination of the foregoing clauses, such owner or operator of any such facility from which oil or a hazardous substance is discharged in violation of subsection (b)(3) of this section shall be liable to the United States Government for the actual costs incurred under subsection (c) for the removal of such oil or substance by the United States Government in an amount not to exceed $50,000,000, except that where the United States can show that such discharge was the result of willful negligence or willful misconduct within the privity and knowledge of the owner, such owner or operator shall be liable to the United States Government for the full amount of such costs. The United States may bring an action against the owner or operator of such facility in any court of competent jurisdiction to recover such costs. The Administrator is authorized, by regulation, after consultation with the Secretary of Commerce and the Small Business Administration, to establish reasonable and equitable classifications, of those onshore facilities having a total

fixed storage capacity of 1,000 barrels or less which he determines because of size, type, and location do not present a substantial risk of the discharge of oil or hazardous substance in violation of subsection (b)(3) of this section, and apply with respect to such classifications differing limits of liability which may be less than the amount contained in this paragraph.

(3) Except where an owner or operator of an offshore facility can prove that a discharge was caused solely by (A) an act of God, (B) an act of war, (C) negligence on the part of the United States Government, or (D) an act or omission of a third party without regard to whether any such act or omission was or was not negligent, or any combination of the foregoing clauses, such owner or operator of any such facility from which oil or a hazardous substance is discharged in violation of subsection (b)(3) of this section shall, notwithstanding any other provision of law, be liable to the United States Government for the actual costs incurred under subsection (c) for the removal of such oil or substance by the United States Government in an amount not to exceed $50,000,000, except that where the United States can show that such discharge was the result of willful negligence or willful misconduct within the privity and knowledge of the owner, such owner or operator shall be liable to the United States Government for the full amount of such costs. The United States may bring an action against the owner or operator of such a facility in any court of competent jurisdiction to recover such costs.

(4) The costs of removal of oil or a hazardous substance for which the owner or operator of a vessel or onshore or offshore facility is liable under subsection (f) of this section shall include any costs or expenses incurred by the Federal Government or any State government in the restoration or replacement of natural resources damaged or destroyed as a result of a discharge of oil or a hazardous substance in violation of subsection (b) of this section.

(5) The President, or the authorized representative of any State, shall act on behalf of the public as trustee of the natural resources to recover for the costs of replacing or restoring such resources. Sums recovered shall be used to restore, rehabilitate, or acquire the equivalent of such natural resources by the appropriate agencies of the Federal Government, or the State government.

(g) Where the owner or operator of a vessel (other than an inland oil barge) carrying oil or hazardous substances as cargo or an onshore or offshore facility which handles or stores oil or hazardous substances in bulk, from which oil or a hazardous substance is discharged in violation of subsection (b) of this section, alleges that such discharge was caused solely by an act or omission of a third party, such owner or operator shall pay to the United States Government the actual costs incurred under subsection (c) for removal of such oil or substance and shall be entitled by subrogation to all rights of the United States Government to recover such costs from such third party under this subsection. In any case where an owner or operator of a vessel, of an onshore facility, or of an offshore facility, from which oil or a hazardous substance is discharged in violation of subsection (b)(3) of this section, proves that such discharge of oil or hazardous substance was caused solely by an act or omission of a third party, or was caused solely by such an act or omission in combination with an act of God, an act of war, or negligence on the part of the United States Government, such third party shall, not withstanding any other provision of law, be liable to the United States Government for the actual costs incurred under subsection (c) for removal of such oil or substance by the United States Government, except where such third party can prove that such discharge was caused solely by (A) an act of God, (B) an act of war, (C) negligence on the part of the United States Government, or (D) an act or omission of another party without regard to whether such act or omission was or was not negligent, or any combination of the foregoing clauses. If such third party was the owner or operator of a vessel which caused the discharge of oil or a hazardous substance in violation of subsection (b)(3) of this section, the liability of such third party under this subsection shall not exceed, in the case of an inland oil barge $125 per gross ton of such barge, $125,000, whichever is greater, and in the case of any other vessel, $150 per gross ton of such vessel (or, for a vessel carrying oil or hazardous substances as cargo, $250,000), whichever is greater. In any other case the liability of such third party shall not exceed the limitation which would have been applicable to the owner or operator of the vessel or the onshore or offshore facility from which the discharge actually occurred if such owner or operator were liable. If the United States can show that the discharge of oil or a hazardous substance in violation of subsection (b)(3) of this section was the result of willful negligence or willful misconduct within the privity and knowledge of such third party, such third party shall be liable to the United States Government for the full amount of such removal costs. The United States may bring an action against the third party in any court of competent jurisdiction to recover such removal costs.

(h) The liabilities established by this section shall in no way affect any rights which (1) the owner or operator of a vessel or of an onshore facility or an offshore facility may have against any third party whose acts may in any way have caused or contributed to such discharge, or (2) The[15] United States Government may have against any third party whose actions may in any way have caused or contributed to the discharge of oil or hazardous substance.

[15] So in law. Should not be capitalized.

(i) In any case where an owner or operator of a vessel or an onshore facility or an offshore facility from which oil or a hazardous substance is discharged in violation of subsection (b)(3) of this section acts to remove such oil or substance in accordance with regulations promulgated pursuant to this section, such owner or operator shall be entitled to recover the reasonable costs incurred in such removal upon establishing, in a suit which may be brought against the United States Government in the United States Claims Court, that such discharge was caused solely by (A) an act of God, (B) an act of war, (C) negligence on the part of the United States Government, or (D) an act or omission of a third party without regard to whether such act or omission was or was not negligent, or of any combination of the foregoing clauses.

(j) National Response System.—

(1) In general.— Consistent with the National Contingency Plan required by subsection (c)(2) of this section, as soon as practicable after the effective date of this section, and from time to time thereafter, the President shall issue regulations consistent with maritime safety and with marine and navigation laws (A) establishing methods and procedures for removal of discharged oil and hazardous substances, (B) establishing criteria for the development and implementation of local and regional oil and hazardous substance removal contingency plans, (C)

establishing procedures, methods, and equipment and other requirements for equipment to prevent discharges of oil and hazardous substances from vessels and from onshore facilities and offshore facilities, and to contain such discharges, and (D) governing the inspection of vessels carrying cargoes of oil and hazardous substances and the inspection of such cargoes in order to reduce the likelihood of discharges of oil from vessels in violation of this section.

(2) NATIONAL RESPONSE UNIT.—The Secretary of the department in which the Coast Guard is operating shall establish a National Response Unit at Elizabeth City, North Carolina. The Secretary, acting through the National Response Unit—

(A) shall compile and maintain a comprehensive computer list of spill removal resources, personnel, and equipment that is available worldwide and within the areas designated by the President pursuant to paragraph (4), and of information regarding previous spills, including data from universities, research institutions, State governments, and other nations, as appropriate, which shall be disseminated as appropriate to response groups and area committees, and which shall be available to Federal and State agencies and the public;

(B) shall provide technical assistance, equipment, and other resources requested by a Federal On-Scene Coordinator;

(C) shall coordinate use of private and public personnel and equipment to remove a worst case discharge, and to mitigate or prevent a substantial threat of such a discharge, from a vessel, offshore facility, or onshore facility operating in or near an area designated by the President pursuant to paragraph (4);

(D) may provide technical assistance in the preparation of Area Contingency Plans required under paragraph (4);

(E) shall administer Coast Guard strike teams established under the National Contingency Plan;

(F) shall maintain on file all Area Contingency Plans approved by the President under this subsection; and

(G) shall review each of those plans that affects its responsibilities under this subsection.

(3) COAST GUARD DISTRICT RESPONSE GROUPS.—(A) The Secretary of the department in which the Coast Guard is operating shall establish in each Coast Guard district a Coast Guard District Response Group.

(B) Each Coast Guard District Response Group shall consist of—

(i) the Coast Guard personnel and equipment, including firefighting equipment, of each port within the district;

(ii) additional prepositioned equipment; and

(iii) a district response advisory staff.

(C) Coast Guard district response groups—

(i) shall provide technical assistance, equipment, and other resources when required by a Federal On-Scene Coordinator;

(ii) shall maintain all Coast Guard response equipment within its district;

(iii) may provide technical assistance in the preparation of Area Contingency Plans required under paragraph (4); and

(iv) shall review each of those plans that affect its area of geographic responsibility.

(4) Area committees and area contingency plans.—(A) There is established for each area designated by the President an Area Committee comprised of members appointed by the President from qualified—

(i) personnel of Federal, State, and local agencies; and

(ii) members of federally recognized Indian tribes, where applicable.

(B) Each Area Committee, under the direction of the Federal On-Scene Coordinator for its area, shall—

(i) prepare for its area the Area Contingency Plan required under subparagraph (C);

(ii) work with State, local, and tribal officials to enhance the contingency planning of those officials and to assure preplanning of joint response efforts, including appropriate procedures for mechanical recovery, dispersal, shoreline cleanup, protection of sensitive environmental areas, and protection, rescue, and rehabilitation of fisheries and wildlife, including advance planning with respect to the closing and reopening of fishing areas following a discharge; and

(iii) work with State, local, and tribal officials to expedite decisions for the use of dispersants and other mitigating substances and devices.

(C) Each Area Committee shall prepare and submit to the President for approval an Area Contingency Plan for its area. The Area Contingency Plan shall—

(i) when implemented in conjunction with the National Contingency Plan, be adequate to remove a worst case discharge, and to mitigate or prevent a substantial threat of such a discharge, from a vessel, offshore facility, or onshore facility operating in or near the area;

(ii) describe the area covered by the plan, including the areas of special economic or environmental importance that might be damaged by a discharge;

(iii) describe in detail the responsibilities of an owner or operator and of Federal, State, and local agencies in removing a discharge, and in mitigating or preventing a substantial threat of a discharge;

(iv) list the equipment (including firefighting equipment), dispersants or other mitigating substances and devices, and personnel available to an owner or operator, Federal, State, and local agencies, and tribal governments, to ensure an effective and immediate removal of a discharge, and to ensure mitigation or prevention of a substantial threat of a discharge;

(v) compile a list of local scientists, both inside and outside Federal

Government service, with expertise in the environmental effects of spills of the types of oil typically transported in the area, who may be contacted to provide information or, where appropriate, participate in meetings of the scientific support team convened in response to a spill, and describe the procedures to be followed for obtaining an expedited decision regarding the use of dispersants;

(vi) describe in detail how the plan is integrated into other Area Contingency Plans and vessel, offshore facility, and onshore facility response plans approved under this subsection, and into operating procedures of the National Response Unit;

(vii) include a framework for advance planning and decisionmaking with respect to the closing and reopening of fishing areas following a discharge, including protocols and standards for the closing and reopening of fishing areas;

(viii) include any other information the President requires; and

(ix) be updated periodically by the Area Committee.

(D) The President shall—

(i) review and approve Area Contingency Plans under this paragraph; and

(ii) periodically review Area Contingency Plans so approved.

(5) Tank vessel, nontank vessel, and facility response plans.—(A)(i) The President shall issue regulations which require an owner or operator of a tank vessel or facility described in subparagraph (C) to prepare and submit to the President a plan for responding, to the maximum extent practicable, to a worst case discharge, and to a substantial threat of such a discharge, of oil or a hazardous substance.

(ii) The President shall also issue regulations which require an owner or operator of a nontank vessel to prepare and submit to the President a plan for responding, to the maximum extent practicable, to a worst case discharge, and to a substantial threat of such a discharge, of oil.

(B) The Secretary of the Department in which the Coast Guard is operating may issue regulations which require an owner or operator of a tank vessel, a nontank vessel, or a facility described in subparagraph (C) that transfers noxious liquid substances in bulk to or from a vessel to prepare and submit to the Secretary a plan for responding, to the maximum extent practicable, to a worst case discharge, and to a substantial threat of such a discharge, of a noxious liquid substance that is not designated as a hazardous substance or regulated as oil in any other law or regulation. For purposes of this paragraph, the term noxious liquid substance has the same meaning when that term is used in the MARPOL Protocol described in section 2(a)(3) of the Act to Prevent Pollution from Ships (33 U.S.C. 1901(a)(3)).

(C) The tank vessels, nontank vessels, and facilities referred to in subparagraphs (A) and (B) are the following:

(i) A tank vessel, as defined under section 2101 of title 46, United States

Code.

(ii) A nontank vessel.

(iii) An offshore facility.

(iv) An onshore facility that, because of its location, could reasonably be expected to cause substantial harm to the environment by discharging into or on the navigable waters, adjoining shorelines, or the exclusive economic zone.

(D) A response plan required under this paragraph shall—

(i) be consistent with the requirements of the National Contingency Plan and Area Contingency Plans;

(ii) identify the qualified individual having full authority to implement removal actions, and require immediate communications between that individual and the appropriate Federal official and the persons providing personnel and equipment pursuant to clause (iii);

(iii) identify, and ensure by contract or other means approved by the President the availability of, private personnel and equipment necessary to remove to the maximum extent practicable a worst case discharge (including a discharge resulting from fire or explosion), and to mitigate or prevent a substantial threat of such a discharge;

(iv) describe the training, equipment testing, periodic unannounced drills, and response actions of persons on the vessel or at the facility, to be carried out under the plan to ensure the safety of the vessel or facility and to mitigate or prevent the discharge, or the substantial threat of a discharge;

(v) be updated periodically; and

(vi) be resubmitted for approval of each significant change.

(E) With respect to any response plan submitted under this paragraph for an onshore facility that, because of its location, could reasonably be expected to cause significant and substantial harm to the environment by discharging into or on the navigable waters or adjoining shorelines or the exclusive economic zone, and with respect to each response plan submitted under this paragraph for a tank vessel, nontank vessel, or offshore facility, the President shall—

(i) promptly review such response plan;

(ii) require amendments to any plan that does not meet the requirements of this paragraph;

(iii) approve any plan that meets the requirements of this paragraph;

(iv) review each plan periodically thereafter; and

(v) in the case of a plan for a nontank vessel, consider any applicable State-mandated response plan in effect on the date of the enactment of the Coast Guard and Maritime Transportation Act of 2004 and ensure consistency to the extent practicable.

(F)[16] A tank vessel, nontank vessel, offshore facility, or onshore facility required to prepare a response plan under this subsection may not handle, store, or transport oil unless—

[16] Subparagraph (F) of section 311(j)(5) (as redesignated) shall take effect 36 months (August 18, 1993) after the date of the enactment of Public Law 101-380. See P.L. 101-380, sec. 4202(b)(4)(C), 104 Stat. 532.

(i) in the case of a tank vessel, nontank vessel, offshore facility, or onshore facility for which a response plan is reviewed by the President under subparagraph (E), the plan has been approved by the President; and

(ii) the vessel or facility is operating in compliance with the plan.

(G) Notwithstanding subparagraph (E), the President may authorize a tank vessel, nontank vessel, offshore facility, or onshore facility to operate without a response plan approved under this paragraph, until not later than 2 years after the date of the submission to the President of a plan for the tank vessel, nontank vessel, or facility, if the owner or operator certifies that the owner or operator has ensured by contract or other means approved by the President the availability of private personnel and equipment necessary to respond, to the maximum extent practicable, to a worst case discharge or a substantial threat of such a discharge.

(H) The owner or operator of a tank vessel, nontank vessel, offshore facility, or onshore facility may not claim as a defense to liability under title I of the Oil Pollution Act of 1990 that the owner or operator was acting in accordance with an approved response plan.

(I) The Secretary shall maintain, in the Vessel Identification System established under chapter 125 of title 46, United States Code, the dates of approval and review of a response plan under this paragraph for each tank vessel and nontank vessel that is a vessel of the United States.

(6) Equipment requirements and inspection.—The President may require—

(A) periodic inspection of containment booms, skimmers, vessels, and other major equipment used to remove discharges; and

(B) vessels operating on navigable waters and carrying oil or a hazardous substance in bulk as cargo, and nontank vessels carrying oil of any kind as fuel for main propulsion, to carry appropriate removal equipment that employs the best technology economically feasible and that is compatible with the safe operation of the vessel.

(7) Area drills.— The President shall periodically conduct drills of removal capability, without prior notice, in areas for which Area Contingency Plans are required under this subsection and under relevant tank vessel, nontank vessel, and facility response plans. The drills may include participation by Federal, State, and local agencies, the owners and operators of vessels and facilities in the area, and private industry. The President may publish annual reports on these drills, including assessments of the effectiveness of the plans and a list of amendments made to improve plans.

(8) United states government not liable.— The United States Government is not liable for any damages arising from its actions or omissions relating to any

response plan required by this section.

(9) Western alaska oil spill planning criteria program.—

(A) Definitions.—In this paragraph:

(i) Alternative planning criteria.— The term alternative planning criteria means criteria submitted under section 155.1065 or 155.5067 of title 33, Code of Federal Regulations (as in effect on the date of enactment of this paragraph), for vessel response plans.

(ii) Prince william sound captain of the port zone.— The term Prince William Sound Captain of the Port Zone means the area described in section 3.85–15(b) of title 33, Code of Federal Regulations (or successor regulations).

(iii) Secretary.— The term Secretary means the Secretary of the department in which the Coast Guard is operating.

(iv) Vessel response plan.— The term vessel response plan means a plan required to be submitted by the owner or operator of a tank vessel or a nontank vessel under regulations issued by the President under paragraph (5).

(v) Western alaska captain of the port zone.— The term Western Alaska Captain of the Port Zone means the area described in section 3.85–15(a) of title 33, Code of Federal Regulations (as in effect on the date of enactment of this paragraph).

(B) Requirement.— Except as provided in subparagraph (I), for any part of the area of responsibility of the Western Alaska Captain of the Port Zone or the Prince William Sound Captain of the Port Zone for which the Secretary has determined that the national planning criteria established pursuant to this subsection are inappropriate for a vessel operating in such area, a vessel response plan with respect to a discharge of oil for such a vessel shall comply with the Western Alaska oil spill planning criteria established under subparagraph (D)(i).

(C) Relation to national planning criteria.— The Western Alaska oil spill planning criteria established under subparagraph (D)(i) shall, with respect to a discharge of oil from a vessel described in subparagraph (B), apply in lieu of any alternative planning criteria accepted for vessels operating, prior to the date on which the Western Alaska oil spill planning criteria are established, in any part of the area of responsibility of the Western Alaska Captain of the Port Zone or the Prince William Sound Captain of the Port Zone for which the Secretary has determined that the national planning criteria established pursuant to this subsection are inappropriate for a vessel operating in such area.

(D) Establishment of western alaska oil spill planning criteria.—

(i) In general.—The President, acting through the Commandant, in consultation with the Western Alaska Oil Spill Criteria Program Manager selected under section 323 of title 14, United States Code, shall establish—

(I) Western Alaska oil spill planning criteria for a worst case discharge of oil, and a substantial threat of such a discharge, within any part of the area of responsibility of the Western Alaska Captain of the Port Zone or Prince William Sound Captain of the Port Zone for which the Secretary has determined that the national planning criteria established pursuant to this subsection are inappropriate for a vessel operating in such area; and

(II) standardized submission, review, approval, and compliance verification processes for the Western Alaska oil spill planning criteria established under this clause, including the quantity and frequency of drills and on-site verifications of vessel response plans approved pursuant to such planning criteria.

(ii) Development of subregions.—

(I) Development.— After establishing the Western Alaska oil spill planning criteria under clause (i), and if necessary to adequately reflect the needs and capabilities of various locations within the Western Alaska Captain of the Port Zone, the President, acting through the Commandant, and in consultation with the Western Alaska Oil Spill Criteria Program Manager selected under section 323 of title 14, United States Code, may develop subregions for which planning criteria may differ from planning criteria for other subregions in the Western Alaska Captain of the Port Zone.

(II) Limitation.— Any planning criteria for a subregion developed under this clause may not be less stringent than the Western Alaska oil spill planning criteria established under clause (i).

(iii) Assessment.—

(I) In general.— Prior to developing a subregion, the President, acting through the Commandant, shall conduct an assessment on any potential impacts to the entire Western Alaska Captain of the Port Zone to include quantity and availability of response resources in the proposed subregion and in surrounding areas and any changes or impacts to surrounding areas resulting in the development of a subregion with different standards.

(II) Consultation.— In conducting an assessment under this clause, the President, acting through the Commandant, shall consult with State and local governments, Tribes (as defined in section 323 of title 14, United States Code), the owners and operators that would operate under the proposed subregions, oil spill removal organizations, Alaska Native organizations, and environmental nongovernmental organizations, and shall take into account any experience with the prior use of subregions within the State of Alaska.

(III) Submission.— The President, acting through the Commandant, shall submit the results of an assessment conducted under this clause to the Committee on Transportation and Infrastructure of the House of Representatives and the Committee on Commerce, Science, and

Transportation of the Senate.

(E) INCLUSIONS.—

(i) REQUIREMENTS.—The Western Alaska oil spill planning criteria established under subparagraph (D)(i) shall include planning criteria for the following:

(I) Mechanical oil spill response resources that are required to be located within any part of the area of responsibility of the Western Alaska Captain of the Port Zone or the Prince William Sound Captain of the Port Zone for which the Secretary has determined that the national planning criteria established pursuant to this subsection are inappropriate for a vessel operating in such area.

(II) Response times for mobilization of oil spill response resources and arrival on the scene of a worst case discharge of oil, or substantial threat of such a discharge, occurring within such part of such area.

(III) Pre-identified vessels for oil spill response that are capable of operating in the ocean environment.

(IV) Ensuring the availability of at least 1 oil spill removal organization that is classified by the Coast Guard and that—

(aa) is capable of responding in all operating environments in such part of such area;

(bb) controls oil spill response resources of dedicated and nondedicated resources within such part of such area, through ownership, contracts, agreements, or other means approved by the President, sufficient—

(AA) to mobilize and sustain a response to a worst case discharge of oil; and

(BB) to contain, recover, and temporarily store discharged oil;

(cc) has pre-positioned oil spill response resources in strategic locations throughout such part of such area in a manner that ensures the ability to support response personnel, marine operations, air cargo, or other related logistics infrastructure;

(dd) has temporary storage capability using both dedicated and non-dedicated assets located within such part of such area;

(ee) has non-mechanical oil spill response resources capable of responding to a discharge of persistent oil and a discharge of nonpersistent oil, whether the discharged oil was carried by a vessel as fuel or cargo; and

(ff) has wildlife response resources for primary, secondary, and tertiary responses to support carcass collection, sampling, deterrence, rescue, and rehabilitation of birds, sea turtles, marine mammals, fishery resources, and other wildlife.

(V) With respect to tank barges carrying nonpersistent oil in bulk as cargo, oil spill response resources that are required to be carried on board.

(VI) Specifying a minimum length of time that approval of a vessel response plan under this paragraph is valid.

(VII) Managing wildlife protection and rehabilitation, including identified wildlife protection and rehabilitation resources in that area.

(ii) ADDITIONAL CONSIDERATIONS.—The Western Alaska oil spill planning criteria established under subparagraph (D)(i) may include planning criteria for the following:

(I) Vessel routing measures consistent with international routing measure deviation protocols.

(II) Maintenance of real-time continuous vessel tracking, monitoring, and engagement protocols with the ability to detect and address vessel operation anomalies.

(F) REQUIREMENT FOR APPROVAL.— The President may approve a vessel response plan for a vessel under this paragraph only if the owner or operator of the vessel demonstrates the availability of the oil spill response resources required to be included in the vessel response plan under the Western Alaska oil spill planning criteria established under subparagraph (D)(i).

(G) PERIODIC AUDITS.— The Secretary shall conduct periodic audits to ensure compliance of vessel response plans and oil spill removal organizations within the Western Alaska Captain of the Port Zone and the Prince William Sound Captain of the Port Zone with the Western Alaska oil spill planning criteria established under subparagraph (D)(i).

(H) REVIEW OF DETERMINATION.— Not less frequently than once every 5 years, the Secretary shall review each determination of the Secretary under subparagraph (B) that the national planning criteria established pursuant to this subsection are inappropriate for a vessel operating in the area of responsibility of the Western Alaska Captain of the Port Zone and the Prince William Sound Captain of the Port Zone.

(I) VESSELS IN COOK INLET.— Unless otherwise authorized by the Secretary, a vessel may only operate in Cook Inlet, Alaska, under a vessel response plan approved under paragraph (5) that meets the requirements of the national planning criteria established pursuant to this subsection.

(J) SAVINGS PROVISIONS.—Nothing in this paragraph affects—

(i) the requirements under this subsection applicable to vessel response plans for vessels operating within the area of responsibility of the Western Alaska Captain of the Port Zone, within Cook Inlet, Alaska;

(ii) the requirements under this subsection applicable to vessel response plans for vessels operating within the area of responsibility of the Prince William Sound Captain of the Port Zone that are subject to section 5005 of the Oil Pollution Act of 1990 (33 U.S.C. 2735); or

(iii) the authority of a Federal On-Scene Coordinator to use any available resources when responding to an oil spill.

[Subsection (k) was repealed by sec. 2002(b)(2) of P.L. 101-380.]

(l) The President is authorized to delegate the administration of this section to the heads of those Federal departments, agencies, and instrumentalities which he determines to be appropriate. Each such department, agency, and instrumentality, in order to avoid duplication of effort, shall, whenever appropriate, utilize the personnel, services, and facilities of other Federal departments, agencies, and instrumentalities.

(m) ADMINISTRATIVE PROVISIONS.—

(1) FOR VESSELS.—Anyone authorized by the President to enforce the provisions of this section with respect to any vessel may, except as to public vessels—

(A) board and inspect any vessel upon the navigable waters of the United States or the waters of the contiguous zone,

(B) with or without a warrant, arrest any person who in the presence or view of the authorized person violates the provisions of this section or any regulation issued thereunder, and

(C) execute any warrant or other process issued by an officer or court of competent jurisdiction.

(2) FOR FACILITIES.—

(A) RECORDKEEPING.— Whenever required to carry out the purposes of this section, the Administrator, the Secretary of Transportation, or the Secretary of the Department in which the Coast Guard is operating shall require the owner or operator of a facility to which this section applies to establish and maintain such records, make such reports, install, use, and maintain such monitoring equipment and methods, and provide such other information as the Administrator, the Secretary of Transportation, or Secretary, as the case may be, may require to carry out the objectives of this section.

(B) ENTRY AND INSPECTION.—Whenever required to carry out the purposes of this section, the Administrator, the Secretary of Transportation, or the Secretary of the Department in which the Coast Guard is operating or an authorized representative of the Administrator, the Secretary of Transportation, or Secretary, upon presentation of appropriate credentials, may—

(i) enter and inspect any facility to which this section applies, including any facility at which any records are required to be maintained under subparagraph (A); and

(ii) at reasonable times, have access to and copy any records, take samples, and inspect any monitoring equipment or methods required under subparagraph (A).

(C) ARRESTS AND EXECUTION OF WARRANTS.—Anyone authorized by the Administrator or the Secretary of the department in which the Coast Guard is operating to enforce the provisions of this section with respect to any facility may—

(i) with or without a warrant, arrest any person who violates the provisions of this section or any regulation issued thereunder in the presence or view of the person so authorized; and

(ii) execute any warrant or process issued by an officer or court of competent jurisdiction.

(D) PUBLIC ACCESS.— Any records, reports, or information obtained under this paragraph shall be subject to the same public access and disclosure requirements which are applicable to records, reports, and information obtained pursuant to section 308.

(n) The several district courts of the United States are invested with jurisdiction for any actions, other than actions pursuant to subsection (i)(1), arising under this section. In the case of Guam and the Trust Territory of the Pacific Islands, such actions may be brought in the district court of Guam, and in the case of the Virgin Islands such actions may be brought in the district court of the Virgin Islands. In the case of American Samoa and the Trust Territory of the Pacific Islands, such actions may be brought in the District Court of the United States for the District of Hawaii and such court shall have jurisdiction of such actions. In the case of the Canal Zone, such actions may be brought in the United States District Court for the District of the Canal Zone.

(o)(1) Nothing in this section shall affect or modify in any way the obligations of any owner or operator of any vessel, or of any owner or operator of any onshore facility or offshore facility to any person or agency under any provision of law for damages to any publicly owned or privately owned property resulting from a discharge of any oil or hazardous substance or from the removal of any such oil or hazardous substance.

(2) Nothing in this section shall be construed as preempting any State or political subdivision thereof from imposing any requirement or liability with respect to the discharge of oil or hazardous substance into any waters within such State, or with respect to any removal activities related to such discharge.

(3) Nothing in this section shall be construed as affecting or modifying any other existing authority of any Federal department, agency, or instrumentality, relative to onshore or offshore facilities under this Act or any other provision of law, or to affect any State or local law not in conflict with this section.

[Subsection (p) was repealed by sec. 2002(b)(4) of Public Law 101-380, 104 Stat. 507.]

(q) The President is authorized to establish, with respect to any class or category of onshore or offshore facilities, a maximum limit of liability under subsections (f)(2) and (3) of this section of less than $50,000,000, but not less than, $8,000,000.

(r) Nothing in this section shall be construed to impose, or authorize the imposition of, any limitation on liability under the Outer Continental Shelf Lands Act or the Deepwater Port Act of 1974.

(s) The Oil Spill Liability Trust Fund established under section 9509 of the Internal Revenue Code of 1986 (26 U.S.C. 9509) shall be available to carry out subsections (b), (c), (d), (j), and (l) as those subsections apply to discharges, and substantial threats of discharges, of oil. Any amounts received by the United States under this section shall be deposited in the Oil Spill Liability Trust Fund except as provided in subsection (t).

(t) GULF COAST RESTORATION AND RECOVERY.—

(1) STATE ALLOCATION AND EXPENDITURES.—

(A) IN GENERAL.— Of the total amounts made available in any fiscal year from the Trust Fund, 35 percent shall be available, in accordance with the requirements of this section, to the Gulf Coast States in equal shares for expenditure for ecological and economic restoration of the Gulf Coast region in accordance with this subsection.

(B) USE OF FUNDS.—

(i) ELIGIBLE ACTIVITIES IN THE GULF COAST REGION.—Subject to clause (iii), amounts provided to the Gulf Coast States under this subsection may only be used to carry out 1 or more of the following activities in the Gulf Coast region:

(I) Restoration and protection of the natural resources, ecosystems, fisheries, marine and wildlife habitats, beaches, and coastal wetlands of the Gulf Coast region.

(II) Mitigation of damage to fish, wildlife, and natural resources.

(III) Implementation of a federally approved marine, coastal, or comprehensive conservation management plan, including fisheries monitoring.

(IV) Workforce development and job creation.

(V) Improvements to or on State parks located in coastal areas affected by the Deepwater Horizon oil spill.

(VI) Infrastructure projects benefitting the economy or ecological resources, including port infrastructure.

(VII) Coastal flood protection and related infrastructure.

(VIII) Planning assistance.

(IX) Administrative costs of complying with this subsection.

(ii) ACTIVITIES TO PROMOTE TOURISM AND SEAFOOD IN THE GULF COAST REGION.—Amounts provided to the Gulf Coast States under this subsection may be used to carry out 1 or more of the following activities:

(I) Promotion of tourism in the Gulf Coast Region, including recreational fishing.

(II) Promotion of the consumption of seafood harvested from the Gulf Coast Region.

(iii) LIMITATION.—

(I) IN GENERAL.— Of the amounts received by a Gulf Coast State under this subsection, not more than 3 percent may be used for administrative costs eligible under clause (i)(IX).

(II) CLAIMS FOR COMPENSATION.— Activities funded under this subsection may not be included in any claim for compensation paid out by the Oil Spill Liability Trust Fund after the date of enactment of this subsection.

(C) COASTAL POLITICAL SUBDIVISIONS.—

(i) DISTRIBUTION.—In the case of a State where the coastal zone includes the entire State—

(I) 75 percent of funding shall be provided directly to the 8 disproportionately affected counties impacted by the Deepwater Horizon oil spill; and

(II) 25 percent shall be provided directly to nondisproportionately impacted counties within the State.

(ii) NONDISPROPORTIONATELY IMPACTED COUNTIES.—The total amounts made available to coastal political subdivisions in the State of Florida under clause (i)(II) shall be distributed according to the following weighted formula:

(I) 34 percent based on the weighted average of the population of the county.

(II) 33 percent based on the weighted average of the county per capita sales tax collections estimated for fiscal year 2012.

(III) 33 percent based on the inverse proportion of the weighted average distance from the Deepwater Horizon oil rig to each of the nearest and farthest points of the shoreline.

(D) LOUISIANA.—

(i) IN GENERAL.—Of the total amounts made available to the State of Louisiana under this paragraph:

(I) 70 percent shall be provided directly to the State in accordance with this subsection.

(II) 30 percent shall be provided directly to parishes in the coastal zone (as defined in section 304 of the Coastal Zone Management Act of 1972 (16 U.S.C. 1453)) of the State of Louisiana according to the following weighted formula:

(aa) 40 percent based on the weighted average of miles of the parish shoreline oiled.

(bb) 40 percent based on the weighted average of the population of the parish.

(cc) 20 percent based on the weighted average of the land mass of the parish.

(ii) CONDITIONS.—

(I) LAND USE PLAN.— As a condition of receiving amounts allocated under this paragraph, the chief executive of the eligible parish shall certify to the Governor of the State that the parish has completed a comprehensive land use plan.

(II) OTHER CONDITIONS.— A coastal political subdivision receiving funding under this paragraph shall meet all of the conditions in subparagraph (E).

(E) CONDITIONS.—As a condition of receiving amounts from the Trust Fund, a Gulf Coast State, including the entities described in subparagraph (F), or a coastal political subdivision shall—

(i) agree to meet such conditions, including audit requirements, as the Secretary of the Treasury determines necessary to ensure that amounts disbursed from the Trust Fund will be used in accordance with this subsection;

(ii) certify in such form and in such manner as the Secretary of the Treasury determines necessary that the project or program for which the Gulf Coast State or coastal political subdivision is requesting amounts—

(I) is designed to restore and protect the natural resources, ecosystems, fisheries, marine and wildlife habitats, beaches, coastal wetlands, or economy of the Gulf Coast;

(II) carries out 1 or more of the activities described in clauses (i) and (ii) of subparagraph (B);

(III) was selected based on meaningful input from the public, including broad-based participation from individuals, businesses, and nonprofit organizations; and

(IV) in the case of a natural resource protection or restoration project, is based on the best available science;

(iii) certify that the project or program and the awarding of a contract for the expenditure of amounts received under this paragraph are consistent with the standard procurement rules and regulations governing a comparable project or program in that State, including all applicable competitive bidding and audit requirements; and

(iv) develop and submit a multiyear implementation plan for the use of such amounts, which may include milestones, projected completion of each activity, and a mechanism to evaluate the success of each activity in helping to restore and protect the Gulf Coast region impacted by the Deepwater Horizon oil spill.

(F) APPROVAL BY STATE ENTITY, TASK FORCE, OR AGENCY.—The following Gulf Coast State entities, task forces, or agencies shall carry out the duties of a Gulf Coast State pursuant to this paragraph:

(i) ALABAMA.—

(I) IN GENERAL.—In the State of Alabama, the Alabama Gulf Coast Recovery Council, which shall be comprised of only the following:

(aa) The Governor of Alabama, who shall also serve as Chairperson and preside over the meetings of the Alabama Gulf Coast Recovery Council.

(bb) The Director of the Alabama State Port Authority, who shall also serve as Vice Chairperson and preside over the meetings of the Alabama Gulf Coast Recovery Council in the absence of the Chairperson.

(cc) The Chairman of the Baldwin County Commission.

(dd) The President of the Mobile County Commission.

(ee) The Mayor of the city of Bayou La Batre.

(ff) The Mayor of the town of Dauphin Island.

(gg) The Mayor of the city of Fairhope.

(hh) The Mayor of the city of Gulf Shores.

(ii) The Mayor of the city of Mobile.

(jj) The Mayor of the city of Orange Beach.

(II) VOTE.— Each member of the Alabama Gulf Coast Recovery Council shall be entitled to 1 vote.

(III) MAJORITY VOTE.— All decisions of the Alabama Gulf Coast Recovery Council shall be made by majority vote.

(IV) LIMITATION ON ADMINISTRATIVE EXPENSES.— Administrative duties for the Alabama Gulf Coast Recovery Council may only be performed by public officials and employees that are subject to the ethics laws of the State of Alabama.

(ii) LOUISIANA.— In the State of Louisiana, the Coastal Protection and Restoration Authority of Louisiana.

(iii) MISSISSIPPI.— In the State of Mississippi, the Mississippi Department of Environmental Quality.

(iv) TEXAS.— In the State of Texas, the Office of the Governor or an appointee of the Office of the Governor.

(G) COMPLIANCE WITH ELIGIBLE ACTIVITIES.—If the Secretary of the Treasury determines that an expenditure by a Gulf Coast State or coastal political subdivision of amounts made available under this subsection does not meet one of the activities described in clauses (i) and (ii) of subparagraph (B), the Secretary shall make no additional amounts from the Trust Fund available to that Gulf Coast State or coastal political subdivision until such time as an amount equal to the amount expended for the unauthorized use—

(i) has been deposited by the Gulf Coast State or coastal political subdivision in the Trust Fund; or

(ii) has been authorized by the Secretary of the Treasury for expenditure by the Gulf Coast State or coastal political subdivision for a project or program that meets the requirements of this subsection.

(H) COMPLIANCE WITH CONDITIONS.— If the Secretary of the Treasury determines that a Gulf Coast State or coastal political subdivision does not meet the requirements of this paragraph, including the conditions of subparagraph (E), where applicable, the Secretary of the Treasury shall make no amounts from the Trust Fund available to that Gulf Coast State or coastal political subdivision until all conditions of this paragraph are met.

(I) PUBLIC INPUT.— In meeting any condition of this paragraph, a Gulf Coast

State may use an appropriate procedure for public consultation in that Gulf Coast State, including consulting with one or more established task forces or other entities, to develop recommendations for proposed projects and programs that would restore and protect the natural resources, ecosystems, fisheries, marine and wildlife habitats, beaches, coastal wetlands, and economy of the Gulf Coast.

(J) PREVIOUSLY APPROVED PROJECTS AND PROGRAMS.—A Gulf Coast State or coastal political subdivision shall be considered to have met the conditions of subparagraph (E) for a specific project or program if, before the date of enactment of the Resources and Ecosystems Sustainability, Tourist Opportunities, and Revived Economies of the Gulf Coast States Act of 2012—

(i) the Gulf Coast State or coastal political subdivision has established conditions for carrying out projects and programs that are substantively the same as the conditions described in subparagraph (E); and

(ii) the applicable project or program carries out 1 or more of the activities described in clauses (i) and (ii) of subparagraph (B).

(K) LOCAL PREFERENCE.— In awarding contracts to carry out a project or program under this paragraph, a Gulf Coast State or coastal political subdivision may give a preference to individuals and companies that reside in, are headquartered in, or are principally engaged in business in the State of project execution.

(L) UNUSED FUNDS.— Funds allocated to a State or coastal political subdivision under this paragraph shall remain in the Trust Fund until such time as the State or coastal political subdivision develops and submits a plan identifying uses for those funds in accordance with subparagraph (E)(iv).

(M) JUDICIAL REVIEW.— If the Secretary of the Treasury determines that a Gulf Coast State or coastal political subdivision does not meet the requirements of this paragraph, including the conditions of subparagraph (E), the Gulf Coast State or coastal political subdivision may obtain expedited judicial review within 90 days after that decision in a district court of the United States, of appropriate jurisdiction and venue, that is located within the State seeking the review.

(N) COST-SHARING.—

(i) IN GENERAL.— A Gulf Coast State or coastal political subdivision may use, in whole or in part, amounts made available under this paragraph to that Gulf Coast State or coastal political subdivision to satisfy the non-Federal share of the cost of any project or program authorized by Federal law that is an eligible activity described in clauses (i) and (ii) of subparagraph (B).

(ii) EFFECT ON OTHER FUNDS.— The use of funds made available from the Trust Fund to satisfy the non-Federal share of the cost of a project or program that meets the requirements of clause (i) shall not affect the priority in which other Federal funds are allocated or awarded.

(2) COUNCIL ESTABLISHMENT AND ALLOCATION.—

(A) IN GENERAL.— Of the total amount made available in any fiscal year from the Trust Fund, 30 percent shall be disbursed to the Council to carry out the Comprehensive Plan.

(B) COUNCIL EXPENDITURES.—

(i) IN GENERAL.— In accordance with this paragraph, the Council shall expend funds made available from the Trust Fund to undertake projects and programs, using the best available science, that would restore and protect the natural resources, ecosystems, fisheries, marine and wildlife habitats, beaches, coastal wetlands, and economy of the Gulf Coast.

(ii) ALLOCATION AND EXPENDITURE PROCEDURES.— The Secretary of the Treasury shall develop such conditions, including audit requirements, as the Secretary of the Treasury determines necessary to ensure that amounts disbursed from the Trust Fund to the Council to implement the Comprehensive Plan will be used in accordance with this paragraph.

(iii) ADMINISTRATIVE EXPENSES.— Of the amounts received by the Council under this paragraph, not more than 3 percent may be used for administrative expenses, including staff.

(C) GULF COAST ECOSYSTEM RESTORATION COUNCIL.—

(i) ESTABLISHMENT.— There is established as an independent entity in the Federal Government a council to be known as the Gulf Coast Ecosystem Restoration Council.

(ii) MEMBERSHIP.—The Council shall consist of the following members, or in the case of a Federal agency, a designee at the level of the Assistant Secretary or the equivalent:

(I) The Secretary of the Interior.

(II) The Secretary of the Army.

(III) The Secretary of Commerce.

(IV) The Administrator of the Environmental Protection Agency.

(V) The Secretary of Agriculture.

(VI) The head of the department in which the Coast Guard is operating.

(VII) The Governor of the State of Alabama.

(VIII) The Governor of the State of Florida.

(IX) The Governor of the State of Louisiana.

(X) The Governor of the State of Mississippi.

(XI) The Governor of the State of Texas.

(iii) ALTERNATE.— A Governor appointed to the Council by the President may designate an alternate to represent the Governor on the Council and vote on behalf of the Governor.

(iv) CHAIRPERSON.— From among the Federal agency members of the Council, the representatives of States on the Council shall select, and the

President shall appoint, 1 Federal member to serve as Chairperson of the Council.

(v) PRESIDENTIAL APPOINTMENT.— All Council members shall be appointed by the President.

(vi) COUNCIL ACTIONS.—

(I) IN GENERAL.—The following actions by the Council shall require the affirmative vote of the Chairperson and a majority of the State members to be effective:

(aa) Approval of a Comprehensive Plan and future revisions to a Comprehensive Plan.

(bb) Approval of State plans pursuant to paragraph (3)(B)(iv).

(cc) Approval of reports to Congress pursuant to clause (vii)(VII).

(dd) Approval of transfers pursuant to subparagraph (E)(ii)(I).

(ee) Other significant actions determined by the Council.

(II) QUORUM.— A majority of State members shall be required to be present for the Council to take any significant action.

(III) AFFIRMATIVE VOTE REQUIREMENT CONSIDERED MET.— For approval of State plans pursuant to paragraph (3)(B)(iv), the certification by a State member of the Council that the plan satisfies all requirements of clauses (i) and (ii) of paragraph (3)(B), when joined by an affirmative vote of the Federal Chairperson of the Council, shall be considered to satisfy the requirements for affirmative votes under subclause (I).

(IV) PUBLIC TRANSPARENCY.— Appropriate actions of the Council, including significant actions and associated deliberations, shall be made available to the public via electronic means prior to any vote.

(vii) DUTIES OF COUNCIL.—The Council shall—

(I) develop the Comprehensive Plan and future revisions to the Comprehensive Plan;

(II) identify as soon as practicable the projects that—

(aa) have been authorized prior to the date of enactment of this subsection but not yet commenced; and

(bb) if implemented quickly, would restore and protect the natural resources, ecosystems, fisheries, marine and wildlife habitats, beaches, barrier islands, dunes, and coastal wetlands of the Gulf Coast region;

(III) establish such other 1 or more advisory committees as may be necessary to assist the Council, including a scientific advisory committee and a committee to advise the Council on public policy issues;

(IV) collect and consider scientific and other research associated with restoration of the Gulf Coast ecosystem, including research, observation, and monitoring carried out pursuant to sections 1604 and 1605 of the Resources and Ecosystems Sustainability, Tourist Opportunities, and Revived Economies of the Gulf Coast States Act of 2012;

(V) develop standard terms to include in contracts for projects and programs awarded pursuant to the Comprehensive Plan that provide a preference to individuals and companies that reside in, are headquartered in, or are principally engaged in business in a Gulf Coast State;

(VI) prepare an integrated financial plan and recommendations for coordinated budget requests for the amounts proposed to be expended by the Federal agencies represented on the Council for projects and programs in the Gulf Coast States; and

(VII) submit to Congress an annual report that—

(aa) summarizes the policies, strategies, plans, and activities for addressing the restoration and protection of the Gulf Coast region;

(bb) describes the projects and programs being implemented to restore and protect the Gulf Coast region, including—

(AA) a list of each project and program;

(BB) an identification of the funding provided to projects and programs identified in subitem (AA);

(CC) an identification of each recipient for funding identified in subitem (BB); and

(DD) a description of the length of time and funding needed to complete the objectives of each project and program identified in subitem (AA);

(cc) makes such recommendations to Congress for modifications of existing laws as the Council determines necessary to implement the Comprehensive Plan;

(dd) reports on the progress on implementation of each project or program—

(AA) after 3 years of ongoing activity of the project or program, if applicable; and

(BB) on completion of the project or program;

(ee) includes the information required to be submitted under section 1605(c)(4) of the Resources and Ecosystems Sustainability, Tourist Opportunities, and Revived Economies of the Gulf Coast States Act of 2012; and

(ff) submits the reports required under item (dd) to—

(AA) the Committee on Science, Space, and Technology, the Committee on Natural Resources, the Committee on Transportation and Infrastructure, and the Committee on Appropriations of the House of Representatives; and

(BB) the Committee on Environment and Public Works, the Committee on Commerce, Science, and Transportation, the Committee on Energy and Natural Resources, and the Committee on Appropriations of the Senate.

(viii) Application of chapter 10 of title 5, United States code.— The Council, or any other advisory committee established under this subparagraph, shall not be considered an advisory committee under chapter 10 of title 5, United States Code.

(ix) Sunset.— The authority for the Council, and any other advisory committee established under this subparagraph, shall terminate on the date all funds in the Trust Fund have been expended.

(D) Comprehensive plan.—

(i) Proposed plan.—

(I) In general.— Not later than 180 days after the date of enactment of the Resources and Ecosystems Sustainability, Tourist Opportunities, and Revived Economies of the Gulf Coast States Act of 2012, the Chairperson, on behalf of the Council and after appropriate public input, review, and comment, shall publish a proposed plan to restore and protect the natural resources, ecosystems, fisheries, marine and wildlife habitats, beaches, and coastal wetlands of the Gulf Coast region.

(II) Inclusions.— The proposed plan described in subclause (I) shall include and incorporate the findings and information prepared by the President's Gulf Coast Restoration Task Force.

(ii) Publication.—

(I) Initial plan.— Not later than 1 year after the date of enactment of the Resources and Ecosystems Sustainability, Tourist Opportunities, and Revived Economies of the Gulf Coast States Act of 2012 and after notice and opportunity for public comment, the Chairperson, on behalf of the Council and after approval by the Council, shall publish in the Federal Register the initial Comprehensive Plan to restore and protect the natural resources, ecosystems, fisheries, marine and wildlife habitats, beaches, and coastal wetlands of the Gulf Coast region.

(II) Cooperation with gulf coast restoration task force.— The Council shall develop the initial Comprehensive Plan in close coordination with the President's Gulf Coast Restoration Task Force.

(III) Considerations.— In developing the initial Comprehensive Plan and subsequent updates, the Council shall consider all relevant findings, reports, or research prepared or funded under section 1604 or 1605 of the Resources and Ecosystems Sustainability, Tourist Opportunities, and Revived Economies of the Gulf Coast States Act of 2012.

(IV) Contents.—The initial Comprehensive Plan shall include—

(aa) such provisions as are necessary to fully incorporate in the Comprehensive Plan the strategy, projects, and programs recommended by the President's Gulf Coast Restoration Task Force;

(bb) a list of any project or program authorized prior to the date of enactment of this subsection but not yet commenced, the completion of which would further the purposes and goals of this subsection and of the Resources and Ecosystems Sustainability, Tourist Opportunities, and Revived Economies of the Gulf Coast States Act of 2012;

(cc) a description of the manner in which amounts from the Trust Fund projected to be made available to the Council for the succeeding 10 years will be allocated; and

(dd) subject to available funding in accordance with clause (iii), a prioritized list of specific projects and programs to be funded and carried out during the 3-year period immediately following the date of publication of the initial Comprehensive Plan, including a table that illustrates the distribution of projects and programs by the Gulf Coast State.

(V) Plan updates.—The Council shall update—

(aa) the Comprehensive Plan every 5 years in a manner comparable to the manner established in this subparagraph for each 5-year period for which amounts are expected to be made available to the Gulf Coast States from the Trust Fund; and

(bb) the 3-year list of projects and programs described in subclause (IV)(dd) annually.

(iii) Restoration priorities.—Except for projects and programs described in clause (ii)(IV)(bb), in selecting projects and programs to include on the 3-year list described in clause (ii)(IV)(dd), based on the best available science, the Council shall give highest priority to projects that address 1 or more of the following criteria:

(I) Projects that are projected to make the greatest contribution to restoring and protecting the natural resources, ecosystems, fisheries, marine and wildlife habitats, beaches, and coastal wetlands of the Gulf Coast region, without regard to geographic location within the Gulf Coast region.

(II) Large-scale projects and programs that are projected to substantially contribute to restoring and protecting the natural resources, ecosystems, fisheries, marine and wildlife habitats, beaches, and coastal wetlands of the Gulf Coast ecosystem.

(III) Projects contained in existing Gulf Coast State comprehensive plans for the restoration and protection of natural resources, ecosystems, fisheries, marine and wildlife habitats, beaches, and coastal wetlands of the Gulf Coast region.

(IV) Projects that restore long-term resiliency of the natural resources, ecosystems, fisheries, marine and wildlife habitats, beaches, and coastal wetlands most impacted by the Deepwater Horizon oil spill.

(E) Implementation.—

(i) In general.— The Council, acting through the Federal agencies represented on the Council and Gulf Coast States, shall expend funds made available from the Trust Fund to carry out projects and programs adopted in the Comprehensive Plan.

(ii) Administrative responsibility.—

(I) In general.— Primary authority and responsibility for each project and program included in the Comprehensive Plan shall be assigned by the Council to a Gulf Coast State represented on the Council or a Federal agency.

(II) Transfer of amounts.— Amounts necessary to carry out each project or program included in the Comprehensive Plan shall be transferred by the Secretary of the Treasury from the Trust Fund to that Federal agency or Gulf Coast State as the project or program is implemented, subject to such conditions as the Secretary of the Treasury, in consultation with the Secretary of the Interior and the Secretary of Commerce, established pursuant to section 1602 of the Resources and Ecosystems Sustainability, Tourist Opportunities, and Revived Economies of the Gulf Coast States Act of 2012.

(III) Limitation on transfers.—

(aa) Grants to nongovernmental entities.— In the case of funds transferred to a Federal or State agency under subclause (II), the agency shall not make 1 or more grants or cooperative agreements to a nongovernmental entity if the total amount provided to the entity would equal or exceed 10 percent of the total amount provided to the agency for that particular project or program, unless the 1 or more grants have been reported in accordance with item (bb).

(bb) Reporting of grantees.— At least 30 days prior to making a grant or entering into a cooperative agreement described in item (aa), the name of each grantee, including the amount and purpose of each grant or cooperative agreement, shall be published in the Federal Register and delivered to the congressional committees listed in subparagraph (C)(vii)(VII)(ff).

(cc) Annual reporting of grantees.— Annually, the name of each grantee, including the amount and purposes of each grant or cooperative agreement, shall be published in the Federal Register and delivered to Congress as part of the report submitted pursuant to subparagraph (C)(vii)(VII).

(IV) Project and program limitation.— The Council, a Federal agency, or a State may not carry out a project or program funded under this paragraph outside of the Gulf Coast region.

(F) Coordination.— The Council and the Federal members of the Council may develop memoranda of understanding establishing integrated funding and implementation plans among the member agencies and authorities.

(3) Oil spill restoration impact allocation.—

(A) In general.—

(i) Disbursement.— Of the total amount made available from the Trust Fund, 30 percent shall be disbursed pursuant to the formula in clause (ii) to the Gulf Coast States on the approval of the plan described in subparagraph (B)(i).

(ii) Formula.—Subject to subparagraph (B), for each Gulf Coast State, the amount disbursed under this paragraph shall be based on a formula established by the Council by regulation that is based on a weighted average of the following criteria:

(I) 40 percent based on the proportionate number of miles of shoreline in each Gulf Coast State that experienced oiling on or before April 10, 2011, compared to the total number of miles of shoreline that experienced oiling as a result of the Deepwater Horizon oil spill.

(II) 40 percent based on the inverse proportion of the average distance from the mobile offshore drilling unit *Deepwater Horizon* at the time of the explosion to the nearest and farthest point of the shoreline that experienced oiling of each Gulf Coast State.

(III) 20 percent based on the average population in the 2010 decennial census of coastal counties bordering the Gulf of Mexico within each Gulf Coast State.

(iii) Minimum allocation.— The amount disbursed to a Gulf Coast State for each fiscal year under clause (ii) shall be at least 5 percent of the total amounts made available under this paragraph.

(B) Disbursement of funds.—

(i) In general.—The Council shall disburse amounts to the respective Gulf Coast States in accordance with the formula developed under subparagraph (A) for projects, programs, and activities that will improve the ecosystems or economy of the Gulf Coast region, subject to the condition that each Gulf Coast State submits a plan for the expenditure of amounts disbursed under this paragraph that meets the following criteria:

(I) All projects, programs, and activities included in the plan are eligible activities pursuant to clauses (i) and (ii) of paragraph (1)(B).

(II) The projects, programs, and activities included in the plan contribute to the overall economic and ecological recovery of the Gulf Coast.

(III) The plan takes into consideration the Comprehensive Plan and is consistent with the goals and objectives of the Plan, as described in paragraph (2)(B)(i).

(ii) FUNDING.—

(I) IN GENERAL.— Except as provided in subclause (II), the plan described in clause (i) may use not more than 25 percent of the funding made available for infrastructure projects eligible under subclauses (VI) and (VII) of paragraph (1)(B)(i).

(II) EXCEPTION.—The plan described in clause (i) may propose to use more than 25 percent of the funding made available for infrastructure projects eligible under subclauses (VI) and (VII) of paragraph (1)(B)(i) if the plan certifies that—

(aa) ecosystem restoration needs in the State will be addressed by the projects in the proposed plan; and

(bb) additional investment in infrastructure is required to mitigate the impacts of the Deepwater Horizon Oil Spill to the ecosystem or economy.

(iii) DEVELOPMENT.—The plan described in clause (i) shall be developed by—

(I) in the State of Alabama, the Alabama Gulf Coast Recovery Council established under paragraph (1)(F)(i);

(II) in the State of Florida, a consortia[17] of local political subdivisions that includes at a minimum 1 representative of each affected county;

[17] So in law. Probably should read consortium.

(III) in the State of Louisiana, the Coastal Protection and Restoration Authority of Louisiana;

(IV) in the State of Mississippi, the Office of the Governor or an appointee of the Office of the Governor; and

(V) in the State of Texas, the Office of the Governor or an appointee of the Office of the Governor.

(iv) APPROVAL.— Not later than 60 days after the date on which a plan is submitted under clause (i), the Council shall approve or disapprove the plan based on the conditions of clause (i).

(C) DISAPPROVAL.—If the Council disapproves a plan pursuant to subparagraph (B)(iv), the Council shall—

(i) provide the reasons for disapproval in writing; and

(ii) consult with the State to address any identified deficiencies with the State plan.

(D) FAILURE TO SUBMIT ADEQUATE PLAN.— If a State fails to submit an adequate plan under this paragraph, any funds made available under this paragraph shall remain in the Trust Fund until such date as a plan is submitted and approved pursuant to this paragraph.

(E) JUDICIAL REVIEW.— If the Council fails to approve or take action within 60 days on a plan, as described in subparagraph (B)(iv), the State may obtain expedited judicial review within 90 days of that decision in a district court of the United States, of appropriate jurisdiction and venue, that is located within the State seeking the review.

(F) COST-SHARING.—

(i) IN GENERAL.—A Gulf Coast State or coastal political subdivision may use, in whole or in part, amounts made available to that Gulf Coast State or coastal political subdivision under this paragraph to satisfy the non-Federal share of any project or program that—

(I) is authorized by other Federal law; and

(II) is an eligible activity described in clause (i) or (ii) of paragraph (1)(B).

(ii) EFFECT ON OTHER FUNDS.— The use of funds made available from the Trust Fund under this paragraph to satisfy the non-Federal share of the cost of a project or program described in clause (i) shall not affect the priority in which other Federal funds are allocated or awarded.

(4) AUTHORIZATION OF INTEREST TRANSFERS.—Of the total amount made available for any fiscal year from the Trust Fund that is equal to the interest earned by the Trust Fund and proceeds from investments made by the Trust Fund in the preceding fiscal year—

(A) 50 percent shall be divided equally between—

(i) the Gulf Coast Ecosystem Restoration Science, Observation, Monitoring, and Technology program authorized in section 1604 of the Resources and Ecosystems Sustainability, Tourist Opportunities, and Revived Economies of the Gulf Coast States Act of 2012; and

(ii) the centers of excellence research grants authorized in section 1605 of that Act; and

(B) 50 percent shall be made available to the Gulf Coast Ecosystem Restoration Council to carry out the Comprehensive Plan pursuant to paragraph (2).

[33 U.S.C. 1321]

SEC. 312. MARINE SANITATION DEVICES; DISCHARGES INCIDENTAL TO THE NORMAL OPERATION OF VESSELS.

(a) DEFINITIONS.—In this section, the term—

(1) new vessel includes every description of watercraft or other artificial contrivance used, or capable of being used, as a means of transportation on the navigable waters, the construction of which is initiated after promulgation of standards and regulations under this section;

(2) existing vessel includes every description of watercraft or other artificial contrivance used, or capable of being used, as a means of transportation on the navigable waters, the construction of which is initiated before promulgation of

standards and regulations under this section;

(3) public vessel means a vessel owned or bareboat chartered and operated by the United States, by a State or political subdivision thereof, or by a foreign nation, except when such vessel is engaged in commerce;

(4) United States includes the States, the District of Columbia, the Commonwealth of Puerto Rico, the Virgin Islands, Guam, American Samoa, the Canal Zone, and the Trust Territory of the Pacific Islands;

(5) marine sanitation device includes any equipment for installation on board a vessel which is designed to receive, retain, treat, or discharge sewage, and any process to treat such sewage;

(6) sewage means human body wastes and the wastes from toilets and other receptacles intended to receive or retain body wastes except that, with respect to commercial vessels on the Great Lakes, such term shall include graywater;

(7) manufacture means any person engaged in the manufacturing, assembling, or importation of marine sanitation devices, marine pollution control device equipment, or vessels subject to standards and regulations promulgated under this section;

(8) person means an individual, partnership, firm, corporation, association, or agency of the United States, but does not include an individual on board a public vessel;

(9) discharge includes, but is not limited to, any spilling, leaking, pumping, pouring, emitting, emptying or dumping;

(10) commercial vessels means those vessels used in the business of transporting property for compensation or hire, or in transporting property in the business of the owner, lessee, or operator of the vessel;

(11) graywater means galley, bath, and shower water;

(12) discharge incidental to the normal operation of a vessel—

(A) means a discharge, including—

(i) graywater, bilge water, cooling water, weather deck runoff, ballast water, oil water separator effluent, and any other pollutant discharge from the operation of a marine propulsion system, shipboard maneuvering system, crew habitability system, or installed major equipment, such as an aircraft carrier elevator or a catapult, or from a protective, preservative, or absorptive application to the hull of the vessel; and

(ii) a discharge in connection with the testing, maintenance, and repair of a system described in clause (i) whenever the vessel is waterborne; and

(B) does not include—

(i) a discharge of rubbish, trash, garbage, or other such material discharged overboard;

(ii) an air emission resulting from the operation of a vessel propulsion system, motor driven equipment, or incinerator; or

(iii) a discharge that is not covered by part 122.3 of title 40, Code of Federal Regulations (as in effect on the date of the enactment of subsection (n));

(13) marine pollution control device means, except as provided in subsection (p), any equipment or management practice, for installation or use on board a vessel of the Armed Forces, that is—

(A) designed to receive, retain, treat, control, or discharge a discharge incidental to the normal operation of a vessel; and

(B) determined by the Administrator and the Secretary of Defense to be the most effective equipment or management practice to reduce the environmental impacts of the discharge consistent with the considerations set forth in subsection (n)(2)(B); and

(14) vessel of the Armed Forces means—

(A) any vessel owned or operated by the Department of Defense, other than a time or voyage chartered vessel; and

(B) any vessel owned or operated by the Department of Transportation that is designated by the Secretary of the department in which the Coast Guard is operating as a vessel equivalent to a vessel described in subparagraph (A).

(b)(1) As soon as possible, after the enactment of this section and subject to the provisions of section 104(j) of this Act, the Administrator, after consultation with the Secretary of the department in which the Coast Guard is operating, after giving appropriate consideration to the economic costs involved, and within the limits of available technology, shall promulgate Federal standards of performance for marine sanitation devices (hereinafter in this section referred to as standards) which shall be designed to prevent the discharge of untreated or inadequately treated sewage into or upon the navigable waters from new vessels and existing vessels, except vessels not equipped with installed toilet facilities. Such standards and standards established under subsection (c)(1)(B) of this section shall be consistent with maritime safety and the marine and navigation laws and regulations and shall be coordinated with the regulations issued under this subsection by the Secretary of the department in which the Coast Guard is operating. The Secretary of the department in which the Coast Guard is operating shall promulgate regulations, which are consistent with standards promulgated under this subsection and subsection (c) of this section and with maritime safety and the marine and navigation laws and regulations governing the design, construction, installation, and operation of any marine sanitation device on board such vessels.

(2) Any existing vessel equipped with a marine sanitation device on the date of promulgation of initial standards and regulations under this section, which device is in compliance with such initial standards and regulations, shall be deemed in compliance with this section until such time as the device is replaced or is found not to be in compliance with such initial standards and regulations.

(c)(1)(A) Initial standards and regulations under this section shall become effective for new vessels two years after promulgation; and for existing vessels five years after promulgation. Revisions of standards and regulations shall be effective upon promulgation, unless another effective date is specified, except that no revision shall take effect before the effective date of the standard or regulation being revised.

(B) The Administrator shall, with respect to commercial vessels on the Great Lakes, establish standards which require at a minimum the equivalent of secondary treatment as defined under section 304(d) of this Act. Such standards and regulations shall take effect for existing vessels after such time as the Administrator determines to be reasonable for the upgrading of marine sanitation devices to attain such standard.

(2) The Secretary of the department in which the Coast Guard is operating with regard to his regulatory authority established by this section, after consultation with the Administrator, may distinguish among classes, type[18], and sizes of vessels as well as between new and existing vessels, and may waive applicability of standards and regulations as necessary or appropriate for such classes, types, and sizes of vessels (including existing vessels equipped with marine sanitation devices on the date of promulgation of the initial standards required by this section), and, upon application, for individual vessels.

[18] So in law. Probably should read types.

(d) The provisions of this section and the standards and regulations promulgated hereunder apply to vessels owned and operated by the United States unless the Secretary of Defense finds that compliance would not be in the interest of national security. With respect to vessels owned and operated by the Department of Defense, regulations under the last sentence of subsection (b)(1) of this section and certifications under subsection (g)(2) of this section shall be promulgated and issued by the Secretary of Defense.

(e) Before the standards and regulations under this section are promulgated, the Administrator and the Secretary of the department in which the Coast Guard is operating shall consult with the Secretary of State; the Secretary of Health, Education, and Welfare; the Secretary of Defense; the Secretary of the Treasury; the Secretary of Commerce; other interested Federal agencies; and the States and industries interested; and otherwise comply with the requirements of section 553 of title 5 of the United States Code.

(f)(1)(A) Except as provided in subparagraph (B), after the effective date of the initial standards and regulations promulgated under this section, no State or political subdivision thereof shall adopt or enforce any statute or regulation of such State or political subdivision with respect to the design, manufacture, or installation or use of any marine sanitation device on any vessel subject to the provisions of this section.

(B) A State may adopt and enforce a statute or regulation with respect to the design, manufacture, or installation or use of any marine sanitation device on a houseboat, if such statute or regulation is more stringent than the standards and regulations promulgated under this section. For purposes of this paragraph, the term houseboat means a vessel which, for a period of time determined by the State in which the vessel is located, is used primarily as a residence and is not used primarily as a means of transportation.

(2) If, after promulgation of the initial standards and regulations and prior to their effective date, a vessel is equipped with a marine sanitation device in compliance with such standards and regulations and the installation and operation

of such device is in accordance with such standards and regulations, such standards and regulations shall, for the purposes of paragraph (1) of this subsection, become effective with respect to such vessel on the date of such compliance.

(3) After the effective date of the initial standards and regulations promulgated under this section, if any State determines that the protection and enhancement of the quality of some or all of the waters within such State require greater environmental protection, such State may completely prohibit the discharge from all vessels of any sewage, whether treated or not, into such waters, except that no such prohibition shall apply until the Administrator determines that adequate facilities for the safe and sanitary removal and treatment of sewage from all vessels are reasonably available for such water to which such prohibition would apply. Upon application of the State, the Administrator shall make such determination within 90 days of the date of such application.

(4)(A) If the Administrator determines upon application by a State that the protection and enhancement of the quality of specified waters within such State requires such a prohibition, he shall by regulation completely prohibit the discharge from a vessel of any sewage (whether treated or not) into such waters.

(B) Upon application by a State, the Administrator shall, by regulation, establish a drinking water intake zone in any waters within such State and prohibit the discharge of sewage from vessels within that zone.

(g)(1) No manufacturer of a marine sanitation device or marine pollution control device equipment shall sell, offer for sale, or introduce or deliver for introduction in interstate commerce, or import into the United States for sale or resale any marine sanitation device or marine pollution control device equipment manufactured after the effective date of the standards and regulations promulgated under this section unless such device or equipment is in all material respects substantially the same as a test device or equipment certified under this subsection.

(2) Upon application of the manufacturer, the Secretary of the department in which the Coast Guard is operating shall so certify a marine sanitation device or marine pollution control device equipment if he determines, in accordance with the provisions of this paragraph, that it meets the appropriate standards and regulations promulgated under this section. The Secretary of the department in which the Coast Guard is operating shall test or require such testing of the device or equipment in accordance with procedures set forth by the Administrator as to standards of performance and for such other purposes as may be appropriate. If the Secretary of the department in which the Coast Guard is operating determines that the device or equipment is satisfactory from the standpoint of safety and any other requirements of maritime law or regulation, and after consideration of the design, installation, operation, material, or other appropriate factors, he shall certify the device or equipment. Any device or equipment manufactured by such manufacturer which is in all material respects substantially the same as the certified test device or equipment shall be deemed to be in conformity with the appropriate standards and regulations established under this section.

(3) Every manufacturer shall establish and maintain such records, make such reports, and provide such information as the Administrator or the Secretary of the

department in which the Coast Guard is operating may reasonably require to enable him to determine whether such manufacturer has acted or is acting in compliance with this section and regulations issued thereunder and shall, upon request of an officer or employee duly designated by the Administrator or the Secretary of the department in which the Coast Guard is operating, permit such officer or employee at reasonable times to have access to and copy such records. All information reported to or otherwise obtained by the Administrator or the Secretary of the department in which the Coast Guard is operating or their representatives pursuant to this subsection which contains or relates to a trade secret or other matter referred in section 1905 of title 18 of the United States Code shall be considered confidential for the purpose of that section, except that such information may be disclosed to other officers or employees concerned with carrying out this section. This paragraph shall not apply in the case of the construction of a vessel by an individual for his own use.

(h) SALE AND RESALE OF PROPERLY EQUIPPED VESSELS; OPERABILITY OF CERTIFIED MARINE SANITATION DEVICES.—

(1) IN GENERAL.—Subject to paragraph (2), after the effective date of standards and regulations promulgated under this section, it shall be unlawful—

(A) for the manufacturer of any vessel subject to such standards and regulations to manufacture for sale, to sell or offer for sale, or to distribute for sale or resale any such vessel unless it is equipped with a marine sanitation device and marine pollution control device equipment which is in all material respects substantially the same as the appropriate test device certified pursuant to this section;

(B) for any person, prior to the sale or delivery of a vessel subject to such standards and regulations to the ultimate purchaser, wrongfully to remove or render inoperative any certified marine sanitation device or element of design of such device or any certified marine pollution control device equipment or element of design of such equipment installed in such vessel;

(C) for any person to fail or refuse to permit access to or copying of records or to fail to make reports or provide information required under this section; and

(D) for a vessel subject to such standards and regulations to operate on the navigable waters of the United States, if such vessel is not equipped with an operable marine sanitation device certified pursuant to this section.

(2) EFFECT OF SUBSECTION.— Nothing in this subsection requires certification of a marine pollution control device for use on any vessel of the Armed Forces.

(i) The district courts of the United States shall have jurisdictions to restrain violations of subsection (g)(1) of this section and subsections (h)(1) through (3) of this section. Actions to restrain such violations shall be brought by, and in, the name of the United States. In case of contumacy or refusal to obey a subpena served upon any person under this subsection, the district court of the United States for any district in which such person is found or resides or transacts business, upon application by the United States and after notice to such person, shall have jurisdiction to issue an order requiring such person to appear and give testimony or to appear and produce documents, and any failure to obey such order of the court may be punished by such court as a contempt thereof.

(j) Any person who violates subsection (g)(1), clause (1) or (2) of subsection (h), or subsection (n)(8) shall be liable to a civil penalty of not more than $5,000 for each violation. Any person who violates clause (4) of subsection (h) of this section or any regulation issued pursuant to this section shall be liable to a civil penalty of not more than $2,000 for each violation. Each violation shall be a separate offense. The Secretary of the department in which the Coast Guard is operating may assess and compromise any such penalty. No penalty shall be assessed until the person charged shall have been given notice and an opportunity for a hearing on such charge. In determining the amount of the penalty, or the amount agreed upon in compromise, the gravity of the violation, and the demonstrated good faith of the person charged in attempting to achieve rapid compliance, after notification of a violation, shall be considered by said Secretary.

(k) ENFORCEMENT AUTHORITY.—

(1) ADMINISTRATOR.— This section shall be enforced by the Administrator, to the extent provided in section 309.

(2) SECRETARY.—

(A) IN GENERAL.— This section shall be enforced by the Secretary of the department in which the Coast Guard is operating, who may use, by agreement, with or without reimbursement, law enforcement officers or other personnel and facilities of the Administrator, other Federal agencies, or the States to carry out the provisions of this section.

(B) INSPECTIONS.—For purposes of ensuring compliance with this section, the Secretary—

(i) may carry out an inspection (including the taking of ballast water samples) of any vessel at any time; and

(ii) shall—

(I) establish procedures for—

(aa) reporting violations of this section; and

(bb) accumulating evidence regarding those violations; and

(II) use appropriate and practicable measures of detection and environmental monitoring of vessels.

(C) DETENTION.—The Secretary may detain a vessel if the Secretary—

(i) has reasonable cause to believe that the vessel—

(I) has failed to comply with an applicable requirement of this section; or

(II) is being operated in violation of such a requirement; and

(ii) the Secretary provides to the owner or operator of the vessel a notice of the intent to detain.

(3) STATES.—

(A) IN GENERAL.— This section may be enforced by a State or political subdivision of a State (including the attorney general of a State), including by filing a civil action in an appropriate Federal district court to enforce any violation of subsection (p).

(B) JURISDICTION.—The appropriate Federal district court shall have jurisdiction with respect to a civil action filed pursuant to subparagraph (A), without regard to the amount in controversy or the citizenship of the parties—

(i) to enforce the requirements of this section; and

(ii) to apply appropriate civil penalties under this section or section 309(d), as appropriate.

(l) Anyone authorized by the Secretary of the department in which the Coast Guard is operating to enforce the provisions of this section may, except as to public vessels, (1) board and inspect any vessel upon the navigable waters of the United States and (2) execute any warrant or other process issued by an officer or court of competent jurisdiction.

(m) In the case of Guam and the Trust Territory of the Pacific Islands, actions arising under this section may be brought in the district court of Guam, and in the case of the Virgin Islands such actions may be brought in the district court of the Virgin Islands. In the case of American Samoa and the Trust Territory of the Pacific Islands, such actions may be brought in the District Court of the United States for the District of Hawaii and such court shall have jurisdiction of such actions. In the case of the Canal Zone, such actions may be brought in the District Court for the District of the Canal Zone.

(n) UNIFORM NATIONAL DISCHARGE STANDARDS FOR VESSELS OF THE ARMED FORCES.—

(1) APPLICABILITY.— This subsection shall apply to vessels of the Armed Forces and discharges, other than sewage, incidental to the normal operation of a vessel of the Armed Forces, unless the Secretary of Defense finds that compliance with this subsection would not be in the national security interests of the United States.

(2) DETERMINATION OF DISCHARGES REQUIRED TO BE CONTROLLED BY MARINE POLLUTION CONTROL DEVICES.—

(A) IN GENERAL.— The Administrator and the Secretary of Defense, after consultation with the Secretary of the department in which the Coast Guard is operating, the Secretary of Commerce, and interested States, shall jointly determine the discharges incidental to the normal operation of a vessel of the Armed Forces for which it is reasonable and practicable to require use of a marine pollution control device to mitigate adverse impacts on the marine environment. Notwithstanding subsection (a)(1) of section 553 of title 5, United States Code, the Administrator and the Secretary of Defense shall promulgate the determinations in accordance with such section. The Secretary of Defense shall require the use of a marine pollution control device on board a vessel of the Armed Forces in any case in which it is determined that the use of such a device is reasonable and practicable.

(B) CONSIDERATIONS.—In making a determination under subparagraph (A), the Administrator and the Secretary of Defense shall take into consideration—

(i) the nature of the discharge;

(ii) the environmental effects of the discharge;

(iii) the practicability of using the marine pollution control device;

(iv) the effect that installation or use of the marine pollution control device would have on the operation or operational capability of the vessel;

(v) applicable United States law;

(vi) applicable international standards; and

(vii) the economic costs of the installation and use of the marine pollution control device.

(3) PERFORMANCE STANDARDS FOR MARINE POLLUTION CONTROL DEVICES.—

(A) IN GENERAL.— For each discharge for which a marine pollution control device is determined to be required under paragraph (2), the Administrator and the Secretary of Defense, in consultation with the Secretary of the department in which the Coast Guard is operating, the Secretary of State, the Secretary of Commerce, other interested Federal agencies, and interested States, shall jointly promulgate Federal standards of performance for each marine pollution control device required with respect to the discharge. Notwithstanding subsection (a)(1) of section 553 of title 5, United States Code, the Administrator and the Secretary of Defense shall promulgate the standards in accordance with such section.

(B) CONSIDERATIONS.— In promulgating standards under this paragraph, the Administrator and the Secretary of Defense shall take into consideration the matters set forth in paragraph (2)(B).

(C) CLASSES, TYPES, AND SIZES OF VESSELS.—The standards promulgated under this paragraph may—

(i) distinguish among classes, types, and sizes of vessels;

(ii) distinguish between new and existing vessels; and

(iii) provide for a waiver of the applicability of the standards as necessary or appropriate to a particular class, type, age, or size of vessel.

(4) REGULATIONS FOR USE OF MARINE POLLUTION CONTROL DEVICES.— The Secretary of Defense, after consultation with the Administrator and the Secretary of the department in which the Coast Guard is operating, shall promulgate such regulations governing the design, construction, installation, and use of marine pollution control devices on board vessels of the Armed Forces as are necessary to achieve the standards promulgated under paragraph (3).

(5) DEADLINES; EFFECTIVE DATE.—

(A) DETERMINATIONS.—The Administrator and the Secretary of Defense shall—

(i) make the initial determinations under paragraph (2) not later than 2 years after the date of the enactment of this subsection; and

(ii) every 5 years—

(I) review the determinations; and

(II) if necessary, revise the determinations based on significant new information.

(B) STANDARDS.—The Administrator and the Secretary of Defense shall—

(i) promulgate standards of performance for a marine pollution control device under paragraph (3) not later than 2 years after the date of a determination under paragraph (2) that the marine pollution control device is required; and

(ii) every 5 years—

(I) review the standards; and

(II) if necessary, revise the standards, consistent with paragraph (3)(B) and based on significant new information.

(C) REGULATIONS.— The Secretary of Defense shall promulgate regulations with respect to a marine pollution control device under paragraph (4) as soon as practicable after the Administrator and the Secretary of Defense promulgate standards with respect to the device under paragraph (3), but not later than 1 year after the Administrator and the Secretary of Defense promulgate the standards. The regulations promulgated by the Secretary of Defense under paragraph (4) shall become effective upon promulgation unless another effective date is specified in the regulations.

(D) PETITION FOR REVIEW.— The Governor of any State may submit a petition requesting that the Secretary of Defense and the Administrator review a determination under paragraph (2) or a standard under paragraph (3), if there is significant new information, not considered previously, that could reasonably result in a change to the particular determination or standard after consideration of the matters set forth in paragraph (2)(B). The petition shall be accompanied by the scientific and technical information on which the petition is based. The Administrator and the Secretary of Defense shall grant or deny the petition not later than 2 years after the date of receipt of the petition.

(6) EFFECT ON OTHER LAWS.—

(A) PROHIBITION ON REGULATION BY STATES OR POLITICAL SUBDIVISIONS OF STATES.—Beginning on the effective date of—

(i) a determination under paragraph (2) that it is not reasonable and practicable to require use of a marine pollution control device regarding a particular discharge incidental to the normal operation of a vessel of the Armed Forces; or

(ii) regulations promulgated by the Secretary of Defense under paragraph (4);

except as provided in paragraph (7), neither a State nor a political subdivision of a State may adopt or enforce any statute or regulation of the State or political subdivision with respect to the discharge or the design, construction, installation, or use of any marine pollution control device required to control discharges from a vessel of the Armed Forces.

(B) FEDERAL LAWS.— This subsection shall not affect the application of section 311 to discharges incidental to the normal operation of a vessel.

(7) ESTABLISHMENT OF STATE NO-DISCHARGE ZONES.—

(A) STATE PROHIBITION.—

(i) IN GENERAL.—After the effective date of—

(I) a determination under paragraph (2) that it is not reasonable and practicable to require use of a marine pollution control device regarding a particular discharge incidental to the normal operation of a vessel of the Armed Forces; or

(II) regulations promulgated by the Secretary of Defense under paragraph (4);

if a State determines that the protection and enhancement of the quality of some or all of the waters within the State require greater environmental protection, the State may prohibit 1 or more discharges incidental to the normal operation of a vessel, whether treated or not treated, into the waters. No prohibition shall apply until the Administrator makes the determinations described in subclauses (II) and (III) of subparagraph (B)(i).

(ii) DOCUMENTATION.— To the extent that a prohibition under this paragraph would apply to vessels of the Armed Forces and not to other types of vessels, the State shall document the technical or environmental basis for the distinction.

(B) PROHIBITION BY THE ADMINISTRATOR.—

(i) IN GENERAL.—Upon application of a State, the Administrator shall by regulation prohibit the discharge from a vessel of 1 or more discharges incidental to the normal operation of a vessel, whether treated or not treated, into the waters covered by the application if the Administrator determines that—

(I) the protection and enhancement of the quality of the specified waters within the State require a prohibition of the discharge into the waters;

(II) adequate facilities for the safe and sanitary removal of the discharge incidental to the normal operation of a vessel are reasonably available for the waters to which the prohibition would apply; and

(III) the prohibition will not have the effect of discriminating against a vessel of the Armed Forces by reason of the ownership or operation by the Federal Government, or the military function, of the vessel.

(ii) APPROVAL OR DISAPPROVAL.— The Administrator shall approve or disapprove an application submitted under clause (i) not later than 90 days after the date on which the application is submitted to the Administrator. Notwithstanding clause (i)(II), the Administrator shall not disapprove an application for the sole reason that there are not adequate facilities to remove any discharge incidental to the normal operation of a vessel from vessels of the Armed Forces.

(C) APPLICABILITY TO FOREIGN FLAGGED VESSELS.—A prohibition under this paragraph—

(i) shall not impose any design, construction, manning, or equipment standard on a foreign flagged vessel engaged in innocent passage unless the prohibition implements a generally accepted international rule or standard; and

(ii) that relates to the prevention, reduction, and control of pollution shall not apply to a foreign flagged vessel engaged in transit passage unless the prohibition implements an applicable international regulation regarding the discharge of oil, oily waste, or any other noxious substance into the waters.

(8) PROHIBITION RELATING TO VESSELS OF THE ARMED FORCES.—After the effective date of the regulations promulgated by the Secretary of Defense under paragraph (4), it shall be unlawful for any vessel of the Armed Forces subject to the regulations to—

(A) operate in the navigable waters of the United States or the waters of the contiguous zone, if the vessel is not equipped with any required marine pollution control device meeting standards established under this subsection; or

(B) discharge overboard any discharge incidental to the normal operation of a vessel in waters with respect to which a prohibition on the discharge has been established under paragraph (7).

(9) ENFORCEMENT.— This subsection shall be enforceable, as provided in subsections (j) and (k), against any agency of the United States responsible for vessels of the Armed Forces notwithstanding any immunity asserted by the agency.

(o) MANAGEMENT PRACTICES FOR RECREATIONAL VESSELS.—

(1) APPLICABILITY.—This subsection applies to any discharge, other than a discharge of sewage, from a recreational vessel that is—

(A) incidental to the normal operation of the vessel; and

(B) exempt from permitting requirements under section 402(r).

(2) DETERMINATION OF DISCHARGES SUBJECT TO MANAGEMENT PRACTICES.—

(A) DETERMINATION.—

(i) IN GENERAL.— The Administrator, in consultation with the Secretary of the department in which the Coast Guard is operating, the Secretary of Commerce, and interested States, shall determine the discharges incidental to the normal operation of a recreational vessel for which it is reasonable and practicable to develop management practices to mitigate adverse impacts on the waters of the United States.

(ii) PROMULGATION.— The Administrator shall promulgate the determinations under clause (i) in accordance with section 553 of title 5, United States Code.

(iii) MANAGEMENT PRACTICES.— The Administrator shall develop management practices for recreational vessels in any case in which the Administrator determines that the use of those practices is reasonable and practicable.

(B) CONSIDERATIONS.—In making a determination under subparagraph (A), the Administrator shall consider—

(i) the nature of the discharge;

(ii) the environmental effects of the discharge;

(iii) the practicability of using a management practice;

(iv) the effect that the use of a management practice would have on the operation, operational capability, or safety of the vessel;

(v) applicable Federal and State law;

(vi) applicable international standards; and

(vii) the economic costs of the use of the management practice.

(C) TIMING.—The Administrator shall—

(i) make the initial determinations under subparagraph (A) not later than 1 year after the date of enactment of this subsection; and

(ii) every 5 years thereafter—

(I) review the determinations; and

(II) if necessary, revise the determinations based on any new information available to the Administrator.

(3) PERFORMANCE STANDARDS FOR MANAGEMENT PRACTICES.—

(A) IN GENERAL.— For each discharge for which a management practice is developed under paragraph (2), the Administrator, in consultation with the Secretary of the department in which the Coast Guard is operating, the Secretary of Commerce, other interested Federal agencies, and interested States, shall promulgate, in accordance with section 553 of title 5, United States Code, Federal standards of performance for each management practice required with respect to the discharge.

(B) CONSIDERATIONS.— In promulgating standards under this paragraph, the Administrator shall take into account the considerations described in paragraph (2)(B).

(C) CLASSES, TYPES, AND SIZES OF VESSELS.—The standards promulgated under this paragraph may—

(i) distinguish among classes, types, and sizes of vessels;

(ii) distinguish between new and existing vessels; and

(iii) provide for a waiver of the applicability of the standards as necessary or appropriate to a particular class, type, age, or size of vessel.

(D) TIMING.—The Administrator shall—

(i) promulgate standards of performance for a management practice under subparagraph (A) not later than 1 year after the date of a determination under paragraph (2) that the management practice is reasonable and practicable; and

(ii) every 5 years thereafter—

(I) review the standards; and

(II) if necessary, revise the standards, in accordance with subparagraph (B) and based on any new information available to the Administrator.

(4) REGULATIONS FOR THE USE OF MANAGEMENT PRACTICES.—

(A) IN GENERAL.— The Secretary of the department in which the Coast Guard is operating shall promulgate such regulations governing the design, construction, installation, and use of management practices for recreational vessels as are necessary to meet the standards of performance promulgated under paragraph (3).

(B) REGULATIONS.—

(i) IN GENERAL.— The Secretary shall promulgate the regulations under this paragraph as soon as practicable after the Administrator promulgates standards with respect to the practice under paragraph (3), but not later than 1 year after the date on which the Administrator promulgates the standards.

(ii) EFFECTIVE DATE.— The regulations promulgated by the Secretary under this paragraph shall be effective upon promulgation unless another effective date is specified in the regulations.

(iii) CONSIDERATION OF TIME.— In determining the effective date of a regulation promulgated under this paragraph, the Secretary shall consider the period of time necessary to communicate the existence of the regulation to persons affected by the regulation.

(5) EFFECT OF OTHER LAWS.— This subsection shall not affect the application of section 311 to discharges incidental to the normal operation of a recreational vessel.

(6) PROHIBITION RELATING TO RECREATIONAL VESSELS.— After the effective date of the regulations promulgated by the Secretary of the department in which the Coast Guard is operating under paragraph (4), the owner or operator of a recreational vessel shall neither operate in nor discharge any discharge incidental to the normal operation of the vessel into, the waters of the United States or the waters of the contiguous zone, if the owner or operator of the vessel is not using any applicable management practice meeting standards established under this subsection.

(p) UNIFORM NATIONAL STANDARDS FOR DISCHARGES INCIDENTAL TO NORMAL OPERATION OF VESSELS.—

(1) DEFINITIONS.—In this subsection:

(A) AQUATIC NUISANCE SPECIES.—The term aquatic nuisance species means a nonindigenous species that threatens—

(i) the diversity or abundance of a native species;

(ii) the ecological stability of—

(I) waters of the United States; or

(II) waters of the contiguous zone; or

(iii) a commercial, agricultural, aquacultural, or recreational activity that is dependent on—

(I) waters of the United States; or

(II) waters of the contiguous zone.

(B) Ballast water.—

(i) In general.—The term ballast water means any water, suspended matter, and other materials taken onboard a vessel—

(I) to control or maintain trim, draught, stability, or stresses of the vessel, regardless of the means by which any such water or suspended matter is carried; or

(II) during the cleaning, maintenance, or other operation of a ballast tank or ballast water management system of the vessel.

(ii) Exclusion.— The term ballast water does not include any substance that is added to the water described in clause (i) that is directly related to the operation of a properly functioning ballast water management system.

(C) Ballast water discharge standard.—The term ballast water discharge standard means—

(i) the numerical ballast water discharge standard established by section 151.1511 or 151.2030 of title 33, Code of Federal Regulations (or successor regulations); or

(ii) if a standard referred to in clause (i) is superseded by a numerical standard of performance under this subsection, that superseding standard.

(D) Ballast water exchange.—The term ballast water exchange means the replacement of water in a ballast water tank using 1 of the following methods:

(i) Flow-through exchange, in which ballast water is flushed out by pumping in midocean water at the bottom of the tank if practicable, and continuously overflowing the tank from the top, until 3 full volumes of water have been changed to minimize the number of original organisms remaining in the tank.

(ii) Empty and refill exchange, in which ballast water taken on in ports, estuarine waters, or territorial waters is pumped out until the pump loses suction, after which the ballast tank is refilled with midocean water.

(E) Ballast water management system.—The term ballast water management system means any marine pollution control device (including all ballast water treatment equipment, ballast tanks, pipes, pumps, and all associated control and monitoring equipment) that processes ballast water—

(i) to kill, render nonviable, or remove organisms; or

(ii) to avoid the uptake or discharge of organisms.

(F) Best available technology economically achievable.—The term best available technology economically achievable means—

(i) best available technology economically achievable (within the meaning of section 301(b)(2)(A));

(ii) best available technology (within the meaning of section 304(b)(2)(B)); and

(iii) best available technology, as determined in accordance with section 125.3(d)(3) of title 40, Code of Federal Regulations (or successor regulations).

(G) Best conventional pollutant control technology.—The term best conventional pollutant control technology means—

(i) best conventional pollutant control technology (within the meaning of section 301(b)(2)(E));

(ii) best conventional pollutant control technology (within the meaning of section 304(b)(4)); and

(iii) best conventional pollutant control technology, as determined in accordance with section 125.3(d)(2) of title 40, Code of Federal Regulations (or successor regulations).

(H) Best management practice.—

(i) In general.—The term best management practice means a schedule of activities, prohibitions of practices, maintenance procedures, and other management practices to prevent or reduce the pollution of—

(I) the waters of the United States; or

(II) the waters of the contiguous zone.

(ii) Inclusions.—The term best management practice includes any treatment requirement, operating procedure, or practice to control—

(I) vessel runoff;

(II) spillage or leaks;

(III) sludge or waste disposal; or

(IV) drainage from raw material storage.

(I) Best practicable control technology currently available.—The term best practicable control technology currently available means—

(i) best practicable control technology currently available (within the meaning of section 301(b)(1)(A));

(ii) best practicable control technology currently available (within the meaning of section 304(b)(1)); and

(iii) best practicable control technology currently available, as determined in accordance with section 125.3(d)(1) of title 40, Code of Federal Regulations (or successor regulations).

(J) Captain of the port zone.— The term Captain of the Port Zone means a Captain of the Port Zone established by the Secretary pursuant to sections 92, 93, and 633 of title 14, United States Code.

(K) EMPTY BALLAST TANK.—The term empty ballast tank means a tank that—

(i) has previously held ballast water that has been drained to the limit of the functional or operational capabilities of the tank (such as loss of suction);

(ii) is recorded as empty on a vessel log; and

(iii) contains unpumpable residual ballast water and sediment.

(L) GREAT LAKES COMMISSION.— The term Great Lakes Commission means the Great Lakes Commission established by article IV A of the Great Lakes Compact to which Congress granted consent in the Act of July 24, 1968 (Public Law 90–419; 82 Stat. 414).

(M) GREAT LAKES STATE.—The term Great Lakes State means any of the States of—

(i) Illinois;

(ii) Indiana;

(iii) Michigan;

(iv) Minnesota;

(v) New York;

(vi) Ohio;

(vii) Pennsylvania; and

(viii) Wisconsin.

(N) GREAT LAKES SYSTEM.— The term Great Lakes System has the meaning given the term in section 118(a)(3).

(O) INTERNAL WATERS.— The term internal waters has the meaning given the term in section 2.24 of title 33, Code of Federal Regulations (or a successor regulation).

(P) MARINE POLLUTION CONTROL DEVICE.—The term marine pollution control device means any equipment or management practice (or combination of equipment and a management practice), for installation or use onboard a vessel, that is—

(i) designed to receive, retain, treat, control, or discharge a discharge incidental to the normal operation of a vessel; and

(ii) determined by the Administrator and the Secretary to be the most effective equipment or management practice (or combination of equipment and a management practice) to reduce the environmental impacts of the discharge, consistent with the factors for consideration described in paragraphs (4) and (5).

(Q) NONINDIGENOUS SPECIES.— The term nonindigenous species means an organism of a species that enters an ecosystem beyond the historic range of the species.

(R) ORGANISM.—The term organism includes—

(i) an animal, including fish and fish eggs and larvae;

(ii) a plant;

(iii) a pathogen;

(iv) a microbe;

(v) a virus;

(vi) a prokaryote (including any archean or bacterium);

(vii) a fungus; and

(viii) a protist.

(S) PACIFIC REGION.—

(i) IN GENERAL.—The term Pacific Region means any Federal or State water—

(I) adjacent to the State of Alaska, California, Hawaii, Oregon, or Washington; and

(II) extending from shore.

(ii) INCLUSION.— The term Pacific Region includes the entire exclusive economic zone (as defined in section 1001 of the Oil Pollution Act of 1990 (33 U.S.C. 2701)) adjacent to each State described in clause (i)(I).

(T) PORT OR PLACE OF DESTINATION.— The term port or place of destination means a port or place to which a vessel is bound to anchor or moor.

(U) RENDER NONVIABLE.— The term render nonviable, with respect to an organism in ballast water, means the action of a ballast water management system that renders the organism permanently incapable of reproduction following treatment.

(V) SALTWATER FLUSH.—

(i) IN GENERAL.—The term saltwater flush means—

(I)(aa) the addition of as much midocean water into each empty ballast tank of a vessel as is safe for the vessel and crew; and

(bb) the mixing of the flushwater with residual ballast water and sediment through the motion of the vessel; and

(II) the discharge of that mixed water, such that the resultant residual water remaining in the tank—

(aa) has the highest salinity possible; and

(bb) is at least 30 parts per thousand.

(ii) MULTIPLE SEQUENCES.— For purposes of clause (i), a saltwater flush may require more than 1 fill-mix-empty sequence, particularly if only small quantities of water can be safely taken onboard a vessel at 1 time.

(W) SECRETARY.— The term Secretary means the Secretary of the department in which the Coast Guard is operating.

(X) SMALL VESSEL GENERAL PERMIT.— The term Small Vessel General Permit means the permit that is the subject of the notice of final permit issuance entitled Final National Pollutant Discharge Elimination System (NPDES) Small Vessel General Permit for Discharges Incidental to the Normal Operation of Vessels Less Than 79 Feet (79 Fed. Reg. 53702 (September 10, 2014)).

(Y) SMALL VESSEL OR FISHING VESSEL.—The term small vessel or fishing vessel means a vessel that is—

(i) less than 79 feet in length; or

(ii) a fishing vessel, fish processing vessel, or fish tender vessel (as those terms are defined in section 2101 of title 46, United States Code), regardless of the length of the vessel.

(Z) VESSEL GENERAL PERMIT.— The term Vessel General Permit means the permit that is the subject of the notice of final permit issuance entitled Final National Pollutant Discharge Elimination System (NPDES) General Permit for Discharges Incidental to the Normal Operation of a Vessel (78 Fed. Reg. 21938 (April 12, 2013)).

(2) APPLICABILITY.—

(A) IN GENERAL.—Except as provided in subparagraph (B), this subsection applies to—

(i) any discharge incidental to the normal operation of a vessel; and

(ii) any discharge incidental to the normal operation of a vessel (such as most graywater) that is commingled with sewage, subject to the conditions that—

(I) nothing in this subsection prevents a State from regulating sewage discharges; and

(II) any such commingled discharge shall comply with all applicable requirements of—

(aa) this subsection; and

(bb) any law applicable to discharges of sewage.

(B) EXCLUSION.—This subsection does not apply to any discharge incidental to the normal operation of a vessel—

(i) from—

(I) a vessel of the Armed Forces subject to subsection (n);

(II) a recreational vessel subject to subsection (o);

(III) a small vessel or fishing vessel, except that this subsection shall apply to any discharge of ballast water from a small vessel or fishing vessel; or

(IV) a floating craft that is permanently moored to a pier, including a floating casino, hotel, restaurant, or bar;

(ii) of ballast water from a vessel—

(I) that continuously takes on and discharges ballast water in a flow-through system, if the Administrator determines that system cannot materially contribute to the spread or introduction of an aquatic nuisance species into waters of the United States;

(II) in the National Defense Reserve Fleet that is scheduled for disposal, if the vessel does not have an operable ballast water management system;

(III) that discharges ballast water consisting solely of water taken onboard from a public or commercial source that, at the time the water is taken onboard, meets the applicable requirements or permit requirements of the Safe Drinking Water Act (42 U.S.C. 300f et seq.);

(IV) that carries all permanent ballast water in sealed tanks that are not subject to discharge; or

(V) that only discharges ballast water into a reception facility; or

(iii) that results from, or contains material derived from, an activity other than the normal operation of the vessel, such as material resulting from an industrial or manufacturing process onboard the vessel.

(3) CONTINUATION IN EFFECT OF EXISTING REQUIREMENTS.—

(A) VESSEL GENERAL PERMIT.— Notwithstanding the expiration date of the Vessel General Permit or any other provision of law, all provisions of the Vessel General Permit shall remain in force and effect, and shall not be modified, until the applicable date described in subparagraph (C).

(B) NONINDIGENOUS AQUATIC NUISANCE PREVENTION AND CONTROL ACT REGULATIONS.— Notwithstanding section 903(a)(2)(A) of the Vessel Incidental Discharge Act of 2018, all regulations promulgated by the Secretary pursuant to section 1101 of the Nonindigenous Aquatic Nuisance Prevention and Control Act of 1990 (16 U.S.C. 4711) (as in effect on the day before the date of enactment of this subsection), including the regulations contained in subparts C and D of part 151 of title 33, Code of Federal Regulations, and subpart 162.060 of part 162 of title 46, Code of Federal Regulations (as in effect on the day before that date of enactment), shall remain in force and effect until the applicable date described in subparagraph (C).

(C) REPEAL ON EXISTENCE OF FINAL, EFFECTIVE, AND ENFORCEABLE REQUIREMENTS.— Effective beginning on the date on which the requirements promulgated by the Secretary under subparagraphs (A), (B), and (C) of paragraph (5) with respect to every discharge incidental to the normal operation of a vessel that is subject to regulation under this subsection are final, effective, and enforceable, the requirements of the Vessel General Permit and the regulations described in subparagraph (B) shall have no force or effect.

(4) NATIONAL STANDARDS OF PERFORMANCE FOR MARINE POLLUTION CONTROL DEVICES AND WATER QUALITY ORDERS.—

(A) ESTABLISHMENT.—

(i) IN GENERAL.— Not later than 2 years after the date of enactment of this subsection, the Administrator, in concurrence with the Secretary (subject to clause (ii)), and in consultation with interested Governors (subject to clause (iii)), shall promulgate Federal standards of performance for marine pollution control devices for each type of discharge incidental to the normal operation of a vessel that is subject to regulation under this subsection.

(ii) CONCURRENCE WITH SECRETARY.—

(I) REQUEST.— The Administrator shall submit to the Secretary a request for written concurrence with respect to a proposed standard of performance under clause (i).

(II) EFFECT OF FAILURE TO CONCUR.—A failure by the Secretary to concur with the Administrator under clause (i) by the date that is 60 days after the date on which the Administrator submits a request for concurrence under subclause (I) shall not prevent the Administrator from promulgating the relevant standard of performance in accordance with the deadline under clause (i), subject to the condition that the Administrator shall include in the administrative record of the promulgation—

(aa) documentation of the request submitted under subclause (I); and

(bb) the response of the Administrator to any written objections received from the Secretary relating to the proposed standard of performance during the 60-day period beginning on the date of submission of the request.

(iii) CONSULTATION WITH GOVERNORS.—

(I) IN GENERAL.—The Administrator, in promulgating a standard of performance under clause (i), shall develop the standard of performance—

(aa) in consultation with interested Governors; and

(bb) in accordance with the deadlines under that clause.

(II) PROCESS.— The Administrator shall develop a process for soliciting input from interested Governors, including information sharing relevant to such process, to allow interested Governors to inform the development of standards of performance under clause (i).

(III) OBJECTION BY GOVERNORS.—

(aa) SUBMISSION.— An interested Governor that objects to a proposed standard of performance under clause (i) may submit to the Administrator in writing a detailed objection to the proposed standard of performance, describing the scientific, technical, or operational factors that form the basis of the objection.

(bb) RESPONSE.— Before finalizing a standard of performance under clause (i) that is subject to an objection under item (aa) from 1 or more interested Governors, the Administrator shall provide a written response to each interested Governor that submitted an objection under that item that details the scientific, technical, or operational factors that form the basis for that standard of performance.

(cc) JUDICIAL REVIEW.— A response of the Administrator under item (bb) shall not be subject to judicial review.

(iv) PROCEDURE.—The Administrator shall promulgate the standards of performance under this subparagraph in accordance with—

(I) this paragraph; and

(II) section 553 of title 5, United States Code.

(B) STRINGENCY.—

(i) IN GENERAL.—Subject to clause (iii), the standards of performance promulgated under this paragraph shall require—

(I) with respect to conventional pollutants, toxic pollutants, and nonconventional pollutants (including aquatic nuisance species), the application of the best practicable control technology currently available;

(II) with respect to conventional pollutants, the application of the best conventional pollutant control technology; and

(III) with respect to toxic pollutants and nonconventional pollutants (including aquatic nuisance species), the application of the best available technology economically achievable for categories and classes of vessels, which shall result in reasonable progress toward the national goal of eliminating discharges of all pollutants.

(ii) BEST MANAGEMENT PRACTICES.—The Administrator shall require the use of best management practices to control or abate any discharge incidental to the normal operation of a vessel if—

(I) numeric standards of performance are infeasible under clause (i); or

(II) the best management practices are reasonably necessary—

(aa) to achieve the standards of performance; or

(bb) to carry out the purpose and intent of this subsection.

(iii) MINIMUM REQUIREMENTS.—Subject to subparagraph (D)(ii)(II), the combination of any equipment or best management practice comprising a marine pollution control device shall not be less stringent than the following provisions of the Vessel General Permit:

(I) All requirements contained in parts 2.1 and 2.2 (relating to effluent limits and related requirements), including with respect to waters subject to Federal protection, in whole or in part, for conservation purposes.

(II) All requirements contained in part 5 (relating to vessel class-specific requirements) that concern effluent limits and authorized discharges (within the meaning of that part), including with respect to waters subject to Federal protection, in whole or in part, for conservation purposes.

(C) CLASSES, TYPES, AND SIZES OF VESSELS.—The standards promulgated under this paragraph may distinguish—

(i) among classes, types, and sizes of vessels; and

(ii) between new vessels and existing vessels.

(D) REVIEW AND REVISION.—

(i) IN GENERAL.—Not less frequently than once every 5 years, the Administrator, in consultation with the Secretary, shall—

(I) review the standards of performance in effect under this paragraph; and

(II) if appropriate, revise those standards of performance—

(aa) in accordance with subparagraphs (A) through (C); and

(bb) as necessary to establish requirements for any discharge that is subject to regulation under this subsection.

(ii) MAINTAINING PROTECTIVENESS.—

(I) IN GENERAL.— Except as provided in subclause (II), the Administrator shall not revise a standard of performance under this subsection to be less stringent than an applicable existing requirement.

(II) EXCEPTIONS.—The Administrator may revise a standard of performance to be less stringent than an applicable existing requirement—

(aa) if information becomes available that—

(AA) was not reasonably available when the Administrator promulgated the initial standard of performance or comparable requirement of the Vessel General Permit, as applicable (including the subsequent scarcity or unavailability of materials used to control the relevant discharge); and

(BB) would have justified the application of a less-stringent standard of performance at the time of promulgation; or

(bb) if the Administrator determines that a material technical mistake or misinterpretation of law occurred when promulgating the existing standard of performance or comparable requirement of the Vessel General Permit, as applicable.

(E) BEST MANAGEMENT PRACTICES FOR AQUATIC NUISANCE SPECIES EMERGENCIES AND FURTHER PROTECTION OF WATER QUALITY.—

(i) IN GENERAL.—Notwithstanding any other provision of this subsection, the Administrator, in concurrence with the Secretary (subject to clause (ii)), and in consultation with States, may require, by order, the use of an emergency best management practice for any region or category of vessels in any case in which the Administrator determines that such a best management practice—

(I) is necessary to reduce the reasonably foreseeable risk of introduction or establishment of an aquatic nuisance species; or

(II) will mitigate the adverse effects of a discharge that contributes to a violation of a water quality requirement under section 303, other than a requirement based on the presence of an aquatic nuisance species.

(ii) CONCURRENCE WITH SECRETARY.—

(I) REQUEST.— The Administrator shall submit to the Secretary a request for written concurrence with respect to an order under clause (i).

(II) EFFECT OF FAILURE TO CONCUR.—A failure by the Secretary to concur with the Administrator under clause (i) by the date that is 60 days after the date on which the Administrator submits a request for concurrence under subclause (I) shall not prevent the Administrator from issuing the relevant order, subject to the condition that the Administrator shall include in the administrative record of the issuance—

(aa) documentation of the request submitted under subclause (I); and

(bb) the response of the Administrator to any written objections received from the Secretary relating to the proposed order during the 60-day period beginning on the date of submission of the request.

(iii) DURATION.— An order issued by the Administrator under clause (i) shall expire not later than the date that is 4 years after the date of issuance.

(iv) EXTENSIONS.— The Administrator may reissue an order under clause (i) for such subsequent periods of not longer than 4 years as the Administrator determines to be appropriate.

(5) IMPLEMENTATION, COMPLIANCE, AND ENFORCEMENT REQUIREMENTS.—

(A) ESTABLISHMENT.—

(i) IN GENERAL.— As soon as practicable, but not later than 2 years, after the date on which the Administrator promulgates any new or revised standard of performance under paragraph (4) with respect to a discharge, the Secretary, in consultation with States, shall promulgate the regulations required under this paragraph with respect to that discharge.

(ii) MINIMUM REQUIREMENTS.—Subject to subparagraph (C)(ii)(II), the regulations promulgated under this paragraph shall not be less stringent with respect to ensuring, monitoring, and enforcing compliance than—

(I) the requirements contained in part 3 of the Vessel General Permit (relating to corrective actions);

(II) the requirements contained in part 4 of the Vessel General Permit (relating to inspections, monitoring, reporting, and recordkeeping), including with respect to waters subject to Federal protection, in whole or in part, for conservation purposes;

(III) the requirements contained in part 5 of the Vessel General Permit (relating to vessel class-specific requirements) regarding monitoring, inspection, and educational and training requirements (within the meaning of that part), including with respect to waters subject to Federal protection, in whole or in part, for conservation purposes; and

(IV) any comparable, existing requirements promulgated under the Nonindigenous Aquatic Nuisance Prevention and Control Act of 1990 (16 U.S.C. 4701 et seq.) (including section 1101 of that Act (16 U.S.C. 4711) (as in effect on the day before the date of enactment of this subsection)) applicable to that discharge.

(iii) COORDINATION WITH STATES.— The Secretary, in coordination with the Governors of the States, shall develop, publish, and periodically update inspection, monitoring, data management, and enforcement procedures for the enforcement by States of Federal standards and requirements under this subsection.

(iv) EFFECTIVE DATE.—In determining the effective date of a regulation promulgated under this paragraph, the Secretary shall take into consideration the period of time necessary—

(I) to communicate to affected persons the applicability of the regulation; and

(II) for affected persons reasonably to comply with the regulation.

(v) PROCEDURE.—The Secretary shall promulgate the regulations under this subparagraph in accordance with—

(I) this paragraph; and

(II) section 553 of title 5, United States Code.

(B) IMPLEMENTATION REGULATIONS FOR MARINE POLLUTION CONTROL DEVICES.— The Secretary shall promulgate such regulations governing the design, construction, testing, approval, installation, and use of marine pollution control devices as are necessary to ensure compliance with the standards of performance promulgated under paragraph (4).

(C) COMPLIANCE ASSURANCE.—

(i) IN GENERAL.—The Secretary shall promulgate requirements (including requirements for vessel owners and operators with respect to inspections, monitoring, reporting, sampling, and recordkeeping) to ensure, monitor, and enforce compliance with—

(I) the standards of performance promulgated by the Administrator under paragraph (4); and

(II) the implementation regulations promulgated by the Secretary under subparagraph (B).

(ii) MAINTAINING PROTECTIVENESS.—

(I) IN GENERAL.— Except as provided in subclause (II), the Secretary shall not revise a requirement under this subparagraph or subparagraph (B) to be less stringent with respect to ensuring, monitoring, or enforcing compliance than an applicable existing requirement.

(II) EXCEPTIONS.—The Secretary may revise a requirement under this subparagraph or subparagraph (B) to be less stringent than an applicable existing requirement—

(aa) in accordance with this subparagraph or subparagraph (B), as applicable;

(bb) if information becomes available that—

(AA) the Administrator determines was not reasonably available when the Administrator promulgated the existing requirement of the Vessel General Permit, or that the Secretary determines was not reasonably available when the Secretary promulgated the existing requirement under the Nonindigenous Aquatic Nuisance Prevention and Control Act of 1990 (16 U.S.C. 4701 et seq.) or the applicable existing requirement under this subparagraph, as applicable (including subsequent scarcity or unavailability of materials used to control the relevant discharge); and

(BB) would have justified the application of a less-stringent requirement at the time of promulgation; or

(cc) if the Administrator determines that a material technical mistake or misinterpretation of law occurred when promulgating an existing requirement of the Vessel General Permit, or if the Secretary determines that a material mistake or misinterpretation of law occurred when promulgating an existing requirement under the Nonindigenous Aquatic Nuisance Prevention and Control Act of 1990 (16 U.S.C. 4701 et seq.) or this subsection.

(D) DATA AVAILABILITY.— Beginning not later than 1 year after the date of enactment of this subsection, the Secretary shall provide to the Governor of a State, on request by the Governor, access to Automated Identification System arrival data for inbound vessels to specific ports or places of destination in the State.

(6) ADDITIONAL PROVISIONS REGARDING BALLAST WATER.—

(A) IN GENERAL.— In addition to the other applicable requirements of this subsection, the requirements of this paragraph shall apply with respect to any discharge incidental to the normal operation of a vessel that is a discharge of ballast water.

(B) EMPTY BALLAST TANKS.—

(i) REQUIREMENTS.—Except as provided in clause (ii), the owner or operator of a vessel with empty ballast tanks bound for a port or place of destination subject to the jurisdiction of the United States shall, prior to arriving at that port or place of destination, conduct a ballast water exchange or saltwater flush—

(I) not less than 200 nautical miles from any shore for a voyage originating outside the United States or Canadian exclusive economic zone; or

(II) not less than 50 nautical miles from any shore for a voyage originating within the United States or Canadian exclusive economic zone.

(ii) Exceptions.—Clause (i) shall not apply—

(I) if the unpumpable residual waters and sediments of an empty ballast tank were subject to treatment, in compliance with applicable requirements, through a type-approved ballast water management system approved by the Secretary;

(II) except as otherwise required under this subsection, if the unpumpable residual waters and sediments of an empty ballast tank were sourced within—

(aa) the same port or place of destination; or

(bb) contiguous portions of a single Captain of the Port Zone;

(III) if complying with an applicable requirement of clause (i)—

(aa) would compromise the safety of the vessel; or

(bb) is otherwise prohibited by any Federal, Canadian, or international law (including regulations) pertaining to vessel safety;

(IV) if design limitations of the vessel prevent a ballast water exchange or saltwater flush from being conducted in accordance with clause (i); or

(V) if the vessel is operating exclusively within the internal waters of the United States or Canada.

(C) Period of use of installed ballast water management systems.—

(i) In general.—Except as provided in clause (ii), a vessel shall be deemed to be in compliance with a standard of performance for a marine pollution control device that is a ballast water management system if the ballast water management system—

(I) is maintained in proper working condition, as determined by the Secretary;

(II) is maintained and used in accordance with manufacturer specifications;

(III) continues to meet the ballast water discharge standard applicable to the vessel at the time of installation, as determined by the Secretary; and

(IV) has in effect a valid type-approval certificate issued by the Secretary.

(ii) LIMITATION.—Clause (i) shall cease to apply with respect to any vessel on, as applicable—

(I) the expiration of the service life, as determined by the Secretary, of—

(aa) the ballast water management system; or

(bb) the vessel;

(II) the completion of a major conversion (as defined in section 2101 of title 46, United States Code) of the vessel; or

(III) a determination by the Secretary that there are other type-approved systems for the vessel or category of vessels, with respect to the use of which the environmental, health, and economic benefits would exceed the costs.

(D) REVIEW OF BALLAST WATER MANAGEMENT SYSTEM TYPE-APPROVAL TESTING METHODS.—

(i) DEFINITION OF LIVE; LIVING.—Notwithstanding any other provision of law (including regulations), for purposes of section 151.1511 of title 33, and part 162 of title 46, Code of Federal Regulations (or successor regulations), the terms live and living shall not—

(I) include an organism that has been rendered nonviable; or

(II) preclude the consideration of any method of measuring the concentration of organisms in ballast water that are capable of reproduction.

(ii) DRAFT POLICY.—Not later than 180 days after the date of enactment of this subsection, the Secretary, in coordination with the Administrator, shall publish a draft policy letter, based on the best available science, describing type-approval testing methods and protocols for ballast water management systems, if any, that—

(I) render nonviable organisms in ballast water; and

(II) may be used in addition to the methods established under subpart 162.060 of title 46, Code of Federal Regulations (or successor regulations)—

(aa) to measure the concentration of organisms in ballast water that are capable of reproduction;

(bb) to certify the performance of each ballast water management system under this subsection; and

(cc) to certify laboratories to evaluate applicable treatment technologies.

(iii) PUBLIC COMMENT.— The Secretary shall provide a period of not more than 60 days for public comment regarding the draft policy letter published under clause (ii).

(iv) FINAL POLICY.—

(I) In general.— Not later than 1 year after the date of enactment of this subsection, the Secretary, in coordination with the Administrator, shall publish a final policy letter describing type-approval testing methods, if any, for ballast water management systems that render nonviable organisms in ballast water.

(II) Method of evaluation.— The ballast water management systems under subclause (I) shall be evaluated by measuring the concentration of organisms in ballast water that are capable of reproduction based on the best available science that may be used in addition to the methods established under subpart 162.060 of title 46, Code of Federal Regulations (or successor regulations).

(III) Revisions.— The Secretary shall revise the final policy letter under subclause (I) in any case in which the Secretary, in coordination with the Administrator, determines that additional testing methods are capable of measuring the concentration of organisms in ballast water that have not been rendered nonviable.

(v) Factors for consideration.—In developing a policy letter under this subparagraph, the Secretary, in coordination with the Administrator—

(I) shall take into consideration a testing method that uses organism grow-out and most probable number statistical analysis to determine the concentration of organisms in ballast water that are capable of reproduction; and

(II) shall not take into consideration a testing method that relies on a staining method that measures the concentration of—

(aa) organisms greater than or equal to 10 micrometers; and

(bb) organisms less than or equal to 50 micrometers.

(E) Intergovernmental response framework.—

(i) In general.— The Secretary, in consultation with the Administrator and acting in coordination with, or through, the Aquatic Nuisance Species Task Force established by section 1201(a) of the Nonindigenous Aquatic Nuisance Prevention and Control Act of 1990 (16 U.S.C. 4721(a)), shall establish a framework for Federal and intergovernmental response to aquatic nuisance species risks from discharges from vessels subject to ballast water and incidental discharge compliance requirements under this subsection, including the introduction, spread, and establishment of aquatic nuisance species populations.

(ii) Ballast discharge risk response.—The Administrator, in coordination with the Secretary and taking into consideration information from the National Ballast Information Clearinghouse developed under section 1102(f) of the Nonindigenous Aquatic Nuisance Prevention and Control Act of 1990 (16 U.S.C. 4712(f)), shall establish a risk assessment and response framework using ballast water discharge data and aquatic nuisance species monitoring data for the purposes of—

(I) identifying and tracking populations of aquatic invasive species;

(II) evaluating the risk of any aquatic nuisance species population tracked under subclause (I) establishing and spreading in waters of the United States or waters of the contiguous zone; and

(III) establishing emergency best management practices that may be deployed rapidly, in a local or regional manner, to respond to emerging aquatic nuisance species threats.

(7) PETITIONS BY GOVERNORS FOR REVIEW.—

(A) IN GENERAL.—The Governor of a State (or a designee) may submit to the Administrator or the Secretary a petition—

(i) to issue an order under paragraph (4)(E); or

(ii) to review any standard of performance, regulation, or policy promulgated under paragraph (4), (5), or (6), respectively, if there exists new information that could reasonably result in a change to—

(I) the standard of performance, regulation, or policy; or

(II) a determination on which the standard of performance, regulation, or policy was based.

(B) INCLUSION.— A petition under subparagraph (A) shall include a description of any applicable scientific or technical information that forms the basis of the petition.

(C) DETERMINATION.—

(i) TIMING.—The Administrator or the Secretary, as applicable, shall grant or deny—

(I) a petition under subparagraph (A)(i) by not later than the date that is 180 days after the date on which the petition is submitted; and

(II) a petition under subparagraph (A)(ii) by not later than the date that is 1 year after the date on which the petition is submitted.

(ii) EFFECT OF GRANT.—If the Administrator or the Secretary determines under clause (i) to grant a petition—

(I) in the case of a petition under subparagraph (A)(i), the Administrator shall immediately issue the relevant order under paragraph (4)(E); or

(II) in the case of a petition under subparagraph (A)(ii), the Administrator or Secretary shall publish in the Federal Register, by not later than 30 days after the date of that determination, a notice of proposed rulemaking to revise the relevant standard, requirement, regulation, or policy under paragraph (4), (5), or (6), as applicable.

(iii) NOTICE OF DENIAL.— If the Administrator or the Secretary determines under clause (i) to deny a petition, the Administrator or Secretary shall publish in the Federal Register, by not later than 30 days after the date of that determination, a detailed explanation of the scientific, technical, or operational factors that form the basis of the determination.

(iv) REVIEW.—A determination by the Administrator or the Secretary under clause (i) to deny a petition shall be—

(I) considered to be a final agency action; and

(II) subject to judicial review in accordance with section 509, subject to clause (v).

(v) EXCEPTIONS.—

(I) VENUE.— Notwithstanding section 509(b), a petition for review of a determination by the Administrator or the Secretary under clause (i) to deny a petition submitted by the Governor of a State under subparagraph (A) may be filed in any United States district court of competent jurisdiction.

(II) DEADLINE FOR FILING.— Notwithstanding section 509(b), a petition for review of a determination by the Administrator or the Secretary under clause (i) shall be filed by not later than 180 days after the date on which the justification for the determination is published in the Federal Register under clause (iii).

(8) PROHIBITION.—

(A) IN GENERAL.—It shall be unlawful for any person to violate—

(i) a provision of the Vessel General Permit in force and effect under paragraph (3)(A);

(ii) a regulation promulgated pursuant to section 1101 of the Nonindigenous Aquatic Nuisance Prevention and Control Act of 1990 (16 U.S.C. 4711) (as in effect on the day before the date of enactment of this subsection) in force and effect under paragraph (3)(B); or

(iii) an applicable requirement or regulation under this subsection.

(B) COMPLIANCE WITH REGULATIONS.—Effective beginning on the effective date of a regulation promulgated under paragraph (4), (5), (6), or (10), as applicable, it shall be unlawful for the owner or operator of a vessel subject to the regulation—

(i) to discharge any discharge incidental to the normal operation of the vessel into waters of the United States or waters of the contiguous zone, except in compliance with the regulation; or

(ii) to operate in waters of the United States or waters of the contiguous zone, if the vessel is not equipped with a required marine pollution control device that complies with the requirements established under this subsection, unless—

(I) the owner or operator of the vessel denotes in an entry in the official logbook of the vessel that the equipment was not operational; and

(II) either—

(aa) the applicable discharge was avoided; or

(bb) an alternate compliance option approved by the Secretary as meeting the applicable standard was employed.

(C) AFFIRMATIVE DEFENSE.—No person shall be found to be in violation of this paragraph if—

(i) the violation was in the interest of ensuring the safety of life at sea, as determined by the Secretary; and

(ii) the applicable emergency circumstance was not the result of negligence or malfeasance on the part of—

(I) the owner or operator of the vessel;

(II) the master of the vessel; or

(III) the person in charge of the vessel.

(D) TREATMENT.— Each day of continuing violation of an applicable requirement of this subsection shall constitute a separate offense.

(E) IN REM LIABILITY.— A vessel operated in violation of this subsection is liable in rem for any civil penalty assessed for the violation.

(F) REVOCATION OF CLEARANCE.— The Secretary shall withhold or revoke the clearance of a vessel required under section 60105 of title 46, United States Code, if the owner or operator of the vessel is in violation of this subsection.

(9) EFFECT ON OTHER LAWS.—

(A) STATE AUTHORITY.—

(i) IN GENERAL.— Except as provided in clauses (ii) through (v) and paragraph (10), effective beginning on the date on which the requirements promulgated by the Secretary under subparagraphs (A), (B), and (C) of paragraph (5) with respect to every discharge incidental to the normal operation of a vessel that is subject to regulation under this subsection are final, effective, and enforceable, no State, political subdivision of a State, or interstate agency may adopt or enforce any law, regulation, or other requirement of the State, political subdivision, or interstate agency with respect to any such discharge.

(ii) IDENTICAL OR LESSER STATE LAWS.—Clause (i) shall not apply to any law, regulation, or other requirement of a State, political subdivision of a State, or interstate agency in effect on or after the date of enactment of this subsection—

(I) that is identical to a Federal requirement under this subsection applicable to the relevant discharge; or

(II) compliance with which would be achieved concurrently in achieving compliance with a Federal requirement under this subsection applicable to the relevant discharge.

(iii) STATE ENFORCEMENT OF FEDERAL REQUIREMENTS.— A State may enforce any standard of performance or other Federal requirement of this subsection in accordance with subsection (k) or other applicable Federal authority.

(iv) EXCEPTION FOR CERTAIN FEES.—

(I) IN GENERAL.— Subject to subclauses (II) and (III), a State that assesses any fee pursuant to any State or Federal law relating to the regulation of a discharge incidental to the normal operation of a vessel before the date of enactment of this subsection may assess or retain a fee to cover the costs of administration, inspection, monitoring, and enforcement activities by the State to achieve compliance with the applicable requirements of this subsection.

(II) MAXIMUM AMOUNT.—

(aa) IN GENERAL.—Except as provided in item (bb), a State may assess a fee for activities under this clause equal to not more than $1,000 against the owner or operator of a vessel that—

(AA) has operated outside of that State; and

(BB) arrives at a port or place of destination in the State (excluding movement entirely within a single port or place of destination).

(bb) VESSELS ENGAGED IN COASTWISE TRADE.— A State may assess against the owner or operator of a vessel registered in accordance with applicable Federal law and lawfully engaged in the coastwise trade not more than $5,000 in fees under this clause per vessel during a calendar year.

(III) ADJUSTMENT FOR INFLATION.—

(aa) IN GENERAL.— A State may adjust the amount of a fee authorized under this clause not more frequently than once every 5 years to reflect the percentage by which the Consumer Price Index for All Urban Consumers published by the Department of Labor for the month of October immediately preceding the date of adjustment exceeds the Consumer Price Index for All Urban Consumers published by the Department of Labor for the month of October that immediately precedes the date that is 5 years before the date of adjustment.

(bb) EFFECT OF SUBCLAUSE.— Nothing in this subclause prevents a State from adjusting a fee in effect before the date of enactment of this subsection to the applicable maximum amount under subclause (II).

(cc) APPLICABILITY.— This subclause applies only to increases in fees to amounts greater than the applicable maximum amount under subclause (II).

(v) ALASKA GRAYWATER.— Clause (i) shall not apply with respect to any discharge of graywater (as defined in section 1414 of the Consolidated Appropriations Act, 2001 (Public Law 106–554; 114 Stat. 2763A–323)) from a passenger vessel (as defined in section 2101 of title 46, United States Code) in the State of Alaska (including all waters in the Alexander Archipelago) carrying 50 or more passengers.

(vi) PRESERVATION OF AUTHORITY.— Nothing in this subsection preempts any State law, public initiative, referendum, regulation, requirement, or other State action, except as expressly provided in this subsection.

(B) ESTABLISHED REGIMES.—Except as expressly provided in this subsection, nothing in this subsection affects the applicability to a vessel of any other provision of Federal law, including—

(i) this section;

(ii) section 311;

(iii) the Act to Prevent Pollution from Ships (33 U.S.C. 1901 et seq.); and

(iv) title X of the Coast Guard Authorization Act of 2010 (33 U.S.C. 3801 et seq.).

(C) PERMITTING.—Effective beginning on the date of enactment of this subsection—

(i) the Small Vessel General Permit is repealed; and

(ii) the Administrator, or a State in the case of a permit program approved under section 402, shall not require, or in any way modify, a permit under that section for—

(I) any discharge that is subject to regulation under this subsection;

(II) any discharge incidental to the normal operation of a vessel from a small vessel or fishing vessel, regardless of whether that discharge is subject to regulation under this subsection; or

(III) any discharge described in paragraph (2)(B)(ii).

(D) NO EFFECT ON CIVIL OR CRIMINAL ACTIONS.—Nothing in this subsection, or any standard, regulation, or requirement established under this subsection, modifies or otherwise affects, preempts, or displaces—

(i) any cause of action; or

(ii) any provision of Federal or State law establishing a remedy for civil relief or criminal penalty.

(E) NO EFFECT ON CERTAIN SECRETARIAL AUTHORITY.— Nothing in this subsection affects the authority of the Secretary of Commerce or the Secretary of the Interior to administer any land or waters under the administrative control of the Secretary of Commerce or the Secretary of the Interior, respectively.

(F) NO LIMITATION ON STATE INSPECTION AUTHORITY.— Nothing in this subsection limits the authority of a State to inspect a vessel pursuant to paragraph (5)(A)(iii) in order to monitor compliance with an applicable requirement of this section.

(10) ADDITIONAL REGIONAL REQUIREMENTS.—

(A) MINIMUM GREAT LAKES SYSTEM REQUIREMENTS.—

(i) IN GENERAL.—Except as provided in clause (ii), the owner or operator of a vessel entering the St. Lawrence Seaway through the mouth of the St. Lawrence River shall conduct a complete ballast water exchange or saltwater flush—

(I) not less than 200 nautical miles from any shore for a voyage originating outside the United States or Canadian exclusive economic zone; or

(II) not less than 50 nautical miles from any shore for a voyage originating within the United States or Canadian exclusive economic zone.

(ii) EXCEPTIONS.—Clause (i) shall not apply to a vessel if—

(I) complying with an applicable requirement of clause (i)—

(aa) would compromise the safety of the vessel; or

(bb) is otherwise prohibited by any Federal, Canadian, or international law (including regulations) pertaining to vessel safety;

(II) design limitations of the vessel prevent a ballast water exchange from being conducted in accordance with an applicable requirement of clause (i);

(III) the vessel—

(aa) is certified by the Secretary as having no residual ballast water or sediments onboard; or

(bb) retains all ballast water while in waters subject to the requirement; or

(IV) empty ballast tanks on the vessel are sealed and certified by the Secretary in a manner that ensures that—

(aa) no discharge or uptake occurs; and

(bb) any subsequent discharge of ballast water is subject to the requirement.

(B) ENHANCED GREAT LAKES SYSTEM REQUIREMENTS.—

(i) PETITIONS BY GOVERNORS FOR PROPOSED ENHANCED STANDARDS AND REQUIREMENTS.—

(I) IN GENERAL.—The Governor of a Great Lakes State (or a State employee designee) may submit a petition in accordance with subclause (II) to propose that other Governors of Great Lakes States endorse an enhanced standard of performance or other requirement with respect to any discharge that—

(aa) is subject to regulation under this subsection; and

(bb) occurs within the Great Lakes System.

(II) SUBMISSION.—A Governor shall submit a petition under subclause

(I), in writing, to—

(aa) the Executive Director of the Great Lakes Commission, in such manner as may be prescribed by the Great Lakes Commission;

(bb) the Governor of each other Great Lakes State; and

(cc) the Director of the Great Lakes National Program Office established by section 118(b).

(III) PRELIMINARY ASSESSMENT BY GREAT LAKES COMMISSION.—

(aa) IN GENERAL.— After the date of receipt of a petition under subclause (II)(aa), the Great Lakes Commission (acting through the Great Lakes Panel on Aquatic Nuisance Species, to the maximum extent practicable) may develop a preliminary assessment regarding each enhanced standard of performance or other requirement described in the petition.

(bb) PROVISIONS.—The preliminary assessment developed by the Great Lakes Commission under item (aa)—

(AA) may be developed in consultation with relevant experts and stakeholders;

(BB) may be narrative in nature;

(CC) may include the preliminary views, if any, of the Great Lakes Commission on the propriety of the proposed enhanced standard of performance or other requirement;

(DD) shall be submitted, in writing, to the Governor of each Great Lakes State and the Director of the Great Lakes National Program Office and published on the internet website of the Great Lakes National Program Office; and

(EE) except as provided in clause (iii), shall not be taken into consideration, or provide a basis for review, by the Administrator or the Secretary for purposes of that clause.

(ii) PROPOSED ENHANCED STANDARDS AND REQUIREMENTS.—

(I) PUBLICATION IN FEDERAL REGISTER.—

(aa) REQUEST BY GOVERNOR.—Not earlier than the date that is 90 days after the date on which the Executive Director of the Great Lakes Commission receives from a Governor of a Great Lakes State a petition under clause (i)(II)(aa), the Governor may request the Director of the Great Lakes National Program Office to publish, for a period requested by the Governor of not less than 30 days, and the Director shall so publish, in the Federal Register for public comment—

(AA) a copy of the petition; and

(BB) if applicable as of the date of publication, any preliminary assessment of the Great Lakes Commission developed under clause (i)(III) relating to the petition.

(bb) REVIEW OF PUBLIC COMMENTS.— On receipt of a written request of a Governor of a Great Lakes State, the Director of the Great Lakes National Program Office shall make available all public comments received in response to the notice under item (aa).

(cc) NO RESPONSE REQUIRED.— Notwithstanding any other provision of law, a Governor of a Great Lakes State or the Director of the Great Lakes National Program Office shall not be required to provide a response to any comment received in response to the publication of a petition or preliminary assessment under item (aa).

(dd) PURPOSE.— Any public comments received in response to the publication of a petition or preliminary assessment under item (aa) shall be used solely for the purpose of providing information and feedback to the Governor of each Great Lakes State regarding the decision to endorse the proposed standard or requirement.

(ee) EFFECT OF PETITION.— A proposed standard or requirement developed under subclause (II) may differ from the proposed standard or requirement described in a petition published under item (aa).

(II) COORDINATION TO DEVELOP PROPOSED STANDARD OR REQUIREMENT.— After the expiration of the public comment period for the petition under subclause (I), any interested Governor of a Great Lakes State may work in coordination with the Great Lakes Commission to develop a proposed standard of performance or other requirement applicable to a discharge referred to in the petition.

(III) REQUIREMENTS.—A proposed standard of performance or other requirement under subclause (II)—

(aa) shall be developed—

(AA) in consultation with representatives from the Federal and provincial governments of Canada;

(BB) after notice and opportunity for public comment on the petition published under subclause (I); and

(CC) taking into consideration the preliminary assessment, if any, of the Great Lakes Commission under clause (i)(III);

(bb) shall be specifically endorsed in writing by—

(AA) the Governor of each Great Lakes State, if the proposed standard or requirement would impose any additional equipment requirement on a vessel; or

(BB) not fewer than 5 Governors of Great Lakes States, if the proposed standard or requirement would not impose any additional equipment requirement on a vessel; and

(cc) in the case of a proposed requirement to prohibit 1 or more types of discharge regulated under this subsection, whether treated or not treated, into waters within the Great Lakes System, shall not apply outside the waters of the Great Lakes States of the Governors endorsing the proposed requirement under item (bb).

(iii) PROMULGATION BY ADMINISTRATOR AND SECRETARY.—

(I) SUBMISSION.—

(aa) IN GENERAL.— The Governors endorsing a proposed standard or requirement under clause (ii)(III)(bb) may jointly submit to the Administrator and the Secretary for approval each proposed standard of performance or other requirement developed and endorsed pursuant to clause (ii).

(bb) INCLUSION.—Each submission under item (aa) shall include an explanation regarding why the applicable standard of performance or other requirement is—

(AA) at least as stringent as a comparable standard of performance or other requirement under this subsection;

(BB) in accordance with maritime safety; and

(CC) in accordance with applicable maritime and navigation laws and regulations.

(cc) WITHDRAWAL.—

(AA) IN GENERAL.— The Governor of any Great Lakes State that endorses a proposed standard or requirement under clause (ii)(III)(bb) may withdraw the endorsement by not later than the date that is 90 days after the date on which the Administrator and the Secretary receive the proposed standard or requirement.

(BB) EFFECT ON FEDERAL REVIEW.— If, after the withdrawal of an endorsement under subitem (AA), the proposed standard or requirement does not have the applicable number of endorsements under clause (ii)(III)(bb), the Administrator and the Secretary shall terminate the review under this clause.

(dd) DISSENTING OPINIONS.— The Governor of a Great Lakes State that does not endorse a proposed standard or requirement under clause (ii)(III)(bb) may submit to the Administrator and the Secretary any dissenting opinions of the Governor.

(II) JOINT NOTICE.—On receipt of a proposed standard of performance or other requirement under subclause (I), the Administrator and the Secretary shall publish in the Federal Register a joint notice that, at minimum—

(aa) states that the proposed standard or requirement is publicly available; and

(bb) provides an opportunity for public comment regarding the proposed standard or requirement during the 90-day period beginning on the date of receipt by the Administrator and the Secretary of the proposed standard or requirement.

(III) REVIEW.—

(aa) IN GENERAL.—As soon as practicable after the date of publication of a joint notice under subclause (II)—

(AA) the Administrator shall commence a review of each proposed standard of performance or other requirement covered by the notice to determine whether that standard or requirement is at least as stringent as comparable standards and requirements under this subsection; and

(BB) the Secretary shall commence a review of each proposed standard of performance or other requirement covered by the notice to determine whether that standard or requirement is in accordance with maritime safety and applicable maritime and navigation laws and regulations.

(bb) CONSULTATION.—In carrying out item (aa), the Administrator and the Secretary—

(AA) shall consult with the Governor of each Great Lakes State and representatives from the Federal and provincial governments of Canada;

(BB) shall take into consideration any relevant data or public comments received under subclause (II)(bb); and

(CC) shall not take into consideration any preliminary assessment by the Great Lakes Commission under clause (i)(III), or any dissenting opinion under subclause (I)(dd), except to the extent that such an assessment or opinion is relevant to the criteria for the applicable determination under item (aa).

(IV) APPROVAL OR DISAPPROVAL.—Not later than 180 days after the date of receipt of each proposed standard of performance or other requirement under subclause (I), the Administrator and the Secretary shall—

(aa) determine, as applicable, whether each proposed standard or other requirement satisfies the criteria under subclause (III)(aa);

(bb) approve each proposed standard or other requirement, unless the Administrator or the Secretary, as applicable, determines under item (aa) that the proposed standard or other requirement does not satisfy the criteria under subclause (III)(aa); and

(cc) submit to the Governor of each Great Lakes State, and publish in the Federal Register, a notice of the determination under item (aa).

(V) ACTION ON DISAPPROVAL.—

(aa) RATIONALE AND RECOMMENDATIONS.—If the Administrator and the Secretary disapprove a proposed standard of performance or other requirement under subclause (IV)(bb), the notices under subclause (IV)(cc) shall include—

(AA) a description of the reasons why the standard or requirement is, as applicable, less stringent than a comparable standard or requirement under this subsection, inconsistent with maritime safety, or inconsistent with applicable maritime and navigation laws and regulations; and

(BB) any recommendations regarding changes the Governors of the Great Lakes States could make to conform the disapproved portion of the standard or requirement to the requirements of this subparagraph.

(bb) Review.— Disapproval of a proposed standard or requirement by the Administrator and the Secretary under this subparagraph shall be considered to be a final agency action subject to judicial review under section 509.

(VI) Action on approval.—On approval by the Administrator and the Secretary of a proposed standard of performance or other requirement under subclause (IV)(bb)—

(aa) the Administrator shall establish, by regulation, the proposed standard or requirement within the Great Lakes System in lieu of any comparable standard or other requirement promulgated under paragraph (4); and

(bb) the Secretary shall establish, by regulation, any requirements necessary to implement, ensure compliance with, and enforce the standard or requirement under item (aa), or to apply the proposed requirement, within the Great Lakes System in lieu of any comparable requirement promulgated under paragraph (5).

(VII) No judicial review for certain actions.— An action or inaction of a Governor of a Great Lakes State or the Great Lakes Commission under this subparagraph shall not be subject to judicial review.

(VIII) Great lakes compact.— Nothing in this subsection limits, alters, or amends the Great Lakes Compact to which Congress granted consent in the Act of July 24, 1968 (Public Law 90–419; 82 Stat. 414).

(IX) Authorization of appropriations.— There is authorized to be appropriated to the Great Lakes Commission $5,000,000, to be available until expended.

(C) Minimum pacific region requirements.—

(i) Definition of commercial vessel.—In this subparagraph, the term commercial vessel means a vessel operating between—

(I) 2 ports or places of destination within the Pacific Region; or

(II) a port or place of destination within the Pacific Region and a port or place of destination on the Pacific Coast of Canada or Mexico north of parallel 20 degrees north latitude, inclusive of the Gulf of California.

(ii) Ballast water exchange.—

(I) IN GENERAL.— Except as provided in subclause (II) and clause (iv), the owner or operator of a commercial vessel shall conduct a complete ballast water exchange in waters more than 50 nautical miles from shore.

(II) EXEMPTIONS.—Subclause (I) shall not apply to a commercial vessel—

(aa) using, in compliance with applicable requirements, a type-approved ballast water management system approved by the Secretary; or

(bb) voyaging—

(AA) between or to a port or place of destination in the State of Washington, if the ballast water to be discharged from the commercial vessel originated solely from waters located between the parallel 46 degrees north latitude, including the internal waters of the Columbia River, and the internal waters of Canada south of parallel 50 degrees north latitude, including the waters of the Strait of Georgia and the Strait of Juan de Fuca;

(BB) between ports or places of destination in the State of Oregon, if the ballast water to be discharged from the commercial vessel originated solely from waters located between the parallel 40 degrees north latitude and the parallel 50 degrees north latitude;

(CC) between ports or places of destination in the State of California within the San Francisco Bay area east of the Golden Gate Bridge, including the Port of Stockton and the Port of Sacramento, if the ballast water to be discharged from the commercial vessel originated solely from ports or places within that area;

(DD) between the Port of Los Angeles, the Port of Long Beach, and the El Segundo offshore marine oil terminal, if the ballast water to be discharged from the commercial vessel originated solely from the Port of Los Angeles, the Port of Long Beach, or the El Segundo offshore marine oil terminal;

(EE) between a port or place of destination in the State of Alaska within a single Captain of the Port Zone;

(FF) between ports or places of destination in different counties of the State of Hawaii, if the vessel may conduct a complete ballast water exchange in waters that are more than 10 nautical miles from shore and at least 200 meters deep; or

(GG) between ports or places of destination within the same county of the State of Hawaii, if the vessel does not transit outside State marine waters during the voyage.

(iii) LOW-SALINITY BALLAST WATER.—

(I) IN GENERAL.—Except as provided in subclause (II) and clause (iv), the owner or operator of a commercial vessel that transports ballast water sourced from waters with a measured salinity of less than 18 parts per thousand and voyages to a Pacific Region port or place of destination with a measured salinity of less than 18 parts per thousand shall conduct a complete ballast water exchange—

(aa) not less than 50 nautical miles from shore, if the ballast water was sourced from a Pacific Region port or place of destination; or

(bb) more than 200 nautical miles from shore, if the ballast water was not sourced from a Pacific Region port or place of destination.

(II) EXCEPTION.—Subclause (I) shall not apply to a commercial vessel voyaging to a port or place of destination in the Pacific Region that is using, in compliance with applicable requirements, a type-approved ballast water management system approved by the Secretary to achieve standards of performance of—

(aa) less than 1 organism per 10 cubic meters, if that organism—

(AA) is living, or has not been rendered nonviable; and

(BB) is 50 or more micrometers in minimum dimension;

(bb) less than 1 organism per 10 milliliters, if that organism—

(AA) is living, or has not been rendered nonviable; and

(BB) is more than 10, but less than 50, micrometers in minimum dimension;

(cc) concentrations of indicator microbes that are less than—

(AA) 1 colony-forming unit of toxicogenic Vibrio cholera (serotypes O1 and O139) per 100 milliliters or less than 1 colony-forming unit of that microbe per gram of wet weight of zoological samples;

(BB) 126 colony-forming units of escherichia coli per 100 milliliters; and

(CC) 33 colony-forming units of intestinal enterococci per 100 milliliters; and

(dd) concentrations of such additional indicator microbes and viruses as may be specified in the standards of performance established by the Administrator under paragraph (4).

(iv) GENERAL EXCEPTIONS.—The requirements of clauses (ii) and (iii) shall not apply to a commercial vessel if—

(I) complying with the requirement would compromise the safety of the commercial vessel;

(II) design limitations of the commercial vessel prevent a ballast water exchange from being conducted in accordance with clause (ii) or (iii), as applicable;

(III) the commercial vessel—

(aa) is certified by the Secretary as having no residual ballast water or sediments onboard; or

(bb) retains all ballast water while in waters subject to those requirements; or

(IV) empty ballast tanks on the commercial vessel are sealed and certified by the Secretary in a manner that ensures that—

(aa) no discharge or uptake occurs; and

(bb) any subsequent discharge of ballast water is subject to those requirements.

(D) ESTABLISHMENT OF STATE NO-DISCHARGE ZONES.—

(i) STATE PROHIBITION.— Subject to clause (ii), after the effective date of regulations promulgated by the Secretary under paragraph (5), if any State determines that the protection and enhancement of the quality of some or all of the waters within the State require greater environmental protection, the State may prohibit 1 or more types of discharge regulated under this subsection, whether treated or not treated, into such waters.

(ii) APPLICABILITY.— A prohibition by a State under clause (i) shall not apply until the date on which the Administrator makes the applicable determinations described in clause (iii).

(iii) PROHIBITION BY ADMINISTRATOR.—

(I) DETERMINATION.—On application of a State, the Administrator, in concurrence with the Secretary (subject to subclause (II)), shall, by regulation, prohibit the discharge from a vessel of 1 or more discharges subject to regulation under this subsection, whether treated or not treated, into the waters covered by the application if the Administrator determines that—

(aa) prohibition of the discharge would protect and enhance the quality of the specified waters within the State;

(bb) adequate facilities for the safe and sanitary removal and treatment of the discharge are reasonably available for the water and all vessels to which the prohibition would apply;

(cc) the discharge can be safely collected and stored until a vessel reaches a discharge facility or other location; and

(dd) in the case of an application for the prohibition of discharges of ballast water in a port (or in any other location where cargo, passengers, or fuel are loaded and unloaded)—

(AA) the adequate facilities described in item (bb) are reasonably available for commercial vessels, after considering, at a minimum, water depth, dock size, pumpout facility capacity and flow rate, availability of year-round operations, proximity to navigation routes, and the ratio of pumpout facilities to the population and discharge capacity of commercial vessels operating in those waters; and

(BB) the prohibition will not unreasonably interfere with the safe loading and unloading of cargo, passengers, or fuel.

(II) CONCURRENCE WITH SECRETARY.—

(aa) REQUEST.— The Administrator shall submit to the Secretary a request for written concurrence with respect to a prohibition under subclause (I).

(bb) EFFECT OF FAILURE TO CONCUR.—A failure by the Secretary to concur with the Administrator under subclause (I) by the date that is 60 days after the date on which the Administrator submits a request for concurrence under item (aa) shall not prevent the Administrator from prohibiting the relevant discharge in accordance with subclause (III), subject to the condition that the Administrator shall include in the administrative record of the promulgation—

(AA) documentation of the request submitted under item (aa); and

(BB) the response of the Administrator to any written objections received from the Secretary relating to the proposed standard of performance during the 60-day period beginning on the date of submission of the request.

(III) TIMING.— The Administrator shall approve or disapprove an application submitted under subclause (I) by not later than 90 days after the date on which the application is submitted to the Administrator.

(E) MAINTENANCE IN EFFECT OF MORE-STRINGENT STANDARDS.— In any case in which a requirement established under this paragraph is more stringent or environmentally protective than a comparable requirement established under paragraph (4), (5), or (6), the more-stringent or more-protective requirement shall control.

[33 U.S.C. 1322]

FEDERAL FACILITIES POLLUTION CONTROL

SEC. 313. (a) Each department, agency, or instrumentality of the executive, legislative, and judicial branches of the Federal Government (1) having jurisdiction over any property or facility, or (2) engaged in any activity resulting, or which may result, in the discharge or runoff of pollutants, and each officer, agent, or employee thereof in the performance of his official duties, shall be subject to, and comply with, all Federal, State, interstate, and local requirements, administrative authority, and process and sanctions respecting the control and abatement of water pollution in the same manner, and to the same extent as any nongovernmental entity including the payment of reasonable service charges. The preceding sentence shall apply (A) to any requirement whether substantive or procedural (including any recordkeeping or reporting requirement, any requirement respecting permits and any other requirement, whatsoever), (B) to the exercise of any Federal, State, or local administrative authority, and (C) to any process and sanction, whether enforced in Federal, State, or local courts or in any other manner. This subsection shall apply notwithstanding any immunity of such agencies, officers, agents, or employees under any law or rule of law. Nothing in this section shall be construed to prevent any department, agency, or instrumentality of the Federal Government, or any officer, agent, or employee thereof in the performance of his official duties, from removing to the appropriate Federal district court any proceeding to which the department, agency, or instrumentality or officer, agent, or employee thereof is subject pursuant to this section, and any such proceeding may be removed in accordance with 28 U.S.C. 1441 et seq. No officer, agent, or employee of the United States shall be personally liable for any civil penalty arising from the performance of his official duties, for which he is not otherwise liable, and the United States shall be liable only for those civil penalties arising under Federal law or imposed by a State or local court to enforce an order or the process of such court. The President may exempt any effluent source of any department, agency, or instrumentality in the executive branch from compliance with any such a requirement if he determines it to be in the paramount interest of the United States to do so; except that no exemption may be granted from the requirements of section 306 or 307 of this Act. No such exemptions shall be granted due to lack of appropriation unless the President shall have specifically requested such appropriation as a part of the budgetary process and the Congress shall have failed to make available such requested appropriation. Any exemption shall be for a period not in excess of one year, but additional exemptions may be granted for periods of not to exceed one year upon the President's making a new determination. The President shall report each January to the Congress all exemptions from the requirements of this section granted during the preceding calendar year, together with his reason for granting such exemption. In addition to any such exemption of a particular effluent source, the President may, if he determines it to be in the paramount interest of the United States to do so, issue regulations exempting from compliance with the requirements of this section any weaponry, equipment, aircraft, vessels, vehicles, or other classes or categories of property, and access to such property, which are owned or operated by the Armed Forces of the United States (including the Coast Guard) or by the National Guard of any State and which are uniquely military in nature. The President shall reconsider the need for such regulations at three-year intervals.

(b)(1) The Administrator shall coordinate with the head of each department, agency, or instrumentality of the Federal Government having jurisdiction over any property or facility utilizing federally owned wastewater facilities to develop a program of cooperation for utilizing wastewater control systems utilizing those innovative treatment processes and techniques for which guidelines have been promulgated under section 304(d)(3). Such program shall include an inventory of property and facilities which could utilize such processes and techniques.

(2) Construction shall not be initiated for facilities for treatment of wastewater at any Federal property or facility after September 30, 1979, if alternative methods for wastewater treatment at such property or facility utilizing innovative treatment processes and techniques, including but not limited to methods utilizing recycle and reuse techniques and land treatment are not utilized, unless the life cycle cost of the alternative treatment works exceeds the life cycle cost of the most cost effective alternative by more than 15 per centum. The Administrator may waive the

application of this paragraph in any case where the Administrator determines it to be in the public interest, or that compliance with this paragraph would interfere with the orderly compliance with the conditions of a permit issued pursuant to section 402 of this Act.

(c) Reasonable Service Charges.—

(1) In general.—For the purposes of this Act, reasonable service charges described in subsection (a) include any reasonable nondiscriminatory fee, charge, or assessment that is—

(A) based on some fair approximation of the proportionate contribution of the property or facility to stormwater pollution (in terms of quantities of pollutants, or volume or rate of stormwater discharge or runoff from the property or facility); and

(B) used to pay or reimburse the costs associated with any stormwater management program (whether associated with a separate storm sewer system or a sewer system that manages a combination of stormwater and sanitary waste), including the full range of programmatic and structural costs attributable to collecting stormwater, reducing pollutants in stormwater, and reducing the volume and rate of stormwater discharge, regardless of whether that reasonable fee, charge, or assessment is denominated a tax.

(2) Limitation on accounts.—

(A) Limitation.— The payment or reimbursement of any fee, charge, or assessment described in paragraph (1) shall not be made using funds from any permanent authorization account in the Treasury.

(B) Reimbursement or payment obligation of Federal government.— Each department, agency, or instrumentality of the executive, legislative, and judicial branches of the Federal Government, as described in subsection (a), shall not be obligated to pay or reimburse any fee, charge, or assessment described in paragraph (1), except to the extent and in an amount provided in advance by any appropriations Act to pay or reimburse the fee, charge, or assessment.

[33 U.S.C. 1323]

CLEAN LAKES

Sec. 314. (a) Establishment and Scope of Program.—

(1) State program requirements.—Each State on a biennial basis shall prepare and submit to the Administrator for his approval—

(A) an identification and classification according to eutrophic condition of all publicly owned lakes in such State;

(B) a description of procedures, processes, and methods (including land use requirements), to control sources of pollution of such lakes;

(C) a description of methods and procedures, in conjunction with appropriate Federal agencies, to restore the quality of such lakes;

(D) methods and procedures to mitigate the harmful effects of high acidity, including innovative methods of neutralizing and restoring buffering capacity of lakes and methods of removing from lakes toxic metals and other toxic substances mobilized by high acidity;

(E) a list and description of those publicly owned lakes in such State for which uses are known to be impaired, including those lakes which are known not to meet applicable water quality standards or which require implementation of control programs to maintain compliance with applicable standards and those lakes in which water quality has deteriorated as a result of high acidity that may reasonably be due to acid deposition; and

(F) an assessment of the status and trends of water quality in lakes in such State, including but not limited to, the nature and extent of pollution loading from point and nonpoint sources and the extent to which the use of lakes is impaired as a result of such pollution, particularly with respect to toxic pollution.

(2) SUBMISSION AS PART OF 305(B)(1) REPORT.— The information required under paragraph (1) shall be included in the report required under section 305(b)(1) of this Act, beginning with the report required under such section by April 1, 1988.

(3) REPORT OF ADMINISTRATOR.— Not later than 180 days after receipt from the States of the biennial information required under paragraph (1), the Administrator shall submit to the Committee on Public Works and Transportation of the House of Representatives and the Committee on Environment and Public Works of the Senate a report on the status of water quality in lakes in the United States, including the effectiveness of the methods and procedures described in paragraph (1)(D).

(4) ELIGIBILITY REQUIREMENT.— Beginning after April 1, 1988, a State must have submitted the information required under paragraph (1) in order to receive grant assistance under this section.

(b) The Administrator shall provide financial assistance to States in order to carry out methods and procedures approved by him under subsection (a) of this section. The Administrator shall provide financial assistance to States to prepare the identification and classification surveys required in subsection (a)(1) of this section.

(c)(1) The amount granted to any State for any fiscal year under subsection (b) of this section shall not exceed 70 per centum of the funds expended by such State in such year for carrying out approved methods and procedures under subsection (a) of this section.

(2) There is authorized to be appropriated $50,000,000 for each of fiscal years 2001 through 2005 for grants to States under subsection (b) of this section which such sums shall remain available until expended. The Administrator shall provide for an equitable distribution of such sums to the States with approved methods and procedures under subsection (a) of this section.

(d) DEMONSTRATION PROGRAM.—

(1) GENERAL REQUIREMENTS.—The Administrator is authorized and directed to establish and conduct at locations throughout the Nation a lake water quality demonstration program. The program shall, at a minimum—

(A) develop cost effective technologies for the control of pollutants to preserve or enhance lake water quality while optimizing multiple lakes uses;

(B) control nonpoint sources of pollution which are contributing to the degradation of water quality in lakes;

(C) evaluate the feasibility of implementing regional consolidated pollution control strategies;

(D) demonstrate environmentally preferred techniques for the removal and disposal of contaminated lake sediments;

(E) develop improved methods for the removal of silt, stumps, aquatic growth, and other obstructions which impair the quality of lakes;

(F) construct and evaluate silt traps and other devices or equipment to prevent or abate the deposit of sediment in lakes; and

(G) demonstrate the costs and benefits of utilizing dredged material from lakes in the reclamation of despoiled land.

(2) GEOGRAPHICAL REQUIREMENTS.— Demonstration projects authorized by this subsection shall be undertaken to reflect a variety of geographical and environmental conditions. As a priority, the Administrator shall undertake demonstration projects at Lake Champlain, New York and Vermont; Lake Houston, Texas; Beaver Lake, Arkansas; Greenwood Lake and Belcher Creek, New Jersey; Deal Lake, New Jersey; Alcyon Lake, New Jersey; Gorton's Pond, Rhode Island; Lake Washington, Rhode Island; Lake Bomoseen, Vermont; Sauk Lake, Minnesota; Otsego Lake, New York; Oneida Lake, New York; Raystown Lake, Pennsylvania; Swan Lake, Itasca County, Minnesota; Walker Lake, Nevada; Lake Tahoe, California and Nevada; Ten Mile Lakes, Oregon; Woahink Lake, Oregon; Highland Lake, Connecticut; Lily Lake, New Jersey; Strawbridge Lake, New Jersey; Baboosic Lake, New Hampshire; French Pond, New Hampshire; Dillon Reservoir, Ohio; Tohopekaliga Lake, Florida; Lake Apopka, Florida; Lake George, New York; Lake Wallenpaupack, Pennsylvania; Lake Allatoona, Georgia; and Lake Worth, Texas.

(3) REPORTS.— Notwithstanding section 3003 of the Federal Reports Elimination and Sunset Act of 1995 (31 U.S.C. 1113 note; 109 Stat. 734–736), by January 1, 1997, and January 1 of every odd-numbered year thereafter, the Administrator shall report to the Committee on Transportation and Infrastructure of the House of Representatives and the Committee on Environment and Public Works of the Senate on work undertaken pursuant to this subsection. Upon completion of the program authorized by this subsection, the Administrator shall submit to such committees a final report on the results of such program, along with recommendations for further measures to improve the water quality of the Nation's lakes.

(4) AUTHORIZATION OF APPROPRIATIONS.—

(A) IN GENERAL.— There is authorized to be appropriated to carry out this subsection not to exceed $40,000,000 for fiscal years beginning after September 30, 1986, to remain available until expended.

(B) SPECIAL AUTHORIZATIONS.—

(i) AMOUNT.— There is authorized to be appropriated to carry out subsection (b) with respect to subsection (a)(1)(D) not to exceed

$25,000,000 for fiscal years beginning after September 30, 1986, to remain available until expended.

(ii) Distribution of funds.— The Administrator shall provide for an equitable distribution of sums appropriated pursuant to this subparagraph among States carrying out approved methods and procedures. Such distribution shall be based on the relative needs of each such State for the mitigation of the harmful effects on lakes and other surface waters of high acidity that may reasonably be due to acid deposition or acid mine drainage.

(iii) Grants as additional assistance.— The amount of any grant to a State under this subparagraph shall be in addition to, and not in lieu of, any other Federal financial assistance.

[33 U.S.C. 1324]

NATIONAL STUDY COMMISSION

Sec. 315. (a) There is established a National Study Commission, which shall make a full and complete investigation and study of all of the technological aspects of achieving, and all aspects of the total economic, social, and environmental effects of achieving or not achieving, the effluent limitations and goals set forth for 1983 in section 301(b)(2) of this Act.

(b) Such Commission shall be composed of fifteen members, including five members of the Senate, who are members of the Public Works committee, appointed by the President of the Senate, five members of the House, who are members of the Public Works committee, appointed by the Speaker of the House, and five members of the public appointed by the President. The Chairman of such Commission shall be elected from among its members.

(c) In the conduct of such study, the Commission is authorized to contract with the National Academy of Sciences and the National Academy of Engineering (acting through the National Research Council), the National Institute of Ecology, Brookings Institution, and other nongovernmental entities, for the investigation of matters within their competence.

(d) The heads of the departments, agencies and instrumentalities of the executive branch of the Federal Government shall cooperate with the Commission in carrying out the requirements of this section, and shall furnish to the Commission such information as the Commission deems necessary to carry out this section.

(e) A report shall be submitted to the Congress of the results of such investigation and study, together with recommendations, not later than three years after the date of enactment of this title.

(f) The members of the Commission who are not officers or employees of the United States, while attending conferences or meetings of the Commission or while otherwise serving at the request of the Chairman shall be entitled to receive compensation at a rate not in excess of the maximum rate of pay for grade GS–18, as provided in the General Schedule under section 5332 of title V of the United States Code, including traveltime and while away from their homes or regular places of business they may be allowed travel expenses, including per diem in lieu of subsistence as authorized by law (5 U.S.C.

73b–2) for persons in the Government service employed intermittently.

(g) In addition to authority to appoint personnel subject to the provisions of title 5, United States Code, governing appointments in the competitive service, and to pay such personnel in accordance with the provisions of chapter 51 and subchapter III of chapter 53 of such title relating to classification and General Schedule pay rates, the Commission shall have authority to enter into contracts with private or public organizations who shall furnish the Commission with such administrative and technical personnel as may be necessary to carry out the purpose of this section. Personnel furnished by such organizations under this subsection are not, and shall not be considered to be, Federal employees for any purposes, but in the performance of their duties shall be guided by the standards which apply to employees of the legislative branches under rules 41 and 43 of the Senate and House of Representatives, respectively.

(h) There is authorized to be appropriated, for use in carrying out this section, not to exceed $17,250,000.

[33 U.S.C. 1325]

THERMAL DISCHARGES

SEC. 316. (a) With respect to any point source otherwise subject to the provisions of section 301 or section 306 of this Act, whenever the owner or operator of any such source, after opportunity for public hearing, can demonstrate to the satisfaction of the Administrator (or, if appropriate, the State) that any effluent limitation proposed for the control of the thermal component of any discharge from such source will require effluent limitations more stringent than necessary to assure the projection and propagation of a balanced, indigenous population of shellfish, fish, and wildlife in and on the body of water into which the discharge is to be made, the Administrator (or, if appropriate, the State) may impose an effluent limitation under such sections for such plant, with respect to the thermal component of such discharge (taking into account the interaction of such thermal component with other pollutants), that will assure the projection and propagation of a balanced, indigenous population of shellfish, fish, and wildlife in and on that body of water.

(b) Any standard established pursuant to section 301 or section 306 of this Act and applicable to a point source shall require that the location, design, construction, and capacity of cooling water intake structures reflect the best technology available for minimizing adverse environmental impact.

(c) Notwithstanding any other provision of this Act, any point source of a discharge having a thermal component, the modification of which point source is commenced after the date of enactment of the Federal Water Pollution Control Act Amendments of 1972 and which, as modified, meets effluent limitations established under section 301 or, if more stringent, effluent limitations established under section 303 and which effluent limitations will assure protection and propagation of a balanced, indigenous population of shellfish, fish, and wildlife in or on the water into which the discharge is made, shall not be subject to any more stringent effluent limitation with respect to the thermal component of its discharge during a ten year period beginning on the date of completion of such modification or during the period of depreciation or amortization of such facility for the purpose of section 167 or 169 (or both) of the Internal Revenue Code of 1954, whichever period ends first.

[33 U.S.C. 1326]

FINANCING STUDY

SEC. 317. (a) The Administrator shall continue to investigate and study the feasibility of alternate methods of financing the cost of preventing, controlling and abating pollution as directed in the Water Quality Improvement Act of 1970 (Public Law 91–224), including, but not limited to, the feasibility of establishing a pollution abatement trust fund. The results of such investigation and study shall be reported to the Congress not later than two years after enactment of this title, together with recommendations of the Administrator for financing the programs for preventing, controlling and abating pollution for the fiscal years beginning after fiscal year 1976, including any necessary legislation.

(b) There is authorized to be appropriated for use in carrying out this section, not to exceed $1,000,000.

[33 U.S.C. 1327]

AQUACULTURE

SEC. 318. (a) The Administrator is authorized, after public hearings, to permit the discharge of a specific pollutant or pollutants under controlled conditions associated with an approved aquaculture project under Federal or State supervision pursuant to section 402 of this Act.

(b) The Administrator shall by regulation establish any procedures and guidelines which the Administrator deems necessary to carry out this section. Such regulations shall require the application to such discharge of each criterion, factor, procedure, and requirement applicable to a permit issued under section 402 of this title, as the Administrator determines necessary to carry out the objective of this Act.

(c) Each State desiring to administer its own permit program within its jurisdiction for discharge of a specific pollutant or pollutants under controlled conditions associated with an approved aquaculture project may do so if upon submission of such program the Administrator determines such program is adequate to carry out the objective of this Act.

[33 U.S.C. 1328]

SEC. 319. NONPOINT SOURCE MANAGEMENT PROGRAMS.

(a) STATE ASSESSMENT REPORTS.—

(1) CONTENTS.—The Governor of each State shall, after notice and opportunity for public comment, prepare and submit to the Administrator for approval, a report which—

(A) identifies those navigable waters within the State which, without additional action to control nonpoint sources of pollution, cannot reasonably be expected to attain or maintain applicable water quality standards or the goals and requirements of this Act;

(B) identifies those categories and subcategories of nonpoint sources or, where appropriate, particular nonpoint sources which add significant pollution to each portion of the navigable waters identified under subparagraph (A) in amounts which contribute to such portion not meeting such water quality standards or such goals and requirements;

(C) describes the process, including intergovernmental coordination and public participation, for identifying best management practices and measures to control each category and subcategory of nonpoint sources and, where appropriate, particular nonpoint sources identified under subparagraph (B) and to reduce, to the maximum extent practicable, the level of pollution resulting from such category, subcategory, or source; and

(D) identifies and describes State and local programs for controlling pollution added from nonpoint sources to, and improving the quality of, each such portion of the navigable waters, including but not limited to those programs which are receiving Federal assistance under subsections (h) and (i).

(2) INFORMATION USED IN PREPARATION.— In developing the report required by this section, the State (A) may rely upon information developed pursuant to sections 208, 303(e), 304(f), 305(b), and 314, and other information as appropriate, and (B) may utilize appropriate elements of the waste treatment management plans developed pursuant to sections 208(b) and 303, to the extent such elements are consistent with and fulfill the requirements of this section.

(b) STATE MANAGEMENT PROGRAMS.—

(1) IN GENERAL.— The Governor of each State, for that State or in combination with adjacent States, shall, after notice and opportunity for public comment, prepare and submit to the Administrator for approval a management program which such State proposes to implement in the first four fiscal years beginning after the date of submission of such management program for controlling pollution added from nonpoint sources to the navigable waters within the State and improving the quality of such waters.

(2) SPECIFIC CONTENTS.—Each management program proposed for implementation under this subsection shall include each of the following:

(A) An identification of the best management practices and measures which will be undertaken to reduce pollutant loadings resulting from each category, subcategory, or particular nonpoint source designated under paragraph (1)(B), taking into account the impact of the practice on ground water quality.

(B) An identification of programs (including, as appropriate, nonregulatory or regulatory programs for enforcement, technical assistance, financial assistance, education, training, technology transfer, and demonstration projects) to achieve implementation of the best management practices by the categories, subcategories, and particular nonpoint sources designated under subparagraph (A).

(C) A schedule containing annual milestones for (i) utilization of the program implementation methods identified in subparagraph (B), and (ii) implementation of the best management practices identified in subparagraph (A) by the categories, subcategories, or particular nonpoint sources designated under paragraph (1)(B). Such schedule shall provide for utilization of the best management practices at the earliest practicable date.

(D) A certification of the attorney general of the State or States (or the chief attorney of any State water pollution control agency which has independent legal counsel) that the laws of the State or States, as the case may be, provide adequate authority to implement such management program or, if there is not such adequate authority, a list of such additional authorities as will be necessary to implement such management program. A schedule and commitment by the State or States to seek such additional authorities as expeditiously as practicable.

(E) Sources of Federal and other assistance and funding (other than assistance provided under subsections (h) and (i)) which will be available in each of such fiscal years for supporting implementation of such practices and measures and the purposes for which such assistance will be used in each of such fiscal years.

(F) An identification of Federal financial assistance programs and Federal development projects for which the State will review individual assistance applications or development projects for their effect on water quality pursuant to the procedures set forth in Executive Order 12372 as in effect on September 17, 1983, to determine whether such assistance applications or development projects would be consistent with the program prepared under this subsection; for the purposes of this subparagraph, identification shall not be limited to the assistance programs or development projects subject to Executive Order 12372 but may include any programs listed in the most recent Catalog of Federal Domestic Assistance which may have an effect on the purposes and objectives of the State's nonpoint source pollution management program.

(3) UTILIZATION OF LOCAL AND PRIVATE EXPERTS.— In developing and implementing a management program under this subsection, a State shall, to the maximum extent practicable, involve local public and private agencies and organizations which have expertise in control of nonpoint sources of pollution.

(4) DEVELOPMENT ON WATERSHED BASIS.— A State shall, to the maximum extent practicable, develop and implement a management program under this subsection on a watershed-by-watershed basis within such State.

(c) ADMINISTRATIVE PROVISIONS.—

(1) COOPERATION REQUIREMENT.— Any report required by subsection (a) and any management program and report required by subsection (b) shall be developed in cooperation with local, substate regional, and interstate entities which are actively planning for the implementation of nonpoint source pollution controls and have either been certified by the Administrator in accordance with section 208, have worked jointly with the State on water quality management planning under section 205(j), or have been designated by the State legislative body or Governor as water quality management planning agencies for their geographic areas.

(2) TIME PERIOD FOR SUBMISSION OF REPORTS AND MANAGEMENT PROGRAMS.— Each report and management program shall be submitted to the Administrator during the 18-month period beginning on the date of the enactment of this section.

(d) APPROVAL OR DISAPPROVAL OF REPORTS AND MANAGEMENT PROGRAMS.—

(1) DEADLINE.— Subject to paragraph (2), not later than 180 days after the date of submission to the Administrator of any report or management program under this section (other than subsections (h), (i), and (k)), the Administrator shall either approve or disapprove such report or management program, as the case may be. The Administrator may approve a portion of a management program under this subsection. If the Administrator does not disapprove a report, management program, or portion of a management program in such 180-day period, such report, management program, or portion shall be deemed approved for purposes of this section.

(2) PROCEDURE FOR DISAPPROVAL.—If, after notice and opportunity for public comment and consultation with appropriate Federal and State agencies and other interested persons, the Administrator determines that—

(A) the proposed management program or any portion thereof does not meet the requirements of subsection (b)(2) of this section or is not likely to satisfy, in whole or in part, the goals and requirements of this Act;

(B) adequate authority does not exist, or adequate resources are not available, to implement such program or portion;

(C) the schedule for implementing such program or portion is not sufficiently expeditious; or

(D) the practices and measures proposed in such program or portion are not adequate to reduce the level of pollution in navigable waters in the State resulting from nonpoint sources and to improve the quality of navigable waters in the State;

the Administrator shall within 6 months of the receipt of the proposed program notify the State of any revisions or modifications necessary to obtain approval. The State shall thereupon have an additional 3 months to submit its revised management program and the Administrator shall approve or disapprove such revised program within three months of receipt.

(3) FAILURE OF STATE TO SUBMIT REPORT.— If a Governor of a State does not submit the report required by subsection (a) within the period specified by subsection (c)(2), the Administrator shall, within 30 months after the date of the enactment of this section, prepare a report for such State which makes the identifications required by paragraphs (1)(A) and (1)(B) of subsection (a). Upon completion of the requirement of the preceding sentence and after notice and opportunity for comment, the Administrator shall report to Congress on his actions pursuant to this section.

(e) LOCAL MANAGEMENT PROGRAMS; TECHNICAL ASSISTANCE.— If a State fails to submit a management program under subsection (b) or the Administrator does not approve such a management program, a local public agency or organization which has expertise in, and authority to, control water pollution resulting from nonpoint sources in any area of such State which the Administrator determines is of sufficient geographic size may, with approval of such State, request the Administrator to provide, and the Administrator shall provide, technical assistance to such agency or organization in developing for such area a management program which is described in subsection (b) and can be approved pursuant to subsection (d). After development of such management program, such agency or organization shall submit such management program to the Administrator for approval. If the Administrator approves such management program, such agency or organization shall be eligible to receive financial assistance under subsection (h) for implementation of such management program as if such agency or organization were a State for which a report submitted under subsection (a) and a management program submitted under subsection (b) were approved under this section. Such financial assistance shall be subject to the same terms and conditions as assistance provided to a State under subsection (h).

(f) Technical Assistance for State.— Upon request of a State, the Administrator may provide technical assistance to such State in developing a management program approved under subsection (b) for those portions of the navigable waters requested by such State.

(g) Interstate Management Conference.—

(1) Convening of conference; notification; purpose.— If any portion of the navigable waters in any State which is implementing a management program approved under this section is not meeting applicable water quality standards or the goals and requirements of this Act as a result, in whole or in part, of pollution from nonpoint sources in another State, such State may petition the Administrator to convene, and the Administrator shall convene, a management conference of all States which contribute significant pollution resulting from nonpoint sources to such portion. If, on the basis of information available, the Administrator determines that a State is not meeting applicable water quality standards or the goals and requirements of this Act as a result, in whole or in part, of significant pollution from nonpoint sources in another State, the Administrator shall notify such States. The Administrator may convene a management conference under this paragraph not later than 180 days after giving such notification, whether or not the State which is not meeting such standards requests such conference. The purpose of such conference shall be to develop an agreement among such States to reduce the level of pollution in such portion resulting from nonpoint sources and to improve the water quality of such portion. Nothing in such agreement shall supersede or abrogate rights to quantities of water which have been established by interstate water compacts, Supreme Court decrees, or State water laws. This subsection shall not apply to any pollution which is subject to the Colorado River Basin Salinity Control Act. The requirement that the Administrator convene a management conference shall not be subject to the provisions of section 505 of this Act.

(2) State management program requirement.— To the extent that the States reach agreement through such conference, the management programs of the States which are parties to such agreements and which contribute significant pollution to the navigable waters or portions thereof not meeting applicable water quality standards or goals and requirements of this Act will be revised to reflect such agreement. Such management programs shall be consistent with Federal and State law.

(h) Grant Program.—

(1) Grants for implementation of management programs.— Upon application of a State for which a report submitted under subsection (a) and a

management program submitted under subsection (b) is approved under this section, the Administrator shall make grants, subject to such terms and conditions as the Administrator considers appropriate, under this subsection to such State for the purpose of assisting the State in implementing such management program. Funds reserved pursuant to section 205(j)(5) of this Act may be used to develop and implement such management program.

(2) Applications.— An application for a grant under this subsection in any fiscal year shall be in such form and shall contain such other information as the Administrator may require, including an identification and description of the best management practices and measures which the State proposes to assist, encourage, or require in such year with the Federal assistance to be provided under the grant.

(3) Federal share.— The Federal share of the cost of each management program implemented with Federal assistance under this subsection in any fiscal year shall not exceed 60 percent of the cost incurred by the State in implementing such management program and shall be made on condition that the non-Federal share is provided from non-Federal sources.

(4) Limitation on grant amounts.— Notwithstanding any other provision of this subsection, not more than 15 percent of the amount appropriated to carry out this subsection may be used to make grants to any one State, including any grants to any local public agency or organization with authority to control pollution from nonpoint sources in any area of such State.

(5) Priority for effective mechanisms.—For each fiscal year beginning after September 30, 1987, the Administrator may give priority in making grants under this subsection, and shall give consideration in determining the Federal share of any such grant, to States which have implemented or are proposing to implement management programs which will—

(A) control particularly difficult or serious nonpoint source pollution problems, including, but not limited to, problems resulting from mining activities;

(B) implement innovative methods or practices for controlling nonpoint sources of pollution, including regulatory programs where the Administrator deems appropriate;

(C) control interstate nonpoint source pollution problems; or

(D) carry out ground water quality protection activities which the Administrator determines are part of a comprehensive nonpoint source pollution control program, including research, planning, ground water assessments, demonstration programs, enforcement, technical assistance, education, and training to protect ground water quality from nonpoint sources of pollution.

(6) Availability for obligation.— The funds granted to each State pursuant to this subsection in a fiscal year shall remain available for obligation by such State for the fiscal year for which appropriated. The amount of any such funds not obligated by the end of such fiscal year shall be available to the Administrator for granting to other States under this subsection in the next fiscal year.

(7) Limitation on use of funds.— States may use funds from grants made

pursuant to this section for financial assistance to persons only to the extent that such assistance is related to the costs of demonstration projects.

(8) SATISFACTORY PROGRESS.— No grant may be made under this subsection in any fiscal year to a State which in the preceding fiscal year received a grant under this subsection unless the Administrator determines that such State made satisfactory progress in such preceding fiscal year in meeting the schedule specified by such State under subsection (b)(2).

(9) MAINTENANCE OF EFFORT.— No grant may be made to a State under this subsection in any fiscal year unless such State enters into such agreements with the Administrator as the Administrator may require to ensure that such State will maintain its aggregate expenditures from all other sources for programs for controlling pollution added to the navigable waters in such State from nonpoint sources and improving the quality of such waters at or above the average level of such expenditures in its two fiscal years preceding the date of enactment of this subsection.

(10) REQUEST FOR INFORMATION.— The Administrator may request such information, data, and reports as he considers necessary to make the determination of continuing eligibility for grants under this section.

(11) REPORTING AND OTHER REQUIREMENTS.— Each State shall report to the Administrator on an annual basis concerning (A) its progress in meeting the schedule of milestones submitted pursuant to subsection (b)(2)(C) of this section, and (B) to the extent that appropriate information is available, reductions in nonpoint source pollutant loading and improvements in water quality for those navigable waters or watersheds within the State which were identified pursuant to subsection (a)(1)(A) of this section resulting from implementation of the management program.

(12) LIMITATION ON ADMINISTRATIVE COSTS.— For purposes of this subsection, administrative costs in the form of salaries, overhead, or indirect costs for services provided and charged against activities and programs carried out with a grant under this subsection shall not exceed in any fiscal year 10 percent of the amount of the grant in such year, except that costs of implementing enforcement and regulatory activities, education, training, technical assistance, demonstration projects, and technology transfer programs shall not be subject to this limitation.

(i) GRANTS FOR PROTECTING GROUNDWATER QUALITY.—

(1) ELIGIBLE APPLICANTS AND ACTIVITIES.— Upon application of a State for which a report submitted under subsection (a) and a plan submitted under subsection (b) is approved under this section, the Administrator shall make grants under this subsection to such State for the purpose of assisting such State in carrying out groundwater quality protection activities which the Administrator determines will advance the State toward implementation of a comprehensive nonpoint source pollution control program. Such activities shall include, but not be limited to, research, planning, groundwater assessments, demonstration programs, enforcement, technical assistance, education and training to protect the quality of groundwater and to prevent contamination of groundwater from nonpoint sources of pollution.

(2) Applications.— An application for a grant under this subsection shall be in such form and shall contain such information as the Administrator may require.

(3) Federal share; maximum amount.— The Federal share of the cost of assisting a State in carrying out groundwater protection activities in any fiscal year under this subsection shall be 50 percent of the costs incurred by the State in carrying out such activities, except that the maximum amount of Federal assistance which any State may receive under this subsection in any fiscal year shall not exceed $150,000.

(4) Report.— The Administrator shall include in each report transmitted under subsection (m) a report on the activities and programs implemented under this subsection during the preceding fiscal year.

(j) Authorization of Appropriations.— There is authorized to be appropriated to carry out subsections (h) and (i) $200,000,000 for each of fiscal years 2023 through 2027; except that for each of such fiscal years not to exceed $7,500,000 may be made available to carry out subsection (i). Sums appropriated pursuant to this subsection shall remain available until expended.

(k) Consistency of Other Programs and Projects With Management Programs.— The Administrator shall transmit to the Office of Management and Budget and the appropriate Federal departments and agencies a list of those assistance programs and development projects identified by each State under subsection (b)(2)(F) for which individual assistance applications and projects will be reviewed pursuant to the procedures set forth in Executive Order 12372 as in effect on September 17, 1983. Beginning not later than sixty days after receiving notification by the Administrator, each Federal department and agency shall modify existing regulations to allow States to review individual development projects and assistance applications under the identified Federal assistance programs and shall accommodate, according to the requirements and definitions of Executive Order 12372, as in effect on September 17, 1983, the concerns of the State regarding the consistency of such applications or projects with the State nonpoint source pollution management program.

(l) Collection of Information.— The Administrator shall collect and make available, through publications and other appropriate means, information pertaining to management practices and implementation methods, including, but not limited to, (1) information concerning the costs and relative efficiencies of best management practices for reducing nonpoint source pollution; and (2) available data concerning the relationship between water quality and implementation of various management practices to control nonpoint sources of pollution.

(m) Reports of Administrator.—

(1) Annual reports.— Not later than January 1, 1988, and each January 1 thereafter, the Administrator shall transmit to the Committee on Public Works and Transportation of the House of Representatives and the Committee on Environment and Public Works of the Senate, a report for the preceding fiscal year on the activities and programs implemented under this section and the progress made in reducing pollution in the navigable waters resulting from nonpoint sources and improving the quality of such waters.

(2) Final report.—Not later than January 1, 1990, the Administrator shall

transmit to Congress a final report on the activities carried out under this section. Such report, at a minimum, shall—

(A) describe the management programs being implemented by the States by types and amount of affected navigable waters, categories and subcategories of nonpoint sources, and types of best management practices being implemented;

(B) describe the experiences of the States in adhering to schedules and implementing best management practices;

(C) describe the amount and purpose of grants awarded pursuant to subsections (h) and (i) of this section;

(D) identify, to the extent that information is available, the progress made in reducing pollutant loads and improving water quality in the navigable waters;

(E) indicate what further actions need to be taken to attain and maintain in those navigable waters (i) applicable water quality standards, and (ii) the goals and requirements of this Act;

(F) include recommendations of the Administrator concerning future programs (including enforcement programs) for controlling pollution from nonpoint sources; and

(G) identify the activities and programs of departments, agencies, and instrumentalities of the United States which are inconsistent with the management programs submitted by the States and recommend modifications so that such activities and programs are consistent with and assist the States in implementation of such management programs.

(n) Set Aside for Administrative Personnel.— Not less than 5 percent of the funds appropriated pursuant to subsection (j) for any fiscal year shall be available to the Administrator to maintain personnel levels at the Environmental Protection Agency at levels which are adequate to carry out this section in such year.

[33 U.S.C. 1329]

SEC. 320. NATIONAL ESTUARY PROGRAM.

(a) Management Conference.—

(1) Nomination of estuaries.— The Governor of any State may nominate to the Administrator an estuary lying in whole or in part within the State as an estuary of national significance and request a management conference to develop a comprehensive management plan for the estuary. The nomination shall document the need for the conference, the likelihood of success, and information relating to the factors in paragraph (2).

(2) Convening of conference.—

(A) In general.— In any case where the Administrator determines, on his own initiative or upon nomination of a State under paragraph (1), that the attainment or maintenance of that water quality in an estuary which assures protection of public water supplies and the protection and propagation of a balanced, indigenous population of shellfish, fish, and wildlife, and allows recreational activities, in and on the water, requires the control of point and nonpoint sources of pollution to supplement existing controls of pollution in more than one State, the Administrator shall select such estuary and convene a management conference.

(B) PRIORITY CONSIDERATION.— The Administrator shall give priority consideration under this section to Long Island Sound, New York and Connecticut; Narragansett Bay, Rhode Island; Buzzards Bay, Massachusetts; Massachusetts Bay, Massachusetts (including Cape Cod Bay and Boston Harbor);[19] Puget Sound, Washington; New York-New Jersey Harbor, New York and New Jersey; Delaware Bay, Delaware and New Jersey; Delaware Inland Bays, Delaware; Albermarle Sound, North Carolina; Sarasota Bay, Florida; San Francisco Bay, California; Santa Monica Bay, California; Galveston Bay, Texas;[20] Barataria-Terrebonne Bay estuary complex, Louisiana; Indian River Lagoon, Florida; Lake Pontchartrain Basin, Louisiana and Mississippi; Peconic Bay, New York; Casco Bay, Maine; Tampa Bay, Florida; Coastal Bend, Texas; San Juan Bay, Puerto Rico; Tillamook Bay, Oregon; Piscataqua Region, New Hampshire; Barnegat Bay, New Jersey; Maryland Coastal Bays, Maryland; Charlotte Harbor, Florida; Mobile Bay, Alabama; Morro Bay, California; Lower Columbia River, Oregon and Washington; and Pensacola and Perdido Bays, Florida.

[19] Both P.L. 100–653 and P.L. 100–658 inserted the same Massachusetts Bay phrase after Buzzards Bay; so that the phrase appears twice.

[20] P.L. 100–688, section 2001(3) inserted the Louisiana, Florida, New York bays after Galveston, Texas; which technically could not be executed.

(3) BOUNDARY DISPUTE EXCEPTION.— In any case in which a boundary between two States passes through an estuary and such boundary is disputed and is the subject of an action in any court, the Administrator shall not convene a management conference with respect to such estuary before a final adjudication has been made of such dispute.

(b) PURPOSES OF CONFERENCE.—The purposes of any management conference convened with respect to an estuary under this subsection shall be to—

(1) assess trends in water quality, natural resources, and uses of the estuary;

(2) collect, characterize, and assess data on toxics, nutrients, and natural resources within the estuarine zone to identify the causes of environmental problems;

(3) develop the relationship between the inplace loads and point and nonpoint loadings of pollutants to the estuarine zone and the potential uses of the zone, water quality, and natural resources;

(4) develop a comprehensive conservation and management plan that—

(A) recommends priority corrective actions and compliance schedules addressing point and nonpoint sources of pollution to restore and maintain the chemical, physical, and biological integrity of the estuary, including restoration and maintenance of water quality, a balanced indigenous population of shellfish, fish and wildlife, and recreational activities in the estuary, and assure that the designated uses of the estuary are protected;

(B) addresses the effects of recurring extreme weather events on the estuary, including the identification and assessment of vulnerabilities in the estuary and the development and implementation of adaptation strategies; and

(C) increases public education and awareness of the ecological health and water quality conditions of the estuary;

(5) develop plans for the coordinated implementation of the plan by the States as well as Federal and local agencies participating in the conference;

(6) monitor the effectiveness of actions taken pursuant to the plan; and

(7) review all Federal financial assistance programs and Federal development projects in accordance with the requirements of Executive Order 12372, as in effect on September 17, 1983, to determine whether such assistance program or project would be consistent with and further the purposes and objectives of the plan prepared under this section.

For purposes of paragraph (7), such programs and projects shall not be limited to the assistance programs and development projects subject to Executive Order 12372, but may include any programs listed in the most recent Catalog of Federal Domestic Assistance which may have an effect on the purposes and objectives of the plan developed under this section.

(c) MEMBERS OF CONFERENCE.—The members of a management conference convened under this section shall include, at a minimum, the Administrator and representatives of—

(1) each State and foreign nation located in whole or in part in the estuarine zone of the estuary for which the conference is convened;

(2) international, interstate, or regional agencies or entities having jurisdiction over all or a significant part of the estuary;

(3) each interested Federal agency, as determined appropriate by the Administrator;

(4) local governments having jurisdiction over any land or water within the estuarine zone, as determined appropriate by the Administrator; and

(5) affected industries, public and private educational institutions, nonprofit organizations, and the general public, as determined appropriate by the Administrator.

(d) UTILIZATION OF EXISTING DATA.— In developing a conservation and management plan under this section, the management conference shall survey and utilize existing reports, data, and studies relating to the estuary that have been developed by or made available to Federal, interstate, State, and local agencies.

(e) PERIOD OF CONFERENCE.— A management conference convened under this section shall be convened for a period not to exceed 5 years. Such conference may be extended by the Administrator, and if terminated after the initial period, may be reconvened by the Administrator at any time thereafter, as may be necessary to meet the requirements of this section.

(f) APPROVAL AND IMPLEMENTATION OF PLANS.—

(1) APPROVAL.— Not later than 120 days after the completion of a conservation and management plan and after providing for public review and comment, the Administrator shall approve such plan if the plan meets the requirements of this section and the affected Governor or Governors concur.

(2) IMPLEMENTATION.— Upon approval of a conservation and management plan under this section, such plan shall be implemented. Funds authorized to be appropriated under titles II and VI and section 319 of this Act may be used in accordance with the applicable requirements of this Act to assist States with the implementation of such plan.

(g) GRANTS.—

(1) RECIPIENTS.— The Administrator is authorized to make grants to State, interstate, and regional water pollution control agencies and entities, State coastal zone management agencies, interstate agencies, other public or nonprofit private agencies, institutions, organizations, and individuals.

(2) PURPOSES.— Grants under this subsection shall be made to pay for activities necessary for the development and implementation of a comprehensive conservation and management plan under this section.

(3) FEDERAL SHARE.—The Federal share of a grant to any person (including a State, interstate, or regional agency or entity) under this subsection for a fiscal year—

(A) shall not exceed—

(i) 75 percent of the annual aggregate costs of the development of a comprehensive conservation and management plan; and

(ii) 50 percent of the annual aggregate costs of the implementation of the plan; and

(B) shall be made on condition that the non-Federal share of the costs are provided from non-Federal sources.

(4) COMPETITIVE AWARDS.—

(A) IN GENERAL.— Using the amounts made available under subsection (i)(2)(B), the Administrator shall make competitive awards under this paragraph.

(B) APPLICATION FOR AWARDS.— The Administrator shall solicit applications for awards under this paragraph from State, interstate, and regional water pollution control agencies and entities, State coastal zone management agencies, interstate agencies, other public or nonprofit private agencies, institutions, organizations, and individuals.

(C) SELECTION OF RECIPIENTS.—In selecting award recipients under this paragraph, the Administrator shall select recipients that are best able to address urgent, emerging, and challenging issues that threaten the ecological and economic well-being of the estuaries selected by the Administrator under subsection (a)(2), or that relate to the coastal resiliency of such estuaries. Such issues shall include—

(i) extensive seagrass habitat losses resulting in significant impacts on fisheries and water quality;

(ii) recurring harmful algae blooms;

(iii) unusual marine mammal mortalities;

(iv) invasive exotic species that may threaten wastewater systems and cause other damage;

(v) jellyfish proliferation limiting community access to water during peak tourism seasons;

(vi) stormwater runoff;

(vii) accelerated land loss;

(viii) flooding that may be related to sea level rise, extreme weather, or wetland degradation or loss; and

(ix) low dissolved oxygen conditions in estuarine waters and related nutrient management.

(h) GRANT REPORTING.— Any person (including a State, interstate, or regional agency or entity) that receives a grant under subsection (g) shall report to the Administrator not later than 18 months after receipt of such grants and biennially thereafter on the progress being made under this section.

(i) AUTHORIZATION OF APPROPRIATIONS.—

(1) IN GENERAL.—There is authorized to be appropriated to the Administrator $26,500,000 for each of fiscal years 2017 through 2021, and $50,000,000 for each of fiscal years 2022 through 2026, for—

(A) expenses relating to the administration of grants or awards by the Administrator under this section, including the award and oversight of grants and awards, except that such expenses may not exceed 5 percent of the amount appropriated under this subsection for a fiscal year; and

(B) making grants and awards under subsection (g).

(2) ALLOCATIONS.—

(A) CONSERVATION AND MANAGEMENT PLANS.— Not less than 80 percent of the amount made available under this subsection for a fiscal year shall be used by the Administrator to provide grant assistance for the development, implementation, and monitoring of each of the conservation and management plans eligible for grant assistance under subsection (g)(2).

(B) COMPETITIVE AWARDS.— Not less than 15 percent of the amount made available under this subsection for a fiscal year shall be used by the Administrator for making competitive awards described in subsection (g)(4).

(j) RESEARCH.—

(1) PROGRAMS.—In order to determine the need to convene a management conference under this section or at the request of such a management conference, the Administrator shall coordinate and implement, through the National Marine Pollution Program Office and the National Marine Fisheries Service of the National

Oceanic and Atmospheric Administration, as appropriate, for one or more estuarine zones—

(A) a long-term program of trend assessment monitoring measuring variations in pollutant concentrations, marine ecology, and other physical or biological environmental parameters which may affect estuarine zones, to provide the Administrator the capacity to determine the potential and actual effects of alternative management strategies and measures;

(B) a program of ecosystem assessment assisting in the development of (i) baseline studies which determine the state of estuarine zones and the effects of natural and anthropogenic changes, and (ii) predictive models capable of translating information on specific discharges or general pollutant loadings within estuarine zones into a set of probable effects on such zones;

(C) a comprehensive water quality sampling program for the continuous monitoring of nutrients, chlorine, acid precipitation dissolved oxygen, and potentially toxic pollutants (including organic chemicals and metals) in estuarine zones, after consultation with interested State, local, interstate, or international agencies and review and analysis of all environmental sampling data presently collected from estuarine zones; and

(D) a program of research to identify the movements of nutrients, sediments and pollutants through estuarine zones and the impact of nutrients, sediments, and pollutants on water quality, the ecosystem, and designated or potential uses of the estuarine zones.

(2) Reports.—The Administrator, in cooperation with the Administrator of the National Oceanic and Atmospheric Administration, shall submit to the Congress no less often than biennially a comprehensive report on the activities authorized under this subsection including—

(A) a listing of priority monitoring and research needs;

(B) an assessment of the state and health of the Nation's estuarine zones, to the extent evaluated under this subsection;

(C) a discussion of pollution problems and trends in pollutant concentrations with a direct or indirect effect on water quality, the ecosystem, and designated or potential uses of each estuarine zone, to the extent evaluated under this subsection; and

(D) an evaluation of pollution abatement activities and management measures so far implemented to determine the degree of improvement toward the objectives expressed in subsection (b)(4) of this section.

(k) Definitions.— For purposes of this section, the terms estuary and estuarine zone have the meanings such terms have in section 104(n)(4) of this Act, except that the term estuarine zone shall also include associated aquatic ecosystems and those portions of tributaries draining into the estuary up to the historic height of migration of anadromous fish or the historic head of tidal influence, whichever is higher.

[33 U.S.C. 1330]

TITLE IV—PERMITS AND LICENCES

TITLE IV—PERMITS AND LICENSES

CERTIFICATION

SEC. 401. (a)(1) Any applicant for a Federal license or permit to conduct any activity including, but not limited to, the construction or operation of facilities, which may result in any discharge into the navigable waters, shall provide the licensing or permitting agency a certification from the State in which the discharge originates or will originate, or, if appropriate, from the interstate water pollution control agency having jurisdiction over the navigable waters at the point where the discharge originates or will originate, that any such discharge will comply with the applicable provisions of sections 301, 302, 303, 306, and 307 of this Act. In the case of any such activity for which there is not an applicable effluent limitation or other limitation under sections 301(b) and 302, and there is not an applicable standard under sections 306 and 307, the State shall so certify, except that any such certification shall not be deemed to satisfy section 511(c) of this Act. Such State or interstate agency shall establish procedures for public notice in the case of all applications for certification by it and, to the extent it deems appropriate, procedures for public hearings in connection with specific applications. In any case where a State or interstate agency has no authority to give such a certification, such certification shall be from the Administrator. If the State, interstate agency, or Administrator, as the case may be, fails or refuses to act on a request for certification, within a reasonable period of time (which shall not exceed one year) after receipt of such request, the certification requirements of this subsection shall be waived with respect to such Federal application. No license or permit shall be granted until the certification required by this section has been obtained or has been waived as provided in the preceding sentence. No license or permit shall be granted if certification has been denied by the State, interstate agency, or the Administrator, as the case may be.

(2) Upon receipt of such application and certification the licensing or permitting agency shall immediately notify the Administrator of such application and certification. Whenever such a discharge may affect, as determined by the Administrator, the quality of the waters of any other State, the Administrator within thirty days of the date of notice of application for such Federal license or permit shall so notify such other State, the licensing or permitting agency, and the applicant. If, within sixty days after receipt of such notification, such other State determines that such discharge will affect the quality of its waters so as to violate any water quality requirement in such State, and within such sixty-day period notifies the Administrator and the licensing or permitting agency in writing of its objection to the issuance of such license or permit and requests a public hearing on such objection, the licensing or permitting agency shall hold such a hearing. The Administrator shall at such hearing submit his evaluation and recommendations with respect to any such objection to the licensing or permitting agency. Such agency, based upon the recommendations of such State, the Administrator, and upon any additional evidence, if any, presented to the agency at the hearing, shall condition such license or permit in such manner as may be necessary to insure compliance with applicable water quality requirements. If the imposition of conditions cannot insure such compliance such agency shall not issue such license or permit.

(3) The certification obtained pursuant to paragraph (1) of this subsection with respect to the construction of any facility shall fulfill the requirements of this subsection with respect to certification in connection with any other Federal license or permit required for the operation of such facility unless, after notice to the certifying State, agency, or Administrator, as the case may be, which shall be given by the Federal agency to whom application is made for such operating license or permit, the State, or if appropriate, the interstate agency or the Administrator, notifies such agency within sixty days after receipt of such notice that there is no longer reasonable assurance that there will be compliance with the applicable provisions of sections 301, 302, 303, 306, and 307 of this Act because of changes since the construction license or permit certification was issued in (A) the construction or operation of the facility, (B) the characteristics of the waters into which such discharge is made, (C) the water quality criteria applicable to such waters or (D) applicable effluent limitations or other requirements. This paragraph shall be inapplicable in any case where the applicant for such operating license or permit has failed to provide the certifying State, or, if appropriate, the interstate agency or the Administrator, with notice of any proposed changes in the construction or operation of the facility with respect to which a construction license or permit has been granted, which changes may result in violation of section 301, 302, 303, 306, or 307 of this Act.

(4) Prior to the initial operation of any federally licensed or permitted facility or activity which may result in any discharge into the navigable waters and with respect to which a certification has been obtained pursuant to paragraph (1) of this subsection, which facility or activity is not subject to a Federal operating license or permit, the licensee or permittee shall provide an opportunity for such certifying State, or, if appropriate, the interstate agency or the Administrator to review the manner in which the facility or activity shall be operated or conducted for the purposes of assuring that applicable effluent limitations or other limitations or other applicable water quality requirements will not be violated. Upon notification by the certifying State, or if appropriate, the interstate agency or the Administrator that the operation of any such federally licensed or permitted facility or activity will violate applicable effluent limitations or other limitations or other water quality requirements such Federal agency may, after public hearing, suspend such license or permit. If such license or permit is suspended, it shall remain suspended until notification is received from the certifying State, agency, or Administrator, as the case may be, that there is reasonable assurance that such facility or activity will not violate the applicable provisions of section 301, 302, 303, 306, or 307 of this Act.

(5) Any Federal license or permit with respect to which a certification has been obtained under paragraph (1) of this subsection may be suspended or revoked by the Federal agency issuing such license or permit upon the entering of a judgment under this Act that such facility or activity has been operated in violation of the applicable provisions of section 301, 302, 303, 306, or 307 of this Act.

(6) Except with respect to a permit issued under section 402 of this Act, in any case where actual construction of a facility has been lawfully commenced prior to April 3, 1970, no certification shall be required under this subsection for a license or permit issued after April 3, 1970, to operate such facility, except that any such

license or permit issued without certification shall terminate April 3, 1973, unless prior to such termination date the person having such license or permit submits to the Federal agency which issued such license or permit a certification and otherwise meets the requirements of this section.

(b) Nothing in this section shall be construed to limit the authority of any department or agency pursuant to any other provision of law to require compliance with any applicable water quality requirements. The Administrator shall, upon the request of any Federal department or agency, or State or interstate agency, or applicant, provide, for the purpose of this section, any relevant information on applicable effluent limitations, or other limitations, standards, regulations, or requirements, or water quality criteria, and shall, when requested by any such department or agency or State or interstate agency, or applicant, comment on any methods to comply with such limitations, standards, regulations, requirements, or criteria.

(c) In order to implement the provisions of this section, the Secretary of the Army, acting through the Chief of Engineers, is authorized, if he deems it to be in the public interest, to permit the use of spoil disposal areas under his jurisdiction by Federal licensees or permittees, and to make an appropriate charge for such use. Moneys received from such licensees or permittees shall be deposited in the Treasury as miscellaneous receipts.

(d) Any certification provided under this section shall set forth any effluent limitations and other limitations, and monitoring requirements necessary to assure that any applicant for a Federal license or permit will comply with any applicable effluent limitations and other limitations, under section 301 or 302 of this Act, standard of performance under section 306 of this Act, or prohibition, effluent standard, or pretreatment standard under section 307 of this Act, and with any other appropriate requirement of State law set forth in such certification, and shall become a condition on any Federal license or permit subject to the provisions of this section.

[33 U.S.C. 1341]

NATIONAL POLLUTANT DISCHARGE ELIMINATION SYSTEM

SEC. 402. (a)(1) Except as provided in sections 318 and 404 of this Act, the Administrator may, after opportunity for public hearing, issue a permit for the discharge of any pollutant, or combination of pollutants, notwithstanding section 301(a), upon condition that such discharge will meet either (A) all applicable requirements under sections 301, 302, 306, 307, 308, and 403 of this Act, or (B) prior to the taking of necessary implementing actions relating to all such requirements, such conditions as the Administrator determines are necessary to carry out the provisions of this Act.

(2) The Administrator shall prescribe conditions for such permits to assure compliance with the requirements of paragraph (1) of this subsection, including conditions on data and information collection, reporting, and such other requirements as he deems appropriate.

(3) The permit program of the Administrator under paragraph (1) of this subsection, and permits issued thereunder, shall be subject to the same terms, conditions, and requirements as apply to a State permit program and permits issued thereunder under subsection (b) of this section.

(4) All permits for discharges into the navigable waters issued pursuant to section 13 of the Act of March 3, 1899, shall be deemed to be permits issued under this title, and permits issued under this title shall be deemed to be permits issued under section 13 of the Act of March 3, 1899, and shall continue in force and effect for their term unless revoked, modified, or suspended in accordance with the provisions of this Act.

(5) No permit for a discharge into the navigable waters shall be issued under section 13 of the Act of March 3, 1899, after the date of enactment of this title. Each application for a permit under section 13 of the Act of March 3, 1899, pending on the date of enactment of this Act shall be deemed to be an application for a permit under this section. The Administrator shall authorize a State, which he determines has the capability of administering a permit program which will carry out the objective of this Act, to issue permits for discharges into the navigable waters within the jurisdiction of such State. The Administrator may exercise the authority granted him by the preceding sentence only during the period which begins on the date of enactment of this Act and ends either on the ninetieth day after the date of the first promulgation of guidelines required by section 304(i)(2) of this Act, or the date of approval by the Administrator of a permit program for such State under subsection (b) of this section, whichever date first occurs, and no such authorization to a State shall extend beyond the last day of such period. Each such permit shall be subject to such conditions as the Administrator determines are necessary to carry out the provisions of this Act. No such permit shall issue if the Administrator objects to such issuance.

(b) At any time after the promulgation of the guidelines required by subsection (i)(2) of section 304 of this Act, the Governor of each State desiring to administer its own permit program for discharges into navigable waters within its jurisdiction may submit to the Administrator a full and complete description of the program it proposes to establish and administer under State law or under an interstate compact. In addition, such State shall submit a statement from the attorney general (or the attorney for those State water pollution control agencies which have independent legal counsel), or from the chief legal officer in the case of an interstate agency, that the laws of such State, or the interstate compact, as the case may be, provide adequate authority to carry out the described program. The Administrator shall approve each such submitted program unless he determines that adequate authority does not exist:

(1) To issue permits which—

(A) apply, and insure compliance with, any applicable requirements of sections 301, 302, 306, 307, and 403;

(B) are for fixed terms not exceeding five years; and

(C) can be terminated or modified for cause including, but not limited to, the following:

(i) violation of any condition of the permit;

(ii) obtaining a permit by misrepresentation, or failure to disclose fully all relevant facts;

(iii) change in any condition that requires either a temporary or permanent reduction or elimination of the permitted discharge;

(D) control the disposal of pollutants into wells;

(2)(A) To issue permits which apply, and insure compliance with, all applicable requirements of section 308 of this Act, or

(B) To inspect, monitor, enter, and require reports to at least the same extent as required in section 308 of this Act;

(3) To insure that the public, and any other State the waters of which may be affected, receive notice of each application for a permit and to provide an opportunity for public hearing before a ruling on each such application;

(4) To insure that the Administrator receives notice of each application (including a copy thereof) for a permit;

(5) To insure that any State (other than the permitting State), whose waters may be affected by the issuance of a permit may submit written recommendations to the permitting State (and the Administrator) with respect to any permit application and, if any part of such written recommendations are not accepted by the permitting State, that the permitting State will notify such affected State (and the Administrator) in writing of its failure to so accept such recommendations together with its reasons for so doing;

(6) To insure that no permit will be issued if, in the judgment of the Secretary of the Army acting through the Chief of Engineers, after consultation with the Secretary of the department in which the Coast Guard is operating, anchorage and navigation of any of the navigable waters would be substantially impaired thereby;

(7) To abate violations of the permit or the permit program, including civil and criminal penalties and other ways and means of enforcement;

(8) To insure that any permit for a discharge from a publicly owned treatment works includes conditions to require the identification in terms of character and volume of pollutants of any significant source introducing pollutants subject to pretreatment standards under section 307(b) of this Act into such works and a program to assure compliance with such pretreatment standards by each such source, in addition to adequate notice to the permitting agency of (A) new introductions into such works of pollutants from any source which would be a new source as defined in section 306 if such source were discharging pollutants, (B) new introductions of pollutants into such works from a source which would be subject to section 301 if it were discharging such pollutants, or (C) a substantial change in volume or character of pollutants being introduced into such works by a source introducing pollutants into such works at the time of issuance of the permit. Such notice shall include information on the quality and quantity of effluent to be introduced into such treatment works and any anticipated impact of such change in the quantity or quality of effluent to be discharged from such publicly owned treatment works; and

(9) To insure that any industrial user of any publicly owned treatment works will comply with sections 204(b), 307, and 308.

(c)(1) Not later than ninety days after the date on which a State has submitted a program (or revision thereof) pursuant to subsection (b) of this section, the

Administrator shall suspend the issuance of permits under subsection (a) of this section as to those discharges subject to such program unless he determines that the State permit program does not meet the requirements of subsection (b) of this section or does not conform to the guidelines issued under section 304(i)(2) of this Act. If the Administrator so determines, he shall notify the State of any revisions or modifications necessary to conform to such requirements or guidelines.

(2) Any State permit program under this section shall at all times be in accordance with this section and guidelines promulgated pursuant to section 304(i)(2) of this Act.

(3) Whenever the Administrator determines after public hearing that a State is not administering a program approved under this section in accordance with requirements of this section, he shall so notify the State and, if appropriate corrective action is not taken within a reasonable time, not to exceed ninety days, the Administrator shall withdraw approval of such program. The Administrator shall not withdraw approval of any such program unless he shall first have notified the State, and made public, in writing, the reasons for such withdrawal.

(4) LIMITATIONS ON PARTIAL PERMIT PROGRAM RETURNS AND WITHDRAWALS.—A State may return to the Administrator administration, and the Administrator may withdraw under paragraph (3) of this subsection approval, of—

(A) a State partial permit program approved under subsection (n)(3) only if the entire permit program being administered by the State department or agency at the time is returned or withdrawn; and

(B) a State partial permit program approved under subsection (n)(4) only if an entire phased component of the permit program being administered by the State at the time is returned or withdrawn.

(d)(1) Each State shall transmit to the Administrator a copy of each permit application received by such State and provide notice to the Administrator of every action related to the consideration of such permit application, including each permit proposed to be issued by such State.

(2) No permit shall issue (A) if the Administrator within ninety days of the date of his notification under subsection (b)(5) of this section objects in writing to the issuance of such permit, or (B) if the Administrator within ninety days of the date of transmittal of the proposed permit by the State objects in writing to the issuance of such permit as being outside the guidelines and requirements of this Act. Whenever the Administrator objects to the issuance of a permit under this paragraph such written objection shall contain a statement of the reasons for such objection and the effluent limitations and conditions which such permit would include if it were issued by the Administrator.

(3) The Administrator may, as to any permit application, waive paragraph (2) of this subsection.

(4) In any case where, after the date of enactment of this paragraph, the Administrator, pursuant to paragraph (2) of this subsection, objects to the issuance of a permit, on request of the State, a public hearing shall be held by the Administrator on such objection. If the State does not resubmit such permit revised to meet

such objection within 30 days after completion of the hearing, or, if no hearing is requested within 90 days after the date of such objection, the Administrator may issue the permit pursuant to subsection (a) of this section for such source in accordance with the guidelines and requirements of this Act.

(e) In accordance with guidelines promulgated pursuant to subsection (i)(2) of section 304 of this Act, the Administrator is authorized to waive the requirements of subsection (d) of this section at the time he approves a program pursuant to subsection (b) of this section for any category (including any class, type, or size within such category) of point sources within the State submitting such program.

(f) The Administrator shall promulgate regulations establishing categories of point sources which he determines shall not be subject to the requirements of subsection (d) of this section in any State with a program approved pursuant to subsection (b) of this section. The Administrator may distinguish among classes, types, and sizes within any category of point sources.

(g) Any permit issued under this section for the discharge of pollutants into the navigable waters from a vessel or other floating craft shall be subject to any applicable regulations promulgated by the Secretary of the Department in which the Coast Guard is operating, establishing specifications for safe transportation, handling, carriage, storage, and stowage of pollutants.

(h) In the event any condition of a permit for discharges from a treatment works (as defined in section 212 of this Act) which is publicly owned is violated, a State with a program approved under subsection (b) of this section or the Administrator, where no State program is approved or where the Administrator determines pursuant to section 309(a) of this Act that a State with an approved program has not commenced appropriate enforcement action with respect to such permit, may proceed in a court of competent jurisdiction to restrict or prohibit the introduction of any pollutant into such treatment works by a source not utilizing such treatment works prior to the finding that such condition was violated.

(i) Nothing in this section shall be construed to limit the authority of the Administrator to take action pursuant to section 309 of this Act.

(j) A copy of each permit application and each permit issued under this section shall be available to the public. Such permit application or permit, or portion thereof, shall further be available on request for the purpose of reproduction.

(k) Compliance with a permit issued pursuant to this section shall be deemed compliance, for purposes of sections 309 and 505, with sections 301, 302, 306, 307, and 403, except any standard imposed under section 307 for a toxic pollutant injurious to human health. Until December 31, 1974, in any case where a permit for discharge has been applied for pursuant to this section, but final administrative disposition of such application has not been made, such discharge shall not be a violation of (1) section 301, 306, or 402 of this Act, or (2) section 13 of the Act of March 3, 1899, unless the Administrator or other plaintiff proves that final administrative disposition of such application has not been made because of the failure of the applicant to furnish information reasonably required or requested in order to process the application. For the 180-day period beginning on the date of enactment of the Federal Water Pollution Control Act Amendments of 1972, in the case of any point source discharging any pollutant or combination of pollutants immediately prior to such date of enactment which source is not subject to section 13 of the Act of March 3, 1899, the discharge by such source shall not be a violation of this Act if such a source applies for a permit for discharge pursuant to this section within such 180-day period.

(l) LIMITATION ON PERMIT REQUIREMENT.—

(1) AGRICULTURAL RETURN FLOWS.— The Administrator shall not require a permit under this section for discharges composed entirely of return flows from irrigated agriculture, nor shall the Administrator directly or indirectly, require any State to require such a permit.

(2) STORMWATER RUNOFF FROM OIL, GAS, AND MINING OPERATIONS.— The Administrator shall not require a permit under this section, nor shall the Administrator directly or indirectly require any State to require a permit, for discharges of stormwater runoff from mining operations or oil and gas exploration, production, processing, or treatment operations or transmission facilities, composed entirely of flows which are from conveyances or systems of conveyances (including but not limited to pipes, conduits, ditches, and channels) used for collecting and conveying precipitation runoff and which are not contaminated by contact with, or do not come into contact with, any overburden, raw material, intermediate products, finished product, byproduct, or waste products located on the site of such operations.

(3) SILVICULTURAL ACTIVITIES.—

(A) NPDES PERMIT REQUIREMENTS FOR SILVICULTURAL ACTIVITIES.— The Administrator shall not require a permit under this section nor directly or indirectly require any State to require a permit under this section for a discharge from runoff resulting from the conduct of the following silviculture activities conducted in accordance with standard industry practice: nursery operations, site preparation, reforestation and subsequent cultural treatment, thinning, prescribed burning, pest and fire control, harvesting operations, surface drainage, or road construction and maintenance.

(B) OTHER REQUIREMENTS.— Nothing in this paragraph exempts a discharge from silvicultural activity from any permitting requirement under section 404, existing permitting requirements under section 402, or from any other federal law.

(C)[21] The authorization provided in Section[22] 505(a) does not apply to any non-permitting program established under 402(p)(6) for the silviculture activities listed in 402(l)(3)(A), or to any other limitations that might be deemed to apply to the silviculture activities listed in 402(l)(3)(A).

[21] So in law. Subparagraph (C) was enacted into law by an amendment made by section 12313 of Public Law 113–79 without including a heading.

[22] So in law. Probably should read section.

(m) ADDITIONAL PRETREATMENT OF CONVENTIONAL POLLUTANTS NOT REQUIRED.— To the extent a treatment works (as defined in section 212 of this Act) which is publicly owned is not meeting the requirements of a permit issued under this section for such treatment works as a result of inadequate design or operation of such treatment works, the Administrator, in issuing a permit under this section, shall not require pretreatment by a person introducing conventional pollutants identified pursuant to a section 304(a)(4) of this Act into such treatment works other than pretreatment required to assure compliance with pretreatment standards under subsection (b)(8) of this section and section 307(b)(1) of this Act. Nothing in this subsection shall affect the Administrator's authority under sections 307 and 309 of this Act, affect State and local authority under sections 307(b)(4) and 510 of this Act, relieve such treatment works of its obligations to meet requirements established under this Act, or otherwise preclude such works from pursuing whatever feasible options are available to meet its responsibility to comply with its permit under this section.

(n) Partial Permit Program.—

(1) State submission.— The Governor of a State may submit under subsection (b) of this section a permit program for a portion of the discharges into the navigable waters in such State.

(2) Minimum coverage.— A partial permit program under this subsection shall cover, at a minimum, administration of a major category of the discharges into the navigable waters of the State or a major component of the permit program required by subsection (b).

(3) Approval of major category partial permit programs.—The Administrator may approve a partial permit program covering administration of a major category of discharges under this subsection if—

(A) such program represents a complete permit program and covers all of the discharges under the jurisdiction of a department or agency of the State; and

(B) the Administrator determines that the partial program represents a significant and identifiable part of the State program required by subsection (b).

(4) Approval of major component partial permit programs.—The Administrator may approve under this subsection a partial and phased permit program covering administration of a major component (including discharge categories) of a State permit program required by subsection (b) if—

(A) the Administrator determines that the partial program represents a significant and identifiable part of the State program required by subsection (b); and

(B) the State submits, and the Administrator approves, a plan for the State to assume administration by phases of the remainder of the State program required by subsection (b) by a specified date not more than 5 years after submission of the partial program under this subsection and agrees to make all reasonable efforts to assume such administration by such date.

(o) Anti-Backsliding.—

(1) General prohibition.— In the case of effluent limitations established on the basis of subsection (a)(1)(B) of this section, a permit may not be renewed, reissued, or modified on the basis of effluent guidelines promulgated under section 304(b) subsequent to the original issuance of such permit, to contain effluent limitations

which are less stringent than the comparable effluent limitations in the previous permit. In the case of effluent limitations established on the basis of section 301(b)(1)(C) or section 303(d) or (e), a permit may not be renewed, reissued, or modified to contain effluent limitations which are less stringent than the comparable effluent limitations in the previous permit except in compliance with section 303(d)(4).

(2) Exceptions.—A permit with respect to which paragraph (1) applies may be renewed, reissued, or modified to contain a less stringent effluent limitation applicable to a pollutant if—

(A) material and substantial alterations or additions to the permitted facility occurred after permit issuance which justify the application of a less stringent effluent limitation;

(B)(i) information is available which was not available at the time of permit issuance (other than revised regulations, guidance, or test methods) and which would have justified the application of a less stringent effluent limitation at the time of permit issuance; or

(ii) the Administrator determines that technical mistakes or mistaken interpretations of law were made in issuing the permit under subsection (a)(1)(B);

(C) a less stringent effluent limitation is necessary because of events over which the permittee has no control and for which there is no reasonably available remedy;

(D) the permittee has received a permit modification under section 301(c), 301(g), 301(h), 301(i), 301(k), 301(n), or 316(a); or

(E) the permittee has installed the treatment facilities required to meet the effluent limitations in the previous permit and has properly operated and maintained the facilities but has nevertheless been unable to achieve the previous effluent limitations, in which case the limitations in the reviewed, reissued, or modified permit may reflect the level of pollutant control actually achieved (but shall not be less stringent than required by effluent guidelines in effect at the time of permit renewal, reissuance, or modification).

Subparagraph (B) shall not apply to any revised waste load allocations or any alternative grounds for translating water quality standards into effluent limitations, except where the cumulative effect of such revised allocations results in a decrease in the amount of pollutants discharged into the concerned waters, and such revised allocations are not the result of a discharger eliminating or substantially reducing its discharge of pollutants due to complying with the requirements of this Act or for reasons otherwise unrelated to water quality.

(3) Limitations.— In no event may a permit with respect to which paragraph (1) applies be renewed, reissued, or modified to contain an effluent limitation which is less stringent than required by effluent guidelines in effect at the time the permit is renewed, reissued, or modified. In no event may such a permit to discharge into waters be renewed, reissued, or modified to contain a less stringent effluent limitation if the implementation of such limitation would result in a violation of a

water quality standard under section 303 applicable to such waters.

(p) Municipal and Industrial Stormwater Discharges.—

(1) General rule.— Prior to October 1, 1994, the Administrator or the State (in the case of a permit program approved under section 402 of this Act) shall not require a permit under this section for discharges composed entirely of stormwater.

(2) Exceptions.—Paragraph (1) shall not apply with respect to the following stormwater discharges:

(A) A discharge with respect to which a permit has been issued under this section before the date of the enactment of this subsection.

(B) A discharge associated with industrial activity.

(C) A discharge from a municipal separate storm sewer system serving a population of 250,000 or more.

(D) A discharge from a municipal separate storm sewer system serving a population of 100,000 or more but less than 250,000.

(E) A discharge for which the Administrator or the State, as the case may be, determines that the stormwater discharge contributes to a violation of a water quality standard or is a significant contributor of pollutants to waters of the United States.

(3) Permit requirements.—

(A) Industrial discharges.— Permits for discharges associated with industrial activity shall meet all applicable provisions of this section and section 301.

(B) Municipal discharge.—Permits for discharges from municipal storm sewers—

(i) may be issued on a system- or jurisdiction-wide basis;

(ii) shall include a requirement to effectively prohibit non-stormwater discharges into the storm sewers; and

(iii) shall require controls to reduce the discharge of pollutants to the maximum extent practicable, including management practices, control techniques and system, design and engineering methods, and such other provisions as the Administrator or the State determines appropriate for the control of such pollutants.

(4) Permit application requirements.—

(A) Industrial and large municipal discharges.— Not later than 2 years after the date of the enactment of this subsection, the Administrator shall establish regulations setting forth the permit application requirements for stormwater discharges described in paragraphs (2)(B) and (2)(C). Applications for permits for such discharges shall be filed no later than 3 years after such date of enactment. Not later than 4 years after such date of enactment the Administrator or the State, as the case may be, shall issue or deny each such permit. Any such permit shall provide for compliance as expeditiously as practicable, but in no event later than 3 years after the date of issuance of such permit.

(B) Other municipal discharges.— Not later than 4 years after the date of the enactment of this subsection, the Administrator shall establish regulations setting forth the permit application requirements for stormwater discharges described in paragraph (2)(D). Applications for permits for such discharges shall be filed no later than 5 years after such date of enactment. Not later than 6 years after such date of enactment, the Administrator or the State, as the case may be, shall issue or deny each such permit. Any such permit shall provide for compliance as expeditiously as practicable, but in no event later than 3 years after the date of issuance of such permit.

(5) Studies.—The Administrator, in consultation with the States, shall conduct a study for the purposes of—

(A) identifying those stormwater discharges or classes of stormwater discharges for which permits are not required pursuant to paragraphs (1) and (2) of this subsection;

(B) determining, to the maximum extent practicable, the nature and extent of pollutants in such discharges; and

(C) establishing procedures and methods to control stormwater discharges to the extent necessary to mitigate impacts on water quality.

Not later than October 1, 1988, the Administrator shall submit to Congress a report on the results of the study described in subparagraphs (A) and (B). Not later than October 1, 1989, the Administrator shall submit to Congress a report on the results of the study described in subparagraph (C).

(6) Regulations.— Not later than October 1, 1993, the Administrator, in consultation with State and local officials, shall issue regulations (based on the results of the studies conducted under paragraph (5)) which designate stormwater discharges, other than those discharges described in paragraph (2), to be regulated to protect water quality and shall establish a comprehensive program to regulate such designated sources. The program shall, at a minimum, (A) establish priorities, (B) establish requirements for State stormwater management programs, and (C) establish expeditious deadlines. The program may include performance standards, guidelines, guidance, and management practices and treatment requirements, as appropriate.

(q) Combined Sewer Overflows.—

(1) Requirement for permits, orders, and decrees.— Each permit, order, or decree issued pursuant to this Act after the date of enactment of this subsection for a discharge from a municipal combined storm and sanitary sewer shall conform to the Combined Sewer Overflow Control Policy signed by the Administrator on April 11, 1994 (in this subsection referred to as the CSO control policy).

(2) Water quality and designated use review guidance.— Not later than July 31, 2001, and after providing notice and opportunity for public comment, the Administrator shall issue guidance to facilitate the conduct of water quality and designated use reviews for municipal combined sewer overflow receiving waters.

(3) Report.— Not later than September 1, 2001, the Administrator shall transmit

to Congress a report on the progress made by the Environmental Protection Agency, States, and municipalities in implementing and enforcing the CSO control policy.

(r) Discharges Incidental to the Normal Operation of Recreational Vessels.— No permit shall be required under this Act by the Administrator (or a State, in the case of a permit program approved under subsection (b)) for the discharge of any graywater, bilge water, cooling water, weather deck runoff, oil water separator effluent, or effluent from properly functioning marine engines, or any other discharge that is incidental to the normal operation of a vessel, if the discharge is from a recreational vessel.

(s) Integrated Plans.—

(1) Definition of integrated plan.— In this subsection, the term integrated plan means a plan developed in accordance with the Integrated Municipal Stormwater and Wastewater Planning Approach Framework, issued by the Environmental Protection Agency and dated June 5, 2012.

(2) In general.— The Administrator (or a State, in the case of a permit program approved by the Administrator) shall inform municipalities of the opportunity to develop an integrated plan that may be incorporated into a permit under this section.

(3) Scope.—

(A) Scope of permit incorporating integrated plan.—A permit issued under this section that incorporates an integrated plan may integrate all requirements under this Act addressed in the integrated plan, including requirements relating to—

(i) a combined sewer overflow;

(ii) a capacity, management, operation, and maintenance program for sanitary sewer collection systems;

(iii) a municipal stormwater discharge;

(iv) a municipal wastewater discharge; and

(v) a water quality-based effluent limitation to implement an applicable wasteload allocation in a total maximum daily load.

(B) Inclusions in integrated plan.—An integrated plan incorporated into a permit issued under this section may include the implementation of—

(i) projects, including innovative projects, to reclaim, recycle, or reuse water; and

(ii) green infrastructure.

(4) Compliance schedules.—

(A) In general.—A permit issued under this section that incorporates an integrated plan may include a schedule of compliance, under which actions taken to meet any applicable water quality-based effluent limitation may be implemented over more than 1 permit term if the schedule of compliance—

(i) is authorized by State water quality standards; and

(ii) meets the requirements of section 122.47 of title 40, Code of Federal Regulations (as in effect on the date of enactment of this subsection).

(B) TIME FOR COMPLIANCE.— For purposes of subparagraph (A)(ii), the requirement of section 122.47 of title 40, Code of Federal Regulations, for compliance by an applicable statutory deadline under this Act does not prohibit implementation of an applicable water quality-based effluent limitation over more than 1 permit term.

(C) REVIEW.— A schedule of compliance incorporated into a permit issued under this section may be reviewed at the time the permit is renewed to determine whether the schedule should be modified.

(5) EXISTING AUTHORITIES RETAINED.—

(A) APPLICABLE STANDARDS.— Nothing in this subsection modifies any obligation to comply with applicable technology and water quality-based effluent limitations under this Act.

(B) FLEXIBILITY.— Nothing in this subsection reduces or eliminates any flexibility available under this Act, including the authority of a State to revise a water quality standard after a use attainability analysis under section 131.10(g) of title 40, Code of Federal Regulations (or a successor regulation), subject to the approval of the Administrator under section 303(c).

(6) CLARIFICATION OF STATE AUTHORITY.—

(A) IN GENERAL.— Nothing in section 301(b)(1)(C) precludes a State from authorizing in the water quality standards of the State the issuance of a schedule of compliance to meet water quality-based effluent limitations in permits that incorporate provisions of an integrated plan.

(B) TRANSITION RULE.— In any case in which a discharge is subject to a judicial order or consent decree, as of the date of enactment of this subsection, resolving an enforcement action under this Act, any schedule of compliance issued pursuant to an authorization in a State water quality standard may not revise a schedule of compliance in that order or decree to be less stringent, unless the order or decree is modified by agreement of the parties and the court.

[33 U.S.C. 1342]

OCEAN DISCHARGE CRITERIA

SEC. 403. (a) No permit under section 402 of this Act for a discharge into the territorial sea, the waters of the contiguous zone, or the oceans shall be issued, after promulgation of guidelines established under subsection (c) of this section, except in compliance with such guidelines. Prior to the promulgation of such guidelines, a permit may be issued under such section 402 if the Administrator determines it to be in the public interest.

(b) The requirements of subsection (d) of section 402 of this Act may not be waived in the case of permits for discharges into the territorial sea.

(c)(1) The Administrator shall, within one hundred and eighty days after enactment of this Act (and from time to time thereafter), promulgate guidelines for determining the degradation of the waters of the territorial seas, the contiguous zone, and the oceans, which shall include:

(A) the effect of disposal of pollutants on human health or welfare, including but not limited to plankton, fish, shellfish, wildlife, shorelines, and beaches;

(B) the effect of disposal of pollutants on marine life including the transfer, concentration, and dispersal of pollutants or their byproducts through biological, physical, and chemical processes; changes in marine ecosystem diversity, productivity, and stability; and species and community population changes;

(C) the effect of disposal, of pollutants on esthetic, recreation, and economic values;

(D) the persistence and permanence of the effects of disposal of pollutants;

(E) the effect of the disposal at varying rates, of particular volumes and concentrations of pollutants;

(F) other possible locations and methods of disposal or recycling of pollutants including land-based alternatives; and

(G) the effect on alternate uses of the oceans, such as mineral exploitation and scientific study.

(2) In any event where insufficient information exists on any proposed discharge to make a reasonable judgment on any of the guidelines established pursuant to this subsection no permit shall be issued under section 402 of this Act.

[33 U.S.C. 1343]

PERMITS FOR DREDGED OR FILL MATERIAL

SEC. 404. (a) The Secretary may issue permits, after notice and opportunity for public hearings for the discharge of dredged or fill material into the navigable waters at specified disposal sites. Not later than the fifteenth day after the date an applicant submits all the information required to complete an application for a permit under this subsection, the Secretary shall publish the notice required by this subsection.

(b) Subject to subsection (c) of this section, each such disposal site shall be specified for each such permit by the Secretary (1) through the application of guidelines developed by the Administrator, in conjunction with the Secretary, which guidelines shall be based upon criteria comparable to the criteria applicable to the territorial seas, the contiguous zone, and the ocean under section 403(c), and (2) in any case where such guidelines under clause (1) alone would prohibit the specification of a site, through the application additionally of the economic impact of the site on navigation and anchorage.

(c) The Administrator is authorized to prohibit the specification (including the withdrawal of specification) of any defined area as a disposal site, and he is authorized to deny or restrict the use of any defined area for specification (including the withdrawal of specification) as a disposal site, whenever he determines, after notice and opportunity for public hearings, that the discharge of such materials into such area will have an unacceptable adverse effect on municipal water supplies, shellfish beds and fishery areas (including spawning and breeding areas), wildlife, or recreational areas. Before making such determination, the Administrator shall consult with the Secretary. The Administrator shall set forth in writing and make public his findings and his reasons for making any determination under this subsection.

(d) The term Secretary as used in this section means the Secretary of the Army, acting through the Chief of Engineers.

(e)(1) In carrying out his functions relating to the discharge of dredged or fill material under this section, the Secretary may, after notice and opportunity for public hearing, issue general permits on a State, regional, or nationwide basis for any category of activities involving discharges of dredged or fill material if the Secretary determines that the activities in such category are similar in nature, will cause only minimal adverse environmental effects when performed separately, and will have only minimal cumulative adverse effect on the environment. Any general permit issued under this subsection shall (A) be based on the guidelines described in subsection (b)(1) of this section, and (B) set forth the requirements and standards which shall apply to any activity authorized by such general permit.

(2) No general permit issued under this subsection shall be for a period of more than five years after the date of its issuance and such general permit may be revoked or modified by the Secretary if, after opportunity for public hearing, the Secretary determines that the activities authorized by such general permit have an adverse impact on the environment or such activities are more appropriately authorized by individual permits.

(f)(1) Except as provided in paragraph (2) of this subsection, the discharge of dredged or fill material—

(A) from normal farming, silviculture, and ranching activities such as plowing, seeding, cultivating, minor drainage, harvesting for the production of food, fiber, and forest products, or upland soil and water conservation practices;

(B) for the purpose of maintenance, including emergency reconstruction of recently damaged parts, of currently serviceable structures such as dikes, dams, levees, groins, riprap, breakwaters, causeways, and bridge abutments or approaches, and transportation structures;

(C) for the purpose of construction or maintenance of farm or stock ponds or irrigation ditches, or the maintenance of drainage ditches;

(D) for the purpose of construction of temporary sedimentation basins on a construction site which does not include placement of fill material into the navigable waters;

(E) for the purpose of construction or maintenance of farm roads or forest roads, or temporary roads for moving mining equipment, where such roads are constructed and maintained, in accordance with best management practices, to assure that flow and circulation patterns and chemical and biological characteristics of the navigable waters are not impaired, that the reach of the navigable waters is not reduced, and that any adverse effect on the aquatic environment will be otherwise minimized;

(F) resulting from any activity with respect to which a State has an approved program under section 208(b)(4) which meets the requirements of subparagraphs (B) and (C) of such section,

is not prohibited by or otherwise subject to regulation under this section or section 301(a) or 402 of this Act (except for effluent standards or prohibitions under section 307).

(2) Any discharge of dredged or fill material into the navigable waters incidental to any activity having as its purpose bringing an area of the navigable waters into a use to which it was not previously subject, where the flow or circulation of navigable waters may be impaired or the reach of such waters be reduced, shall be required to have a permit under this section.

(g)(1) The Governor of any State desiring to administer its own individual and general permit program for the discharge of dredged or fill material into the navigable waters (other than those waters which are presently used, or are susceptible to use in their natural condition or by reasonable improvement as a means to transport interstate or foreign commerce shoreward to their ordinary high water mark, including all waters which are subject to the ebb and flow of the tide shoreward to their mean high water mark, or mean higher high water mark on the west coast, including wetlands adjacent thereto) within its jurisdiction may submit to the Administrator a full and complete description of the program it proposes to establish and administer under State law or under an interstate compact. In addition, such State shall submit a statement from the attorney general (or the attorney for those State agencies which have independent legal counsel), or from the chief legal officer in the case of an interstate agency, that the laws of such State, or the interstate compact, as the case may be, provide adequate authority to carry out the described program.

(2) Not later than the tenth day after the date of the receipt of the program and statement submitted by any State under paragraph (1) of this subsection, the Administrator shall provide copies of such program and statement to the Secretary and the Secretary of the Interior, acting through the Director of the United States Fish and Wildlife Service.

(3) Not later than the ninetieth day after the date of the receipt by the Administrator of the program and statement submitted by any State, under paragraph (1) of this subsection, the Secretary and the Secretary of the Interior, acting through the Director of the United States Fish and Wildlife Service, shall submit any comments with respect to such program and statement to the Administrator in writing.

(h)(1) Not later than the one-hundred-twentieth day after the date of the receipt by the Administrator of a program and statement submitted by any State under paragraph (1) of this subsection, the Administrator shall determine, taking into account any comments submitted by the Secretary and the Secretary of the Interior, acting through the Director of the United States Fish and Wildlife Service, pursuant to subsection (g) of this section, whether such State has the following authority with respect to the issuance of permits pursuant to such program:

(A) To issue permits which—

(i) apply, and assure compliance with, any applicable requirements of this section, including, but not limited to, the guidelines established under subsection (b)(1) of this section, and sections 307 and 403 of this Act;

(ii) are for fixed terms not exceeding five years; and

(iii) can be terminated or modified for cause including, but not limited to, the following:

(I) violation of any condition of the permit;

(II) obtaining a permit by misrepresentation, or failure to disclose fully all relevant facts;

(III) change in any condition that requires either a temporary or permanent reduction or elimination of the permitted discharge.

(B) To issue permits which apply, and assure compliance with, all applicable requirements of section 308 of this Act, or to inspect, monitor, enter, and require reports to at least the same extent as required in section 308 of this Act.

(C) To assure that the public, and any other State the waters of which may be affected, receive notice of each application for a permit and to provide an opportunity for public hearing before a ruling on each such application.

(D) To assure that the Administrator receives notice of each application (including a copy thereof) for a permit.

(E) To assure that any State (other than the permitting State), whose waters may be affected by the issuance of a permit may submit written recommendations to the permitting State (and the Administrator) with respect to any permit application and, if any part of such written recommendations are not accepted by the permitting State, that the permitting State will notify such affected State (and the Administrator) in writing of its failure to so accept such recommendations together with its reasons for so doing.

(F) To assure that no permit will be issued if, in the judgment of the Secretary, after consultation with the Secretary of the department in which the Coast Guard is operating, anchorage and navigation of any of the navigable waters would be substantially impaired thereby.

(G) To abate violations of the permit or the permit program, including civil and criminal penalties and other ways and means of enforcement.

(H) To assure continued coordination with Federal and Federal-State water-related planning and review processes.

(2) If, with respect to a State program submitted under subsection (g)(1) of this section, the Administrator determines that such State—

(A) has the authority set forth in paragraph (1) of this subsection, the Administrator shall approve the program and so notify (i) such State and (ii) the Secretary, who upon subsequent notification from such State that it is administering such program, shall suspend the issuance of permits under subsection (a) and (e) of this section for activities with respect to which a permit may be issued pursuant to such State program; or

(B) does not have the authority set forth in paragraph (1) of this subsection, the Administrator shall so notify such State, which notification shall also describe the revisions or modifications necessary so that such State may resubmit such program for a determination by the Administrator under this subsection.

(3) If the Administrator fails to make a determination with respect to any program submitted by a State under subsection (g)(1) of this section within one-

hundred-twenty days after the date of the receipt of such program, such program shall be deemed approved pursuant to paragraph (2)(A) of this subsection and the Administrator shall so notify such State and the Secretary who, upon subsequent notification from such State that it is administering such program, shall suspend the issuance of permits under subsection (a) and (e) of this section for activities with respect to which a permit may be issued by such State.

(4) After the Secretary receives notification from the Administrator under paragraph (2) or (3) of this subsection that a State permit program has been approved, the Secretary shall transfer any applications for permits pending before the Secretary for activities with respect to which a permit may be issued pursuant to such State program to such State for appropriate action.

(5) Upon notification from a State with a permit program approved under this subsection that such State intends to administer and enforce the terms and conditions of a general permit issued by the Secretary under subsection (e) of this section with respect to activities in such State to which such general permit applies, the Secretary shall suspend the administration and enforcement of such general permit with respect to such activities.

(i) Whenever the Administrator determines after public hearing that a State is not administering a program approved under section (h)(2)(A) of this section, in accordance with this section, including, but not limited to, the guidelines established under subsection (b)(1) of this section, the Administrator shall so notify the State, and, if appropriate corrective action is not taken within a reasonable time, not to exceed ninety days after the date of the receipt of such notification, the Administrator shall (1) withdraw approval of such program until the Administrator determines such corrective action has been taken, and (2) notify the Secretary that the Secretary shall resume the program for the issuance of permits under subsections (a) and (e) of this section for activities with respect to which the State was issuing permits and that such authority of the Secretary shall continue in effect until such time as the Administrator makes the determination described in clause (1) of this subsection and such State again has an approved program.

(j) Each State which is administering a permit program pursuant to this section shall transmit to the Administrator (1) a copy of each permit application received by such State and provide notice to the Administrator of every action related to the consideration of such permit application, including each permit proposed to be issued by such State, and (2) a copy of each proposed general permit which such State intends to issue. Not later than the tenth day after the date of the receipt of such permit application or such proposed general permit, the Administrator shall provide copies of such permit application or such proposed general permit to the Secretary and the Secretary of the Interior, acting through the Director of the United States Fish and Wildlife Service. If the Administrator intends to provide written comments to such State with respect to such permit application or such proposed general permit, he shall so notify such State not later than the thirtieth day after the date of the receipt of such application or such proposed general permit and provide such written comments to such State, after consideration of any comments made in writing with respect to such application or such proposed general permit by the Secretary and the Secretary of the Interior, acting through the Director of the United States Fish and Wildlife Service, not later than the ninetieth day after the date of such receipt. If such State is so notified by the Administrator, it shall not issue the proposed permit until after the receipt of such comments from the Administrator, or after such ninetieth day, whichever first occurs. Such State shall not issue such proposed permit after such ninetieth day if it has received such written comments in which the Administrator objects (A) to the issuance of such proposed permit and such proposed permit is one that has been submitted to the Administrator pursuant to subsection (h)(1)(E), or (B) to the issuance of such proposed permit as being outside the requirements of this section, including, but not limited to, the guidelines developed under subsection (b)(1) of this section unless it modifies such proposed permit in accordance with such comments. Whenever the Administrator objects to the issuance of a permit under the preceding sentence such written objection shall contain a statement of the reasons for such objection and the conditions which such permit would include if it were issued by the Administrator. In any case where the Administrator objects to the issuance of a permit, on request of the State, a public hearing shall be held by the Administrator on such objection. If the State does not resubmit such permit revised to meet such objection within 30 days after completion of the hearing or, if no hearing is requested within 90 days after the date of such objection, the Secretary may issue the permit pursuant to subsection (a) or (e) of this section, as the case may be, for such source in accordance with the guidelines and requirements of this Act.

(k) In accordance with guidelines promulgated pursuant to subsection (i)(2) of section 304 of this Act, the Administrator is authorized to waive the requirements of subsection (j) of this section at the time of the approval of a program pursuant to subsection (h)(2)(A) of this section for any category (including any class, type, or size within such category) of discharge within the State submitting such program.

(l) The Administrator shall promulgate regulations establishing categories of discharges which he determines shall not be subject to the requirements of subsection (j) of this section in any State with a program approved pursuant to subsection (h)(2)(A) of this section. The Administrator may distinguish among classes, types, and sizes within any category of discharges.

(m) Not later than the ninetieth day after the date on which the Secretary notifies the Secretary of the Interior, acting through the Director of the United States Fish and Wildlife Service that (1) an application for a permit under subsection (a) of this section has been received by the Secretary, or (2) the Secretary proposes to issue a general permit under subsection (e) of this section, the Secretary of the Interior, acting through the Director of the United States Fish and Wildlife Service, shall submit any comments with respect to such application or such proposed general permit in writing to the Secretary.

(n) Nothing in this section shall be construed to limit the authority of the Administrator to take action pursuant to section 309 of this Act.

(o) A copy of each permit application and each permit issued under this section shall be available to the public. Such permit application or portion thereof, shall further be available on request for the purpose of reproduction.

(p) Compliance with a permit issued pursuant to this section, including any activity carried out pursuant to a general permit issued under this section, shall be deemed compliance, for purposes of sections 309 and 505, with sections 301, 307, and 403.

(q) Not later than the one-hundred-eightieth day after the date of enactment of this subsection, the Secretary shall enter into agreements with the Administrator, the Secretaries of the Departments of Agriculture, Commerce, Interior, and Transportation, and the heads of other appropriate Federal agencies to minimize, to the maximum extent practicable, duplication, needless paperwork, and delays in the issuance of permits under this section. Such agreements shall be developed to assure that, to the maximum extent practicable, a decision with respect to an application for a permit under subsection (a) of this section will be made not later than the ninetieth day after the date the notice of such application is published under subsection (a) of this section.

(r) The discharge of dredged or fill material as part of the construction of a Federal project specifically authorized by Congress, whether prior to or on or after the date of enactment of this subsection, is not prohibited by or otherwise subject to regulation under this section, or a State program approved under this section, or section 301(a) or 402 of the Act (except for effluent standards or prohibitions under section 307), if information on the effects of such discharge, including consideration of the guidelines developed under subsection (b)(1) of this section, is included in an environmental impact statement for such project pursuant to the National Environmental Policy Act of 1969 and such environmental impact statement has been submitted to Congress before the actual discharge of dredged or fill material in connection with the construction of such project and prior to either authorization of such project or an appropriation of funds for such construction.

(s)(1) Whenever on the basis of any information available to him the Secretary finds that any person is in violation of any condition or limitation set forth in a permit issued by the Secretary under this section, the Secretary shall issue an order requiring such persons to comply with such condition or limitation, or the Secretary shall bring a civil action in accordance with paragraph (3) of this subsection.

(2) A copy of any order issued under this subsection shall be sent immediately by the Secretary to the State in which the violation occurs and other affected States. Any order issued under this subsection shall be by personal service and shall state with reasonable specificity the nature of the violation, specify a time for compliance, not to exceed thirty days, which the Secretary determines is reasonable, taking into account the seriousness of the violation and any good faith efforts to comply with applicable requirements. In any case in which an order under this subsection is issued to a corporation, a copy of such order shall be served on any appropriate corporate officers.

(3) The Secretary is authorized to commence a civil action for appropriate relief, including a permanent or temporary injunction for any violation for which he is authorized to issue a compliance order under paragraph (1) of this subsection. Any action under this paragraph may be brought in the district court of the United States for the district in which the defendant is located or resides or is doing business, and such court shall have jurisdiction to restrain such violation and to require compliance. Notice of the commencement of such acton[23] shall be given immediately to the appropriate State.

---

[23] So in law. Probably should be action.

(4) Any person who violates any condition or limitation in a permit issued by the Secretary under this section, and any person who violates any order issued by the Secretary under paragraph (1) of this subsection, shall be subject to a civil penalty not to exceed $25,000 per day for each violation. In determining the amount of a civil penalty the court shall consider the seriousness of the violation or violations, the economic benefit (if any) resulting from the violation, any history of such violations, any good-faith efforts to comply with the applicable requirements, the economic impact of the penalty on the violator, and such other matters as justice may require.

(t) Nothing in the section shall preclude or deny the right of any State or interstate agency to control the discharge of dredged or fill material in any portion of the navigable waters within the jurisdiction of such State, including any activity of any Federal agency, and each such agency shall comply with such State or interstate requirements both substantive and procedural to control the discharge of dredged or fill material to the same extent that any person is subject to such requirements. This section shall not be construed as affecting or impairing the authority of the Secretary to maintain navigation.

[33 U.S.C. 1344]

DISPOSAL OF SEWAGE SLUDGE

SEC. 405. (a) Notwithstanding any other provision of this Act or of any other law, in the case where the disposal of sewage sludge resulting from the operation of a treatment works as defined in section 212 of this Act (including the removal of in-place sewage sludge from one location and its deposit at another location) would result in any pollutant from such sewage sludge entering the navigable waters, such disposal is prohibited except in accordance with a permit issued by the Administrator under section 402 of this Act.

(b) The Administrator shall issue regulations governing the issuance of permits for the disposal of sewage sludge subject to subsection (a) of this section and section 402 of this Act. Such regulations shall require the application to such disposal of each criterion, factor, procedure, and requirement applicable to a permit issued under section 402 of this title.

(c) Each State desiring to administer its own permit program for disposal of sewage sludge subject to subsection (a) of this section within its jurisdiction may do so in accordance with section 402 of this Act.

(d) REGULATIONS.—

(1) REGULATIONS.—The Administrator, after consultation with appropriate Federal and State agencies and other interested persons, shall develop and publish, within one year after the date of enactment of this subsection and from time to time thereafter, regulations providing guidelines for the disposal of sludge and the utilization of sludge for various purposes. Such regulations shall—

(A) identify uses for sludge, including disposal;

(B) specify factors to be taken into account in determining the measures and practices applicable to each such use or disposal (including publication of information on costs);

(C) identify concentrations of pollutants which interfere with each such use or disposal.

The Administrator is authorized to revise any regulation issued under this subsection.

(2) IDENTIFICATION AND REGULATION OF TOXIC POLLUTANTS.—

(A) ON BASIS OF AVAILABLE INFORMATION.—

(i) PROPOSED REGULATIONS.— Not later than November 30, 1986, the Administrator shall identify those toxic pollutants which, on the basis of available information on their toxicity, persistence, concentration, mobility, or potential for exposure, may be present in sewage sludge in concentrations which may adversely affect public health or the environment, and propose regulations specifying acceptable management practices for sewage sludge containing each such toxic pollutant and establishing numerical limitations for each such pollutant for each use identified under paragraph (1)(A).

(ii) FINAL REGULATIONS.— Not later than August 31, 1987, and after opportunity for public hearing, the Administrator shall promulgate the regulations required by subparagraph (A)(i).

(B) OTHERS.—

(i) PROPOSED REGULATIONS.— Not later than July 31, 1987, the Administrator shall identify those toxic pollutants not identified under subparagraph (A)(i) which may be present in sewage sludge in concentrations which may adversely affect public health or the environment, and propose regulations specifying acceptable management practices for sewage sludge containing each such toxic pollutant and establishing numerical limitations for each pollutant for each such use identified under paragraph (1)(A).

(ii) FINAL REGULATIONS.— Not later than June 15, 1988, the Administrator shall promulgate the regulations required by subparagraph (B)(i).

(C) REVIEW.— From time to time, but not less often than every 2 years, the Administrator shall review the regulations promulgated under this paragraph for the purpose of identifying additional toxic pollutants and promulgating regulations for such pollutants consistent with the requirements of this paragraph.

(D) MINIMUM STANDARDS; COMPLIANCE DATE.— The management practices and numerical criteria established under subparagraphs (A), (B), and (C) shall be adequate to protect public health and the environment from any reasonably anticipated adverse effects of each pollutant. Such regulations shall require compliance as expeditiously as practicable but in no case later than 12 months after their publication, unless such regulations require the construction of new pollution control facilities, in which case the regulations shall require compliance as expeditiously as practicable but in no case later than two years from the date of their publication.

(3) ALTERNATIVE STANDARDS.— For purposes of this subsection, if, in the

judgment of the Administrator, it is not feasible to prescribe or enforce a numerical limitation for a pollutant identified under paragraph (2), the Administrator may instead promulgate a design, equipment, management practice, or operational standard, or combination thereof, which in the Administrator's judgment is adequate to protect public health and the environment from any reasonably anticipated adverse effects of such pollutant. In the event the Administrator promulgates a design or equipment standard under this subsection, the Administrator shall include as part of such standard such requirements as will assure the proper operation and maintenance of any such element of design or equipment.

(4) Conditions on permits.— Prior to the promulgation of the regulations required by paragraph (2), the Administrator shall impose conditions in permits issued to publicly owned treatment works under section 402 of this Act or take such other measures as the Administrator deems appropriate to protect public health and the environment from any adverse effects which may occur from toxic pollutants in sewage sludge.

(5) Limitation on statutory construction.— Nothing in this section is intended to waive more stringent requirements established by this Act or any other law.

(e) Manner of Sludge Disposal.— The determination of the manner of disposal or use of sludge is a local determination, except that it shall be unlawful for any person to dispose of sludge from a publicly owned treatment works or any other treatment works treating domestic sewage for any use for which regulations have been established pursuant to subsection (d) of this section, except in accordance with such regulations.

(f) Implementation of Regulations.—

(1) Through section 402 permits.— Any permit issued under section 402 of this Act to a publicly owned treatment works or any other treatment works treating domestic sewage shall include requirements for the use and disposal of sludge that implement the regulations established pursuant to subsection (d) of this section, unless such requirements have been included in a permit issued under the appropriate provisions of subtitle C of the Solid Waste Disposal Act, part C of the Safe Drinking Water Act, the Marine Protection, Research, and Sanctuaries Act of 1972, or the Clean Air Act, or under State permit programs approved by the Administrator, where the Administrator determines that such programs assure compliance with any applicable requirements of this section. Not later than December 15, 1986, the Administrator shall promulgate procedures for approval of State programs pursuant to this paragraph.

(2) Through other permits.— In the case of a treatment works described in paragraph (1) that is not subject to section 402 of this Act and to which none of the other above listed permit programs nor approved State permit authority apply, the Administrator may issue a permit to such treatment works solely to impose requirements for the use and disposal of sludge that implement the regulations established pursuant to subsection (d) of this section. The Administrator shall include in the permit appropriate requirements to assure compliance with the regulations established pursuant to subsection (d) of this section. The Administrator shall establish procedures for issuing permits pursuant to this paragraph.

(g) Studies and Projects.—

(1) Grant program; information gathering.— The Administrator is authorized to conduct or initiate scientific studies, demonstration projects, and public information and education projects which are designed to promote the safe and beneficial management or use of sewage sludge for such purposes as aiding the restoration of abandoned mine sites, conditioning soil for parks and recreation areas, agricultural and horticultural uses, and other beneficial purposes. For the purposes of carrying out this subsection, the Administrator may make grants to State water pollution control agencies, other public or nonprofit agencies, institutions, organizations, and individuals. In cooperation with other Federal departments and agencies, other public and private agencies, institutions, and organizations, the Administrator is authorized to collect and disseminate information pertaining to the safe and beneficial use of sewage sludge.

(2) Authorization of appropriations.— For the purposes of carrying out the scientific studies, demonstration projects, and public information and education projects authorized in this section, there is authorized to be appropriated for fiscal years beginning after September 30, 1986, not to exceed $5,000,000.

[33 U.S.C. 1345]

SEC. 406. COASTAL RECREATION WATER QUALITY MONITORING AND NOTIFICATION.

(a) Monitoring and Notification.—

(1) In general.—Not later than 18 months after the date of the enactment of this section, after consultation and in cooperation with appropriate Federal, State, tribal, and local officials (including local health officials), and after providing public notice and an opportunity for comment, the Administrator shall publish performance criteria for—

(A) monitoring and assessment (including specifying available methods for monitoring) of coastal recreation waters adjacent to beaches or similar points of access that are used by the public for attainment of applicable water quality standards for pathogens and pathogen indicators; and

(B) the prompt notification of the public, local governments, and the Administrator of any exceeding of or likelihood of exceeding applicable water quality standards for coastal recreation waters described in subparagraph (A).

(2) Level of protection.— The performance criteria referred to in paragraph (1) shall provide that the activities described in subparagraphs (A) and (B) of that paragraph shall be carried out as necessary for the protection of public health and safety.

(b) Program Development and Implementation Grants.—

(1) In general.— The Administrator may make grants to States and local governments to develop and implement programs for monitoring and notification for coastal recreation waters adjacent to beaches or similar points of access that are used by the public.

(2) Limitations.—

(A) In general.—The Administrator may award a grant to a State or a local government to implement a monitoring and notification program if—

(i) the program is consistent with the performance criteria published by the Administrator under subsection (a);

(ii) the State or local government prioritizes the use of grant funds for particular coastal recreation waters based on the use of the water and the risk to human health presented by pathogens or pathogen indicators;

(iii) the State or local government makes available to the Administrator the factors used to prioritize the use of funds under clause (ii);

(iv) the State or local government provides a list of discrete areas of coastal recreation waters that are subject to the program for monitoring and notification for which the grant is provided that specifies any coastal recreation waters for which fiscal constraints will prevent consistency with the performance criteria under subsection (a); and

(v) the public is provided an opportunity to review the program through a process that provides for public notice and an opportunity for comment.

(B) GRANTS TO LOCAL GOVERNMENTS.— The Administrator may make a grant to a local government under this subsection for implementation of a monitoring and notification program only if, after the 1-year period beginning on the date of publication of performance criteria under subsection (a)(1), the Administrator determines that the State is not implementing a program that meets the requirements of this subsection, regardless of whether the State has received a grant under this subsection.

(3) OTHER REQUIREMENTS.—

(A) REPORT.—A State recipient of a grant under this subsection shall submit to the Administrator, in such format and at such intervals as the Administrator determines to be appropriate, a report that describes—

(i) data collected as part of the program for monitoring and notification as described in subsection (c); and

(ii) actions taken to notify the public when water quality standards are exceeded.

(B) DELEGATION.— A State recipient of a grant under this subsection shall identify each local government to which the State has delegated or intends to delegate responsibility for implementing a monitoring and notification program consistent with the performance criteria published under subsection (a) (including any coastal recreation waters for which the authority to implement a monitoring and notification program would be subject to the delegation).

(4) FEDERAL SHARE.—

(A) IN GENERAL.— The Administrator, through grants awarded under this section, may pay up to 100 percent of the costs of developing and implementing a program for monitoring and notification under this subsection.

(B) NON-FEDERAL SHARE.—The non-Federal share of the costs of developing and implementing a monitoring and notification program may be—

(i) in an amount not to exceed 50 percent, as determined by the Administrator in consultation with State, tribal, and local government representatives; and

(ii) provided in cash or in kind.

(c) CONTENT OF STATE AND LOCAL GOVERNMENT PROGRAMS.—As a condition of receipt of a grant under subsection (b), a State or local government program for monitoring and notification under this section shall identify—

(1) lists of coastal recreation waters in the State, including coastal recreation waters adjacent to beaches or similar points of access that are used by the public;

(2) in the case of a State program for monitoring and notification, the process by which the State may delegate to local governments responsibility for implementing the monitoring and notification program;

(3) the frequency and location of monitoring and assessment of coastal recreation waters based on—

(A) the periods of recreational use of the waters;

(B) the nature and extent of use during certain periods;

(C) the proximity of the waters to known point sources and nonpoint sources of pollution; and

(D) any effect of storm events on the waters;

(4)(A) the methods to be used for detecting levels of pathogens and pathogen indicators that are harmful to human health; and

(B) the assessment procedures for identifying short-term increases in pathogens and pathogen indicators that are harmful to human health in coastal recreation waters (including increases in relation to storm events);

(5) measures for prompt communication of the occurrence, nature, location, pollutants involved, and extent of any exceeding of, or likelihood of exceeding, applicable water quality standards for pathogens and pathogen indicators to—

(A) the Administrator, in such form as the Administrator determines to be appropriate; and

(B) a designated official of a local government having jurisdiction over land adjoining the coastal recreation waters for which the failure to meet applicable standards is identified;

(6) measures for the posting of signs at beaches or similar points of access, or functionally equivalent communication measures that are sufficient to give notice to the public that the coastal recreation waters are not meeting or are not expected to meet applicable water quality standards for pathogens and pathogen indicators; and

(7) measures that inform the public of the potential risks associated with water contact activities in the coastal recreation waters that do not meet applicable water quality standards.

(d) FEDERAL AGENCY PROGRAMS.—Not later than 3 years after the date of the enactment of this section, each Federal agency that has jurisdiction over coastal recreation waters adjacent to beaches or similar points of access that are used by the public shall develop and implement, through a process that provides for public notice and an opportunity for comment, a monitoring and notification program for the coastal recreation waters that—

(1) protects the public health and safety;

(2) is consistent with the performance criteria published under subsection (a);

(3) includes a completed report on the information specified in subsection (b)(3)(A), to be submitted to the Administrator; and

(4) addresses the matters specified in subsection (c) .

(e) DATABASE.—The Administrator shall establish, maintain, and make available to the public by electronic and other means a national coastal recreation water pollution occurrence database that provides—

(1) the data reported to the Administrator under subsections (b)(3)(A)(i) and (d)(3); and

(2) other information concerning pathogens and pathogen indicators in coastal recreation waters that—

(A) is made available to the Administrator by a State or local government, from a coastal water quality monitoring program of the State or local government; and

(B) the Administrator determines should be included.

(f) TECHNICAL ASSISTANCE FOR MONITORING FLOATABLE MATERIAL.— The Administrator shall provide technical assistance to States and local governments for the development of assessment and monitoring procedures for floatable material to protect public health and safety in coastal recreation waters.

(g) LIST OF WATERS.—

(1) IN GENERAL.—Beginning not later than 18 months after the date of publication of performance criteria under subsection (a), based on information made available to the Administrator, the Administrator shall identify, and maintain a list of, discrete coastal recreation waters adjacent to beaches or similar points of access that are used by the public that—

(A) specifies any waters described in this paragraph that are subject to a monitoring and notification program consistent with the performance criteria established under subsection (a); and

(B) specifies any waters described in this paragraph for which there is no monitoring and notification program (including waters for which fiscal constraints will prevent the State or the Administrator from performing monitoring and notification consistent with the performance criteria established under subsection (a)).

(2) AVAILABILITY.—The Administrator shall make the list described in paragraph (1) available to the public through—

(A) publication in the Federal Register; and

(B) electronic media.

(3) UPDATES.— The Administrator shall update the list described in paragraph (1) periodically as new information becomes available.

(h) EPA IMPLEMENTATION.—In the case of a State that has no program for monitoring and notification that is consistent with the performance criteria published under subsection (a) after the last day of the 3-year period beginning on the date on which the Administrator lists waters in the State under subsection (g)(1)(B), the Administrator shall conduct a monitoring and notification program for the listed waters based on a priority ranking established by the Administrator using funds appropriated for grants under subsection (i)—

(1) to conduct monitoring and notification; and

(2) for related salaries, expenses, and travel.

(i) AUTHORIZATION OF APPROPRIATIONS.— There is authorized to be appropriated for making grants under subsection (b), including implementation of monitoring and notification programs by the Administrator under subsection (h), $30,000,000 for each of fiscal years 2001 through 2005.

[33 U.S.C. 1346]

TITLE V—GENERAL PROVISIONS

TITLE V—GENERAL PROVISIONS

ADMINISTRATION

SEC. 501. (a) The Administrator is authorized to prescribe such regulations as are necessary to carry out his functions under this Act.

(b) The Administrator, with the consent of the head of any other agency of the United States, may utilize such officers and employees of such agency as may be found necessary to assist in carrying out the purposes of this Act.

(c) Each recipient of financial assistance under this Act shall keep such records as the Administrator shall prescribe, including records which fully disclose the amount and disposition by such recipient of the proceeds of such assistance, the total cost of the project or undertaking in connection with which such assistance is given or used, and the amount of that portion of the cost of the project or undertaking supplied by other sources, and such other records as will facilitate an effective audit.

(d) The Administrator and the Comptroller General of the United States, or any of their duly authorized representatives, shall have access, for the purpose of audit and examination, to any books, documents, papers, and records of the recipients that are pertinent to the grants received under this Act. For the purpose of carrying out audits and examinations with respect to recipients of Federal assistance under this Act, the Administrator is authorized to enter into noncompetitive procurement contracts with independent State audit organizations, consistent with chapter 75 of title 31, United States Code. Such contracts may only be entered into to the extent and in such amounts as may be provided in advance in appropriation Acts.

(e)(1) It is the purpose of this subsection to authorize a program which will provide official recognition by the United States Government to those industrial organizations and political subdivisions of States which during the preceding year demonstrated an outstanding technological achievement or an innovative process, method, or device in their waste treatment and pollution abatement programs. The Administrator shall, in consultation with the appropriate State water pollution control agencies, establish regulations under which such recognition may be applied for and granted, except that no applicant shall be eligible for an award under this subsection if such applicant is not in total compliance with all applicable water quality requirements under this Act, or otherwise does not have a satisfactory record with respect to environmental quality.

(2) The Administrator shall award a certificate or plaque of suitable design to each industrial organization or political subdivision which qualifies for such recognition under regulations established under this subsection.

(3) The President of the United States, the Governor of the appropriate State, the Speaker of the House of Representatives, and the President pro tempore of the Senate shall be notified of the award by the Administrator and the awarding of such recognition shall be published in the Federal Register.

(f) Upon the request of a State water pollution control agency, personnel of the Environmental Protection Agency may be detailed to such agency for the purpose of carrying out the provisions of this Act.

[33 U.S.C. 1361]

GENERAL DEFINITIONS

SEC. 502. Except as otherwise specifically provided, when used in this Act:

(1) The term State water pollution control agency means the State agency designated by the Governor having responsibility for enforcing State laws relating to the abatement of pollution.

(2) The term interstate agency means an agency of two or more States established by or pursuant to an agreement or compact approved by the Congress, or any other agency of two or more States, having substantial powers or duties pertaining to the control of pollution as determined and approved by the Administrator.

(3) The term State means a State, the District of Columbia, the Commonwealth of Puerto Rico, the Virgin Islands, Guam, American Samoa, the Commonwealth of the Northern Mariana Islands, and the Trust Territory of the Pacific Islands.

(4) The term municipality means a city, town, borough, county, parish, district, association, or other public body created by or pursuant to State law and having jurisdiction over disposal of sewage, industrial wastes, or other wastes, or an Indian tribe or an authorized Indian tribal organization, or a designated and approved management agency under section 208 of this Act.

(5) The term person means an individual, corporation, partnership, association, State, municipality, commission, or political subdivision of a State, or any interstate body.

(6) The term pollutant means dredged spoil, solid waste, incinerator residue, sewage, garbage, sewage sludge, munitions, chemical wastes, biological materials, radioactive materials, heat, wrecked or discarded equipment, rock, sand, cellar dirt and industrial, municipal, and agricultural waste discharged into water. This term does not mean (A) sewage from vessels or a discharge incidental to the normal operation of a vessel of the Armed Forces within the meaning of section 312 of this Act; or (B) water, gas, or other material which is injected into a well to facilitate production of oil or gas, or water derived in association with oil or gas production and disposed of in a well, if the well used either to facilitate production or for disposal purposes is approved by authority of the State in which the well is located, and if such State determines that such injection or disposal will not result in the degradation of ground or surface water resources.

(7) The term navigable waters means the waters of the United States, including the territorial seas.

(8) The term territorial seas means the belt of the seas measured from the line of ordinary low water along that portion of the coast which is in direct contact with the open sea and the line marking the seaward limit of inland waters, and extending seaward a distance of three miles.

(9) The term contiguous zone means the entire zone established or to be established by the United States under article 24 of the Convention of the Territorial Sea and the Contiguous Zone.

(10) The term ocean means any portion of the high seas beyond the contiguous zone.

(11) The term effluent limitation means any restriction established by a State or the Administrator on quantities, rates, and concentrations of chemical, physical, biological, and other constituents which are discharged from point sources into navigable waters, the waters of the contiguous zone, or the ocean, including schedules of compliance.

(12) The term discharge of a pollutant and the term discharge of pollutants each means (A) any addition of any pollutant to navigable waters from any point source, (B) any addition of any pollutant to the waters of the contiguous zone or the ocean from any point source other than a vessel or other floating craft.

(13) The term toxic pollutant means those pollutants, or combinations of pollutants, including disease-causing agents, which after discharge and upon exposure, ingestion, inhalation or assimilation into any organism, either directly from the environment or indirectly by ingestion through food chains, will, on the basis of information available to the Administrator, cause death, disease, behavioral abnormalities, cancer, genetic mutations, physiological malfunctions (including malfunctions in reproduction) or physical deformations, in such organisms or their offspring.

(14) The term point source means any discernible, confined and discrete conveyance, including but not limited to any pipe, ditch, channel, tunnel, conduit, well, discrete fissure, container, rolling stock, concentrated animal feeding operation, or vessel or other floating craft, from which pollutants are or may be discharged. This term does not include agricultural stormwater discharges and return flows from irrigated agriculture.[24]

[24] Section 507 of Public Law 100–4 provided that: For the purposes of the Federal Water Pollution Control Act, the term‘point source’includes a landfill leachate collection system..

(15) The term biological monitoring shall mean the determination of the effects on aquatic life, including accumulation of pollutants in tissue, in receiving waters due to the discharge of pollutants (A) by techniques and procedures, including sampling of organisms representative of appropriate levels of the food chain appropriate to the volume and the physical, chemical, and biological characteristics of the effluent, and (B) at appropriate frequencies and locations.

(16) The term discharge when used without qualification includes a discharge of a pollutant, and a discharge of pollutants.

(17) The term schedule of compliance means a schedule of remedial measures including an enforceable sequence of actions or operations leading to compliance with an effluent limitation, other limitation, prohibition, or standard.

(18) The term industrial user means those industries identified in the Standard Industrial Classification Manual, Bureau of the Budget, 1967, as amended and supplemented, under the category Division D—Manufacturing and such other classes of significant waste producers as, by regulation, the Administrator deems appropriate.

(19) The term pollution means the man-made or man-induced alteration of the chemical, physical, biological, and radiological integrity of water.

(20) The term medical waste means isolation wastes; infectious agents; human blood and blood products; pathological wastes; sharps; body parts; contaminated bedding; surgical wastes and potentially contaminated laboratory wastes; dialysis wastes; and such additional medical items as the Administrator shall prescribe by regulation.

(21) Coastal recreation waters.—

(A) In general.—The term coastal recreation waters means—

(i) the Great Lakes; and

(ii) marine coastal waters (including coastal estuaries) that are designated under section 303(c) by a State for use for swimming, bathing, surfing, or similar water contact activities.

(B) Exclusions.—The term coastal recreation waters does not include—

(i) inland waters; or

(ii) waters upstream of the mouth of a river or stream having an unimpaired natural connection with the open sea.

(22) Floatable material.—

(A) In general.— The term floatable material means any foreign matter that may float or remain suspended in the water column.

(B) Inclusions.—The term floatable material includes—

(i) plastic;

(ii) aluminum cans;

(iii) wood products;

(iv) bottles; and

(v) paper products.

(23) Pathogen indicator.— The term pathogen indicator means a substance that indicates the potential for human infectious disease.

(24) Oil and gas exploration and production.— The term oil and gas exploration, production, processing, or treatment operations or transmission facilities means all field activities or operations associated with exploration, production, processing, or treatment operations, or transmission facilities, including activities necessary to prepare a site for drilling and for the movement and placement of drilling equipment, whether or not such field activities or operations may be considered to be construction activities.

(25) Recreational vessel.—

(A) In general.—The term recreational vessel means any vessel that is—

(i) manufactured or used primarily for pleasure; or

(ii) leased, rented, or chartered to a person for the pleasure of that person.

(B) Exclusion.—The term recreational vessel does not include a vessel that is subject to Coast Guard inspection and that—

(i) is engaged in commercial use; or

(ii) carries paying passengers.

(26) TREATMENT WORKS.— The term treatment works has the meaning given the term in section 212.

(27) GREEN INFRASTRUCTURE.— The term green infrastructure means the range of measures that use plant or soil systems, permeable pavement or other permeable surfaces or substrates, stormwater harvest and reuse, or landscaping to store, infiltrate, or evapotranspirate stormwater and reduce flows to sewer systems or to surface waters.

[33 U.S.C. 1362]

WATER POLLUTION CONTROL ADVISORY BOARD

SEC. 503. (a)(1) There is hereby established in the Environmental Protection Agency a Water Pollution Control Advisory Board, composed of the Administrator or his designee, who shall be Chairman, and nine members appointed by the President, none of whom shall be Federal officers or employees. The appointed members, having due regard for the purposes of this Act, shall be selected from among representatives of various State, interstate, and local governmental agencies, of public or private interests contributing to, affected by, or concerned with pollution, and of other public and private agencies, organizations, or groups demonstrating an active interest in the field of pollution prevention and control, as well as other individuals who are expert in this field.

(2)(A) Each member appointed by the President shall hold office for a term of three years, except that (i) any member appointed to fill a vacancy occurring prior to the expiration of the term for which his predecessor was appointed shall be appointed for the remainder of such term, and (ii) the terms of office of the members first taking office after June 30, 1956, shall expire as follows: three at the end of one year after such date, three at the end of two years after such date, and three at the end of three years after such date, as designated by the President at the time of appointment, and (iii) the term of any member under the preceding provisions shall be extended until the date on which his successor's appointment is effective. None of the members appointed by the President shall be eligible for reappointment within one year after the end of his preceding term.

(B) The members of the Board who are not officers or employees of the United States, while attending conferences or meetings of the Board or while otherwise serving at the request of the Administrator, shall be entitled to receive compensation at a rate to be fixed by the Administrator, but not exceeding $100 per diem, including traveltime, and while away from their homes or regular places of business they may be allowed travel expenses, including per diem in lieu of subsistence, as authorized by law (5 U.S.C. 73b–2) for persons in the Government service employed intermittently.

(b) The Board shall advise, consult with, and make recommendations to the Administrator on matters of policy relating to the activities and functions of the Administrator under this Act.

(c) Such clerical and technical assistance as may be necessary to discharge the duties of the Board shall be provided from the personnel of the Environmental Protection Agency.

[33 U.S.C. 1363]

EMERGENCY POWERS

SEC. 504. (a) Notwithstanding any other provision of this Act, the Administrator upon receipt of evidence that a pollution source or combination of sources is presenting an imminent and substantial endangerment to the health of persons or to the welfare of persons where such endangerment is to the livelihood of such persons, such as inability to market shellfish, may bring suit on behalf of the United States in the appropriate district court to immediately restrain any person causing or contributing to the alleged pollution to stop the discharge of pollutants causing or contributing to such pollution or to take such other action as may be necessary.

(b) [Repealed by §304(a) of P.L. 96–510, Dec. 11, 1980, 94 Stat. 2809.]

[33 U.S.C. 1364]

CITIZEN SUITS

SEC. 505. (a) Except as provided in subsection (b) of this section and section 309(g)(6), any citizen may commence a civil action on his own behalf—

(1) against any person (including (i) the United States, and (ii) any other governmental instrumentality or agency to the extent permitted by the eleventh amendment to the Constitution) who is alleged to be in violation of (A) an effluent standard or limitation under this Act or (B) an order issued by the Administrator or a State with respect to such a standard or limitation, or

(2) against the Administrator where there is alleged a failure of the Administrator to perform any act or duty under this Act which is not discretionary with the Administrator.

The district courts shall have jurisdiction, without regard to the amount in controversy or the citizenship of the parties, to enforce such an effluent standard or limitation, or such an order, or to order the Administrator to perform such act or duty, as the case may be, and to apply any appropriate civil penalties under section 309(d) of this Act.

(b) No action may be commenced—

(1) under subsection (a)(1) of this section—

(A) prior to sixty days after the plaintiff has given notice of the alleged violation (i) to the Administrator, (ii) to the State in which the alleged violation occurs, and (iii) to any alleged violator of the standard, limitation, or order, or

(B) if the Administrator or State has commenced and is diligently prosecuting a civil or criminal action in a court of the United States, or a State to require compliance with the standard, limitation, or order, but in any such action in a court of the United States any citizen may intervene as a matter of right.

(2) under subsection (a)(2) of this section prior to sixty days after the plaintiff has given notice of such action to the Administrator,

except that such action may be brought immediately after such notification in the case of an action under this section respecting a violation of sections 306 and 307(a) of this

Act. Notice under this subsection shall be given in such manner as the Administrator shall prescribe by regulation.

(c)(1) Any action respecting a violation by a discharge source of an effluent standard or limitation or an order respecting such standard or limitation may be brought under this section only in the judicial district in which such source is located.

(2) In such action under this section, the Administrator, if not a party, may intervene as a matter of right.

(3) Protection of interests of United States.— Whenever any action is brought under this section in a court of the United States, the plaintiff shall serve a copy of the complaint on the Attorney General and the Administrator. No consent judgment shall be entered in an action in which the United States is not a party prior to 45 days following the receipt of a copy of the proposed consent judgment by the Attorney General and the Administrator.

(d) The court, in issuing any final order in any action brought pursuant to this section, may award costs of litigation (including reasonable attorney and expert witness fees) to any prevailing or substantially prevailing party, whenever the court determines such award is appropriate. The court may, if a temporary restraining order or preliminary injunction is sought, require the filing of a bond or equivalent security in accordance with the Federal Rules of Civil Procedure.

(e) Nothing in this section shall restrict any right which any person (or class of persons) may have under any statute or common law to seek enforcement of any effluent standard or limitation or to seek any other relief (including relief against the Administrator or a State agency).

(f) For purposes of this section, the term effluent standard or limitation under this Act means (1) effective July 1, 1973, an unlawful act under subsection (a) of section 301 of this Act; (2) an effluent limitation or other limitation under section 301 or 302 of this Act; (3) standard or performance under section 306 of this Act; (4) prohibition, effluent standard or pretreatment standards under section 307 of this Act; (5) a standard of performance or requirement under section 312(p); (6) a certification under section 401; (7) a permit or condition of a permit issued under section 402 that is in effect under this Act (including a requirement applicable by reason of section 313); or (8) a regulation under section 405(d).

(g) For the purposes of this section the term citizen means a person or persons having an interest which is or may be adversely affected.

(h) A Governor of a State may commence a civil action under subsection (a), without regard to the limitations of subsection (b) of this section, against the Administrator where there is alleged a failure of the Administrator to enforce an effluent standard or limitation under this Act the violation of which is occurring in another State and is causing an adverse effect on the public health or welfare in his State, or is causing a violation of any water quality requirement in his State.

[33 U.S.C. 1365]

APPEARANCE

Sec. 506. The Administrator shall request the Attorney General to appear and represent the United States in any civil or criminal action instituted under this Act

to which the Administrator is a party. Unless the Attorney General notifies the Administrator within a reasonable time, that he will appear in a civil action, attorneys who are officers or employees of the Environmental Protection Agency shall appear and represent the United States in such action.
[33 U.S.C. 1366]

EMPLOYEE PROTECTION

SEC. 507. (a) No person shall fire, or in any other way discriminate against, or cause to be fired or discriminated against, any employee or any authorized representative or employees by reason of the fact that such employee or representative has filed, instituted, or caused to be filed or instituted any proceeding under this Act, or has testified or is about to testify in any proceeding resulting from the administration or enforcement of the provisions of this Act.

(b) Any employee or a representative of employees who believes that he has been fired or otherwise discriminated against by any person in violation of subsection (a) of this section may, within thirty days after such alleged violation occurs, apply to the Secretary of Labor for a review of such firing or alleged discrimination. A copy of the application shall be sent to such person who shall be the respondent. Upon receipt of such application, the Secretary of Labor shall cause such investigation to be made as he deems appropriate. Such investigation shall provide an opportunity for a public hearing at the request of any party to such review to enable the parties to present information relating to such alleged violation. The parties shall be given written notice of the time and place of the hearing at least five days prior to the hearing. Any such hearing shall be of record and shall be subject to section 554 of title 5 of the United States Code. Upon receiving the report of such investigation, the Secretary of Labor shall make findings of fact. If he finds that such violation did occur, he shall issue a decision, incorporating an order therein and his findings, requiring the party committing such violation to take such affirmative action to abate the violation as the Secretary of Labor deems appropriate, including, but not limited to, the rehiring or reinstatement of the employee or representative of employees to his former position with compensation. If he finds that there was no such violation, he shall issue an order denying the application. Such order issued by the Secretary of Labor under this subparagraph shall be subject to judicial review in the same manner as orders and decisions of the Administrator are subject to judicial review under this Act.

(c) Whenever an order is issued under this section to abate such violation, at the request of the applicant, a sum equal to the aggregate amount of all costs and expenses (including the attorney's fees), as determined by the Secretary of Labor, to have been reasonably incurred by the applicant for, or in connection with, the institution and prosecution of such proceedings, shall be assessed against the person committing such violation.

(d) This section shall have no application to any employee who, acting without direction from his employer (or his agent) deliberately violates any prohibition of effluent limitation or other limitation under section 301 or 302 of this Act, standards of performance under section 306 of this Act, effluent standard, prohibition or pretreatment standard under section 307 of this Act, or any other prohibition or limitation established under this Act.

(e) The Administrator shall conduct continuing evaluations of potential loss or shifts of employment which may result from the issuance of any effluent limitation or order under this Act, including, where appropriate, investigating threatened plant closures or reductions in employment allegedly resulting from such limitation or order. Any employee who is discharged or laid off, threatened with discharge or laid-off, or otherwise discriminated against by any person because of the alleged results of any effluent limitation or order issued under this Act, or any representative of such employee, may request the Administrator to conduct a full investigation of the matter. The Administrator shall thereupon investigate the matter and, at the request of any party, shall hold public hearings on not less than five days notice, and shall at such hearings require the parties, including the employer involved, to present information relating to the actual or potential effect of such limitation or order on employment and on any alleged discharge, lay-off, or other discrimination and the detailed reasons or justification therefor. Any such hearing shall be of record and shall be subject to section 554 of title 5 of the United States Code. Upon receiving the report of such investigation, the Administrator shall make findings of fact as to the effect of such effluent limitation or order on employment and on the alleged discharge, lay-off, or discrimination and shall make such recommendations as he deems appropriate. Such report, findings, and recommendations shall be available to the public. Nothing in this subsection shall be construed to require or authorize the Administrator to modify or withdraw any effluent limitation or order issued under this Act.

[33 U.S.C. 1367]

FEDERAL PROCUREMENT

SEC. 508. (a) No Federal agency may enter into any contract with any person, who has been convicted of any offense under section 309(c) of this Act, for the procurement of goods, materials, and services if such contract is to be performed at any facility at which the violation which gave rise to such conviction occurred, and if such facility is owned, leased, or supervised by such person. The prohibition in the preceding sentence shall continue until the Administrator certifies that the condition giving rise to such conviction has been corrected.

(b) The Administrator shall establish procedures to provide all Federal agencies with the notification necessary for the purposes of subsection (a) of this section.

(c) In order to implement the purposes and policy of this Act to protect and enhance the quality of the Nation's water, the President shall, not more than one hundred and eighty days after enactment of this Act, cause to be issued an order (1) requiring each Federal agency authorized to enter into contracts and each Federal agency which is empowered to extend Federal assistance by way of grant, loan, or contract to effectuate the purpose and policy of this Act in such contracting or assistance activities, and (2) setting forth procedures, sanctions, penalties, and such other provisions, as the President determines necessary to carry out such requirement.

(d) The President may exempt any contract, loan, or grant from all or part of the provisions of this section where he determines such exemption is necessary in the paramount interest of the United States and he shall notify the Congress of such exemption.

(e) The President shall annually report to the Congress on measures taken in compliance with the purpose and intent of this section, including, but not limited to, the progress and problems associated with such compliance.

(f)(1) No certification by a contractor, and no contract clause, may be required in the case of a contract for the acquisition of commercial products or commercial services in order to implement a prohibition or requirement of this section or a prohibition or requirement issued in the implementation of this section.

(2) In paragraph (1), the terms commercial product and commercial service have the meanings given those terms in sections 103 and 103a, respectively, of title 41, United States Code.

[33 U.S.C. 1368]

ADMINISTRATIVE PROCEDURE AND JUDICIAL REVIEW

SEC. 509. (a)(1) For purposes of obtaining information under section 305 of this Act, or carrying out section 507(e) of this Act, the Administrator may issue subpenas for the attendance and testimony of witnesses and the production of relevant papers, books, and documents, and he may administer oaths. Except for effluent data, upon a showing satisfactory to the Administrator that such papers, books, documents, or information or particular part thereof, if made public, would divulge trade secrets or secret processes, the Administrator shall consider such record, report, or information or particular portion thereof confidential in accordance with the purposes of section 1905 of title 18 of the United States Code, except that such paper, book, document, or information may be disclosed to other officers, employees, or authorized representatives of the United States concerned with carrying out this Act, or when relevant in any proceeding under this Act. Witnesses summoned shall be paid the same fees and mileage that are paid witnesses in the courts of the United States. In case of contumacy or refusal to obey a subpena served upon any person under this subsection, the district court of the United States for any district in which such person is found or resides or transacts business, upon application by the United States and after notice to such person, shall have jurisdiction to issue an order requiring such person to appear and give testimony before the Administrator, to appear and produce papers, books, and documents before the Administrator, or both, and any failure to obey such order of the court may be punished by such court as a contempt thereof.

(2) The district courts of the United States are authorized, upon application by the Administrator, to issue subpenas for attendance and testimony of witnesses and the production of relevant papers, books, and documents, for purposes of obtaining information under sections 304 (b) and (c) of this Act. Any papers, books, documents, or other information or part thereof, obtained by reason of such a subpena shall be subject to the same requirements as are provided in paragraph (1) of this subsection.

(b)(1) Review of the Administrator's action (A) in promulgating any standard of performance under section 306, (B) in making any determination pursuant to section 306(b)(1)(C), (C) in promulgating any effluent standard, prohibition, or pretreatment standard under section 307, (D) in making any determination as to a State permit program submitted under section 402(b), (E) in approving or promulgating any effluent limitation or other limitation under sections 301, 302, 306, or 405, (F) in issuing or denying any permit under section 402, and (G) in promulgating any individual control strategy under section 304(l), may be had by any interested person in the Circuit Court of Appeals of the United States for the Federal judicial district in which such person resides or transacts business which is directly affected by such action upon application by such person. Any such application shall be made within 120 days from the date of such determination, approval, promulgation, issuance or denial, or after such date only if such application is based solely on grounds which arose after such 120th day.

(2) Action of the Administrator with respect to which review could have been obtained under paragraph (1) of this subsection shall not be subject to judicial review in any civil or criminal proceeding for enforcement.

(3) Award of fees.— In any judicial proceeding under this subsection, the court may award costs of litigation (including reasonable attorney and expert witness fees) to any prevailing or substantially prevailing party whenever it determines that such award is appropriate.

(4) Discharges incidental to normal operation of vessels.—

(A) In general.— Except as provided in subparagraph (B), any interested person may file a petition for review of a final agency action under section 312(p) of the Administrator or the Secretary of the department in which the Coast Guard is operating in accordance with the requirements of this subsection.

(B) Venue exception.— Subject to section 312(p)(7)(C)(v), a petition for review of a final agency action under section 312(p) of the Administrator or the Secretary of the department in which the Coast Guard is operating may be filed only in the United States Court of Appeals for the District of Columbia Circuit.

(c) In any judicial proceeding brought under subsection (b) of this section in which review is sought of a determination under this Act required to be made on the record after notice and opportunity for hearing, if any party applies to the court for leave to adduce additional evidence, and shows to the satisfaction of the court that such additional evidence is material and that there were reasonable grounds for the failure to adduce such evidence in the proceeding before the Administrator, the court may order such additional evidence (and evidence in rebuttal thereof) to be taken before the Administrator, in such manner and upon such terms and conditions as the court may deem proper. The Administrator may modify his findings as to the facts, or make new findings, by reason of the additional evidence so taken and he shall file such modified or new findings, and his recommendation, if any, for the modification or setting aside of his original determination, with the return of such additional evidence.

[33 U.S.C. 1369]

STATE AUTHORITY

Sec. 510. Except as expressly provided in this Act, nothing in this Act shall (1) preclude or deny the right of any State or political subdivision thereof or interstate agency to adopt or enforce (A) any standard or limitation respecting discharges of pollutants, or (B) any requirement respecting control or abatement of pollution; except that if an effluent limitation, or other limitation, effluent standard, prohibition, pretreatment standard, or standard of performance is in effect under this Act, such State or political subdivision or interstate agency may not adopt or enforce any effluent

limitation, or other limitation, effluent standard, prohibition, pretreatment standard, or standard of performance which is less stringent than the effluent limitation, or other limitation, effluent standard prohibition, pretreatment standard, or standard of performance under this Act; or (2) be construed as impairing or in any manner affecting any right or jurisdiction of the States with respect to the waters (including boundary waters) of such States.
[33 U.S.C. 1370]

OTHER AFFECTED AUTHORITY

SEC. 511. (a) This Act shall not be construed as (1) limiting the authority or functions of any officer or agency of the United States under any other law or regulation not inconsistent with this Act; (2) affecting or impairing the authority of the Secretary of the Army (A) to maintain navigation or (B) under the Act of March 3, 1899 (30 Stat. 1112); except that any permit issued under section 404 of this Act shall be conclusive as to the effect on water quality of any discharge resulting from any activity subject to section 10 of the Act of March 3, 1899, or (3) affecting or impairing the provisions of any treaty of the United States.

(b) Discharges of pollutants into the navigable waters subject to the Rivers and Harbors Act of 1910 (36 Stat. 593; 33 U.S.C. 421) and the Supervisory Harbors, Act of 1888 (25 Stat. 209; 33 U.S.C. 441–451b) shall be regulated pursuant to this Act, and not subject to such Act of 1910 and the Act of 1888 except as to effect on navigation and anchorage.

(c)(1) Except for the provision of Federal financial assistance for the purpose of assisting the construction of publicly owned treatment works as authorized by section 201 of this Act, and the issuance of a permit under section 402 of this Act for the discharge of any pollutant by a new source as defined in section 306 of this Act, no action of the Administrator taken pursuant to this Act shall be deemed a major Federal action significantly affecting the quality of the human environment within the meaning of the National Environmental Policy Act of 1969 (83 Stat. 852); and

(2) Nothing in the National Environmental Policy Act of 1969 (83 Stat. 852) shall be deemed to—

(A) authorize any Federal agency authorized to license or permit the conduct of any activity which may result in the discharge of a pollutant into the navigable waters to review any effluent limitation or other requirement established pursuant to this Act or the adequacy of any certification under section 401 of this Act; or

(B) authorize any such agency to impose, as a condition precedent to the issuance of any license or permit, any effluent limitation other than any such limitation established pursuant to this Act.

(d) Notwithstanding this Act or any other provisions of law, the Administrator (1) shall not require any State to consider in the development of the ranking in order of priority of needs for the construction of treatment works (as defined in title II of this Act), any water pollution control agreement which may have been entered into between the United States and any other nation, and (2) shall not consider any such agreement in the approval of any such priority ranking.

[33 U.S.C. 1371]

SEPARABILITY

SEC. 512. If any provision of this Act, or the application of any provision of this Act to any person or circumstance, is held invalid, the application of such provision to other persons or circumstances, and the remainder of this Act, shall not be affected thereby.
[33 U.S.C. 1251 note]

LABOR STANDARDS

SEC. 513. The Administrator shall take such action as may be necessary to insure that all laborers and mechanics employed by contractors or subcontractors on treatment works for which grants are made under this Act shall be paid wages at rates not less than those prevailing for the same type of work on similar construction in the immediate locality, as determined by the Secretary of Labor, in accordance with the Act of March 3, 1931, as amended, known as the Davis-Bacon Act (46 Stat. 1494; 40 U.S.C., sec. 276a through 276a–5). The Secretary of Labor shall have, with respect to the labor standards specified in this subsection, the authority and functions set forth in Reorganization Plan Numbered 14 of 1950 (15 F.R. 3176) and section 2 of the Act of June 13, 1934, as amended (48 Stat. 948; 40 U.S.C. 276c).
[33 U.S.C. 1372]

PUBLIC HEALTH AGENCY COORDINATION

SEC. 514. The permitting agency under section 402 shall assist the applicant for a permit under such section in coordinating the requirements of this Act with those of the appropriate public health agencies.
[33 U.S.C. 1373]

EFFLUENT STANDARDS AND WATER QUALITY INFORMATION ADVISORY COMMITTEE

SEC. 515. (a)(1) There is established on[25] Effluent Standards and Water Quality Information Advisory Committee, which shall be composed of a Chairman and eight members who shall be appointed by the Administrator within sixty days after the date of enactment of this Act.

[25] So in law. Probably should read an.

(2) All members of the Committee shall be selected from the scientific community, qualified by education, training, and experience to provide, assess, and evaluate scientific and technical information on effluent standards and limitations.

(3) Members of the Committee shall serve for a term of four years, and may be reappointed.

(b)(1) No later than one hundred and eighty days prior to the date on which the Administrator is required to publish any proposed regulations required by section 304(b) of this Act, any proposed standard of performance for new sources required by section 306 of this Act, or any proposed toxic effluent standard required by section 307 of this Act, he shall transmit to the Committee a notice of intent to propose such regulations. The Chairman of the Committee within ten days after receipt of such notice may publish a notice of a public hearing by the Committee, to be held within thirty days.

(2) No later than one hundred and twenty days after receipt of such notice, the Committee shall transmit to the Administrator such scientific and technical information as is in its possession, including that presented at any public hearing, related to the subject matter contained in such notice.

(3) Information so transmitted to the Administrator shall constitute a part of the administrative record and comments on any proposed regulations or standards as information to be considered with other comments and information in making any final determinations.

(4) In preparing information for transmittal, the Committee shall avail itself of the technical and scientific services of any Federal agency, including the United States Geological Survey and any national environmental laboratories which may be established.

(c)(1) The Committee shall appoint and prescribe the duties of a Secretary, and such legal counsel as it deems necessary. The Committee shall appoint such other employees as it deems necessary to exercise and fulfill its powers and responsibilities. The compensation of all employees appointed by the Committee shall be fixed in accordance with chapter 51 and subchapter III of chapter 53 of title V of the United States Code.

(2) Members of the Committee shall be entitled to receive compensation at a rate to be fixed by the President but not in excess of the maximum rate of pay grade for GS–18, as provided in the General Schedule under section 5332 of title V of the United States Code.

(d) Five members of the Committee shall constitute a quorum, and official actions of the Committee shall be taken only on the affirmative vote of at least five members. A special panel composed of one or more members upon order of the Committee shall conduct any hearing authorized by this section and submit the transcript of such hearing to the entire Committee for its action thereon.

(e) The Committee is authorized to make such rules as are necessary for the orderly transaction of its business.

[33 U.S.C. 1374]

REPORTS TO CONGRESS

SEC. 516. (a) Within ninety days following the convening of each session of Congress, the Administrator shall submit to the Congress a report, in addition to any other report required by this Act, on measures taken toward implementing the objective of this Act, including, but not limited to, (1) the progress and problems associated with developing comprehensive plans under section 102 of this Act, areawide plans under section 208 of this Act, basin plans under section 209 of this Act, and plans under section 303 (e) of this Act; (2) a summary of actions taken and results achieved in the field of water pollution control research, experiments, studies, and related matters by the Administrator and other Federal agencies and by other persons and agencies under Federal grants or contracts; (3) the progress and problems associated with the development of effluent limitations and recommended control techniques; (4) the status of State programs, including a detailed summary of the progress obtained as compared to that planned under State program plans for development and enforcement of water quality requirements; (5) the identification and status of enforcement actions pending or completed under such Act during the preceding year; (6) the status of State, interstate, and local pollution control programs established pursuant to, and assisted by, this Act; (7) a summary of the results of the survey required to be taken under section 210 of this Act; (8) his activities including recommendations under sections 109 through 111 of this Act; and (9) all reports and recommendations made by the Water Pollution Control Advisory Board.

(b)(1) The Administrator, in cooperation with the States, including water pollution control agencies and other water pollution control planning agencies, shall make (A) a detailed estimate of the cost of carrying out the provisions of this Act; (B) a detailed estimate, biennially revised, of the cost of construction of all needed publicly owned treatment works in all of the States and of the cost of construction of all needed publicly owned treatment works in each of the States; (C) a comprehensive study of the economic impact on affected units of government of the cost of installation of treatment facilities; and (D) a comprehensive analysis of the national requirements for and the cost of treating municipal, industrial, and other effluent to attain the water quality objectives as established by this Act or applicable State law. The Administrator shall submit such detailed estimate and such comprehensive study of such cost to the Congress no later than February 10 of each odd-numbered year. Whenever the Administrator, pursuant to this subsection, requests and receives an estimate of cost from a State, he shall furnish copies of such estimate together with such detailed estimate to Congress.

(2) Notwithstanding the second sentence of paragraph (1) of this subsection, the Administrator shall make a preliminary detailed estimate called for by subparagraph (B) of such paragraph and shall submit such preliminary detailed estimate to the Congress no later than September 3, 1974. The Administrator shall require each State to prepare an estimate of cost for such State, and shall utilize the survey form EPA-1, O.M.B. No. 158-R0017, prepared for the 1973 detailed estimate, except that such estimate shall include all costs of compliance with section 201(g)(2)(A) of this Act and water quality standards established pursuant to section 303 of this Act, and all costs of treatment works as defined in section 212(2), including all eligible costs of constructing sewage collection systems and correcting excessive infiltration or inflow and all eligible costs of correcting combined storm and sanitary sewer problems and treating storm water flows. The survey form shall be distributed by the Administrator to each State no later than January 31, 1974.

(c) The Administrator shall submit to the Congress by October 1, 1978, a report on the status of combined sewer overflows in municipal treatment works operations. The report shall include (1) the status of any projects funded under this Act to address combined sewer overflows (2) a listing by State of combined sewer overflow needs identified in the 1977 State priority listings, (3) an estimate for each applicable municipality of the number of years necessary, assuming an annual authorization and appropriation for the construction grants program of $5,000,000,000, to correct combined sewer overflow problems, (4) an analysis using representative municipalities faced with major combined sewer overflow needs, of the annual discharges of pollutants from overflows in comparison to treated effluent discharges, (5) an analysis of the technological alternatives available to municipalities to correct major combined sewer overflow problems, and (6) any recommendations of the Administrator for legislation to address the problem of combined sewer overflows, including whether a separate authorization and grant program should be established by the Congress to address combined sewer overflows.

(d) The Administrator, in cooperation with the States, including water pollution control agencies, and other water pollution control planning agencies, and water supply and water resources agencies of the States and the United States shall submit to Congress, within two years of the date of enactment of this section, a report with recommendations for legislation on a program to require coordination between water supply and wastewater control plans as a condition to grants for construction of treatment works under this Act. No such report shall be submitted except after opportunity for public hearings on such proposed report.

(e) State Revolving Fund Report.—

(1) In general.— Not later than February 10, 1990, the Administrator shall submit to Congress a report on the financial status and operations of water pollution control revolving funds established by the States under title VI of this Act. The Administrator shall prepare such report in cooperation with the States, including water pollution control agencies and other water pollution control planning and financing agencies.

(2) Contents.—The report under this subsection shall also include the following:

(A) an inventory of the facilities that are in significant noncompliance with the enforceable requirements of this Act;

(B) an estimate of the cost of construction necessary to bring such facilities into compliance with such requirements;

(C) an assessment of the availability of sources of funds for financing such needed construction, including an estimate of the amount of funds available for providing assistance for such construction through September 30, 1999, from the water pollution control revolving funds established by the States under title VI of this Act;

(D) an assessment of the operations, loan portfolio, and loan conditions of such revolving funds;

(E) an assessment of the effect on user charges of the assistance provided by such revolving funds compared to the assistance provided with funds appropriated pursuant to section 207 of this Act; and

(F) an assessment of the efficiency of the operation and maintenance of treatment works constructed with assistance provided by such revolving funds compared to the efficiency of the operation and maintenance of treatment works constructed with assistance provided under section 201 of this Act.

[33 U.S.C. 1375]

GENERAL AUTHORIZATION

Sec. 517. There are authorized to be appropriated to carry out this Act, other than sections 104, 105, 106(a), 107, 108, 112, 113, 114, 115, 206, 207, 208 (f) and (h), 209, 304, 311 (c), (d), (i), (l), and (k), 314, 315, and 317, $250,000,000 for the fiscal year ending June 30, 1973, $300,000,000 for the fiscal year ending June 30, 1974, $350,000,000 for the fiscal year ending June 30, 1975, $100,000,000 for the fiscal year ending September 30, 1977, $150,000,000 for the fiscal year ending September 30, 1978, $150,000,000 for the fiscal year ending September 30, 1979, $150,000,000 for the fiscal year ending September 30, 1980, $150,000,000 for the fiscal year ending September 30, 1981, $161,000,000 for the fiscal year ending September 30, 1982, such sums as may be necessary for fiscal years 1983 through 1985, and $135,000,000 per fiscal year for each of the fiscal years 1986 through 1990.

[33 U.S.C. 1376]

SEC. 518. INDIAN TRIBES.

(a) POLICY.— Nothing in this section shall be construed to affect the application of section 101(g) of this Act, and all of the provisions of this section shall be carried out in accordance with the provisions of such section 101(g). Indian tribes shall be treated as States for purposes of such section 101(g).

(b) ASSESSMENT OF SEWAGE TREATMENT NEEDS; REPORT.— The Administrator, in cooperation with the Director of the Indian Health Service, shall assess the need for sewage treatment works to serve Indian tribes, the degree to which such needs will be met through funds allotted to States under section 205 of this Act and priority lists under section 216 of this Act, and any obstacles which prevent such needs from being met. Not later than one year after the date of the enactment of this section, the Administrator shall submit a report to Congress on the assessment under this subsection, along with recommendations specifying (1) how the Administrator intends to provide assistance to Indian tribes to develop waste treatment management plans and to construct treatment works under this Act, and (2) methods by which the participation in and administration of programs under this Act by Indian tribes can be maximized.

(c) RESERVATION OF FUNDS.—

(1) FISCAL YEARS 1987–2014.— The Administrator shall reserve each of fiscal years 1987 through 2014, before allotments to the States under section 205(e), one-half of one percent of the sums appropriated under section 207.

(2) FISCAL YEAR 2015 AND THEREAFTER.— For fiscal year 2015 and each fiscal year thereafter, the Administrator shall reserve, before allotments to the States under section 604(a), not less than 0.5 percent and not more than 2.0 percent of the funds made available to carry out title VI.

(3) USE OF FUNDS.—Funds reserved under this subsection shall be available only for grants for projects and activities eligible for assistance under section 603(c) to serve—

(A) Indian tribes (as defined in subsection (h));

(B) former Indian reservations in Oklahoma (as determined by the Secretary of the Interior); and

(C) Native villages (as defined in section 3 of the Alaska Native Claims Settlement Act (43 U.S.C. 1602)).

(d) COOPERATIVE AGREEMENTS.— In order to ensure the consistent implementation of the requirements of this Act, an Indian tribe and the State or States in which the lands of such tribe are located may enter into a cooperative agreement, subject to the review and approval of the Administrator, to jointly plan and administer the requirements of this Act.

(e) TREATMENT AS STATES.—The Administrator is authorized to treat an Indian tribe as a State for purposes of title II and sections 104, 106, 303, 305, 308, 309, 314, 319, 401, 402, 404, and 406 of this Act to the degree necessary to carry out the objectives of this section, but only if—

(1) the Indian tribe has a governing body carrying out substantial governmental duties and powers;

(2) the functions to be exercised by the Indian tribe pertain to the management and protection of water resources which are held by an Indian tribe, held by the United States in trust for Indians, held by a member of an Indian tribe if such property interest is subject to a trust restriction on alienation, or otherwise within the borders of an Indian reservation; and

(3) the Indian tribe is reasonably expected to be capable, in the Administrator's judgment, of carrying out the functions to be exercised in a manner consistent with the terms and purposes of this Act and of all applicable regulations.

Such treatment as a State may include the direct provision of funds reserved under subsection (c) to the governing bodies of Indian tribes, and the determination of priorities by Indian tribes, where not determined by the Administrator in cooperation with the Director of the Indian Health Service. The Administrator, in cooperation with the Director of the Indian Health Service, is authorized to make grants under title II of this Act in an amount not to exceed 100 percent of the cost of a project. Not later than 18 months after the date of the enactment of this section, the Administrator shall, in consultation with Indian tribes, promulgate final regulations which specify how Indian tribes shall be treated as States for purposes of this Act. The Administrator shall, in promulgating such regulations, consult affected States sharing common water bodies and provide a mechanism for the resolution of any unreasonable consequences that may arise as a result of differing water quality standards that may be set by States and Indian tribes located on common bodies of water. Such mechanism shall provide for explicit consideration of relevant factors including, but not limited to, the effects of differing water quality permit requirements on upstream and downstream dischargers, economic impacts, and present and historical uses and quality of the waters subject to such standards. Such mechanism should provide for the avoidance of such unreasonable consequences in a manner consistent with the objective of this Act.

(f) GRANTS FOR NONPOINT SOURCE PROGRAMS.— The Administrator shall make grants to an Indian tribe under section 319 of this Act as though such tribe was a State. Not more than one-third of one percent of the amount appropriated for any fiscal year under section 319 may be used to make grants under this subsection. In addition to the requirements of section 319, an Indian tribe shall be required to meet the requirements of paragraphs (1), (2), and (3) of subsection (d)[26] of this section in order to receive such a grant.

[26] Probably should be subsection (e).

(g) ALASKA NATIVE ORGANIZATIONS.—No provision of this Act shall be construed to—

(1) grant, enlarge, or diminish, or in any way affect the scope of the

governmental authority, if any, of any Alaska Native organization, including any federally-recognized tribe, traditional Alaska Native council, or Native council organized pursuant to the Act of June 18, 1934 (48 Stat. 987), over lands or persons in Alaska;

(2) create or validate any assertion by such organization or any form of governmental authority over lands or persons in Alaska; or

(3) in any way affect any assertion that Indian country, as defined in section 1151 of title 18, United States Code, exists or does not exist in Alaska.

(h) Definitions.—For purposes of this section, the term—

(1) Federal Indian reservation means all land within the limits of any Indian reservation under the jurisdiction of the United States Government, notwithstanding the issuance of any patent, and including rights-of-way running through the reservation; and

(2) Indian tribe means any Indian tribe, band, group, or community recognized by the Secretary of the Interior and exercising governmental authority over a Federal Indian reservation.

[33 U.S.C. 1377]

SEC. 519. GREEN INFRASTRUCTURE PROMOTION.

(a) In General.— The Administrator shall promote the use of green infrastructure in, and coordinate the integration of green infrastructure into, permitting and enforcement under this Act, planning efforts, research, technical assistance, and funding guidance of the Environmental Protection Agency.

(b) Coordination of Efforts.—The Administrator shall ensure that the Office of Water coordinates efforts to increase the use of green infrastructure with—

(1) other Federal departments and agencies;

(2) State, tribal, and local governments; and

(3) the private sector.

(c) Regional Green Infrastructure Promotion.—The Administrator shall direct each regional office of the Environmental Protection Agency, as appropriate based on local factors, and consistent with the requirements of this Act, to promote and integrate the use of green infrastructure within the region, including through—

(1) outreach and training regarding green infrastructure implementation for State, tribal, and local governments, tribal communities, and the private sector; and

(2) the incorporation of green infrastructure into permitting and other regulatory programs, codes, and ordinance development, including the requirements under consent decrees and settlement agreements in enforcement actions.

(d) Green Infrastructure Information-sharing.—The Administrator shall promote green infrastructure information-sharing, including through an internet website, to share information with, and provide technical assistance to, State, tribal, and local governments, tribal communities, the private sector, and the public, regarding green infrastructure approaches for—

(1) reducing water pollution;

(2) protecting water resources;

(3) complying with regulatory requirements; and

(4) achieving other environmental, public health, and community goals.

[33 U.S.C. 1377a]

SHORT TITLE

SEC. 520. This Act may be cited as the "Federal Water Pollution Control Act" (commonly referred to as the Clean Water Act).

[33 U.S.C. 1251 note]

TITLE VI—STATE WATER POLLUTION CONTROL REVOLVING FUNDS

TITLE VI—STATE WATER POLLUTION CONTROL REVOLVING FUNDS

SEC. 601. GRANTS TO STATES FOR ESTABLISHMENT OF REVOLVING FUNDS.

(a) GENERAL AUTHORITY.— Subject to the provisions of this title, the Administrator shall make capitalization grants to each State for the purpose of establishing a water pollution control revolving fund to accomplish the objectives, goals, and policies of this Act by providing assistance for projects and activities identified in section 603(c).

(b) SCHEDULE OF GRANT PAYMENTS.—The Administrator and each State shall jointly establish a schedule of payments under which the Administrator will pay to the State the amount of each grant to be made to the State under this title. Such schedule shall be based on the State's intended use plan under section 606(c) of this Act, except that—

(1) such payments shall be made in quarterly installments, and

(2) such payments shall be made as expeditiously as possible, but in no event later than the earlier of—

(A) 8 quarters after the date such funds were obligated by the State, or

(B) 12 quarters after the date such funds were allotted to the State.

[33 U.S.C. 1381]

SEC. 602. CAPITALIZATION GRANT AGREEMENTS.

(a) GENERAL RULE.— To receive a capitalization grant with funds made available under this title and section 205(m) of this Act, a State shall enter into an agreement with the Administrator which shall include but not be limited to the specifications set forth in subsection (b) of this section.

(b) SPECIFIC REQUIREMENTS.—The Administrator shall enter into an agreement under this section with a State only after the State has established to the satisfaction of the Administrator that—

(1) the State will accept grant payments with funds to be made available under this title and section 205(m) of this Act in accordance with a payment schedule established jointly by the Administrator under section 601(b) of this Act and will deposit all such payments in the water pollution control revolving fund established by the State in accordance with this title;

(2) the State will deposit in the fund from State moneys an amount equal to at least 20 percent of the total amount of all capitalization grants which will be made to the State with funds to be made available under this title and section 205(m) of this Act on or before the date on which each quarterly grant payment will be made to the State under this title;

(3) the State will enter into binding commitments to provide assistance in accordance with the requirements of this title in an amount equal to 120 percent of the amount of each such grant payment within 1 year after the receipt of such grant payment;

(4) all funds in the fund will be expended in an expeditious and timely manner;

(5) all funds in the fund as a result of capitalization grants under this title and section 205(m) of this Act will first be used to assure maintenance of progress, as determined by the Governor of the State, toward compliance with enforceable deadlines, goals, and requirements of this Act, including the municipal compliance deadline;

(6) treatment works eligible under this Act which will be constructed in whole or in part with assistance made available by a State water pollution control revolving fund authorized under this title, or section 205(m) of this Act, or both, will meet the requirements of, or otherwise be treated (as determined by the Governor of the State) under sections 511(c)(1) and 513 of this Act in the same manner as treatment works constructed with assistance under title II of this Act;

(7) in addition to complying with the requirements of this title, the State will commit or expend each quarterly grant payment which it will receive under this title in accordance with laws and procedures applicable to the commitment or expenditure of revenues of the State;

(8) in carrying out the requirements of section 606 of this Act, the State will use accounting, audit, and fiscal procedures conforming to generally accepted government accounting standards;

(9) the State will require as a condition of making a loan or providing other assistance, as described in section 603(d) of this Act, from the fund that the recipient of such assistance will maintain project accounts in accordance with generally accepted government accounting standards, including standards relating to the reporting of infrastructure assets;

(10) the State will make annual reports to the Administrator on the actual use of funds in accordance with section 606(d) of this Act;

(11) the State will establish, maintain, invest, and credit the fund with repayments, such that the fund balance will be available in perpetuity for activities under this Act;

(12) any fees charged by the State to recipients of assistance that are considered program income will be used for the purpose of financing the cost of administering the fund or financing projects or activities eligible for assistance from the fund;

(13) beginning in fiscal year 2016, the State will require as a condition of providing assistance to a municipality or intermunicipal, interstate, or State agency that the recipient of such assistance certify, in a manner determined by the Governor of the State, that the recipient—

(A) has studied and evaluated the cost and effectiveness of the processes, materials, techniques, and technologies for carrying out the proposed project or activity for which assistance is sought under this title; and

(B) has selected, to the maximum extent practicable, a project or activity that maximizes the potential for efficient water use, reuse, recapture, and conservation, and energy conservation, taking into account—

(i) the cost of constructing the project or activity;

(ii) the cost of operating and maintaining the project or activity over the life of the project or activity; and

(iii) the cost of replacing the project or activity; and

(14) a contract to be carried out using funds directly made available by a capitalization grant under this title for program management, construction management, feasibility studies, preliminary engineering, design, engineering, surveying, mapping, or architectural related services shall be negotiated in the same manner as a contract for architectural and engineering services is negotiated under chapter 11 of title 40, United States Code, or an equivalent State qualifications-based requirement (as determined by the Governor of the State).

[33 U.S.C. 1382]

SEC. 603. WATER POLLUTION CONTROL REVOLVING LOAN FUNDS.[27]

(a) Requirements for Obligation of Grant Funds.— Before a State may receive a capitalization grant with funds made available under this title and section 205(m) of this Act, the State shall first establish a water pollution control revolving fund which complies with the requirements of this section.

[27] See section 104B of the Marine Protection, Research and Sanctuaries Act of 1972 (33 U.S.C. 1414G) for additional amounts that are to be deposited into a State's fund and treatment of such deposits.

(b) Administrator.— Each State water pollution control revolving fund shall be administered by an instrumentality of the State with such powers and limitations as may be required to operate such fund in accordance with the requirements and objectives of this Act.

(c) Projects and Activities Eligible for Assistance.—The amounts of funds available to each State water pollution control revolving fund shall be used only for providing financial assistance—[28]

[28] Section 1006 of the Ocean Dumping Ban Act of 1988 (P.L. 100–688) is as follows:

SEC. 1066. USE OF STATE WATER POLLUTION CONTROL REVOLVING FUND GRANTS FOR DEVELOPING ALTERNATIVE SYSTEMS.

(a) General Requirement.—Notwithstanding the provisions of title VI of the Federal Water Pollution Control Act, each of the States of New York and New Jersey shall use 10 percent of the amount of a grant payment made to such State under such title for each of the fiscal years 1990 and 1991 and 10 percent of the State's contribution associated with such grant payment in the 6-month period beginning on the date of receipt of such grant payment for making loans and providing other assistance as described in section 603(d) of the Federal Water Pollution Control Act to any governmental entity in such State which has entered into a compliance agreement or enforcement agreement under section 104B of the Marine Protection, Research, and Sanctuaries Act of 1972 for identifying, developing, and implementing pursuant to such section alternative systems for management of sewage sludge.

(b) Limitation.—If, after the last day of the 6-month period beginning on the date of receipt of a grant payment by the State of New York or New Jersey under title VI of the Federal Water Pollution Control Act for each of fiscal years 1990 and 1991, 10 percent of the amount of such grant payment and the State's contribution associated with such grant payment has not been used for providing assistance described in subsection (a) as a result of insufficient applications for such assistance from persons eligible for such assistance, the 10 percent limitations set forth in subsection (a) shall not be applicable with respect to such grant payment and associated State contribution.

(1) to any municipality or intermunicipal, interstate, or State agency for construction of publicly owned treatment works (as defined in section 212);

(2) for the implementation of a management program established under section 319;

(3) for development and implementation of a conservation and management plan under section 320;

(4) for the construction, repair, or replacement of decentralized wastewater treatment systems that treat municipal wastewater or domestic sewage;

(5) for measures to manage, reduce, treat, or recapture stormwater or subsurface drainage water;

(6) to any municipality or intermunicipal, interstate, or State agency for measures to reduce the demand for publicly owned treatment works capacity through water conservation, efficiency, or reuse;

(7) for the development and implementation of watershed projects meeting the criteria set forth in section 122;

(8) to any municipality or intermunicipal, interstate, or State agency for measures to reduce the energy consumption needs for publicly owned treatment works;

(9) for reusing or recycling wastewater, stormwater, or subsurface drainage water;

(10) for measures to increase the security of publicly owned treatment works;

(11) to any qualified nonprofit entity, as determined by the Administrator, to provide assistance to owners and operators of small and medium publicly owned treatment works—

(A) to plan, develop, and obtain financing for eligible projects under this subsection, including planning, design, and associated preconstruction activities; and

(B) to assist such treatment works in achieving compliance with this Act; and

(12) to any qualified nonprofit entity, as determined by the Administrator, to provide assistance to an eligible individual (as defined in subsection (j))—

(A) for the repair or replacement of existing individual household decentralized wastewater treatment systems; or

(B) in a case in which an eligible individual resides in a household that could be cost-effectively connected to an available publicly owned treatment works, for the connection of the applicable household to such treatment works.

(d) Types of Assistance.—Except as otherwise limited by State law and provided in subsection (k), a water pollution control revolving fund of a State under this section may be used only—

(1) to make loans, on the condition that—

(A) such loans are made at or below market interest rates, including interest free loans, at terms not to exceed the lesser of 30 years and the projected useful life (as determined by the State) of the project to be financed with the proceeds of the loan;

(B) annual principal and interest payments will commence not later than 1 year after completion of any project and all loans will be fully amortized upon the expiration of the term of the loan;

(C) the recipient of a loan will establish a dedicated source of revenue for repayment of loans;

(D) the fund will be credited with all payments of principal and interest on all loans; and

(E) for a treatment works proposed for repair, replacement, or expansion, and eligible for assistance under subsection (c)(1), the recipient of a loan shall—

(i) develop and implement a fiscal sustainability plan that includes—

(I) an inventory of critical assets that are a part of the treatment works;

(II) an evaluation of the condition and performance of inventoried assets or asset groupings;

(III) a certification that the recipient has evaluated and will be implementing water and energy conservation efforts as part of the plan; and

(IV) a plan for maintaining, repairing, and, as necessary, replacing the treatment works and a plan for funding such activities; or

(ii) certify that the recipient has developed and implemented a plan that meets the requirements under clause (i);

(2) to buy or refinance the debt obligation of municipalities and intermunicipal and interstate agencies within the State at or below market rates, where such debt obligations were incurred after March 7, 1985;

(3) to guarantee, or purchase insurance for, local obligations where such action would improve credit market access or reduce interest rates;

(4) as a source of revenue or security for the payment of principal and interest on revenue or general obligation bonds issued by the State if the proceeds of the sale of such bonds will be deposited in the fund;

(5) to provide loan guarantees for similar revolving funds established by municipalities or intermunicipal agencies;

(6) to earn interest on fund accounts; and

(7) for the reasonable costs of administering the fund and conducting activities under this title, except that such amounts shall not exceed 4 percent of all grant awards to such fund under this title, $400,000 per year, or ⅕ percent per year of the current valuation of the fund, whichever amount is greatest, plus the amount of any fees collected by the State for such purpose regardless of the source.

(e) LIMITATION TO PREVENT DOUBLE BENEFITS.— If a State makes, from its water pollution revolving fund, a loan which will finance the cost of facility planning and the preparation of plans, specifications, and estimates for construction of publicly owned treatment works, the State shall ensure that if the recipient of such loan receives a grant under section 201(g) of this Act for construction of such treatment works and an allowance under section 201(l)(1) of this Act for non-federal funds expended for such planning and preparation, such recipient will promptly repay such loan to the extent of such allowance.

(f) CONSISTENCY WITH PLANNING REQUIREMENTS.— A State may provide financial assistance from its water pollution control revolving fund only with respect to a project which is consistent with plans, if any, developed under sections 205(j), 208, 303(e), 319, and 320 of this Act.

(g) PRIORITY LIST REQUIREMENT.— The State may provide financial assistance from its water pollution control revolving fund only with respect to a project for construction of a treatment works described in subsection (c)(1) if such project is on the State's priority list under section 216 of this Act. Such assistance may be provided regardless of the rank of such project on such list.

(h) ELIGIBILITY OF NON-FEDERAL SHARE OF CONSTRUCTION GRANT PROJECTS.— A State water pollution control revolving fund may provide assistance (other than under subsection (d)(1) of this section) to a municipality or intermunicipal or interstate agency with respect to the non-Federal share of the costs of a treatment works project for which such municipality or agency is receiving assistance from the Administrator under any other authority only if such assistance is necessary to allow such project to proceed.

(i) ADDITIONAL SUBSIDIZATION.—

(1) IN GENERAL.—In any case in which a State provides assistance to an eligible recipient under subsection (d), the State may provide additional subsidization (including forgiveness of principal, grants, negative interest loans, other loan forgiveness, and through buying, refinancing, or restructuring debt)—

(A) in assistance to a municipality or intermunicipal, interstate, or State agency to benefit a municipality that—

(i) meets the affordability criteria of the State established under paragraph (2); or

(ii) does not meet the affordability criteria of the State if the recipient—

(I) seeks additional subsidization to benefit individual ratepayers in the residential user rate class;

(II) demonstrates to the State that such ratepayers will experience a significant hardship from the increase in rates necessary to finance the project or activity for which assistance is sought; and

(III) ensures, as part of an assistance agreement between the State and the recipient, that the additional subsidization provided under this paragraph is directed through a user charge rate system (or other appropriate method) to such ratepayers; or

(B) to implement a process, material, technique, or technology—

(i) to address water-efficiency goals;

(ii) to address energy-efficiency goals;

(iii) to mitigate stormwater runoff; or

(iv) to encourage sustainable project planning, design, and construction.

(2) AFFORDABILITY CRITERIA.—

(A) ESTABLISHMENT.—

(i) IN GENERAL.— Not later than September 30, 2015, and after providing notice and an opportunity for public comment, a State shall establish affordability criteria to assist in identifying municipalities that would experience a significant hardship raising the revenue necessary to finance a project or activity eligible for assistance under subsection (c)(1) if additional subsidization is not provided.

(ii) CONTENTS.— The criteria under clause (i) shall be based on income and unemployment data, population trends, and other data determined relevant by the State, including whether the project or activity is to be carried out in an economically distressed area, as described in section 301 of the Public Works and Economic Development Act of 1965 (42 U.S.C. 3161).

(B) EXISTING CRITERIA.—If a State has previously established, after providing notice and an opportunity for public comment, affordability criteria that meet the requirements of subparagraph (A)—

(i) the State may use the criteria for the purposes of this subsection; and

(ii) those criteria shall be treated as affordability criteria established under this paragraph.

(C) INFORMATION TO ASSIST STATES.— The Administrator may publish information to assist States in establishing affordability criteria under subparagraph (A).

(3) LIMITATIONS.—

(A) IN GENERAL.— A State may provide additional subsidization in a fiscal year under this subsection only if the total amount appropriated for making capitalization grants to all States under this title for the fiscal year exceeds $1,000,000,000.

(B) TOTAL AMOUNT OF SUBSIDIZATION.—

(i) IN GENERAL.—For each fiscal year, of the amount of the capitalization grant received by the State under this title, the total amount of additional subsidization made available by a State under paragraph (1)—

(I) may not exceed 30 percent; and

(II) to the extent that there are sufficient applications for assistance to communities described in that paragraph, may not be less than 10 percent.

(ii) EXCLUSION.— A loan from the water pollution control revolving fund of a State with an interest rate equal to or greater than 0 percent shall not be considered additional subsidization for purposes of this subparagraph.

(C) APPLICABILITY.— The authority of a State to provide additional subsidization under this subsection shall apply to amounts received by the State in capitalization grants under this title for fiscal years beginning after September 30, 2014.

(D) CONSIDERATION.— If the State provides additional subsidization to a municipality or intermunicipal, interstate, or State agency under this subsection that meets the criteria under paragraph (1)(A), the State shall take the criteria set forth in section 602(b)(5) into consideration.

(j) DEFINITION OF ELIGIBLE INDIVIDUAL.— In subsection (c)(12), the term eligible individual means a member of a household, the members of which have a combined income (for the most recent 12-month period for which information is available) equal to not more than 50 percent of the median nonmetropolitan household income for the State in which the household is located, according to the most recent decennial census.

(k) ADDITIONAL USE OF FUNDS.— A State may use an additional 2 percent of the funds annually awarded to each State under this title for nonprofit organizations (as defined in section 104(w)) or State, regional, interstate, or municipal entities to provide technical assistance to rural, small, and tribal publicly owned treatment works (within the meaning of section 104(b)(8)(B)) in the State.

[33 U.S.C. 1383]

SEC. 604. ALLOTMENT OF FUNDS.

(a) FORMULA.— Sums authorized to be appropriated to carry out this section for each of fiscal years 1989 and 1990 shall be allotted by the Administrator in accordance with section 205(c) of this Act.

(b) RESERVATION OF FUNDS FOR PLANNING.— Each State shall reserve each fiscal year 1 percent of the sums allotted to such State under this section for such fiscal year, or $100,000, whichever amount is greater, to carry out planning under sections 205(j) and 303(e) of this Act.

(c) ALLOTMENT PERIOD.—

(1) PERIOD OF AVAILABILITY FOR GRANT AWARD.— Sums allotted to a State under this section for a fiscal year shall be available for obligation by the State during the fiscal year for which sums are authorized and during the following fiscal year.

(2) REALLOTMENT OF UNOBLIGATED FUNDS.— The amount of any allotment not obligated by the State by the last day of the 2-year period of availability established by paragraph (1) shall be immediately reallotted by the Administrator on the basis of the same ratio as is applicable to sums allotted under title II of this Act for the second fiscal year of such 2-year period. None of the funds reallotted by the Administrator shall be reallotted to any State which has not obligated all sums allotted to such State in the first fiscal year of such 2-year period.

[33 U.S.C. 1384]

SEC. 605. CORRECTIVE ACTION.

(a) NOTIFICATION OF NONCOMPLIANCE.— If the Administrator determines that a State has not complied with its agreement with the Administrator under section 602 of this Act or any other requirement of this title, the Administrator shall notify the State of such noncompliance and the necessary corrective action.

(b) WITHHOLDING OF PAYMENTS.— If a State does not take corrective action within 60 days after the date a State receives notification of such action under subsection (a), the Administrator shall withhold additional payments to the State until the Administrator is satisfied that the State has taken the necessary corrective action.

(c) REALLOTMENT OF WITHHELD PAYMENTS.— If the Administrator is not satisfied that adequate corrective actions have been taken by the State within 12 months after the State is notified of such actions under subsection (a), the payments withheld from the State by the Administrator under subsection (b) shall be made available for reallotment in accordance with the most recent formula for allotment of funds under this title.

[33 U.S.C. 1385]

SEC. 606. AUDITS, REPORTS, AND FISCAL CONTROLS; INTENDED USE PLAN.

(a) FISCAL CONTROL AND AUDITING PROCEDURES.—Each State electing to establish a water pollution control revolving fund under this title shall establish fiscal controls and accounting procedures sufficient to assure proper accounting during appropriate accounting periods for—

(1) payments received by the fund;

(2) disbursements made by the fund; and

(3) fund balances at the beginning and end of the accounting period.

(b) ANNUAL FEDERAL AUDITS.— The Administrator shall, at least on an annual basis, conduct or require each State to have independently conducted reviews and audits as may be deemed necessary or appropriate by the Administrator to carry out the objectives of this section. Audits of the use of funds deposited in the water pollution revolving fund established by such State shall be conducted in accordance with the auditing procedures of the General Accounting Office, including chapter 75 of title 31, United States Code.

(c) INTENDED USE PLAN.—After providing for public comment and review, each State shall annually prepare a plan identifying the intended uses of the amounts available to its water pollution control revolving fund. Such intended use plan shall include, but not be limited to—

(1) a list of those projects for construction of publicly owned treatment works on the State's priority list developed pursuant to section 216 of this Act and a list of activities eligible for assistance under sections 319 and 320 of this Act;

(2) a description of the short- and long-term goals and objectives of its water pollution control revolving fund;

(3) information on the activities to be supported, including a description of project categories, discharge requirements under titles III and IV of this Act, terms of financial assistance, and communities served;

(4) assurances and specific proposals for meeting the requirements of paragraphs (3), (4), (5), and (6) of section 602(b) of this Act; and

(5) the criteria and method established for the distribution of funds.

(d) ANNUAL REPORT.— Beginning the first fiscal year after the receipt of payments under this title, the State shall provide an annual report to the Administrator describing how the State has met the goals and objectives for the previous fiscal year as identified in the plan prepared for the previous fiscal year pursuant to subsection (c), including identification of loan recipients, loan amounts, and loan terms and similar details on other forms of financial assistance provided from the water pollution control revolving fund.

(e) Annual Federal Oversight Review.— The Administrator shall conduct an annual oversight review of each State plan prepared under subsection (c), each State report prepared under subsection (d), and other such materials as are considered necessary and appropriate in carrying out the purposes of this title. After reasonable notice by the Administrator to the State or the recipient of a loan from a water pollution control revolving fund, the State or loan recipient shall make available to the Administrator such records as the Administrator reasonably requires to review and determine compliance with this title.

(f) Applicability of Title II Provisions.— Except to the extent provided in this title, the provisions of title II shall not apply to grants under this title.

[33 U.S.C. 1386]

SEC. 607. AUTHORIZATION OF APPROPRIATIONS.

There are authorized to be appropriated to carry out the purposes of this title—

(1) $2,400,000,000 for fiscal year 2022;

(2) $2,750,000,000 for fiscal year 2023;

(3) $3,000,000,000 for fiscal year 2024; and

(4) $3,250,000,000 for each of fiscal years 2025 and 2026.

[33 U.S.C. 1387]

SEC. 608. REQUIREMENTS.

(a) In General.— Funds made available from a State water pollution control revolving fund established under this title may not be used for a project for the construction, alteration, maintenance, or repair of treatment works unless all of the iron and steel products used in the project are produced in the United States.

(b) Definition of Iron and Steel Products.— In this section, the term iron and steel products means the following products made primarily of iron or steel: lined or unlined pipes and fittings, manhole covers and other municipal castings, hydrants, tanks, flanges, pipe clamps and restraints, valves, structural steel, reinforced precast concrete, construction materials.

(c) Application.—Subsection (a) shall not apply in any case or category of cases in which the Administrator finds that—

(1) applying subsection (a) would be inconsistent with the public interest;

(2) iron and steel products are not produced in the United States in sufficient and reasonably available quantities and of a satisfactory quality; or

(3) inclusion of iron and steel products produced in the United States will increase the cost of the overall project by more than 25 percent.

(d) Waiver.— If the Administrator receives a request for a waiver under this section, the Administrator shall make available to the public, on an informal basis, a copy of the request and information available to the Administrator concerning the request, and shall allow for informal public input on the request for at least 15 days prior to making a finding based on the request. The Administrator shall make the request and accompanying information available by electronic means, including on the official public Internet site of the Environmental Protection Agency.

(e) INTERNATIONAL AGREEMENTS.— This section shall be applied in a manner consistent with United States obligations under international agreements.

(f) MANAGEMENT AND OVERSIGHT.— The Administrator may retain up to 0.25 percent of the funds appropriated for this title for management and oversight of the requirements of this section.

(g) EFFECTIVE DATE.— This section does not apply with respect to a project if a State agency approves the engineering plans and specifications for the project, in that agency's capacity to approve such plans and specifications prior to a project requesting bids, prior to the date of enactment of the Water Resources Reform and Development Act of 2014.

[33 U.S.C. 1388]

SEC. 609. CLEAN WATERSHEDS NEEDS SURVEY.

(a) REQUIREMENT.—Not later than 2 years after the date of enactment of this section, and not less frequently than once every 4 years thereafter, the Administrator shall—

(1) conduct and complete an assessment of capital improvement needs for all projects that are eligible under section 603(c) for assistance from State water pollution control revolving funds; and

(2) submit to Congress a report describing the results of the assessment completed under paragraph (1).

(b) AUTHORIZATION OF APPROPRIATIONS.— There is authorized to be appropriated to carry out the initial needs survey under subsection (a) $5,000,000, to remain available until expended.

[33 U.S.C. 1389]

SELECTED PROVISIONS OF THE OIL POLLUTION ACT OF 1990

PUBLIC LAW 101-380
AS AMENDED THROUGH PUBLIC LAW 11728

TITLE I—OIL POLLUTION LIABILITY AND COMPENSATION

OIL POLLUTION ACT OF 1990

[Public Law 101-380]

[As Amended Through P.L. 117–286, Enacted December 27, 2022]

AN ACT To establish limitations on liability for damages resulting from oil pollution, to establish a fund for the payment of compensation for such damages, and for other purposes.

Be it enacted by the Senate and House of Representatives of the United States of America in Congress assembled,

SECTION 1. SHORT TITLE.

This Act may be cited as the "Oil Pollution Act of 1990".

[33 U.S.C. 2701 note]

SEC. 2. TABLE OF CONTENTS.

The contents of this Act are as follows:

TITLE I—OIL POLLUTION LIABILITY AND COMPENSATION

TITLE I—OIL POLLUTION LIABILITY AND COMPENSATION

SEC. 1001. DEFINITIONS.

For the purposes of this Act, the term—

(1) act of God means an unanticipated grave natural disaster or other natural phenomenon of an exceptional, inevitable, and irresistible character the effects of which could not have been prevented or avoided by the exercise of due care or foresight;

(2) barrel means 42 United States gallons at 60 degrees fahrenheit;

(3) claim means a request, made in writing for a sum certain, for compensation for damages or removal costs resulting from an incident;

(4) claimant means any person or government who presents a claim for compensation under this title;

(5) damages means damages specified in section 1002(b) of this Act, and includes the cost of assessing these damages;

(6) deepwater port is a facility licensed under the Deepwater Port Act of 1974 (33 U.S.C. 1501–1524);

(7) discharge means any emission (other than natural seepage), intentional or unintentional, and includes, but is not limited to, spilling, leaking, pumping, pouring, emitting, emptying, or dumping;

(8) exclusive economic zone means the zone established by Presidential Proclamation Numbered 5030, dated March 10, 1983, including the ocean waters of the areas referred to as eastern special areas in Article 3(1) of the Agreement between the United States of America and the Union of Soviet Socialist Republics on the Maritime Boundary, signed June 1, 1990;

(9) facility means any structure, group of structures, equipment, or device (other than a vessel) which is used for one or more of the following purposes: exploring for, drilling for, producing, storing, handling, transferring, processing, or transporting oil. This term includes any motor vehicle, rolling stock, or pipeline used for one or more of these purposes;

(10) foreign offshore unit means a facility which is located, in whole or in part, in the territorial sea or on the continental shelf of a foreign country and which is or was used for one or more of the following purposes: exploring for, drilling for, producing, storing, handling, transferring, processing, or transporting oil produced from the seabed beneath the foreign country's territorial sea or from the foreign country's continental shelf;

(11) Fund means the Oil Spill Liability Trust Fund, established by section 9509 of the Internal Revenue Code of 1986 (26 U.S.C. 9509);

(12) gross ton has the meaning given that term by the Secretary under part J of title 46, United States Code;

(13) guarantor means any person, other than the responsible party, who provides

evidence of financial responsibility for a responsible party under this Act;

(14) incident means any occurrence or series of occurrences having the same origin, involving one or more vessels, facilities, or any combination thereof, resulting in the discharge or substantial threat of discharge of oil;

(15) Indian tribe means any Indian tribe, band, nation, or other organized group or community, but not including any Alaska Native regional or village corporation, which is recognized as eligible for the special programs and services provided by the United States to Indians because of their status as Indians and has governmental authority over lands belonging to or controlled by the tribe;

(16) lessee means a person holding a leasehold interest in an oil or gas lease on lands beneath navigable waters (as that term is defined in section 2(a) of the Submerged Lands Act (43 U.S.C. 1301(a))) or on submerged lands of the Outer Continental Shelf, granted or maintained under applicable State law or the Outer Continental Shelf Lands Act (43 U.S.C. 1331 et seq.);

(17) liable or liability shall be construed to be the standard of liability which obtains under section 311 of the Federal Water Pollution Control Act (33 U.S.C. 1321);

(18) mobile offshore drilling unit means a vessel (other than a self-elevating lift vessel) capable of use as an offshore facility;

(19) National Contingency Plan means the National Contingency Plan prepared and published under section 311(d) of the Federal Water Pollution Control Act, as amended by this Act, or revised under section 105 of the Comprehensive Environmental Response, Compensation, and Liability Act (42 U.S.C. 9605);

(20) natural resources includes land, fish, wildlife, biota, air, water, ground water, drinking water supplies, and other such resources belonging to, managed by, held in trust by, appertaining to, or otherwise controlled by the United States (including the resources of the exclusive economic zone), any State or local government or Indian tribe, or any foreign government;

(21) navigable waters means the waters of the United States, including the territorial sea;

(22) offshore facility means any facility of any kind located in, on, or under any of the navigable waters of the United States, and any facility of any kind which is subject to the jurisdiction of the United States and is located in, on, or under any other waters, other than a vessel or a public vessel;

(23) oil means oil of any kind or in any form, including petroleum, fuel oil, sludge, oil refuse, and oil mixed with wastes other than dredged spoil, but does not include any substance which is specifically listed or designated as a hazardous substance under subparagraphs (A) through (F) of section 101(14) of the Comprehensive Environmental Response, Compensation, and Liability Act (42 U.S.C. 9601) and which is subject to the provisions of that Act;

(24) onshore facility means any facility (including, but not limited to, motor vehicles and rolling stock) of any kind located in, on, or under, any land within the United States other than submerged land;

(25) the term Outer Continental Shelf facility means an offshore facility which is located, in whole or in part, on the Outer Continental Shelf and is or was used for one or more of the following purposes: exploring for, drilling for, producing, storing, handling, transferring, processing, or transporting oil produced from the Outer Continental Shelf;

(26) owner or operator—

(A) means—

(i) in the case of a vessel, any person owning, operating, or chartering by demise, the vessel;

(ii) in the case of an onshore facility, offshore facility, or foreign offshore unit or other facility located seaward of the exclusive economic zone, any person or entity owning or operating such facility;

(iii) in the case of any abandoned offshore facility or foreign offshore unit or other facility located seaward of the exclusive economic zone, the person or entity that owned or operated such facility immediately prior to such abandonment;

(iv) in the case of any facility, title or control of which was conveyed due to bankruptcy, foreclosure, tax delinquency, abandonment, or similar means to a unit of State or local government, any person who owned, operated, or otherwise controlled activities at such facility immediately beforehand;

(v) notwithstanding subparagraph (B)(i), and in the same manner and to the same extent, both procedurally and substantively, as any nongovernmental entity, including for purposes of liability under section 1002, any State or local government that has caused or contributed to a discharge or substantial threat of a discharge of oil from a vessel or facility ownership or control of which was acquired involuntarily through—

(I) seizure or otherwise in connection with law enforcement activity;

(II) bankruptcy;

(III) tax delinquency;

(IV) abandonment; or

(V) other circumstances in which the government involuntarily acquires title by virtue of its function as sovereign;

(vi) notwithstanding subparagraph (B)(ii), a person that is a lender and that holds indicia of ownership primarily to protect a security interest in a vessel or facility if, while the borrower is still in possession of the vessel or facility encumbered by the security interest, the person—

(I) exercises decision making control over the environmental compliance related to the vessel or facility, such that the person has undertaken responsibility for oil handling or disposal practices related to the vessel or facility; or

(II) exercises control at a level comparable to that of a manager of the vessel or facility, such that the person has assumed or manifested responsibility—

(aa) for the overall management of the vessel or facility encompassing day-to-day decision making with respect to environmental compliance; or

(bb) over all or substantially all of the operational functions (as distinguished from financial or administrative functions) of the vessel or facility other than the function of environmental compliance; and

(B) does not include—

(i) A unit of state or local government that acquired ownership or control of a vessel or facility involuntarily through—

(I) seizure or otherwise in connection with law enforcement activity;

(II) bankruptcy;

(III) tax delinquency;

(IV) abandonment; or

(V) other circumstances in which the government involuntarily acquires title by virtue of its function as sovereign;

(ii) a person that is a lender that does not participate in management of a vessel or facility, but holds indicia of ownership primarily to protect the security interest of the person in the vessel or facility; or

(iii) a person that is a lender that did not participate in management of a vessel or facility prior to foreclosure, notwithstanding that the person—

(I) forecloses on the vessel or facility; and

(II) after foreclosure, sells, re-leases (in the case of a lease finance transaction), or liquidates the vessel or facility, maintains business activities, winds up operations, undertakes a removal action under section 311(c) of the Federal Water Pollution Control Act (33 U.S.C. 1321(c)) or under the direction of an on-scene coordinator appointed under the National Contingency Plan, with respect to the vessel or facility, or takes any other measure to preserve, protect, or prepare the vessel or facility prior to sale or disposition,

if the person seeks to sell, re-lease (in the case of a lease finance transaction), or otherwise divest the person of the vessel or facility at the earliest practicable, commercially reasonable time, on commercially reasonable terms, taking into account market conditions and legal and regulatory requirements;

(27) person means an individual, corporation, partnership, association, State, municipality, commission, or political subdivision of a State, or any interstate body;

(28) permittee means a person holding an authorization, license, or permit for geological exploration issued under section 11 of the Outer Continental Shelf Lands

Act (43 U.S.C. 1340) or applicable State law;

(29) public vessel means a vessel owned or bareboat chartered and operated by the United States, or by a State or political subdivision thereof, or by a foreign nation, except when the vessel is engaged in commerce;

(30) remove or removal means containment and removal of oil or a hazardous substance from water and shorelines or the taking of other actions as may be necessary to minimize or mitigate damage to the public health or welfare, including, but not limited to, fish, shellfish, wildlife, and public and private property, shorelines, and beaches;

(31) removal costs means the costs of removal that are incurred after a discharge of oil has occurred or, in any case in which there is a substantial threat of a discharge of oil, the costs to prevent, minimize, or mitigate oil pollution from such an incident;

(32) responsible party means the following:

(A) VESSELS.— In the case of a vessel, any person owning, operating, or demise chartering the vessel. In the case of a vessel, the term responsible party also includes the owner of oil being transported in a tank vessel with a single hull after December 31, 2010.

(B) ONSHORE FACILITIES.— In the case of an onshore facility (other than a pipeline), any person owning or operating the facility, except a Federal agency, State, municipality, commission, or political subdivision of a State, or any interstate body, that as the owner transfers possession and right to use the property to another person by lease, assignment, or permit.

(C) OFFSHORE FACILITIES.— In the case of an offshore facility (other than a pipeline or a deepwater port licensed under the Deepwater Port Act of 1974 (33 U.S.C. 1501 et seq.)), the lessee or permittee of the area in which the facility is located or the holder of a right of use and easement granted under applicable State law or the Outer Continental Shelf Lands Act (43 U.S.C. 1301–1356) for the area in which the facility is located (if the holder is a different person than the lessee or permittee), except a Federal agency, State, municipality, commission, or political subdivision of a State, or any interstate body, that as owner transfers possession and right to use the property to another person by lease, assignment, or permit.

(D) FOREIGN FACILITIES.— In the case of a foreign offshore unit or other facility located seaward of the exclusive economic zone, any person or other entity owning or operating the facility, and any leaseholder, permit holder, assignee, or holder of a right of use and easement granted under applicable foreign law for the area in which the facility is located.

(E) DEEPWATER PORTS.— In the case of a deepwater port licensed under the Deepwater Port Act of 1974 (33 U.S.C. 1501–1524), the licensee.

(F) PIPELINES.— In the case of a pipeline, any person owning or operating the pipeline.

(G) ABANDONMENT.— In the case of an abandoned vessel, onshore facility, deepwater port, pipeline, ,[1] offshore facility, or foreign offshore unit or other facility located seaward of the exclusive economic zone, the persons or entities that would have been responsible parties immediately prior to the abandonment of the vessel or facility.

[1] Two commas are so in law. See amendment made by section 3508(b)(1)(A)(ii)(III) of division C of Public Law 115–91.

(33) Secretary means the Secretary of the department in which the Coast Guard is operating;

(34) tank vessel means a vessel that is constructed or adapted to carry, or that carries, oil or hazardous material in bulk as cargo or cargo residue, and that—

(A) is a vessel of the United States;

(B) operates on the navigable waters; or

(C) transfers oil or hazardous material in a place subject to the jurisdiction of the United States;

(35) territorial seas means the belt of the seas measured from the line of ordinary low water along that portion of the coast which is in direct contact with the open sea and the line marking the seaward limit of inland waters, and extending seaward a distance of 3 miles;

(36) United States and State mean the several States of the United States, the District of Columbia, the Commonwealth of Puerto Rico, Guam, American Samoa, the United States Virgin Islands, the Commonwealth of the Northern Marianas, and any other territory or possession of the United States;

(37) vessel means every description of watercraft or other artificial contrivance used, or capable of being used, as a means of transportation on water, other than a public vessel;

(38) participate in management—

(A)(i) means actually participating in the management or operational affairs of a vessel or facility; and

(ii) does not include merely having the capacity to influence, or the unexercised right to control, vessel or facility operations; and

(B) does not include—

(i) performing an act or failing to act prior to the time at which a security interest is created in a vessel or facility;

(ii) holding a security interest or abandoning or releasing a security interest;

(iii) including in the terms of an extension of credit, or in a contract or security agreement relating to the extension, a covenant, warranty, or other term or condition that relates to environmental compliance;

(iv) monitoring or enforcing the terms and conditions of the extension of credit or security interest;

(v) monitoring or undertaking one or more inspections of the vessel or facility;

(vi) requiring a removal action or other lawful means of addressing a discharge or substantial threat of a discharge of oil in connection with the vessel or facility prior to, during, or on the expiration of the term of the extension of credit;

(vii) providing financial or other advice or counseling in an effort to mitigate, prevent, or cure default or diminution in the value of the vessel or facility;

(viii) restructuring, renegotiating, or otherwise agreeing to alter the terms and conditions of the extension of credit or security interest, exercising forbearance;

(ix) exercising other remedies that may be available under applicable law for the breach of a term or condition of the extension of credit or security agreement; or

(x) conducting a removal action under 311(c) of the Federal Water Pollution Control Act (33 U.S.C. 1321(c)) or under the direction of an on-scene coordinator appointed under the National Contingency Plan,

if such actions do not rise to the level of participating in management under subparagraph (A) of this paragraph and paragraph (26)(A)(vi);

(39) extension of credit has the meaning provided in section 101(20)(G)(i) of the Comprehensive Environmental Response, Compensation and Liability Act of 1980 (42 U.S.C. 9601(20)(G)(i));

(40) financial or administrative function has the meaning provided in section 101(20)(G)(ii) of the Comprehensive Environmental Response, Compensation and Liability Act of 1980 (42 U.S.C. 9601(20)(G)(ii));

(41) foreclosure and foreclose each has the meaning provided in section 101(20)(G)(iii) of the Comprehensive Environmental Response, Compensation and Liability Act of 1980 (42 U.S.C. 9601(20)(G)(iii));

(42) lender has the meaning provided in section 101(20)(G)(iv) of the Comprehensive Environmental Response, Compensation and Liability Act of 1980 (42 U.S.C. 9601(20)(G)(iv));

(43) operational function has the meaning provided in section 101(20)(G)(v) of the Comprehensive Environmental Response, Compensation and Liability Act of 1980 (42 U.S.C. 9601(20)(G)(v)); and

(44) security interest has the meaning provided in section 101(20)(G)(vi) of the Comprehensive Environmental Response, Compensation and Liability Act of 1980 (42 U.S.C. 9601(20)(G)(vi)).

[33 U.S.C. 2701]

SEC. 1002. ELEMENTS OF LIABILITY.

(a) In General.— Notwithstanding any other provision or rule of law, and subject to the provisions of this Act, each responsible party for a vessel or a facility from which oil is discharged, or which poses the substantial threat of a discharge of oil, into or upon the navigable waters or adjoining shorelines or the exclusive economic zone is liable for the removal costs and damages specified in subsection (b) that result from such incident.

(b) Covered Removal Costs and Damages.—

(1) Removal costs.—The removal costs referred to in subsection (a) are—

(A) all removal costs incurred by the United States, a State, or an Indian tribe under subsection (c), (d), (e), or (l) of section 311 of the Federal Water Pollution Control Act (33 U.S.C. 1321), as amended by this Act, under the Intervention on the High Seas Act (33 U.S.C. 1471 et seq.), or under State law; and

(B) any removal costs incurred by any person for acts taken by the person which are consistent with the National Contingency Plan.

(2) Damages.—The damages referred to in subsection (a) are the following:

(A) Natural resources.— Damages for injury to, destruction of, loss of, or loss of use of, natural resources, including the reasonable costs of assessing the damage, which shall be recoverable by a United States trustee, a State trustee, an Indian tribe trustee, or a foreign trustee.

(B) Real or personal property.— Damages for injury to, or economic losses resulting from destruction of, real or personal property, which shall be recoverable by a claimant who owns or leases that property.

(C) Subsistence use.— Damages for loss of subsistence use of natural resources, which shall be recoverable by any claimant who so uses natural resources which have been injured, destroyed, or lost, without regard to the ownership or management of the resources.

(D) Revenues.— Damages equal to the net loss of taxes, royalties, rents, fees, or net profit shares due to the injury, destruction, or loss of real property, personal property, or natural resources, which shall be recoverable by the Government of the United States, a State, or a political subdivision thereof.

(E) Profits and earning capacity.— Damages equal to the loss of profits or impairment of earning capacity due to the injury, destruction, or loss of real property, personal property, or natural resources, which shall be recoverable by any claimant.

(F) Public services.— Damages for net costs of providing increased or additional public services during or after removal activities, including protection from fire, safety, or health hazards, caused by a discharge of oil, which shall be recoverable by a State, or a political subdivision of a State.

(c) Excluded Discharges.—This title does not apply to any discharge—

(1) permitted by a permit issued under Federal, State, or local law;

(2) from a public vessel; or

(3) from an onshore facility which is subject to the Trans-Alaska Pipeline Authorization Act (43 U.S.C. 1651 et seq.).

(d) Liability of Third Parties.—

(1) In general.—

(A) Third party treated as responsible party.— Except as provided in subparagraph (B), in any case in which a responsible party establishes that a discharge or threat of a discharge and the resulting removal costs and damages were caused solely by an act or omission of one or more third parties described in section 1003(a)(3) (or solely by such an act or omission in combination with an act of God or an act of war), the third party or parties shall be treated as the responsible party or parties for purposes of determining liability under this title.

(B) Subrogation of responsible party.—If the responsible party alleges that the discharge or threat of a discharge was caused solely by an act or omission of a third party, the responsible party—

(i) in accordance with section 1013, shall pay removal costs and damages to any claimant; and

(ii) shall be entitled by subrogation to all rights of the United States Government and the claimant to recover removal costs or damages from the third party or the Fund paid under this subsection.

(2) Limitation applied.—

(A) Owner or operator of vessel or facility.— If the act or omission of a third party that causes an incident occurs in connection with a vessel or facility owned or operated by the third party, the liability of the third party shall be subject to the limits provided in section 1004 as applied with respect to the vessel or facility.

(B) Other cases.— In any other case, the liability of a third party or parties shall not exceed the limitation which would have been applicable to the responsible party of the vessel or facility from which the discharge actually occurred if the responsible party were liable.

[33 U.S.C. 2702]

SEC. 1003. DEFENSES TO LIABILITY.

(a) Complete Defenses.—A responsible party is not liable for removal costs or damages under section 1002 if the responsible party establishes, by a preponderance of the evidence, that the discharge or substantial threat of a discharge of oil and the resulting damages or removal costs were caused solely by—

(1) an act of God;

(2) an act of war;

(3) an act or omission of a third party, other than an employee or agent of the responsible party or a third party whose act or omission occurs in connection with any contractual relationship with the responsible party (except where the sole contractual arrangement arises in connection with carriage by a common carrier by rail), if the responsible party establishes, by a preponderance of the evidence, that the responsible party—

(A) exercised due care with respect to the oil concerned, taking into consideration the characteristics of the oil and in light of all relevant facts and circumstances; and

(B) took precautions against foreseeable acts or omissions of any such third party and the foreseeable consequences of those acts or omissions; or

(4) any combination of paragraphs (1), (2), and (3).

(b) DEFENSES AS TO PARTICULAR CLAIMANTS.— A responsible party is not liable under section 1002 to a claimant, to the extent that the incident is caused by the gross negligence or willful misconduct of the claimant.

(c) LIMITATION ON COMPLETE DEFENSE.—Subsection (a) does not apply with respect to a responsible party who fails or refuses—

(1) to report the incident as required by law if the responsible party knows or has reason to know of the incident;

(2) to provide all reasonable cooperation and assistance requested by a responsible official in connection with removal activities; or

(3) without sufficient cause, to comply with an order issued under subsection (c) or (e) of section 311 of the Federal Water Pollution Control Act (33 U.S.C. 1321), as amended by this Act, or the Intervention on the High Seas Act (33 U.S.C. 1471 et seq.).

(d) DEFINITION OF CONTRACTUAL RELATIONSHIP.—

(1) IN GENERAL.—For purposes of subsection (a)(3) the term contractual relationship includes, but is not limited to, land contracts, deeds, easements, leases, or other instruments transferring title or possession, unless—

(A) the real property on which the facility concerned is located was acquired by the responsible party after the placement of the oil on, in, or at the real property on which the facility concerned is located;

(B) one or more of the circumstances described in subparagraph (A), (B), or (C) of paragraph (2) is established by the responsible party by a preponderance of the evidence; and

(C) the responsible party complies with paragraph (3).

(2) REQUIRED CIRCUMSTANCE.—The circumstances referred to in paragraph (1)(B) are the following:

(A) At the time the responsible party acquired the real property on which the facility is located the responsible party did not know and had no reason to know that oil that is the subject of the discharge or substantial threat of discharge was located on, in, or at the facility.

(B) The responsible party is a government entity that acquired the facility—

(i) by escheat;

(ii) through any other involuntary transfer or acquisition; or

(iii) through the exercise of eminent domain authority by purchase or condemnation.

(C) The responsible party acquired the facility by inheritance or bequest.

(3) ADDITIONAL REQUIREMENTS.—For purposes of paragraph (1)(C), the responsible party must establish by a preponderance of the evidence that the responsible party—

(A) has satisfied the requirements of section 1003(a)(3)(A) and (B);

(B) has provided full cooperation, assistance, and facility access to the persons that are authorized to conduct removal actions, including the cooperation and access necessary for the installation, integrity, operation, and maintenance of any complete or partial removal action;

(C) is in compliance with any land use restrictions established or relied on in connection with the removal action; and

(D) has not impeded the effectiveness or integrity of any institutional control employed in connection with the removal action.

(4) REASON TO KNOW.—

(A) APPROPRIATE INQUIRIES.—To establish that the responsible party had no reason to know of the matter described in paragraph (2)(A), the responsible party must demonstrate to a court that—

(i) on or before the date on which the responsible party acquired the real property on which the facility is located, the responsible party carried out all appropriate inquiries, as provided in subparagraphs (B) and (D), into the previous ownership and uses of the real property on which the facility is located in accordance with generally accepted good commercial and customary standards and practices; and

(ii) the responsible party took reasonable steps to—

(I) stop any continuing discharge;

(II) prevent any substantial threat of discharge; and

(III) prevent or limit any human, environmental, or natural resource exposure to any previously discharged oil.

(B) REGULATIONS ESTABLISHING STANDARDS AND PRACTICES.— Not later than 2 years after the date of the enactment of this paragraph, the Secretary, in consultation with the Administrator of the Environmental Protection Agency, shall by regulation establish standards and practices for the purpose of satisfying the requirement to carry out all appropriate inquiries under subparagraph (A).

(C) CRITERIA.—In promulgating regulations that establish the standards and practices referred to in subparagraph (B), the Secretary shall include in such standards and practices provisions regarding each of the following:

(i) The results of an inquiry by an environmental professional.

(ii) Interviews with past and present owners, operators, and occupants of the facility and the real property on which the facility is located for the purpose of gathering information regarding the potential for oil at the facility and on the real property on which the facility is located.

(iii) Reviews of historical sources, such as chain of title documents, aerial photographs, building department records, and land use records, to determine previous uses and occupancies of the real property on which the facility is located since the property was first developed.

(iv) Searches for recorded environmental cleanup liens against the facility and the real property on which the facility is located that are filed under Federal, State, or local law.

(v) Reviews of Federal, State, and local government records, waste disposal records, underground storage tank records, and waste handling, generation, treatment, disposal, and spill records, concerning oil at or near the facility and on the real property on which the facility is located.

(vi) Visual inspections of the facility, the real property on which the facility is located, and adjoining properties.

(vii) Specialized knowledge or experience on the part of the responsible party.

(viii) The relationship of the purchase price to the value of the facility and the real property on which the facility is located, if oil was not at the facility or on the real property.

(ix) Commonly known or reasonably ascertainable information about the facility and the real property on which the facility is located.

(x) The degree of obviousness of the presence or likely presence of oil at the facility and on the real property on which the facility is located, and the ability to detect the oil by appropriate investigation.

(D) INTERIM STANDARDS AND PRACTICES.—

(i) REAL PROPERTY PURCHASED BEFORE MAY 31, 1997.—With respect to real property purchased before May 31, 1997, in making a determination with respect to a responsible party described in subparagraph (A), a court shall take into account—

(I) any specialized knowledge or experience on the part of the responsible party;

(II) the relationship of the purchase price to the value of the facility and the real property on which the facility is located, if the oil was not at the facility or on the real property;

(III) commonly known or reasonably ascertainable information about the facility and the real property on which the facility is located;

(IV) the obviousness of the presence or likely presence of oil at the facility and on the real property on which the facility is located; and

(V) the ability of the responsible party to detect oil by appropriate inspection.

(ii) REAL PROPERTY PURCHASED ON OR AFTER MAY 31, 1997.— With respect to real property purchased on or after May 31, 1997, until the Secretary promulgates the regulations described in clause (ii), the procedures of the American Society for Testing and Materials, including the document known as Standard E1527–97, entitled Standard Practice for Environmental

Site Assessment: Phase I Environmental Site Assessment Process, shall satisfy the requirements in subparagraph (A).

(E) SITE INSPECTION AND TITLE SEARCH.— In the case of real property for residential use or other similar use purchased by a nongovernmental or noncommercial entity, inspection and title search of the facility and the real property on which the facility is located that reveal no basis for further investigation shall be considered to satisfy the requirements of this paragraph.

(5) PREVIOUS OWNER OR OPERATOR.— Nothing in this paragraph or in section 1003(a)(3) shall diminish the liability of any previous owner or operator of such facility who would otherwise be liable under this Act. Notwithstanding this paragraph, if a responsible party obtained actual knowledge of the discharge or substantial threat of discharge of oil at such facility when the responsible party owned the facility and then subsequently transferred ownership of the facility or the real property on which the facility is located to another person without disclosing such knowledge, the responsible party shall be treated as liable under section 1002(a) and no defense under section 1003(a) shall be available to such responsible party.

(6) LIMITATION ON DEFENSE.— Nothing in this paragraph shall affect the liability under this Act of a responsible party who, by any act or omission, caused or contributed to the discharge or substantial threat of discharge of oil which is the subject of the action relating to the facility.

[33 U.S.C. 2703]

SEC. 1004. LIMITS ON LIABILITY.

(a) GENERAL RULE.—Except as otherwise provided in this section, the total of the liability of a responsible party under section 1002 and any removal costs incurred by, or on behalf of, the responsible party, with respect to each incident shall not exceed—

(1) for a tank vessel, the greater of—

(A) with respect to a single-hull vessel, including a single-hull vessel fitted with double sides only or a double bottom only, $3,000 per gross ton;

(B) with respect to a vessel other than a vessel referred to in subparagraph (A), $1,900 per gross ton; or

(C)(i) with respect to a vessel greater than 3,000 gross tons that is—

(I) a vessel described in subparagraph (A), $22,000,000; or

(II) a vessel described in subparagraph (B), $16,000,000; or

(ii) with respect to a vessel of 3,000 gross tons or less that is—

(I) a vessel described in subparagraph (A), $6,000,000; or

(II) a vessel described in subparagraph (B), $4,000,000;

(2) for any other vessel, $950 per gross ton or $800,000, whichever is greater;

(3) for an offshore facility except a deepwater port, the total of all removal costs plus $75,000,000; and

(4) for any onshore facility and a deepwater port, $350,000,000.

(b) DIVISION OF LIABILITY FOR MOBILE OFFSHORE DRILLING UNITS.—

(1) TREATED FIRST AS TANK VESSEL.— For purposes of determining the responsible party and applying this Act and except as provided in paragraph (2), a mobile offshore drilling unit which is being used as an offshore facility is deemed to be a tank vessel with respect to the discharge, or the substantial threat of a discharge, of oil on or above the surface of the water.

(2) TREATED AS FACILITY FOR EXCESS LIABILITY.— To the extent that removal costs and damages from any incident described in paragraph (1) exceed the amount for which a responsible party is liable (as that amount may be limited under subsection (a)(1)), the mobile offshore drilling unit is deemed to be an offshore facility. For purposes of applying subsection (a)(3), the amount specified in that subsection shall be reduced by the amount for which the responsible party is liable under paragraph (1).

(c) EXCEPTIONS.—

(1) ACTS OF RESPONSIBLE PARTY.—Subsection (a) does not apply if the incident was proximately caused by—

(A) gross negligence or willful misconduct of, or

(B) the violation of an applicable Federal safety, construction, or operating regulation by,

the responsible party, an agent or employee of the responsible party, or a person acting pursuant to a contractual relationship with the responsible party (except where the sole contractual arrangement arises in connection with carriage by a common carrier by rail).

(2) FAILURE OR REFUSAL OF RESPONSIBLE PARTY.—Subsection (a) does not apply if the responsible party fails or refuses—

(A) to report the incident as required by law and the responsible party knows or has reason to know of the incident;

(B) to provide all reasonable cooperation and assistance requested by a responsible official in connection with removal activities; or

(C) without sufficient cause, to comply with an order issued under subsection (c) or (e) of section 311 of the Federal Water Pollution Control Act (33 U.S.C. 1321), as amended by this Act, or the Intervention on the High Seas Act (33 U.S.C. 1471 et seq.).

(3) OCS FACILITY OR VESSEL.— Notwithstanding the limitations established under subsection (a) and the defenses of section 1003, all removal costs incurred by the United States Government or any State or local official or agency in connection with a discharge or substantial threat of a discharge of oil from any Outer Continental Shelf facility or a vessel carrying oil as cargo from such a facility shall be borne by the owner or operator of such facility or vessel.

(4) CERTAIN TANK VESSELS.—Subsection (a)(1) shall not apply to—

(A) a tank vessel on which the only oil carried as cargo is an animal fat or vegetable oil, as those terms are used in section 2 of the Edible Oil Regulatory Reform Act; and

(B) a tank vessel that is designated in its certificate of inspection as an oil spill response vessel (as that term is defined in section 2101 of title 46, United States Code) and that is used solely for removal.

(d) Adjusting Limits of Liability.—

(1) Onshore facilities.— Subject to paragraph (2), the President may establish by regulation, with respect to any class or category of onshore facility, a limit of liability under this section of less than $350,000,000, but not less than $8,000,000, taking into account size, storage capacity, oil throughput, proximity to sensitive areas, type of oil handled, history of discharges, and other factors relevant to risks posed by the class or category of facility.

(2) Deepwater ports and associated vessels.—

(A) Study.— The Secretary shall conduct a study of the relative operational and environmental risks posed by the transportation of oil by vessel to deepwater ports (as defined in section 3 of the Deepwater Port Act of 1974 (33 U.S.C. 1502)) versus the transportation of oil by vessel to other ports. The study shall include a review and analysis of offshore lightering practices used in connection with that transportation, an analysis of the volume of oil transported by vessel using those practices, and an analysis of the frequency and volume of oil discharges which occur in connection with the use of those practices.

(B) Report.— Not later than 1 year after the date of the enactment of this Act, the Secretary shall submit to the Congress a report on the results of the study conducted under subparagraph (A).

(C) Rulemaking proceeding.— If the Secretary determines, based on the results of the study conducted under subparagraph (A), that the use of deepwater ports in connection with the transportation of oil by vessel results in a lower operational or environmental risk than the use of other ports, the Secretary shall initiate, not later than the 180th day following the date of submission of the report to the Congress under subparagraph (B), a rulemaking proceeding to lower the limits of liability under this section for deepwater ports as the Secretary determines appropriate. The Secretary may establish a limit of liability of less than $350,000,000, but not less than $50,000,000, in accordance with paragraph (1).

(3) Periodic reports.— The President shall, within 6 months after the date of the enactment of this Act, and from time to time thereafter, report to the Congress on the desirability of adjusting the limits of liability specified in subsection (a).

(4) Adjustment to reflect consumer price index.— The President, by regulations issued not later than 3 years after the date of enactment of the Delaware River Protection Act of 2006 and not less than every 3 years thereafter, shall adjust the limits on liability specified in subsection (a) to reflect significant increases in the Consumer Price Index.

[33 U.S.C. 2704]

SEC. 1005. INTEREST; PARTIAL PAYMENT OF CLAIMS.

(a) General Rule.— The responsible party or the responsible party's guarantor is liable to a claimant for interest on the amount paid in satisfaction of a claim under this Act for the period described in subsection (b). The responsible party shall establish a procedure for the payment or settlement of claims for interim, short-term damages. Payment or settlement of a claim for interim, short-term damages representing less than the full amount of damages to which the claimant ultimately may be entitled shall not preclude recovery by the claimant for damages not reflected in the paid or settled partial claim.

(b) PERIOD.—

(1) IN GENERAL.— Except as provided in paragraph (2), the period for which interest shall be paid is the period beginning on the 30th day following the date on which the claim is presented to the responsible party or guarantor and ending on the date on which the claim is paid.

(2) EXCLUSION OF PERIOD DUE TO OFFER BY GUARANTOR.— If the guarantor offers to the claimant an amount equal to or greater than that finally paid in satisfaction of the claim, the period described in paragraph (1) does not include the period beginning on the date the offer is made and ending on the date the offer is accepted. If the offer is made within 60 days after the date on which the claim is presented under section 1013(a), the period described in paragraph (1) does not include any period before the offer is accepted.

(3) EXCLUSION OF PERIODS IN INTERESTS OF JUSTICE.— If in any period a claimant is not paid due to reasons beyond the control of the responsible party or because it would not serve the interests of justice, no interest shall accrue under this section during that period.

(4) CALCULATION OF INTEREST.—

(A) IN GENERAL.— The interest paid for claims, other than Federal Government cost recovery claims, under this section shall be calculated at the average of the highest rate for commercial and finance company paper of maturities of 180 days or less obtaining on each of the days included within the period for which interest must be paid to the claimant, as published in the Federal Reserve Bulletin.

(B) FEDERAL COST RECOVERY CLAIMS.— The interest paid for Federal Government cost recovery claims under this section shall be calculated in accordance with section 3717 of title 31, United States Code.

(5) INTEREST NOT SUBJECT TO LIABILITY LIMITS.—

(A) IN GENERAL.— Interest (including prejudgment interest) under this paragraph is in addition to damages and removal costs for which claims may be asserted under section 1002 and shall be paid without regard to any limitation of liability under section 1004.

(B) PAYMENT BY GUARANTOR.— The payment of interest under this subsection by a guarantor is subject to section 1016(g).

[33 U.S.C. 2705]

SEC. 1006. NATURAL RESOURCES.

(a) LIABILITY.—In the case of natural resource damages under section 1002(b)(2)(A), liability shall be—

(1) to the United States Government for natural resources belonging to, managed by, controlled by, or appertaining to the United States;

(2) to any State for natural resources belonging to, managed by, controlled by, or appertaining to such State or political subdivision thereof;

(3) to any Indian tribe for natural resources belonging to, managed by, controlled by, or appertaining to such Indian tribe; and

(4) in any case in which section 1007 applies, to the government of a foreign country for natural resources belonging to, managed by, controlled by, or appertaining to such country.

(b) DESIGNATION OF TRUSTEES.—

(1) IN GENERAL.— The President, or the authorized representative of any State, Indian tribe, or foreign government, shall act on behalf of the public, Indian tribe, or foreign country as trustee of natural resources to present a claim for and to recover damages to the natural resources.

(2) FEDERAL TRUSTEES.— The President shall designate the Federal officials who shall act on behalf of the public as trustees for natural resources under this Act.

(3) STATE TRUSTEES.— The Governor of each State shall designate State and local officials who may act on behalf of the public as trustee for natural resources under this Act and shall notify the President of the designation.

(4) INDIAN TRIBE TRUSTEES.— The governing body of any Indian tribe shall designate tribal officials who may act on behalf of the tribe or its members as trustee for natural resources under this Act and shall notify the President of the designation.

(5) FOREIGN TRUSTEES.— The head of any foreign government may designate the trustee who shall act on behalf of that government as trustee for natural resources under this Act.

(c) FUNCTIONS OF TRUSTEES.—

(1) FEDERAL TRUSTEES.—The Federal officials designated under subsection (b)(2)—

(A) shall assess natural resource damages under section 1002(b)(2)(A) for the natural resources under their trusteeship;

(B) may, upon request of and reimbursement from a State or Indian tribe and at the Federal officials' discretion, assess damages for the natural resources under the State's or tribe's trusteeship; and

(C) shall develop and implement a plan for the restoration, rehabilitation, replacement, or acquisition of the equivalent, of the natural resources under their trusteeship.

(2) STATE TRUSTEES.—The State and local officials designated under subsection (b)(3)—

(A) shall assess natural resource damages under section 1002(b)(2)(A) for the purposes of this Act for the natural resources under their trusteeship; and

(B) shall develop and implement a plan for the restoration, rehabilitation, replacement, or acquisition of the equivalent, of the natural resources under their trusteeship.

(3) INDIAN TRIBE TRUSTEES.—The tribal officials designated under subsection (b)(4)—

(A) shall assess natural resource damages under section 1002(b)(2)(A) for the purposes of this Act for the natural resources under their trusteeship; and

(B) shall develop and implement a plan for the restoration, rehabilitation, replacement, or acquisition of the equivalent, of the natural resources under their trusteeship.

(4) FOREIGN TRUSTEES.—The trustees designated under subsection (b)(5)—

(A) shall assess natural resource damages under section 1002(b)(2)(A) for the purposes of this Act for the natural resources under their trusteeship; and

(B) shall develop and implement a plan for the restoration, rehabilitation, replacement, or acquisition of the equivalent, of the natural resources under their trusteeship.

(5) NOTICE AND OPPORTUNITY TO BE HEARD.— Plans shall be developed and implemented under this section only after adequate public notice, opportunity for a hearing, and consideration of all public comment.

(d) MEASURE OF DAMAGES.—

(1) IN GENERAL.—The measure of natural resource damages under section 1002(b)(2)(A) is—

(A) the cost of restoring, rehabilitating, replacing, or acquiring the equivalent of, the damaged natural resources;

(B) the diminution in value of those natural resources pending restoration; plus

(C) the reasonable cost of assessing those damages.

(2) DETERMINE COSTS WITH RESPECT TO PLANS.— Costs shall be determined under paragraph (1) with respect to plans adopted under subsection (c).

(3) NO DOUBLE RECOVERY.— There shall be no double recovery under this Act for natural resource damages, including with respect to the costs of damage assessment or restoration, rehabilitation, replacement, or acquisition for the same incident and natural resource.

(e) DAMAGE ASSESSMENT REGULATIONS.—

(1) REGULATIONS.— The President, acting through the Under Secretary of Commerce for Oceans and Atmosphere and in consultation with the Administrator of the Environmental Protection Agency, the Director of the United States Fish and Wildlife Service, and the heads of other affected agencies, not later than 2 years after the date of the enactment of this Act, shall promulgate regulations for the assessment of natural resource damages under section 1002(b)(2)(A) resulting from a discharge

of oil for the purpose of this Act.

(2) REBUTTABLE PRESUMPTION.— Any determination or assessment of damages to natural resources for the purposes of this Act made under subsection (d) by a Federal, State, or Indian trustee in accordance with the regulations promulgated under paragraph (1) shall have the force and effect of a rebuttable presumption on behalf of the trustee in any administrative or judicial proceeding under this Act.

(f) USE OF RECOVERED SUMS.— Sums recovered under this Act by a Federal, State, Indian, or foreign trustee for natural resource damages under section 1002(b)(2)(A) shall be retained by the trustee in a revolving trust account, without further appropriation, for use only to reimburse or pay costs incurred by the trustee under subsection (c) with respect to the damaged natural resources. Any amounts in excess of those required for these reimbursements and costs shall be deposited in the Fund.

(g) COMPLIANCE.— Review of actions by any Federal official where there is alleged to be a failure of that official to perform a duty under this section that is not discretionary with that official may be had by any person in the district court in which the person resides or in which the alleged damage to natural resources occurred. The court may award costs of litigation (including reasonable attorney and expert witness fees) to any prevailing or substantially prevailing party. Nothing in this subsection shall restrict any right which any person may have to seek relief under any other provision of law.

[33 U.S.C. 2706]

SEC. 1007. RECOVERY BY FOREIGN CLAIMANTS.

(a) REQUIRED SHOWING BY FOREIGN CLAIMANTS.—

(1) IN GENERAL.—In addition to satisfying the other requirements of this Act, to recover removal costs or damages resulting from an incident a foreign claimant shall demonstrate that—

(A) the claimant has not been otherwise compensated for the removal costs or damages; and

(B) recovery is authorized by a treaty or executive agreement between the United States and the claimant's country, or the Secretary of State, in consultation with the Attorney General and other appropriate officials, has certified that the claimant's country provides a comparable remedy for United States claimants.

(2) EXCEPTIONS.— Paragraph (1)(B) shall not apply with respect to recovery by a resident of Canada in the case of an incident described in subsection (b)(4).

(b) DISCHARGES IN FOREIGN COUNTRIES.—A foreign claimant may make a claim for removal costs and damages resulting from a discharge, or substantial threat of a discharge, of oil in or on the territorial sea, internal waters, or adjacent shoreline of a foreign country, only if the discharge is from—

(1) an Outer Continental Shelf facility or a deepwater port;

(2) a vessel in the navigable waters;

(3) a vessel carrying oil as cargo between 2 places in the United States; or

(4) a tanker that received the oil at the terminal of the pipeline constructed

under the Trans-Alaska Pipeline Authorization Act (43 U.S.C. 1651 et seq.), for transportation to a place in the United States, and the discharge or threat occurs prior to delivery of the oil to that place.

(c) FOREIGN CLAIMANT DEFINED.—In this section, the term foreign claimant means—

(1) a person residing in a foreign country;

(2) the government of a foreign country; and

(3) an agency or political subdivision of a foreign country.

[33 U.S.C. 2707]

SEC. 1008. RECOVERY BY RESPONSIBLE PARTY.

(a) IN GENERAL.—The responsible party for a vessel or facility from which oil is discharged, or which poses the substantial threat of a discharge of oil, may assert a claim for removal costs and damages under section 1013 only if the responsible party demonstrates that—

(1) the responsible party is entitled to a defense to liability under section 1003; or

(2) the responsible party is entitled to a limitation of liability under section 1004.

(b) EXTENT OF RECOVERY.— A responsible party who is entitled to a limitation of liability may assert a claim under section 1013 only to the extent that the sum of the removal costs and damages incurred by the responsible party plus the amounts paid by the responsible party, or by the guarantor on behalf of the responsible party, for claims asserted under section 1013 exceeds the amount to which the total of the liability under section 1002 and removal costs and damages incurred by, or on behalf of, the responsible party is limited under section 1004.

[33 U.S.C. 2708]

SEC. 1009. CONTRIBUTION.

A person may bring a civil action for contribution against any other person who is liable or potentially liable under this Act or another law. The action shall be brought in accordance with section 1017.

[33 U.S.C. 2709]

SEC. 1010. INDEMNIFICATION AGREEMENTS.

(a) AGREEMENTS NOT PROHIBITED.— Nothing in this Act prohibits any agreement to insure, hold harmless, or indemnify a party to such agreement for any liability under this Act.

(b) LIABILITY NOT TRANSFERRED.— No indemnification, hold harmless, or similar agreement or conveyance shall be effective to transfer liability imposed under this Act from a responsible party or from any person who may be liable for an incident under this Act to any other person.

(c) RELATIONSHIP TO OTHER CAUSES OF ACTION.— Nothing in this Act, including the provisions of subsection (b), bars a cause of action that a responsible party subject to liability under this Act, or a guarantor, has or would have, by reason of subrogation or otherwise, against any person.

[33 U.S.C. 2710]

SEC. 1011. CONSULTATION ON REMOVAL ACTIONS.

The President shall consult with the affected trustees designated under section 1006 on the appropriate removal action to be taken in connection with any discharge of oil. For the purposes of the National Contingency Plan, removal with respect to any discharge shall be considered completed when so determined by the President in consultation with the Governor or Governors of the affected States. However, this determination shall not preclude additional removal actions under applicable State law.

[33 U.S.C. 2711]

SEC. 1012. USES OF THE FUND.

(a) USES GENERALLY.—The Fund shall be available to the President for—

(1) the payment of removal costs, including the costs of monitoring removal actions, determined by the President to be consistent with the National Contingency Plan—

(A) by Federal authorities; or

(B) by a State, a political subdivision of a State, or an Indian tribe, pursuant to a cost-reimbursable agreement under subsection (d);

(2) the payment of costs incurred by Federal, State, or Indian tribe trustees in carrying out their functions under section 1006 for assessing natural resource damages and for developing and implementing plans for the restoration, rehabilitation, replacement, or acquisition of the equivalent of damaged resources determined by the President to be consistent with the National Contingency Plan;

(3) the payment of removal costs determined by the President to be consistent with the National Contingency Plan as a result of, and damages resulting from, a discharge, or a substantial threat of a discharge, of oil from a foreign offshore unit;

(4) the payment of claims in accordance with section 1013 for uncompensated removal costs determined by the President to be consistent with the National Contingency Plan or uncompensated damages, including, in the case of a spill of national significance that results in extraordinary Coast Guard claims processing activities, the administrative and personnel costs of the Coast Guard to process such claims (including the costs of commercial claims processing, expert services, training, and technical services), subject to the condition that the Coast Guard shall submit to Congress a report describing each spill of national significance not later than 30 days after the date on which the Coast Guard determines it necessary to process such claims; and

(5) the payment of Federal administrative, operational, and personnel costs and expenses reasonably necessary for and incidental to the implementation, administration, and enforcement of this Act (including, but not limited to, sections 1004(d)(2), 1006(e), 4107, 4110, 4111, 4112, 4117, 5006, 8103, and title VII) and subsections (b), (c), (d), (j), and (l) of section 311 of the Federal Water Pollution Control Act (33 U.S.C. 1321), as amended by this Act, with respect to prevention,

removal, and enforcement related to oil discharges, provided that—

(A) not more than $25,000,000 in each fiscal year shall be available to the Secretary for operations and support incurred by the Coast Guard;

(B) not more than $15,000,000 in each fiscal year shall be available to the Under Secretary of Commerce for Oceans and Atmosphere for expenses incurred by, and activities related to, response and damage assessment capabilities of the National Oceanic and Atmospheric Administration;

(C) not more than $30,000,000 each year through the end of fiscal year 1992 shall be available to establish the National Response System under section 311(j) of the Federal Water Pollution Control Act, as amended by this Act, including the purchase and prepositioning of oil spill removal equipment; and

(D) not more than $27,250,000 in each fiscal year shall be available to carry out title VII of this Act.

(b) Defense to Liability for Fund.—

(1) In general.— The Fund shall not be available to pay any claim for removal costs or damages to a particular claimant, to the extent that the incident, removal costs, or damages are caused by the gross negligence or willful misconduct of that claimant.

(2) Subrogated rights.— Except for a guarantor claim pursuant to a defense under section 1016(f)(1), Fund compensation of any claim by an insurer or other indemnifier of a responsible party or injured third party is subject to the subrogated rights of that responsible party or injured third party to such compensation.

(c) Obligation of Fund by Federal Officials.— The President may promulgate regulations designating one or more Federal officials who may obligate money in accordance with subsection (a).

(d) Cost-reimbursable Agreement.—

(1) In general.— In carrying out section 311(c) of the Federal Water Pollution Control Act (33 U.S.C. 1321(c)), the President may enter into cost-reimbursable agreements with a State, a political subdivision of a State, or an Indian tribe to obligate the Fund for the payment of removal costs consistent with the National Contingency Plan.

(2) Inapplicability.— Chapter 63 and section 1535 of title 31, United States Code shall not apply to a cost-reimbursable agreement entered into under this subsection.

(e) Rights of Subrogation.— Payment of any claim or obligation by the Fund under this Act shall be subject to the United States Government acquiring by subrogation all rights of the claimant or State to recover from the responsible party.

(f) Period of Limitations for Claims.—

(1) Removal costs.— No claim may be presented under this title for recovery of removal costs for an incident unless the claim is presented within 6 years after the date of completion of all removal actions for that incident.

(2) Damages.— No claim may be presented under this section for recovery

of damages unless the claim is presented within 3 years after the date on which the injury and its connection with the discharge in question were reasonably discoverable with the exercise of due care, or in the case of natural resource damages under section 1002(b)(2)(A), if later, the date of completion of the natural resources damage assessment under section 1006(e).

(3) MINORS AND INCOMPETENTS.—The time limitations contained in this subsection shall not begin to run—

(A) against a minor until the earlier of the date when such minor reaches 18 years of age or the date on which a legal representative is duly appointed for the minor, or

(B) against an incompetent person until the earlier of the date on which such incompetent's incompetency ends or the date on which a legal representative is duly appointed for the incompetent.

(g) LIMITATION ON PAYMENT FOR SAME COSTS.— In any case in which the President has paid an amount from the Fund for any removal costs or damages specified under subsection (a), no other claim may be paid from the Fund for the same removal costs or damages.

(h) OBLIGATION IN ACCORDANCE WITH PLAN.—

(1) IN GENERAL.— Except as provided in paragraph (2), amounts may be obligated from the Fund for the restoration, rehabilitation, replacement, or acquisition of natural resources only in accordance with a plan adopted under section 1006(c).

(2) EXCEPTION.— Paragraph (1) shall not apply in a situation requiring action to avoid irreversible loss of natural resources or to prevent or reduce any continuing danger to natural resources or similar need for emergency action.

(i) PREFERENCE FOR PRIVATE PERSONS IN AREA AFFECTED BY DISCHARGE.—

(1) IN GENERAL.— In the expenditure of Federal funds for removal of oil, including for distribution of supplies, construction, and other reasonable and appropriate activities, under a contract or agreement with a private person, preference shall be given, to the extent feasible and practicable, to private persons residing or doing business primarily in the area affected by the discharge of oil.

(2) LIMITATION.— This subsection shall not be considered to restrict the use of Department of Defense resources.

(j) REPORTS.—

(1) IN GENERAL.—Each year, on the date on which the President submits to Congress a budget under section 1105 of title 31, United States Code, the President, through the Secretary of the Department in which the Coast Guard is operating, shall—

(A) provide a report on disbursements for the preceding fiscal year from the Fund, regardless of whether those disbursements were subject to annual appropriations, to—

(i) the Senate Committee on Commerce, Science, and Transportation; and

(ii) the House of Representatives Committee on Transportation and Infrastructure; and

(B) make the report available to the public on the National Pollution Funds Center Internet website.

(2) CONTENTS.—The report shall include—

(A) a list of each incident that—

(i) occurred in the preceding fiscal year; and

(ii) resulted in disbursements from the Fund, for removal costs and damages, totaling $500,000 or more;

(B) a list of each incident that—

(i) occurred in the fiscal year preceding the preceding fiscal year; and

(ii) resulted in disbursements from the Fund, for removal costs and damages, totaling $500,000 or more; and

(C) an accounting of any amounts reimbursed to the Fund in the preceding fiscal year that were recovered from a responsible party for an incident that resulted in disbursements from the Fund, for removal costs and damages, totaling $500,000 or more.

(3) AGENCY RECORDKEEPING.— Each Federal agency that receives amounts from the Fund shall maintain records describing the purposes for which such funds were obligated or expended in such detail as the Secretary may require for purposes of the report required under paragraph (1).

[33 U.S.C. 2712]

SEC. 1013. CLAIMS PROCEDURE.

(a) PRESENTATION.— Except as provided in subsection (b), all claims for removal costs or damages shall be presented first to the responsible party or guarantor of the source designated under section 1014(a).

(b) PRESENTATION TO FUND.—

(1) IN GENERAL.—Claims for removal costs or damages may be presented first to the Fund—

(A) if the President has advertised or otherwise notified claimants in accordance with section 1014(c);

(B) by a responsible party who may assert a claim under section 1008;

(C) by the Governor of a State for removal costs incurred by that State; or

(D) by a United States claimant in a case where a foreign offshore unit has discharged oil causing damage for which the Fund is liable under section 1012(a).

(2) LIMITATION ON PRESENTING CLAIM.— No claim of a person against the Fund may be approved or certified during the pendency of an action by the person in court to recover costs which are the subject of the claim.

(c) ELECTION.—If a claim is presented in accordance with subsection (a) and—

(1) each person to whom the claim is presented denies all liability for the claim, or

(2) the claim is not settled by any person by payment within 90 days after the date upon which (A) the claim was presented, or (B) advertising was begun pursuant to section 1014(b), whichever is later,

the claimant may elect to commence an action in court against the responsible party or guarantor or to present the claim to the Fund.

(d) UNCOMPENSATED DAMAGES.— If a claim is presented in accordance with this section, including a claim for interim, short-term damages representing less than the full amount of damages to which the claimant ultimately may be entitled, and full and adequate compensation is unavailable, a claim for the uncompensated damages and removal costs may be presented to the Fund.

(e) PROCEDURE FOR CLAIMS AGAINST FUND.— The President shall promulgate, and may from time to time amend, regulations for the presentation, filing, processing, settlement, and adjudication of claims under this Act against the Fund.

[33 U.S.C. 2713]

SEC. 1014. DESIGNATION OF SOURCE AND ADVERTISEMENT.

(a) DESIGNATION OF SOURCE AND NOTIFICATION.— When the President receives information of an incident, the President shall, where possible and appropriate, designate the source or sources of the discharge or threat. If a designated source is a vessel or a facility, the President shall immediately notify the responsible party and the guarantor, if known, of that designation.

(b) ADVERTISEMENT BY RESPONSIBLE PARTY OR GUARANTOR.—(1) If a responsible party or guarantor fails to inform the President, within 5 days after receiving notification of a designation under subsection (a), of the party's or the guarantor's denial of the designation, such party or guarantor shall advertise the designation and the procedures by which claims may be presented, in accordance with regulations promulgated by the President. Advertisement under the preceding sentence shall begin no later than 15 days after the date of the designation made under subsection (a). If advertisement is not otherwise made in accordance with this subsection, the President shall promptly and at the expense of the responsible party or the guarantor involved, advertise the designation and the procedures by which claims may be presented to the responsible party or guarantor. Advertisement under this subsection shall continue for a period of no less than 30 days.

(2) An advertisement under paragraph (1) shall state that a claimant may present a claim for interim, short-term damages representing less than the full amount of damages to which the claimant ultimately may be entitled and that payment of such a claim shall not preclude recovery for damages not reflected in the paid or settled partial claim.

(c) ADVERTISEMENT BY PRESIDENT.—If—

(1) the responsible party and the guarantor both deny a designation within 5 days after receiving notification of a designation under subsection (a),

(2) the source of the discharge or threat was a public vessel, or

(3) the President is unable to designate the source or sources of the discharge or threat under subsection (a),

the President shall advertise or otherwise notify potential claimants of the procedures by which claims may be presented to the Fund.

[33 U.S.C. 2714]

SEC. 1015. SUBROGATION.[2]

(a) IN GENERAL.— Any person, including the Fund, who pays compensation pursuant to this Act to any claimant for removal costs or damages shall be subrogated to all rights, claims, and causes of action that the claimant has under any other law.

---

[2] Section 1142(d) of Public Law 104–324 (110 Stat. 3991) stated that [s]ection 1015(a) of the Oil Pollution Act of 1990 (33 U.S.C. 2715(a)) is amended by redesignating subsection (b) as subsection (c) and by inserting after subsection (a) a new subsection (b). The amendments were executed as amendments to section 1015.

(b) INTERIM DAMAGES.—

(1) IN GENERAL.— If a responsible party, a guarantor, or the Fund has made payment to a claimant for interim, short-term damages representing less than the full amount of damages to which the claimant ultimately may be entitled, subrogation under subsection (a) shall apply only with respect to the portion of the claim reflected in the paid interim claim.

(2) FINAL DAMAGES.— Payment of such a claim shall not foreclose a claimant's right to recovery of all damages to which the claimant otherwise is entitled under this Act or under any other law.

(c) ACTIONS ON BEHALF OF FUND.— At the request of the Secretary, the Attorney General shall commence an action on behalf of the Fund to recover any compensation paid by the Fund to any claimant pursuant to this Act, and all costs incurred by the Fund by reason of the claim, including interest (including prejudgment interest), administrative and adjudicative costs, and attorney's fees. Such an action may be commenced against any responsible party or (subject to section 1016) guarantor, or against any other person who is liable, pursuant to any law, to the compensated claimant or to the Fund, for the cost or damages for which the compensation was paid. Such an action shall be commenced against the responsible foreign government or other responsible party to recover any removal costs or damages paid from the Fund as the result of the discharge, or substantial threat of discharge, of oil from a foreign offshore unit or other facility located seaward of the exclusive economic zone.

(d) AUTHORITY TO SETTLE.— The head of any department or agency responsible for recovering amounts for which a person is liable under this title may consider, compromise, and settle a claim for such amounts, including such costs paid from the Fund, if the claim has not been referred to the Attorney General. In any case in which the total amount to be recovered may exceed $500,000 (excluding interest), a claim may be compromised and settled under the preceding sentence only with the prior written approval of the Attorney General.

[33 U.S.C. 2715]

SEC. 1016. FINANCIAL RESPONSIBILITY.

(a) REQUIREMENT.—The responsible party for—

(1) any vessel over 300 gross tons (except a non-self-propelled vessel that does not carry oil as cargo or fuel) using any place subject to the jurisdiction of the United States;

(2) any vessel using the waters of the exclusive economic zone to transship or lighter oil destined for a place subject to the jurisdiction of the United States; or

(3) any tank vessel over 100 gross tons using any place subject to the jurisdiction of the United States;

shall establish and maintain, in accordance with regulations promulgated by the Secretary, evidence of financial responsibility sufficient to meet the maximum amount of liability to which the responsible party could be subjected under section 1004(a) or (d) of this Act, in a case where the responsible party would be entitled to limit liability under that section. If the responsible party owns or operates more than one vessel, evidence of financial responsibility need be established only to meet the amount of the maximum liability applicable to the vessel having the greatest maximum liability.

(b) SANCTIONS.—

(1) WITHHOLDING CLEARANCE.— The Secretary of the Treasury shall withhold or revoke the clearance required by section 4197 of the Revised Statutes of the United States of any vessel subject to this section that does not have the evidence of financial responsibility required for the vessel under this section.

(2) DENYING ENTRY TO OR DETAINING VESSELS.—The Secretary may—

(A) deny entry to any vessel to any place in the United States, or to the navigable waters, or

(B) detain at the place,

any vessel that, upon request, does not produce the evidence of financial responsibility required for the vessel under this section.

(3) SEIZURE OF VESSEL.— Any vessel subject to the requirements of this section which is found in the navigable waters without the necessary evidence of financial responsibility for the vessel shall be subject to seizure by and forfeiture to the United States.

(c) OFFSHORE FACILITIES.—

(1) IN GENERAL.—

(A) EVIDENCE OF FINANCIAL RESPONSIBILITY REQUIRED.—Except as provided in paragraph (2), a responsible party with respect to an offshore facility that—

(i)(I) is located seaward of the line of ordinary low water along that portion of the coast that is in direct contact with the open sea and the line marking the seaward limit of inland waters; or

(II) is located in coastal inland waters, such as bays or estuaries, seaward of the line of ordinary low water along that portion of the coast that is not in direct contact with the open sea;

(ii) is used for exploring for, drilling for, producing, or transporting oil from facilities engaged in oil exploration, drilling, or production; and

(iii) has a worst-case oil spill discharge potential of more than 1,000 barrels of oil (or a lesser amount if the President determines that the risks posed by such facility justify it),

shall establish and maintain evidence of financial responsibility in the amount required under subparagraph (B) or (C), as applicable.

(B) AMOUNT REQUIRED GENERALLY.—Except as provided in subparagraph (C), the amount of financial responsibility for offshore facilities that meet the criteria of subparagraph (A) is—

(i) $35,000,000 for an offshore facility located seaward of the seaward boundary of a State; or

(ii) $10,000,000 for an offshore facility located landward of the seaward boundary of a State.

(C) GREATER AMOUNT.— If the President determines that an amount of financial responsibility for a responsible party greater than the amount required by subparagraph (B) is justified based on the relative operational, environmental, human health, and other risks posed by the quantity or quality of oil that is explored for, drilled for, produced, or transported by the responsible party, the evidence of financial responsibility required shall be for an amount determined by the President not exceeding $150,000,000.

(D) MULTIPLE FACILITIES.— In a case in which a person is a responsible party for more than one facility subject to this subsection, evidence of financial responsibility need be established only to meet the amount applicable to the facility having the greatest financial responsibility requirement under this subsection.

(E) DEFINITION.— For the purpose of this paragraph, the seaward boundary of a State shall be determined in accordance with section 2(b) of the Submerged Lands Act (43 U.S.C. 1301(b)).

(2) DEEPWATER PORTS.— Each responsible party with respect to a deepwater port shall establish and maintain evidence of financial responsibility sufficient to meet the maximum amount of liability to which the responsible party could be subjected under section 1004(a) of this Act in a case where the responsible party would be entitled to limit liability under that section. If the Secretary exercises the authority under section 1004(d)(2) to lower the limit of liability for deepwater ports, the responsible party shall establish and maintain evidence of financial responsibility sufficient to meet the maximum amount of liability so established. In a case in which a person is the responsible party for more than one deepwater port, evidence of financial responsibility need be established only to meet the maximum liability applicable to the deepwater port having the greatest maximum liability.

(e) METHODS OF FINANCIAL RESPONSIBILITY.— Financial responsibility under this section may be established by any one, or by any combination, of the following methods which the Secretary (in the case of a vessel) or the President (in the case of a facility) determines to be acceptable: evidence of insurance, surety bond, guarantee, letter of credit, qualification as a self-insurer, or other evidence of financial responsibility. Any bond filed shall be issued by a bonding company authorized to do business in the United States. In promulgating requirements under this section, the Secretary or the President, as appropriate, may specify policy or other contractual terms, conditions, or defenses which are necessary, or which are unacceptable, in establishing evidence of financial responsibility to effectuate the purposes of this Act.

(f) CLAIMS AGAINST GUARANTOR.—

(1) IN GENERAL.—Subject to paragraph (2), a claim for which liability may be established under section 1002 may be asserted directly against any guarantor providing evidence of financial responsibility for a responsible party liable under that section for removal costs and damages to which the claim pertains. In defending against such a claim, the guarantor may invoke—

(A) all rights and defenses which would be available to the responsible party under this Act;

(B) any defense authorized under subsection (e); and

(C) the defense that the incident was caused by the willful misconduct of the responsible party.

The guarantor may not invoke any other defense that might be available in proceedings brought by the responsible party against the guarantor.

(2) FURTHER REQUIREMENT.—A claim may be asserted pursuant to paragraph (1) directly against a guarantor providing evidence of financial responsibility under subsection (c)(1) with respect to an offshore facility only if—

(A) the responsible party for whom evidence of financial responsibility has been provided has denied or failed to pay a claim under this Act on the basis of being insolvent, as defined under section 101(32) of title 11, United States Code, and applying generally accepted accounting principles;

(B) the responsible party for whom evidence of financial responsibility has been provided has filed a petition for bankruptcy under title 11, United States Code; or

(C) the claim is asserted by the United States for removal costs and damages or for compensation paid by the Fund under this Act, including costs incurred by the Fund for processing compensation claims.

(3) RULEMAKING AUTHORITY.— Not later than 1 year after the date of enactment of this paragraph, the President shall promulgate regulations to establish a process for implementing paragraph (2) in a manner that will allow for the orderly and expeditious presentation and resolution of claims and effectuate the purposes of this Act.

(g) LIMITATION ON GUARANTOR'S LIABILITY.— Nothing in this Act shall impose liability with respect to an incident on any guarantor for damages or removal costs which exceed, in the aggregate, the amount of financial responsibility which that guarantor has provided for a responsible party pursuant to this section. The total liability of the guarantor on direct action for claims brought under this Act with respect to an incident shall be limited to that amount.

(h) CONTINUATION OF REGULATIONS.— Any regulation relating to financial responsibility, which has been issued pursuant to any provision of law repealed or superseded by this Act, and which is in effect on the date immediately preceding the effective date of this Act, is deemed and shall be construed to be a regulation issued pursuant to this section. Such a regulation shall remain in full force and effect unless and until superseded by a new regulation issued under this section.

(i) Unified Certificate.— The Secretary may issue a single unified certificate of financial responsibility for purposes of this Act and any other law.

[33 U.S.C. 2716]

SEC. 1017. LITIGATION, JURISDICTION, AND VENUE.

(a) Review of Regulations.— Review of any regulation promulgated under this Act may be had upon application by any interested person only in the Circuit Court of Appeals of the United States for the District of Columbia. Any such application shall be made within 90 days from the date of promulgation of such regulations. Any matter with respect to which review could have been obtained under this subsection shall not be subject to judicial review in any civil or criminal proceeding for enforcement or to obtain damages or recovery of response costs.

(b) Jurisdiction.— Except as provided in subsections (a) and (c), the United States district courts shall have exclusive original jurisdiction over all controversies arising under this Act, without regard to the citizenship of the parties or the amount in controversy. Venue shall lie in any district in which the discharge or injury or damages occurred, or in which the defendant resides, may be found, has its principal office, or has appointed an agent for service of process. For the purposes of this section, the Fund shall reside in the District of Columbia.

(c) State Court Jurisdiction.— A State trial court of competent jurisdiction over claims for removal costs or damages, as defined under this Act, may consider claims under this Act or State law and any final judgment of such court (when no longer subject to ordinary forms of review) shall be recognized, valid, and enforceable for all purposes of this Act.

(d) Assessment and Collection of Tax.— The provisions of subsections (a), (b), and (c) shall not apply to any controversy or other matter resulting from the assessment or collection of any tax, or to the review of any regulation promulgated under the Internal Revenue Code of 1986.

(e) Savings Provision.— Nothing in this title shall apply to any cause of action or right of recovery arising from any incident which occurred prior to the date of enactment of this title. Such claims shall be adjudicated pursuant to the law applicable on the date of the incident.

(f) Period of Limitations.—

(1) Damages.—Except as provided in paragraphs (3) and (4), an action for damages under this Act shall be barred unless the action is brought within 3 years after—

(A) the date on which the loss and the connection of the loss with the discharge in question are reasonably discoverable with the exercise of due care, or

(B) in the case of natural resource damages under section 1002(b)(2)(A), the date of completion of the natural resources damage assessment under section 1006(c).

(2) REMOVAL COSTS.— An action for recovery of removal costs referred to in section 1002(b)(1) must be commenced within 3 years after completion of the removal action. In any such action described in this subsection, the court shall enter a declaratory judgment on liability for removal costs or damages that will be binding on any subsequent action or actions to recover further removal costs or damages. Except as otherwise provided in this paragraph, an action may be commenced under this title for recovery of removal costs at any time after such costs have been incurred.

(3) CONTRIBUTION.—No action for contribution for any removal costs or damages may be commenced more than 3 years after—

(A) the date of judgment in any action under this Act for recovery of such costs or damages, or

(B) the date of entry of a judicially approved settlement with respect to such costs or damages.

(4) SUBROGATION.— No action based on rights subrogated pursuant to this Act by reason of payment of a claim may be commenced under this Act more than 3 years after the date of payment of such claim.

(5) COMMENCEMENT.—The time limitations contained herein shall not begin to run—

(A) against a minor until the earlier of the date when such minor reaches 18 years of age or the date on which a legal representative is duly appointed for such minor, or

(B) against an incompetent person until the earlier of the date on which such incompetent's incompetency ends or the date on which a legal representative is duly appointed for such incompetent.

[33 U.S.C. 2717]

SEC. 1018. RELATIONSHIP TO OTHER LAW.

(a) PRESERVATION OF STATE AUTHORITIES; SOLID WASTE DISPOSAL ACT.—Nothing in this Act or the Act of March 3, 1851 shall—

(1) affect, or be construed or interpreted as preempting, the authority of any State or political subdivision thereof from imposing any additional liability or requirements with respect to—

(A) the discharge of oil or other pollution by oil within such State; or

(B) any removal activities in connection with such a discharge; or

(2) affect, or be construed or interpreted to affect or modify in any way the obligations or liabilities of any person under the Solid Waste Disposal Act (42 U.S.C. 6901 et seq.) or State law, including common law.

(b) PRESERVATION OF STATE FUNDS.—Nothing in this Act or in section 9509 of the Internal Revenue Code of 1986 (26 U.S.C. 9509) shall in any way affect, or be construed to affect, the authority of any State—

(1) to establish, or to continue in effect, a fund any purpose of which is to pay for costs or damages arising out of, or directly resulting from, oil pollution or the

substantial threat of oil pollution; or

(2) to require any person to contribute to such a fund.

(c) ADDITIONAL REQUIREMENTS AND LIABILITIES; PENALTIES.—Nothing in this Act, the Act of March 3, 1851 (46 U.S.C. 183 et seq.), or section 9509 of the Internal Revenue Code of 1986 (26 U.S.C. 9509), shall in any way affect, or be construed to affect, the authority of the United States or any State or political subdivision thereof—

(1) to impose additional liability or additional requirements; or

(2) to impose, or to determine the amount of, any fine or penalty (whether criminal or civil in nature) for any violation of law;

relating to the discharge, or substantial threat of a discharge, of oil.

(d) FEDERAL EMPLOYEE LIABILITY.— For purposes of section 2679(b)(2)(B) of title 28, United States Code, nothing in this Act shall be construed to authorize or create a cause of action against a Federal officer or employee in the officer's or employee's personal or individual capacity for any act or omission while acting within the scope of the officer's or employee's office or employment.

[33 U.S.C. 2718]

SEC. 1019. STATE FINANCIAL RESPONSIBILITY.

A State may enforce, on the navigable waters of the State, the requirements for evidence of financial responsibility under section 1016.

[33 U.S.C. 2719]

SEC. 1020. APPLICATION.

This Act shall apply to an incident occurring after the date of the enactment of this Act.

[33 U.S.C. 2701 note]

TITLE II—CONFORMING AMENDMENTS

TITLE II—CONFORMING AMENDMENTS

* * * * * * *

SEC. 2002. FEDERAL WATER POLLUTION CONTROL ACT.

(a) APPLICATION.— Subsections (f), (g), (h), and (i) of section 311 of the Federal Water Pollution Control Act (33 U.S.C. 1321) shall not apply with respect to any incident for which liability is established under section 1002 of this Act.

(b) * * *

[33 U.S.C. 1321 note]

SEC. 2003. DEEPWATER PORT ACT.

(a) * * *

(b) AMOUNTS REMAINING IN DEEPWATER PORT FUND.— Any amounts remaining in the Deepwater Port Liability Fund established under section 18(f) of the Deepwater Port Act of 1974 (33 U.S.C. 1517(f)) shall be deposited in the Oil Spill Liability Trust Fund established under section 9509 of the Internal Revenue Code of 1986 (26 U.S.C. 9509). The Oil Spill Liability Trust Fund shall assume all liability incurred by the Deepwater Port Liability Fund.

[26 U.S.C. 9509 note]

SEC. 2004. OUTER CONTINENTAL SHELF LANDS ACT AMENDMENTS OF 1978.

Title III of the Outer Continental Shelf Lands Act Amendments of 1978 (43 U.S.C. 1811–1824) is repealed. Any amounts remaining in the Offshore Oil Pollution Compensation Fund established under section 302 of that title (43 U.S.C. 1812) shall be deposited in the Oil Spill Liability Trust Fund established under section 9509 of the Internal Revenue Code of 1986 (26 U.S.C. 9509). The Oil Spill Liability Trust Fund shall assume all liability incurred by the Offshore Oil Pollution Compensation Fund.

[26 U.S.C. 9509 note]

TITLE III—INTERNATIONAL OIL POLLUTION PREVENTION AND REMOVAL

TITLE III—INTERNATIONAL OIL POLLUTION PREVENTION AND REMOVAL

SEC. 3001. SENSE OF CONGRESS REGARDING PARTICIPATION IN INTERNATIONAL REGIME.

It is the sense of the Congress that it is in the best interests of the United States to participate in an international oil pollution liability and compensation regime that is at least as effective as Federal and State laws in preventing incidents and in guaranteeing full and prompt compensation for damages resulting from incidents.

SEC. 3002. UNITED STATES-CANADA GREAT LAKES OIL SPILL COOPERATION.

(a) Review.—The Secretary of State shall review relevant international agreements and treaties with the Government of Canada, including the Great Lakes Water Quality Agreement, to determine whether amendments or additional international agreements are necessary to—

(1) prevent discharges of oil on the Great Lakes;

(2) ensure an immediate and effective removal of oil on the Great Lakes; and

(3) fully compensate those who are injured by a discharge of oil on the Great Lakes.

(b) Consultation.— In carrying out this section, the Secretary of State shall consult with the Department of Transportation, the Environmental Protection Agency, the National Oceanic and Atmospheric Administration, the Great Lakes States, the International Joint Commission, and other appropriate agencies.

(c) Report.— The Secretary of State shall submit a report to the Congress on the results of the review under this section within 6 months after the date of the enactment of this Act.

SEC. 3003. UNITED STATES-CANADA LAKE CHAMPLAIN OIL SPILL COOPERATION.

(a) Review.—The Secretary of State shall review relevant international agreements and treaties with the Government of Canada, to determine whether amendments or additional international agreements are necessary to—

(1) prevent discharges of oil on Lake Champlain;

(2) ensure an immediate and effective removal of oil on Lake Champlain; and

(3) fully compensate those who are injured by a discharge of oil on Lake Champlain.

(b) Consultation.— In carrying out this section, the Secretary of State shall consult with the Department of Transportation, the Environmental Protection Agency, the National Oceanic and Atmospheric Administration, the States of Vermont and New York, the International Joint Commission, and other appropriate agencies.

(c) Report.— The Secretary of State shall submit a report to the Congress on the results of the review under this section within 6 months after the date of the enactment of this Act.

SEC. 3004. INTERNATIONAL INVENTORY OF REMOVAL EQUIPMENT AND PERSONNEL.

The President shall encourage appropriate international organizations to establish an international inventory of spill removal equipment and personnel.

SEC. 3005. NEGOTIATIONS WITH CANADA CONCERNING TUG ESCORTS IN PUGET SOUND.

Congress urges the Secretary of State to enter into negotiations with the Government of Canada to ensure that tugboat escorts are required for all tank vessels with a capacity over 40,000 deadweight tons in the Strait of Juan de Fuca and in Haro Strait.

TITLE IV—PREVENTION AND REMOVAL

TITLE IV—PREVENTION AND REMOVAL

Subtitle A—Prevention

* * * * * * *

SEC. 4102. TERM OF LICENSES, CERTIFICATES OF REGISTRY, AND MERCHANT MARINERS' DOCUMENTS; CRIMINAL RECORD REVIEWS IN RENEWALS.

(a) * * *

* * * * * * *

(d) Termination of Existing Licenses, Certificates, and Documents.—A license, certificate of registry, or merchant mariner's document issued before the date of the enactment of this section terminates on the day it would have expired if—

(1) subsections (a), (b), and (c) were in effect on the date it was issued; and

(2) it was renewed at the end of each 5-year period under section 7106, 7107, or 7302 of title 46, United States Code.

[46 U.S.C. 7106 note]

* * * * * * *

SEC. 4107. VESSEL TRAFFIC SERVICE SYSTEMS.

(a) * * *

(b) Direction of Vessel Movement.—

(1) Study.—The Secretary shall conduct a study—

(A) of whether the Secretary should be given additional authority to direct the movement of vessels on navigable waters and should exercise such authority; and

(B) to determine and prioritize the United States ports and channels that are in need of new, expanded, or improved vessel traffic service systems, by evaluating—

(i) the nature, volume, and frequency of vessel traffic;

(ii) the risks of collisions, spills, and damages associated with that traffic;

(iii) the impact of installation, expansion, or improvement of a vessel traffic service system; and

(iv) all other relevant costs and data.

(2) Report.— Not later than 1 year after the date of the enactment of this Act, the Secretary shall submit to the Congress a report on the results of the study conducted under paragraph (1) and recommendations for implementing the results of that study.

* * * * * * *

SEC. 4109. PERIODIC GAUGING OF PLATING THICKNESS OF COMMERCIAL VESSELS.

Not later than 1 year after the date of the enactment of this Act, the Secretary shall issue regulations for vessels constructed or adapted to carry, or that carry, oil in bulk as cargo or cargo residue—

(1) establishing minimum standards for plating thickness; and

(2) requiring, consistent with generally recognized principles of international law, periodic gauging of the plating thickness of all such vessels over 30 years old operating on the navigable waters or the waters of the exclusive economic zone.

[46 U.S.C. 3703 note]

SEC. 4110. OVERFILL AND TANK LEVEL OR PRESSURE MONITORING DEVICES.

(a) STANDARDS.— The Secretary may establish, by regulation, minimum standards for devices for warning persons of overfills and tank levels of oil in cargo tanks and devices for monitoring the pressure of oil cargo tanks.

(b) USE.—No sooner than 1 year after the Secretary prescribes regulations under subsection (a), the Secretary may issue regulations establishing, consistent with generally recognized principles of international law, requirements concerning the use of—

(1) overfill devices, and

(2) tank level or pressure monitoring devices,

which are referred to in subsection (a) and which meet any standards established by the Secretary under subsection (a), on vessels constructed or adapted to carry, or that carry, oil in bulk as cargo or cargo residue on the navigable waters and the waters of the exclusive economic zone.

[46 U.S.C. 3703 note]

SEC. 4111. STUDY ON TANKER NAVIGATION SAFETY STANDARDS.

(a) IN GENERAL.— Not later than 1 year after the date of enactment of this Act, the Secretary shall initiate a study to determine whether existing laws and regulations are adequate to ensure the safe navigation of vessels transporting oil or hazardous substances in bulk on the navigable waters and the waters of the exclusive economic zone.

(b) CONTENT.—In conducting the study required under subsection (a), the Secretary shall—

(1) determine appropriate crew sizes on tankers;

(2) evaluate the adequacy of qualifications and training of crewmembers on tankers;

(3) evaluate the ability of crewmembers on tankers to take emergency actions to prevent or remove a discharge of oil or a hazardous substance from their tankers;

(4) evaluate the adequacy of navigation equipment and systems on tankers (including sonar, electronic chart display, and satellite technology);

(5) evaluate and test electronic means of position-reporting and identification on tankers, consider the minimum standards suitable for equipment for that purpose, and determine whether to require that equipment on tankers;

(6) evaluate the adequacy of navigation procedures under different operating conditions, including such variables as speed, daylight, ice, tides, weather, and other conditions;

(7) evaluate whether areas of navigable waters and the exclusive economic zone should be designated as zones where the movement of tankers should be limited or prohibited;

(8) evaluate whether inspection standards are adequate;

(9) review and incorporate the results of past studies, including studies conducted by the Coast Guard and the Office of Technology Assessment;

(10) evaluate the use of computer simulator courses for training bridge officers and pilots of vessels transporting oil or hazardous substances on the navigable waters and waters of the exclusive economic zone, and determine the feasibility and practicality of mandating such training;

(11) evaluate the size, cargo capacity, and flag nation of tankers transporting oil or hazardous substances on the navigable waters and the waters of the exclusive economic zone—

(A) identifying changes occurring over the past 20 years in such size and cargo capacity and in vessel navigation and technology; and

(B) evaluating the extent to which the risks or difficulties associated with tanker navigation, vessel traffic control, accidents, oil spills, and the containment and cleanup of such spills are influenced by or related to an increase in tanker size and cargo capacity; and

(12) evaluate and test a program of remote alcohol testing for masters and pilots aboard tankers carrying significant quantities of oil.

(c) REPORT.— Not later than 2 years after the date of enactment of this Act, the Secretary shall transmit to the Congress a report on the results of the study conducted under subsection (a), including recommendations for implementing the results of that study.

[46 U.S.C. 3703 note]

SEC. 4112. DREDGE MODIFICATION STUDY.

(a) STUDY.— The Secretary of the Army shall conduct a study and demonstration to determine the feasibility of modifying dredges to make them usable in removing discharges of oil and hazardous substances.

(b) REPORT.— Not later than 1 year after the date of enactment of this Act, the Secretary of the Army shall submit to the Congress a report on the results of the study conducted under subsection (a) and recommendations for implementing the results of that study.

SEC. 4113. USE OF LINERS.

(a) STUDY.— The President shall conduct a study to determine whether liners or other secondary means of containment should be used to prevent leaking or to aid in leak detection at onshore facilities used for the bulk storage of oil and located near navigable waters.

(b) REPORT.— Not later than 1 year after the date of enactment of this Act, the President shall submit to the Congress a report on the results of the study conducted under subsection (a) and recommendations to implement the results of the study.

(c) IMPLEMENTATION.— Not later than 6 months after the date the report required under subsection (b) is submitted to the Congress, the President shall implement the recommendations contained in the report.

SEC. 4114. TANK VESSEL MANNING.

(a) RULEMAKING.— In order to protect life, property, and the environment, the Secretary shall initiate a rulemaking proceeding within 180 days after the date of the enactment of this Act to define the conditions under, and designate the waters upon, which tank vessels subject to section 3703 of title 46, United States Code, may operate in the navigable waters with the auto-pilot engaged or with an unattended engine room.

(b) * * *

[46 U.S.C. 3703 note]

* * * * * * *

SEC. 4115. ESTABLISHMENT OF DOUBLE HULL REQUIREMENT FOR TANK VESSELS.

(a) * * *

(b) RULEMAKING.— The Secretary shall, within 12 months after the date of the enactment of this Act, complete a rulemaking proceeding and issue a final rule to require that tank vessels over 5,000 gross tons affected by section 3703a of title 46, United States Code, as added by this section, comply until January 1, 2015, with structural and operational requirements that the Secretary determines will provide as substantial protection to the environment as is economically and technologically feasible.

[46 U.S.C. 3703a note]

* * * * * * *

(e) SECRETARIAL STUDIES.—

(1) OTHER REQUIREMENTS.— Not later than 6 months after the date of enactment of this Act, the Secretary shall determine, based on recommendations from the National Academy of Sciences or other qualified organizations, whether other structural and operational tank vessel requirements will provide protection to the marine environment equal to or greater than that provided by double hulls, and shall report to the Congress that determination and recommendations for legislative action.

(2) REVIEW AND ASSESSMENT.—The Secretary shall—

(A) periodically review recommendations from the National Academy of Sciences and other qualified organizations on methods for further increasing the environmental and operational safety of tank vessels;

(B) not later than 5 years after the date of enactment of this Act, assess the impact of this section on the safety of the marine environment and the economic viability and operational makeup of the maritime oil transportation industry; and

(C) report the results of the review and assessment to the Congress with recommendations for legislative or other action.

(3) No later than one year after the date of enactment of the Coast Guard and Maritime Transportation Act of 2004, the Secretary shall, taking into account the recommendations contained in the report by the Marine Board of the National Research Council entitled Environmental Performance of Tanker Design in Collision and Grounding and dated 2001, establish and publish an environmental equivalency evaluation index (including the methodology to develop that index) to assess overall outflow performance due to collisions and groundings for double hull tank vessels and alternative designs.

* * * * * * *

SEC. 4116. PILOTAGE.

(a) * * *

* * * * * * *

(c) ESCORTS FOR CERTAIN TANKERS.—(1)[3] IN GENERAL.— The Secretary shall initiate issuance of regulations under section 3703(a)(3) of title 46, United States Code, to define those areas, including Prince William Sound, Alaska, and Rosario Strait and Puget Sound, Washington (including those portions of the Strait of Juan de Fuca east of Port Angeles, Haro Strait, and the Strait of Georgia subject to United States jurisdiction), on which single hulled tankers over 5,000 gross tons transporting oil in bulk shall be escorted by at least two towing vessels (as defined under section 2101 of title 46, United States Code) or other vessels considered appropriate by the Secretary.

[3] Margin of paragraph (1) so in law. The amendment made by section 711(b)(1)(A) of Public Law 111–281 amends subsection (c) which is reflected above. The amendment results in designation of text in subsection (c) as paragraph (1); however, the margin for paragraph (1) probably should appear on its own margin rather than run-in to the heading for subsection (c).

(2) PRINCE WILLIAM SOUND, ALASKA.—

(A) IN GENERAL.— The requirement in paragraph (1) relating to single hulled tankers in Prince William Sound, Alaska, described in that paragraph being escorted by at least 2 towing vessels or other vessels considered to be appropriate by the Secretary (including regulations promulgated in accordance with section 3703(a)(3) of title 46, United States Code, as set forth in part 168 of title 33, Code of Federal Regulations (as in effect on March 1, 2009) implementing this subsection with respect to those tankers) shall apply to double hulled tankers over 5,000 gross tons transporting oil in bulk in Prince William Sound, Alaska.

(B) IMPLEMENTATION OF REQUIREMENTS.— The Secretary of the department in which the Coast Guard is operating shall prescribe interim final regulations to carry out subparagraph (A) as soon as practicable without notice and hearing pursuant to section 553 of title 5 of the United States Code.

(d) Tanker Defined.— In this section the term tanker has the same meaning the term has in section 2101 of title 46, United States Code.

[46 U.S.C. 3703 note]

SEC. 4117. MARITIME POLLUTION PREVENTION TRAINING PROGRAM STUDY.

The Secretary shall conduct a study to determine the feasibility of a Maritime Oil Pollution Prevention Training program to be carried out in cooperation with approved maritime training institutions. The study shall assess the costs and benefits of transferring suitable vessels to selected maritime training institutions, equipping the vessels for oil spill response, and training students in oil pollution response skills. The study shall be completed and transmitted to the Congress no later than one year after the date of the enactment of this Act.

[46 U.S.C. app. 1295 note]

SEC. 4118. VESSEL COMMUNICATION EQUIPMENT REGULATIONS.

The Secretary shall, not later than one year after the date of the enactment of this Act, issue regulations necessary to ensure that vessels subject to the Vessel Bridge-to-Bridge Radiotelephone Act of 1971 (33 U.S.C. 1203) are also equipped as necessary to—

(1) receive radio marine navigation safety warnings; and

(2) engage in radio communications on designated frequencies with the Coast Guard, and such other vessels and stations as may be specified by the Secretary.

[33 U.S.C. 1203 note]

Subtitle B—Removal

SEC. 4201. FEDERAL REMOVAL AUTHORITY.

(a) * * *

* * * * * * *

(c)[4] Revision of National Contingency Plan.— Not later than one year after the date of the enactment of this Act, the President shall revise and republish the National Contingency Plan prepared under section 311(c)(2) of the Federal Water Pollution Control Act (as in effect immediately before the date of the enactment of this Act) to implement the amendments made by this section and section 4202.

[4] So in law. Probably should be redesignated as subsection (d).

[33 U.S.C. 1321 note]

SEC. 4202. NATIONAL PLANNING AND RESPONSE SYSTEM.

(a) * * *

(b) Implementation.—

(1) Area committees and contingency plans.—(A) Not later than 6 months after the date of the enactment of this Act, the President shall designate the areas for which Area Committees are established under section 311(j)(4) of the Federal

Water Pollution Control Act, as amended by this Act. In designating such areas, the President shall ensure that all navigable waters, adjoining shorelines, and waters of the exclusive economic zone are subject to an Area Contingency Plan under that section.

(B) Not later than 18 months after the date of the enactment of this Act, each Area Committee established under that section shall submit to the President the Area Contingency Plan required under that section.

(C) Not later than 24 months after the date of the enactment of this Act, the President shall—

(i) promptly review each plan;

(ii) require amendments to any plan that does not meet the requirements of section 311(j)(4) of the Federal Water Pollution Control Act; and

(iii) approve each plan that meets the requirements of that section.

(2) NATIONAL RESPONSE UNIT.— Not later than one year after the date of the enactment of this Act, the Secretary of the department in which the Coast Guard is operating shall establish a National Response Unit in accordance with section 311(j)(2) of the Federal Water Pollution Control Act, as amended by this Act.

(3) COAST GUARD DISTRICT RESPONSE GROUPS.— Not later than 1 year after the date of the enactment of this Act, the Secretary of the department in which the Coast Guard is operating shall establish Coast Guard District Response Groups in accordance with section 311(j)(3) of the Federal Water Pollution Control Act, as amended by this Act.

(4) TANK VESSEL AND FACILITY RESPONSE PLANS; TRANSITION PROVISION; EFFECTIVE DATE OF PROHIBITION.—(A) Not later than 24 months after the date of the enactment of this Act, the President shall issue regulations for tank vessel and facility response plans under section 311(j)(5) of the Federal Water Pollution Control Act, as amended by this Act.

(B) During the period beginning 30 months after the date of the enactment of this paragraph and ending 36 months after that date of enactment, a tank vessel or facility for which a response plan is required to be prepared under section 311(j)(5) of the Federal Water Pollution Control Act, as amended by this Act, may not handle, store, or transport oil unless the owner or operator thereof has submitted such a plan to the President.

(C) Subparagraph (E) of section 311(j)(5) of the Federal Water Pollution Control Act, as amended by this Act, shall take effect 36 months after the date of the enactment of this Act.

[33 U.S.C. 1321 note]

* * * * * * *

SEC. 4203. COAST GUARD VESSEL DESIGN.

The Secretary shall ensure that vessels designed and constructed to replace Coast Guard buoy tenders are equipped with oil skimming systems that are readily available and operable, and that complement the primary mission of servicing aids to navigation.

* * * * * * *

Subtitle C—Penalties and Miscellaneous

* * * * * * *

SEC. 4303. FINANCIAL RESPONSIBILITY CIVIL PENALTIES.

(a) Administrative.— Any person who, after notice and an opportunity for a hearing, is found to have failed to comply with the requirements of section 1016 or the regulations issued under that section, or with a denial or detention order issued under subsection (b)(2) of that section, shall be liable to the United States for a civil penalty, not to exceed $25,000 per day of violation. The amount of the civil penalty shall be assessed by the President by written notice. In determining the amount of the penalty, the President shall take into account the nature, circumstances, extent, and gravity of the violation, the degree of culpability, any history of prior violation, ability to pay, and such other matters as justice may require. The President may compromise, modify, or remit, with or without conditions, any civil penalty which is subject to imposition or which has been imposed under this paragraph. If any person fails to pay an assessed civil penalty after it has become final, the President may refer the matter to the Attorney General for collection.

(b) Judicial.— In addition to, or in lieu of, assessing a penalty under subsection (a), the President may request the Attorney General to secure such relief as necessary to compel compliance with section 1016, including a judicial order terminating operations. The district courts of the United States shall have jurisdiction to grant any relief as the public interest and the equities of the case may require.

[33 U.S.C. 2716a]

SEC. 4304. DEPOSIT OF CERTAIN PENALTIES INTO OIL SPILL LIABILITY TRUST FUND.

Penalties paid pursuant to section 311 of the Federal Water Pollution Control Act, section 309(c) of that Act, as a result of violations of section 311 of that Act, and the Deepwater Port Act of 1974, shall be deposited in the Oil Spill Liability Trust Fund created under section 9509 of the Internal Revenue Code of 1986 (26 U.S.C. 9509).

[26 U.S.C. 9509 note]

* * * * * * *

TITLE V—PRINCE WILLIAM SOUND PROVISIONS

TITLE V—PRINCE WILLIAM SOUND PROVISIONS

SEC. 5001. OIL SPILL RECOVERY INSTITUTE.

(a) ESTABLISHMENT OF INSTITUTE.— The Secretary of Commerce shall provide for the establishment of a Prince William Sound Oil Spill Recovery Institute (hereinafter in this section referred to as the Institute) through the Prince William Sound Science and Technology Institute located in Cordova, Alaska.

(b) FUNCTIONS.—The Institute shall conduct research and carry out educational and demonstration projects designed to—

(1) identify and develop the best available techniques, equipment, and materials for dealing with oil spills in the arctic and subarctic marine environment; and

(2) complement Federal and State damage assessment efforts and determine, document, assess, and understand the long-range effects of Arctic or Subarctic oil spills on the natural resources of Prince William Sound and its adjacent waters (as generally depicted on the map entitled EXXON VALDEZ oil spill dated March 1990), and the environment, the economy, and the lifestyle and well-being of the people who are dependent on them, except that the Institute shall not conduct studies or make recommendations on any matter which is not directly related to Arctic or Subarctic oil spills or the effects thereof.

(c) ADVISORY BOARD.—

(1) IN GENERAL.—The policies of the Institute shall be determined by an advisory board, composed of 16 members appointed as follows:

(A) One representative appointed by each of the Commissioners of Fish and Game, Environmental Conservation, and Natural Resources of the State of Alaska, all of whom shall be State employees.

(B) One representative appointed by each of the Secretaries of Commerce and the Interior and the Commandant of the Coast Guard, who shall be Federal employees.

(C) Two representatives from the fishing industry appointed by the Governor of the State of Alaska from among residents of communities in Alaska that were affected by the EXXON VALDEZ oil spill, who shall serve terms of 2 years each. Interested organizations from within the fishing industry may submit the names of qualified individuals for consideration by the Governor.

(D) Two Alaska Natives who represent Native entities affected by the EXXON VALDEZ oil spill, at least one of whom represents an entity located in Prince William Sound, appointed by the Governor of Alaska from a list of 4 qualified individuals submitted by the Alaska Federation of Natives, who shall serve terms of 2 years each.

(E) Two representatives from the oil and gas industry to be appointed by the Governor of the State of Alaska who shall serve terms of 2 years each. Interested organizations from within the oil and gas industry may submit the names of qualified individuals for consideration by the Governor.

(F) Two at-large representatives from among residents of communities in Alaska that were affected by the EXXON VALDEZ oil spill who are knowledgeable about the marine environment and wildlife within Prince William Sound, and who shall serve terms of 2 years each, appointed by the remaining members of the Advisory Board. Interested parties may submit the names of qualified individuals for consideration by the Advisory Board.

(G) One nonvoting representative of the Institute of Marine Science.

(H) One nonvoting representative appointed by the Prince William Sound Science and Technology Institute.

(2) CHAIRMAN.— The representative of the Secretary of Commerce shall serve as Chairman of the Advisory Board.

(3) POLICIES.— Policies determined by the Advisory Board under this subsection shall include policies for the conduct and support, through contracts and grants awarded on a nationally competitive basis, of research, projects, and studies to be supported by the Institute in accordance with the purposes of this section.

(4) SCIENTIFIC REVIEW.— The Advisory Board may request a scientific review of the research program every five years by the National Academy of Sciences which shall perform the review, if requested, as part of its responsibilities under section 7001(b)(2).

(d) SCIENTIFIC AND TECHNICAL COMMITTEE.—

(1) IN GENERAL.— The Advisory Board shall establish a scientific and technical committee, composed of specialists in matters relating to oil spill containment and cleanup technology, arctic and subarctic marine ecology, and the living resources and socioeconomics of Prince William Sound and its adjacent waters, from the University of Alaska, the Institute of Marine Science, the Prince William Sound Science and Technology Institute, and elsewhere in the academic community.

(2) FUNCTIONS.— The Scientific and Technical Committee shall provide such advice to the Advisory Board as the Advisory Board shall request, including recommendations regarding the conduct and support of research, projects, and studies in accordance with the purposes of this section. The Advisory Board shall not request, and the Committee shall not provide, any advice which is not directly related to Arctic or Subarctic oil spills or the effects thereof.

(e) DIRECTOR.— The Institute shall be administered by a Director appointed by the Advisory Board. The Prince William Sound Science and Technology Institute and the Scientific and Technical Committee may each submit independent recommendations for the Advisory Board's consideration for appointment as Director. The Director may hire such staff and incur such expenses on behalf of the Institute as are authorized by the Advisory Board.

(f) EVALUATION.— The Secretary of Commerce may conduct an ongoing evaluation of the activities of the Institute to ensure that funds received by the Institute are used in a manner consistent with this section.

(g) AUDIT.— The Comptroller General of the United States, and any of his or her duly authorized representatives, shall have access, for purposes of audit and examination, to any books, documents, papers, and records of the Institute and its administering agency that are pertinent to the funds received and expended by the Institute and its administering agency.

(h) Status of Employees.— Employees of the Institute shall not, by reason of such employment, be considered to be employees of the Federal Government for any purpose.

(i) Termination.— The authorization in section 5006(b) providing funding for the Institute shall terminate 1 year after the date on which the Secretary, in consultation with the Secretary of the Interior, determines that oil and gas exploration, development, and production in the State of Alaska have ceased.

(j) Use of Funds.— No funds made available to carry out this section may be used to initiate litigation. No funds made available to carry out this section may be used for the acquisition of real property (including buildings) or construction of any building. No more than 20 percent of funds made available to carry out this section may be used to lease necessary facilities and to administer the Institute. The Advisory Board may compensate its Federal representatives for their reasonable travel costs. None of the funds authorized by this section shall be used for any purpose other than the functions specified in subsection (b).

(k) Research.— The Institute shall publish and make available to any person upon request the results of all research, educational, and demonstration projects conducted by the Institute. The Administrator shall provide a copy of all research, educational, and demonstration projects conducted by the Institute to the National Oceanic and Atmospheric Administration.

(l) Definitions.— In this section, the term Prince William Sound and its adjacent waters means such sound and waters as generally depicted on the map entitled EXXON VALDEZ oil spill dated March 1990.

[33 U.S.C. 2731]

SEC. 5002. TERMINAL AND TANKER OVERSIGHT AND MONITORING.

(a) Short Title and Findings.—

(1) Short title.— This section may be cited as the "Oil Terminal and Oil Tanker Environmental Oversight and Monitoring Act of 1990".

(2) Findings.—The Congress finds that—

(A) the March 24, 1989, grounding and rupture of the fully loaded oil tanker, the EXXON VALDEZ, spilled 11 million gallons of crude oil in Prince William Sound, an environmentally sensitive area;

(B) many people believe that complacency on the part of the industry and government personnel responsible for monitoring the operation of the Valdez terminal and vessel traffic in Prince William Sound was one of the contributing factors to the EXXON VALDEZ oil spill;

(C) one way to combat this complacency is to involve local citizens in the process of preparing, adopting, and revising oil spill contingency plans;

(D) a mechanism should be established which fosters the long-term partnership of industry, government, and local communities in overseeing compliance with environmental concerns in the operation of crude oil terminals;

(E) such a mechanism presently exists at the Sullom Voe terminal in the Shetland Islands and this terminal should serve as a model for others;

(F) because of the effective partnership that has developed at Sullom Voe, Sullom Voe is considered the safest terminal in Europe;

(G) the present system of regulation and oversight of crude oil terminals in the United States has degenerated into a process of continual mistrust and confrontation;

(H) only when local citizens are involved in the process will the trust develop that is necessary to change the present system from confrontation to consensus;

(I) a pilot program patterned after Sullom Voe should be established in Alaska to further refine the concepts and relationships involved; and

(J) similar programs should eventually be established in other major crude oil terminals in the United States because the recent oil spills in Texas, Delaware, and Rhode Island indicate that the safe transportation of crude oil is a national problem.

(b) DEMONSTRATION PROGRAMS.—

(1) ESTABLISHMENT.— There are established 2 Oil Terminal and Oil Tanker Environmental Oversight and Monitoring Demonstration Programs (hereinafter referred to as Programs) to be carried out in the State of Alaska.

(2) ADVISORY FUNCTION.— The function of these Programs shall be advisory only.

(3) PURPOSE.— The Prince William Sound Program shall be responsible for environmental monitoring of the terminal facilities in Prince William Sound and the crude oil tankers operating in Prince William Sound. The Cook Inlet Program shall be responsible for environmental monitoring of the terminal facilities and crude oil tankers operating in Cook Inlet located South of the latitude at Point Possession and North of the latitude at Amatuli Island, including offshore facilities in Cook Inlet.

(4) SUITS BARRED.— No program, association, council, committee or other organization created by this section may sue any person or entity, public or private, concerning any matter arising under this section except for the performance of contracts.

(c) OIL TERMINAL FACILITIES AND OIL TANKER OPERATIONS ASSOCIATION.—

(1) ESTABLISHMENT.— There is established an Oil Terminal Facilities and Oil Tanker Operations Association (hereinafter in this section referred to as the Association) for each of the Programs established under subsection (b).

(2) MEMBERSHIP.—Each Association shall be comprised of 4 individuals as follows:

(A) One individual shall be designated by the owners and operators of the terminal facilities and shall represent those owners and operators.

(B) One individual shall be designated by the owners and operators of the crude oil tankers calling at the terminal facilities and shall represent those owners and operators.

(C) One individual shall be an employee of the State of Alaska, shall be designated by the Governor of the State of Alaska, and shall represent the State government.

(D) One individual shall be an employee of the Federal Government, shall be designated by the President, and shall represent the Federal Government.

(3) RESPONSIBILITIES.— Each Association shall be responsible for reviewing policies relating to the operation and maintenance of the oil terminal facilities and crude oil tankers which affect or may affect the environment in the vicinity of their respective terminals. Each Association shall provide a forum among the owners and operators of the terminal facilities, the owners and operators of crude oil tankers calling at those facilities, the United States, and the State of Alaska to discuss and to make recommendations concerning all permits, plans, and site-specific regulations governing the activities and actions of the terminal facilities which affect or may affect the environment in the vicinity of the terminal facilities and of crude oil tankers calling at those facilities.

(4) DESIGNATION OF EXISTING ORGANIZATION.— The Secretary may designate an existing nonprofit organization as an Association under this subsection if the organization is organized to meet the purposes of this section and consists of at least the individuals listed in paragraph (2).

(d) REGIONAL CITIZENS' ADVISORY COUNCILS.—

(1) MEMBERSHIP.— There is established a Regional Citizens' Advisory Council (hereinafter in this section referred to as the Council) for each of the programs established by subsection (b).

(2) MEMBERSHIP.—Each Council shall be composed of voting members and nonvoting members, as follows:

(A) VOTING MEMBERS.—Voting members shall be Alaska residents and, except as provided in clause (vii) of this paragraph, shall be appointed by the Governor of the State of Alaska from a list of nominees provided by each of the following interests, with one representative appointed to represent each of the following interests, taking into consideration the need for regional balance on the Council:

(i) Local commercial fishing industry organizations, the members of which depend on the fisheries resources of the waters in the vicinity of the terminal facilities.

(ii) Aquaculture associations in the vicinity of the terminal facilities.

(iii) Alaska Native Corporations and other Alaska Native organizations the members of which reside in the vicinity of the terminal facilities.

(iv) Environmental organizations the members of which reside in the vicinity of the terminal facilities.

(v) Recreational organizations the members of which reside in or use the vicinity of the terminal facilities.

(vi) The Alaska State Chamber of Commerce, to represent the locally based tourist industry.

(vii)(I) For the Prince William Sound Terminal Facilities Council, one representative selected by each of the following municipalities: Cordova, Whittier, Seward, Valdez, Kodiak, the Kodiak Island Borough, and the Kenai Peninsula Borough.

(II) For the Cook Inlet Terminal Facilities Council, one representative selected by each of the following municipalities: Homer, Seldovia, Anchorage, Kenai, Kodiak, the Kodiak Island Borough, and the Kenai Peninsula Borough.

(B) NONVOTING MEMBERS.—One ex-officio, nonvoting representative shall be designated by, and represent, each of the following:

(i) The Environmental Protection Agency.

(ii) The Coast Guard.

(iii) The National Oceanic and Atmospheric Administration.

(iv) The United States Forest Service.

(v) The Bureau of Land Management.

(vi) The Alaska Department of Environmental Conservation.

(vii) The Alaska Department of Fish and Game.

(viii) The Alaska Department of Natural Resources.

(ix) The Division of Emergency Services, Alaska Department of Military and Veterans Affairs.

(3) TERMS.—

(A) DURATION OF COUNCILS.— The term of the Councils shall continue throughout the life of the operation of the Trans-Alaska Pipeline System and so long as oil is transported to or from Cook Inlet.

(B) THREE YEARS.— The voting members of each Council shall be appointed for a term of 3 years except as provided for in subparagraph (C).

(C) INITIAL APPOINTMENTS.—The terms of the first appointments shall be as follows:

(i) For the appointments by the Governor of the State of Alaska, one-third shall serve for 3 years, one-third shall serve for 2 years, and one-third shall serve for one year.

(ii) For the representatives of municipalities required by subsection (d)(2)(A)(vii), a drawing of lots among the appointees shall determine that one-third of that group serves for 3 years, one-third serves for 2 years, and the remainder serves for 1 year.

(4) SELF-GOVERNING.— Each Council shall elect its own chairperson, select its own staff, and make policies with regard to its internal operating procedures. After the initial organizational meeting called by the Secretary under subsection (i), each

Council shall be self-governing.

(5) DUAL MEMBERSHIP AND CONFLICTS OF INTEREST PROHIBITED.—(A) No individual selected as a member of the Council shall serve on the Association.

(B) No individual selected as a voting member of the Council shall be engaged in any activity which might conflict with such individual carrying out his functions as a member thereof.

(6) DUTIES.—Each Council shall—

(A) provide advice and recommendations to the Association on policies, permits, and site-specific regulations relating to the operation and maintenance of terminal facilities and crude oil tankers which affect or may affect the environment in the vicinity of the terminal facilities;

(B) monitor through the committee established under subsection (e), the environmental impacts of the operation of the terminal facilities and crude oil tankers;

(C) monitor those aspects of terminal facilities' and crude oil tankers' operations and maintenance which affect or may affect the environment in the vicinity of the terminal facilities;

(D) review through the committee established under subsection (f), the adequacy of oil spill prevention and contingency plans for the terminal facilities and the adequacy of oil spill prevention and contingency plans for crude oil tankers, operating in Prince William Sound or in Cook Inlet;

(E) provide advice and recommendations to the Association on port operations, policies and practices;

(F) recommend to the Association—

(i) standards and stipulations for permits and site-specific regulations intended to minimize the impact of the terminal facilities' and crude oil tankers' operations in the vicinity of the terminal facilities;

(ii) modifications of terminal facility operations and maintenance intended to minimize the risk and mitigate the impact of terminal facilities, operations in the vicinity of the terminal facilities and to minimize the risk of oil spills;

(iii) modifications of crude oil tanker operations and maintenance in Prince William Sound and Cook Inlet intended to minimize the risk and mitigate the impact of oil spills; and

(iv) modifications to the oil spill prevention and contingency plans for terminal facilities and for crude oil tankers in Prince William Sound and Cook Inlet intended to enhance the ability to prevent and respond to an oil spill; and

(G) create additional committees of the Council as necessary to carry out the above functions, including a scientific and technical advisory committee to the Prince William Sound Council.

(7) NO ESTOPPEL.— No Council shall be held liable under State or Federal law

for costs or damages as a result of rendering advice under this section. Nor shall any advice given by a voting member of a Council, or program representative or agent, be grounds for estopping the interests represented by the voting Council members from seeking damages or other appropriate relief.

(8) SCIENTIFIC WORK.— In carrying out its research, development and monitoring functions, each Council is authorized to conduct its own scientific research and shall review the scientific work undertaken by or on behalf of the terminal operators or crude oil tanker operators as a result of a legal requirement to undertake that work. Each Council shall also review the relevant scientific work undertaken by or on behalf of any government entity relating to the terminal facilities or crude oil tankers. To the extent possible, to avoid unnecessary duplication, each Council shall coordinate its independent scientific work with the scientific work performed by or on behalf of the terminal operators and with the scientific work performed by or on behalf of the operators of the crude oil tankers.

(e) COMMITTEE FOR TERMINAL AND OIL TANKER OPERATIONS AND ENVIRONMENTAL MONITORING.—

(1) MONITORING COMMITTEE.— Each Council shall establish a standing Terminal and Oil Tanker Operations and Environmental Monitoring Committee (hereinafter in this section referred to as the Monitoring Committee) to devise and manage a comprehensive program of monitoring the environmental impacts of the operations of terminal facilities and of crude oil tankers while operating in Prince William Sound and Cook Inlet. The membership of the Monitoring Committee shall be made up of members of the Council, citizens, and recognized scientific experts selected by the Council.

(2) DUTIES.—In fulfilling its responsibilities, the Monitoring Committee shall—

(A) advise the Council on a monitoring strategy that will permit early detection of environmental impacts of terminal facility operations and crude oil tanker operations while in Prince William Sound and Cook Inlet;

(B) develop monitoring programs and make recommendations to the Council on the implementation of those programs;

(C) at its discretion, select and contract with universities and other scientific institutions to carry out specific monitoring projects authorized by the Council pursuant to an approved monitoring strategy;

(D) complete any other tasks assigned by the Council; and

(E) provide written reports to the Council which interpret and assess the results of all monitoring programs.

(f) COMMITTEE FOR OIL SPILL PREVENTION, SAFETY, AND EMERGENCY RESPONSE.—

(1) TECHNICAL OIL SPILL COMMITTEE.— Each Council shall establish a standing technical committee (hereinafter referred to as Oil Spill Committee) to review and assess measures designed to prevent oil spills and the planning and preparedness for responding to, containing, cleaning up, and mitigating impacts of oil spills. The membership of the Oil Spill Committee shall be made up of members of the Council, citizens, and recognized technical experts selected by the Council.

(2) DUTIES.—In fulfilling its responsibilities, the Oil Spill Committee shall—

(A) periodically review the respective oil spill prevention and contingency plans for the terminal facilities and for the crude oil tankers while in Prince William Sound or Cook Inlet, in light of new technological developments and changed circumstances;

(B) monitor periodic drills and testing of the oil spill contingency plans for the terminal facilities and for crude oil tankers while in Prince William Sound and Cook Inlet;

(C) study wind and water currents and other environmental factors in the vicinity of the terminal facilities which may affect the ability to prevent, respond to, contain, and clean up an oil spill;

(D) identify highly sensitive areas which may require specific protective measures in the event of a spill in Prince William Sound or Cook Inlet;

(E) monitor developments in oil spill prevention, containment, response, and cleanup technology;

(F) periodically review port organization, operations, incidents, and the adequacy and maintenance of vessel traffic service systems designed to assure safe transit of crude oil tankers pertinent to terminal operations;

(G) periodically review the standards for tankers bound for, loading at, exiting from, or otherwise using the terminal facilities;

(H) complete any other tasks assigned by the Council; and

(I) provide written reports to the Council outlining its findings and recommendations.

(g) AGENCY COOPERATION.— On and after the expiration of the 180-day period following the date of the enactment of this section, each Federal department, agency, or other instrumentality shall, with respect to all permits, site-specific regulations, and other matters governing the activities and actions of the terminal facilities which affect or may affect the vicinity of the terminal facilities, consult with the appropriate Council prior to taking substantive action with respect to the permit, site-specific regulation, or other matter. This consultation shall be carried out with a view to enabling the appropriate Association and Council to review the permit, site-specific regulation, or other matters and make appropriate recommendations regarding operations, policy or agency actions. Prior consultation shall not be required if an authorized Federal agency representative reasonably believes that an emergency exists requiring action without delay.

(h) RECOMMENDATIONS OF THE COUNCIL.— In the event that the Association does not adopt, or significantly modifies before adoption, any recommendation of the Council made pursuant to the authority granted to the Council in subsection (d), the Association shall provide to the Council, in writing, within 5 days of its decision, notice of its decision and a written statement of reasons for its rejection or significant modification of the recommendation.

(i) ADMINISTRATIVE ACTIONS.— Appointments, designations, and selections of individuals to serve as members of the Associations and Councils under this section shall be submitted to the Secretary prior to the expiration of the 120-day period following the date of the enactment of this section. On or before the expiration of the 180-day period following that date of enactment of this section, the Secretary shall call an initial meeting of each Association and Council for organizational purposes.

(j) LOCATION AND COMPENSATION.—

(1) LOCATION.— Each Association and Council established by this section shall be located in the State of Alaska.

(2) COMPENSATION.— No member of an Association or Council shall be compensated for the member's services as a member of the Association or Council, but shall be allowed travel expenses, including per diem in lieu of subsistence, at a rate established by the Association or Council not to exceed the rates authorized for employees of agencies under sections 5702 and 5703 of title 5, United States Code. However, each Council may enter into contracts to provide compensation and expenses to members of the committees created under subsections (d), (e), and (f).

(k) FUNDING.—

(1) REQUIREMENT.— Approval of the contingency plans required of owners and operators of the Cook Inlet and Prince William Sound terminal facilities and crude oil tankers while operating in Alaskan waters in commerce with those terminal facilities shall be effective only so long as the respective Association and Council for a facility are funded pursuant to paragraph (2).

(2) PRINCE WILLIAM SOUND PROGRAM.—The owners or operators of terminal facilities or crude oil tankers operating in Prince William Sound shall provide, on an annual basis, an aggregate amount of not more than $2,000,000, as determined by the Secretary. Such amount—

(A) shall provide for the establishment and operation on the environmental oversight and monitoring program in Prince William Sound;

(B) shall be adjusted annually by the Anchorage Consumer Price Index; and

(C) may be adjusted periodically upon the mutual consent of the owners or operators of terminal facilities or crude oil tankers operating in Prince William Sound and the Prince William Sound terminal facilities Council.

(3) COOK INLET PROGRAM.—The owners or operators of terminal facilities, offshore facilities, or crude oil tankers operating in Cook Inlet shall provide, on an annual basis, an aggregate amount of not less than $1,400,000, as determined by the Secretary. Such amount—

(A) shall provide for the establishment and operation of the environmental oversight and monitoring program in Cook Inlet;

(B) shall be adjusted annually by the Anchorage Consumer Price Index; and

(C) may be adjusted periodically upon the mutual consent of the owners or operators of terminal facilities, offshore facilities, or crude oil tankers operating in Cook Inlet and the Cook Inlet Council.

(l) REPORTS.—

(1) Associations and councils.— Prior to the expiration of the 36-month period following the date of the enactment of this section, each Association and Council established by this section shall report to the President and the Congress concerning its activities under this section, together with its recommendations.

(2) GAO.— Prior to the expiration of the 36-month period following the date of the enactment of this section, the Government Accountability Office shall report to the President and the Congress as to the handling of funds, including donated funds, by the entities carrying out the programs under this section, and the effectiveness of the demonstration programs carried out under this section, together with its recommendations.

(m) Definitions.—As used in this section, the term—

(1) terminal facilities means—

(A) in the case of the Prince William Sound Program, the entire oil terminal complex located in Valdez, Alaska, consisting of approximately 1,000 acres including all buildings, docks (except docks owned by the City of Valdez if those docks are not used for loading of crude oil), pipes, piping, roads, ponds, tanks, crude oil tankers only while at the terminal dock, tanker escorts owned or operated by the operator of the terminal, vehicles, and other facilities associated with, and necessary for, assisting tanker movement of crude oil into and out of the oil terminal complex; and

(B) in the case of the Cook Inlet Program, the entire oil terminal complex including all buildings, docks, pipes, piping, roads, ponds, tanks, vessels, vehicles, crude oil tankers only while at the terminal dock, tanker escorts owned or operated by the operator of the terminal, emergency spill response vessels owned or operated by the operator of the terminal, and other facilities associated with, and necessary for, assisting tanker movement of crude oil into and out of the oil terminal complex;

(2) crude oil tanker means a tanker (as that term is defined under section 2101 of title 46, United States Code)—

(A) in the case of the Prince William Sound Program, calling at the terminal facilities for the purpose of receiving and transporting oil to refineries, operating north of Middleston Island and bound for or exiting from Prince William Sound; and

(B) in the case of the Cook Inlet Program, calling at the terminal facilities for the purpose of receiving and transporting oil to refineries and operating in Cook Inlet and the Gulf of Alaska north of Amatuli Island, including tankers transiting to Cook Inlet from Prince William Sound;

(3) vicinity of the terminal facilities means that geographical area surrounding the environment of terminal facilities which is directly affected or may be directly affected by the operation of the terminal facilities; and

(4) Secretary means the Secretary of the department in which the Coast Guard is operating.

(n) Savings Clause.—

(1) REGULATORY AUTHORITY.—Nothing in this section shall be construed as modifying, repealing, superseding, or preempting any municipal, State or Federal law or regulation, or in any way affecting litigation arising from oil spills or the rights and responsibilities of the United States or the State of Alaska, or municipalities thereof, to preserve and protect the environment through regulation of land, air, and water uses, of safety, and of related development. The monitoring provided for by this section shall be designed to help assure compliance with applicable laws and regulations and shall only extend to activities—

(A) that would affect or have the potential to affect the vicinity of the terminal facilities and the area of crude oil tanker operations included in the Programs; and

(B) are subject to the United States or State of Alaska, or municipality thereof, law, regulation, or other legal requirement.

(2) RECOMMENDATIONS.— This subsection is not intended to prevent the Association or Council from recommending to appropriate authorities that existing legal requirements should be modified or that new legal requirements should be adopted.

(o) ALTERNATIVE VOLUNTARY ADVISORY GROUP IN LIEU OF COUNCIL.—The requirements of subsections (c) through (l), as such subsections apply respectively to the Prince William Sound Program and the Cook Inlet Program, are deemed to have been satisfied so long as the following conditions are met:

(1) PRINCE WILLIAM SOUND.— With respect to the Prince William Sound Program, the Alyeska Pipeline Service Company or any of its owner companies enters into a contract for the duration of the operation of the Trans-Alaska Pipeline System with the Alyeska Citizens Advisory Committee in existence on the date of enactment of this section, or a successor organization, to fund that Committee or organization on an annual basis in the amount provided for by subsection (k)(2)(A) and the President annually certifies that the Committee or organization fosters the general goals and purposes of this section and is broadly representative of the communities and interests in the vicinity of the terminal facilities and Prince William Sound.

(2) COOK INLET.— With respect to the Cook Inlet Program, the terminal facilities, offshore facilities, or crude oil tanker owners and operators enter into a contract with a voluntary advisory organization to fund that organization on an annual basis and the President annually certifies that the organization fosters the general goals and purposes of this section and is broadly representative of the communities and interests in the vicinity of the terminal facilities and Cook Inlet.

[33 U.S.C. 2732]

SEC. 5003. BLIGH REEF LIGHT.

The Secretary of Transportation shall within one year after the date of the enactment of this title install and ensure operation of an automated navigation light on or adjacent to Bligh Reef in Prince William Sound, Alaska, of sufficient power and height to provide long-range warning of the location of Bligh Reef.

[33 U.S.C. 2733]

SEC. 5004. VESSEL TRAFFIC SERVICE SYSTEM.

The Secretary of Transportation shall within one year after the date of the enactment of this title—

(1) acquire, install, and operate such additional equipment (which may consist of radar, closed circuit television, satellite tracking systems, or other shipboard dependent surveillance), train and locate such personnel, and issue such final regulations as are necessary to increase the range of the existing VTS system in the Port of Valdez, Alaska, sufficiently to track the locations and movements of tank vessels carrying oil from the Trans-Alaska Pipeline when such vessels are transiting Prince William Sound, Alaska, and to sound an audible alarm when such tankers depart from designated navigation routes; and

(2) submit to the Committee on Commerce, Science, and Transportation of the Senate and the Committee on Transportation and Infrastructure of the House of Representatives a report on the feasibility and desirability of instituting positive control of tank vessel movements in Prince William Sound by Coast Guard personnel using the Port of Valdez, Alaska, VTS system, as modified pursuant to paragraph (1).

[33 U.S.C. 2734]

SEC. 5005. EQUIPMENT AND PERSONNEL REQUIREMENTS UNDER TANK VESSEL AND FACILITY RESPONSE PLANS.

(a) IN GENERAL.—In addition to the requirements for response plans for vessels established by section 311(j) of the Federal Water Pollution Control Act, as amended by this Act, a response plan for a tanker loading cargo at a facility permitted under the Trans-Alaska Pipeline Authorization Act (43 U.S.C. 1651 et seq.),[5] shall provide for—

[5] Section 354(2) of P.L. 102–388 attempted to amend section 5005(a) by inserting and a response plan for such a facility, after (43 U.S.C. 1651 et seq.).. The amendment probably should have made the insertion after (43 U.S.C. 1651 et seq.),.

(1) prepositioned oil spill containment and removal equipment in communities and other strategic locations within the geographic boundaries of Prince William Sound, including escort vessels with skimming capability; barges to receive recovered oil; heavy duty sea boom, pumping, transferring, and lightering equipment; and other appropriate removal equipment for the protection of the environment, including fish hatcheries;

(2) the establishment of an oil spill removal organization at appropriate locations in Prince William Sound, consisting of trained personnel in sufficient numbers to immediately remove, to the maximum extent practicable, a worst case discharge or a discharge of 200,000 barrels of oil, whichever is greater;

(3) training in oil removal techniques for local residents and individuals engaged in the cultivation or production of fish or fish products in Prince William Sound;

(4) practice exercises not less than 2 times per year which test the capacity of the equipment and personnel required under this paragraph; and

(5) periodic testing and certification of equipment required under this paragraph,

as required by the Secretary.

(b) DEFINITIONS.—In this section—

(1) the term Prince William Sound means all State and Federal waters within Prince William Sound, Alaska, including the approach to Hinchenbrook Entrance out to and encompassing Seal Rocks; and

(2) the term worst case discharge means—

(A) in the case of a vessel, a discharge in adverse weather conditions of its entire cargo; and

(B) in the case of a facility, the largest foreseeable discharge in adverse weather conditions.

[33 U.S.C. 2735]

SEC. 5006. FUNDING.

(a) SECTIONS 5001, 5003 AND 5004.— Amounts in the Fund shall be available, without further appropriations and without fiscal year limitation, to carry out section 5001 in the amount as determined in section 5006(b), and to carry out sections 5003 and 5004, in an amount not to exceed $5,000,000.

(b) USE OF INTEREST ONLY.— The amount of funding to be made available annually to carry out section 5001 shall be the interest produced by the Fund's investment of the $22,500,000 remaining funding authorized for the Prince William Sound Oil Spill Recovery Institute and currently deposited in the Fund and invested by the Secretary of the Treasury in income producing securities along with other funds comprising the Fund. The National Pollution Funds Center shall transfer all such accrued interest, including the interest earned from the date funds in the Trans-Alaska Liability Pipeline Fund were transferred into the Oil Spill Liability Trust Fund pursuant to section 8102(a)(2)(B)(ii), to the Prince William Sound Oil Spill Recovery Institute annually, beginning 60 days after the date of enactment of the Coast Guard Authorization Act of 1996.

(c) USE FOR SECTION 1012.— Beginning 1 year after the date on which the Secretary, in consultation with the Secretary of the Interior, determines that oil and gas exploration, development, and production in the State of Alaska have ceased, the funding authorized for the Prince William Sound Oil Spill Recovery Institute and deposited in the Fund shall thereafter be made available for purposes of section 1012 in Alaska.

(d) SECTION 5008.— Amounts in the Fund shall be available, without further appropriation and without fiscal year limitation, to carry out section 5008(b), in an annual[6] amount not to exceed $5,000,000 of which up to $3,000,000 may be used for the lease payment to the Alaska SeaLife Center under section 5008(b)(2): *Provided*, That the entire amount is designated by the Congress as an emergency requirement pursuant to section 251(b)(2)(A) of the Balanced Budget and Emergency Deficit Control Act of 1985, as amended: *Provided further*, That the entire amount shall be available only to the extent an official budget request that includes designation of the entire amount of the request as an emergency requirement as defined in the Balanced Budget and Emergency Deficit Control Act of 1985, as amended, is transmitted by the President to the Congress.

[6] Section 4413 of Public Law 109–59 (119 Stat. 1779) amended this subsection by inserting annual before amount. The amendment has been carried out by inserting annual before amount the first place it appears to reflect the probable intent of Congress.

[33 U.S.C. 2736]

SEC. 5007. LIMITATION.

Notwithstanding any other law, tank vessels that have spilled more than 1,000,000 gallons of oil into the marine environment after March 22, 1989, are prohibited from operating on the navigable waters of Prince William Sound, Alaska.

[33 U.S.C. 2737]

SEC. 5008. NORTH PACIFIC MARINE RESEARCH INSTITUTE.

(a) Institute Established.— The Secretary of Commerce shall establish a North Pacific Marine Research Institute (hereafter in this section referred to as the Institute) to be administered at the Alaska SeaLife Center by the North Pacific Research Board.

(b) Functions.—The Institute shall—

(1) conduct research and carry out education and demonstration projects on or relating to the North Pacific marine ecosystem with particular emphasis on marine mammal, sea bird, fish, and shellfish populations in the Bering Sea and Gulf of Alaska including populations located in or near Kenai Fjords National Park and the Alaska Maritime National Wildlife Refuge; and

(2) lease, maintain, operate, and upgrade the necessary research equipment and related facilities necessary to conduct such research at the Alaska SeaLife Center.

(c) Evaluation and Audit.— The Secretary of Commerce may periodically evaluate the activities of the Institute to ensure that funds received by the Institute are used in a manner consistent with this section. Chapter 10 of title 5, United States Code, shall not apply to the Institute.

(d) Status of Employees.— Employees of the Institute shall not, by reason of such employment, be considered to be employees of the Federal Government for any purpose.

(e) Use of Funds.— No funds made available to carry out this section may be used to initiate litigation, or for the acquisition of real property (other than facilities leased at the Alaska SeaLife Center). No more than 10 percent of the funds made available to carry out subsection (b)(1) may be used to administer the Institute. The administrative funds of the Institute and the administrative funds of the North Pacific Research Board created under Public Law 105–83 may be used to jointly administer such programs at the discretion of the North Pacific Research Board.

(f) Availability of Research.— The Institute shall publish and make available to any person on request the results of all research, educational, and demonstration projects conducted by the Institute. The Institute shall provide a copy of all research, educational, and demonstration projects conducted by the Institute to the National Park Service, the United States Fish and Wildlife Service, and the National Oceanic and Atmospheric Administration.

[33 U.S.C. 2738]

TITLE VI—MISCELLANEOUS

TITLE VI—MISCELLANEOUS

SEC. 6001. SAVINGS PROVISIONS.

(a) Cross-References.— A reference to a law replaced by this Act, including a reference in a regulation, order, or other law, is deemed to refer to the corresponding provision of this Act.

(b) Continuation of Regulations.— An order, rule, or regulation in effect under a law replaced by this Act continues in effect under the corresponding provision of this Act until repealed, amended, or superseded.

(c) Rule of Construction.— An inference of legislative construction shall not be drawn by reason of the caption or catch line of a provision enacted by this Act.

(d) Actions and Rights.— Nothing in this Act shall apply to any rights and duties that matured, penalties that were incurred, and proceedings that were begun before the date of enactment of this Act, except as provided by this section, and shall be adjudicated pursuant to the law applicable on the date prior to the date of the enactment of this Act.

(e) Admiralty and Maritime Law.—Except as otherwise provided in this Act, this Act does not affect—

(1) admiralty and maritime law; or

(2) the jurisdiction of the district courts of the United States with respect to civil actions under admiralty and maritime jurisdiction, saving to suitors in all cases all other remedies to which they are otherwise entitled.

[33 U.S.C. 2751]

SEC. 6002. ANNUAL APPROPRIATIONS.

(a) Required.— Except as provided in subsection (b), amounts in the Fund shall be available only as provided in annual appropriation Acts.

(b) Exceptions.—

(1) In general.—Subsection (a) shall not apply to—

(A) section 1006(f), 1012(a)(4), or 5006; or

(B) an amount, which may not exceed $50,000,000 in any fiscal year, made available by the President from the Fund—

(i) to carry out section 311(c) of the Federal Water Pollution Control Act (33 U.S.C. 1321(c)); and

(ii) to initiate the assessment of natural resources damages required under section 1006.

(2) Fund advances.—

(A) In general.— To the extent that the amount described in subparagraph (B) of paragraph (1) is not adequate to carry out the activities described in such subparagraph, the Coast Guard may obtain 1 or more advances from the Fund as may be necessary, up to a maximum of $100,000,000 for each advance, with the total amount of advances not to exceed the amounts available under section 9509(c)(2) of the Internal Revenue Code of 1986.

(B) NOTIFICATION TO CONGRESS.—Not later than 30 days after the date on which the Coast Guard obtains an advance under subparagraph (A), the Coast Guard shall notify Congress of—

(i) the amount advanced; and

(ii) the facts and circumstances that necessitated the advance.

(C) REPAYMENT.— Amounts advanced under this paragraph shall be repaid to the Fund when, and to the extent that, removal costs are recovered by the Coast Guard from responsible parties for the discharge or substantial threat of discharge.

(3) AVAILABILITY.— Amounts to which this subsection applies shall remain available until expended.

[33 U.S.C. 2752]

[Section 6003—Repealed by section 109 of P.L. 104–134]

SEC. 6004. COOPERATIVE DEVELOPMENT OF COMMON HYDROCARBON-BEARING AREAS.

(a) * * *

(b) EXCEPTION FOR WEST DELTA FIELD.— Section 5(j) of the Outer Continental Shelf Lands Act, as added by this section, shall not be applicable with respect to Blocks 17 and 18 of the West Delta Field offshore Louisiana.

(c) AUTHORIZATION OF APPROPRIATIONS.— There are hereby authorized to be appropriated such sums as may be necessary to provide compensation, including interest, to the State of Louisiana and its lessees, for net drainage of oil and gas resources as determined in the Third Party Factfinder Louisiana Boundary Study dated March 21, 1989. For purposes of this section, such lessees shall include those persons with an ownership interest in State of Louisiana leases SL10087, SL10088 or SL10187, or ownership interests in the production or proceeds therefrom, as established by assignment, contract or otherwise. Interest shall be computed for the period March 21, 1989 until the date of payment.

Title VII—Oil Pollution Research and Development Program

TITLE VII—OIL POLLUTION RESEARCH AND DEVELOPMENT PROGRAM

SEC. 7001. OIL POLLUTION RESEARCH AND DEVELOPMENT PROGRAM.

(a) DEFINITIONS.—In this section—

(1) the term Chair means the Chairperson of the Interagency Committee designated under subsection (c)(2);

(2) the term Commandant means the Commandant of the Coast Guard;

(3) the term institution of higher education means an institution of higher education, as defined in section 101(a) of the Higher Education Act of 1965 (20 U.S.C. 1001(a));

(4) the term Interagency Committee means the Interagency Coordinating Committee on Oil Pollution Research established under subsection (b);

(5) the term Under Secretary means the Under Secretary of Commerce for Oceans and Atmosphere; and

(6) the term Vice Chair means the Vice Chairperson of the Interagency Committee designated under subsection (c)(3).

(b) ESTABLISHMENT OF INTERAGENCY COORDINATING COMMITTEE ON OIL POLLUTION RESEARCH.—

(1) ESTABLISHMENT.— There is established an Interagency Coordinating Committee on Oil Pollution Research.

(2) PURPOSE.— The Interagency Committee shall coordinate a comprehensive program of oil pollution research, technology development, and demonstration among the Federal agencies, in cooperation and coordination with industry, 4-year institutions of higher education and research institutions, State governments, and other nations, as appropriate, and shall foster cost-effective research mechanisms, including the joint funding of research.

(c) MEMBERSHIP.—

(1) COMPOSITION.—The Interagency Committee shall be composed of—

(A) at least 1 representative of the Coast Guard;

(B) at least 1 representative of the National Oceanic and Atmospheric Administration;

(C) at least 1 representative of the Environmental Protection Agency;

(D) at least 1 representative of the Department of the Interior;

(E) at least 1 representative of the Bureau of Safety and Environmental Enforcement;

(F) at least 1 representative of the Bureau of Ocean Energy Management;

(G) at least 1 representative of the United States Fish and Wildlife Service;

(H) at least 1 representative of the Department of Energy;

(I) at least 1 representative of the Pipeline and Hazardous Materials Safety Administration;

(J) at least 1 representative of the Federal Emergency Management Agency;

(K) at least 1 representative of the Navy;

(L) at least 1 representative of the Corps of Engineers;

(M) at least 1 representative of the United States Arctic Research Commission; and

(N) at least 1 representative of each of such other Federal agencies as the President considers to be appropriate.

(2) CHAIRPERSON.— The Commandant shall designate a Chairperson from among the members of the Interagency Committee selected under paragraph (1)(A).

(3) VICE CHAIRPERSON.— The Under Secretary shall designate a Vice Chairperson from among the members of the Interagency Committee selected under paragraph (1)(B).

(4) MEETINGS.—

(A) QUARTERLY MEETINGS.— At a minimum, the members of the Interagency Committee shall meet once each quarter.

(B) PUBLIC SUMMARIES.— After each meeting, a summary shall be made available by the Chair or Vice Chair, as appropriate.

(d) DUTIES OF THE INTERAGENCY COMMITTEE.—

(1) RESEARCH.—The Interagency Committee shall—

(A) coordinate a comprehensive program of oil pollution research, technology development, and demonstration among the Federal agencies, in cooperation and coordination with industry, 4-year institutions of higher education and research institutions, States, Indian tribes, and other countries, as appropriate; and

(B) foster cost-effective research mechanisms, including the joint funding of research and the development of public-private partnerships for the purpose of expanding research.

(2) OIL POLLUTION RESEARCH AND TECHNOLOGY PLAN.—

(A) IMPLEMENTATION PLAN.—Not later than 180 days after the date of enactment of the Elijah E. Cummings Coast Guard Authorization Act of 2020, the Interagency Committee shall submit to Congress a research plan to report on the state of oil discharge prevention and response capabilities that—

(i) identifies current research programs conducted by Federal agencies, States, Indian tribes, 4-year institutions of higher education, and corporate entities;

(ii) assesses the current status of knowledge on oil pollution prevention, response, and mitigation technologies and effects of oil pollution on the environment;

(iii) identifies significant oil pollution research gaps, including an assessment of major technological deficiencies in responses to past oil discharges;

(iv) establishes national research priorities and goals for oil pollution technology development related to prevention, response, mitigation, and environmental effects;

(v) assesses the research on the applicability and effectiveness of the prevention, response, and mitigation technologies to each class of oil;

(vi) estimates the resources needed to conduct the oil pollution research and development program established pursuant to subsection (e), and timetables for completing research tasks;

(vii) summarizes research on response equipment in varying environmental conditions, such as in currents, ice cover, and ice floes; and

(viii) includes such other information or recommendations as the Interagency Committee determines to be appropriate.

(B) ADVICE AND GUIDANCE.—

(i) NATIONAL ACADEMY OF SCIENCES CONTRACT.—The Chair, through the department in which the Coast Guard is operating, shall contract with the National Academy of Sciences to—

(I) provide advice and guidance in the preparation and development of the research plan;

(II) assess the adequacy of the plan as submitted, and submit a report to Congress on the conclusions of such assessment; and

(III) provide organization guidance regarding the implementation of the research plan, including delegation of topics and research among Federal agencies represented on the Interagency Committee.

(ii) NIST ADVICE AND GUIDANCE.— The National Institute of Standards and Technology shall provide the Interagency Committee with advice and guidance on issues relating to quality assurance and standards measurements relating to its activities under this section.

(C) 10-YEAR UPDATES.— Not later than 10 years after the date of enactment of the Elijah E. Cummings Coast Guard Authorization Act of 2020, and every 10 years thereafter, the Interagency Committee shall submit to Congress a research plan that updates the information contained in the previous research plan submitted under this subsection.

(e) OIL POLLUTION RESEARCH AND DEVELOPMENT PROGRAM.—

(1) ESTABLISHMENT.— The Interagency Committee shall coordinate the establishment, by the agencies represented on the Interagency Committee, of a program for conducting oil pollution research, technology, and development, as provided in this subsection.

(2) INNOVATIVE OIL POLLUTION TECHNOLOGY.—The program established under

paragraph (1) shall provide for research, development, and demonstration of new or improved technologies and methods that are effective in preventing, mitigating, or restoring damage from oil discharges and that protect the environment, including—

(A) development of improved designs for vessels and facilities, and improved operational practices;

(B) research, development, and demonstration of improved technologies to measure the ullage of a vessel tank, prevent discharges from tank vents, prevent discharges during lightering and bunkering operations, contain discharges on the deck of a vessel, prevent discharges through the use of vacuums in tanks, and otherwise contain discharges of oil from vessels and facilities;

(C) research, development, and demonstration of new or improved systems of mechanical, chemical, biological, and other methods (including the use of dispersants, solvents, and bioremediation) for the recovery, removal, and disposal of oil, including evaluation of the environmental effects of the use of such systems;

(D) research and training, in consultation with the National Response Team, to improve industry's and Government's ability to quickly and effectively remove an oil discharge, including the long-term use, as appropriate, of the National Spill Control School in Corpus Christi, Texas, and the Center for Marine Training and Safety in Galveston, Texas;

(E) research to improve information systems for decisionmaking, including the use of data from coastal mapping, baseline data, and other data related to the environmental effects of oil discharges, and cleanup technologies;

(F) development of technologies and methods to protect public health and safety from oil discharges, including the population directly exposed to an oil discharge;

(G) development of technologies, methods, and standards for protecting removal personnel, including training, adequate supervision, protective equipment, maximum exposure limits, and decontamination procedures;

(H) research and development of methods to restore and rehabilitate natural resources damaged by oil discharges;

(I) research to evaluate the relative effectiveness and environmental impacts of bioremediation technologies; and

(J) the demonstration of a satellite-based, dependent surveillance vessel traffic system in Narragansett Bay to evaluate the utility of such system in reducing the risk of oil discharges from vessel collisions and groundings in confined waters.

(3) OIL POLLUTION TECHNOLOGY EVALUATION.—The program established under paragraph (1) shall provide for oil pollution prevention and mitigation technology evaluation including—

(A) the evaluation and testing of technologies developed independently of the research and development program established under paragraph (1);

(B) the establishment, where appropriate, of standards and testing protocols traceable to national standards to measure the performance of oil pollution prevention or mitigation technologies; and

(C) the use, where appropriate, of controlled field testing to evaluate real-world application of oil discharge prevention or mitigation technologies.

(4) OIL POLLUTION EFFECTS RESEARCH.—(A) The Committee shall establish a research program to monitor and evaluate the environmental effects of acute and chronic oil discharges on coastal and marine resources (including impacts on protected areas such as sanctuaries) and protected species, and such program shall include the following elements:

(i) The development of improved models and capabilities for predicting the environmental fate, transport, and effects of oil discharges.

(ii) The development of methods, including economic methods, to assess damages to natural resources resulting from oil discharges.

(iii) Research to understand and quantify the effects of sublethal impacts of oil discharge on living natural marine resources, including impacts on pelagic fish species, marine mammals, and commercially and recreationally targeted fish and shellfish species.

(iv) The identification of types of ecologically sensitive areas at particular risk to oil discharges and the preparation of scientific monitoring and evaluation plans, one for each of several types of ecological conditions, to be implemented in the event of major oil discharges in such areas.

(v) The collection of environmental baseline data in ecologically sensitive areas at particular risk to oil discharges where such data are insufficient.

(vi) Research to understand the long-term effects of major oil discharges and the long-term effects of smaller endemic oil discharges.

(vii) The identification of potential impacts on ecosystems, habitat, and wildlife from the additional toxicity, heavy metal concentrations, and increased corrosiveness of mixed crude, such as diluted bitumen crude.

(viii) The development of methods to restore and rehabilitate natural resources and ecosystem functions damaged by oil discharges.

(B) The Department of Commerce in consultation with the Environmental Protection Agency shall monitor and scientifically evaluate the long-term environmental effects of oil discharges if—

(i) the amount of oil discharged exceeds 250,000 gallons;

(ii) the oil discharge has occurred on or after January 1, 1989; and

(iii) the Interagency Committee determines that a study of the long-term environmental effects of the discharge would be of significant scientific value, especially for preventing or responding to future oil discharges.

Areas for study may include the following sites where oil discharges have occurred: the New York/New Jersey Harbor area, where oil was discharged by an Exxon underwater pipeline, the T/B CIBRO SAVANNAH, and the M/V BT NAUTILUS; Narragansett Bay where oil was discharged by the WORLD

PRODIGY; the Houston Ship Channel where oil was discharged by the RACHEL B; the Delaware River, where oil was discharged by the PRESIDENTE RIVERA and the T/V ATHOS I, and Huntington Beach, California, where oil was discharged by the AMERICAN TRADER.

(C) Research conducted under this paragraph by, or through, the United States Fish and Wildlife Service shall be directed and coordinated by the National Wetland Research Center.

(5) MARINE SIMULATION RESEARCH.—The program established under paragraph (1) shall include research on the greater use and application of geographic and vessel response simulation models, including the development of additional data bases and updating of existing data bases using, among others, the resources of the National Maritime Research Center. It shall include research and vessel simulations for—

(A) contingency plan evaluation and amendment;

(B) removal and strike team training;

(C) tank vessel personnel training; and

(D) those geographic areas where there is a significant likelihood of a major oil discharge.

(6) DEMONSTRATION PROJECTS.— The United States Coast Guard, in conjunction with such agencies as the President may designate, shall conduct 4[7] port oil pollution minimization demonstration projects, one each with (A) the Port Authority of New York and New Jersey, (B) the Ports of Los Angeles and Long Beach, California,[7] (C) the Port of New Orleans, Louisiana, and (D) a port on the Great Lakes[7] for the purpose of developing and demonstrating integrated port oil pollution prevention and cleanup systems which utilize the information and implement the improved practices and technologies developed from the research, development, and demonstration program established in this section. Such systems shall utilize improved technologies and management practices for reducing the risk of oil discharges, including, as appropriate, improved data access, computerized tracking of oil shipments, improved vessel tracking and navigation systems, advanced technology to monitor pipeline and tank conditions, improved oil spill response capability, improved capability to predict the flow and effects of oil discharges in both the inner and outer harbor areas for the purposes of making infrastructure decisions, and such other activities necessary to achieve the purposes of this section.

[7] Section 2002(1) of P.L. 101–537 and section 4002(1) of P.L. 101–646 made almost identical amendments to section 7001(c)(6). The amendments made by P.L. 101–537 have been executed.

(7) SIMULATED ENVIRONMENTAL TESTING.—

(A) IN GENERAL.— Agencies represented on the Interagency Committee shall ensure the long-term use and operation of the Oil and Hazardous Materials Simulated Environmental Test Tank (OHMSETT) Research Center in New Jersey for oil pollution technology testing and evaluations.

(B) OTHER TESTING FACILITIES.— Nothing in subparagraph (A) shall be construed as limiting the ability of the Interagency Committee to contract or partner with a facility or facilities other than the Center described in subparagraph (A) for the purpose of oil pollution technology testing and evaluations, provided such a facility or facilities have testing and evaluation capabilities equal to or greater than those of such Center.

(C) IN-KIND CONTRIBUTIONS.—

(i) IN GENERAL.— The Secretary of the department in which the Coast Guard is operating and the Administrator of the Environmental Protection Agency may accept donations of crude oil and crude oil product samples in the form of in-kind contributions for use by the Federal Government for product testing, research and development, and for other purposes as the Secretary and the Administrator determine appropriate.

(ii) USE OF DONATED OIL.— Oil accepted under clause (i) may be used directly by the Secretary and shall be provided to other Federal agencies or departments through interagency agreements to carry out the purposes of this Act.

(8) REGIONAL RESEARCH PROGRAM.—(A) Consistent with the research plan in subsection (d), the Interagency Committee shall coordinate a program of competitive grants to universities or other research institutions, or groups of universities or research institutions, for the purposes of conducting a coordinated research program related to the regional aspects of oil pollution, such as prevention, removal, mitigation, and the effects of discharged oil on regional environments. For the purposes of this paragraph, a region means a Coast Guard district as set out in part 3 of title 33, Code of Federal Regulations (2010).

(B) The Interagency Committee shall coordinate the publication by the agencies represented on the Interagency Committee of a solicitation for grants under this subsection. The application shall be in such form and contain such information as may be required in the published solicitation. The applications shall be reviewed by the Interagency Committee, which shall make recommendations to the appropriate granting agency represented on the Interagency Committee for awarding the grant. The granting agency shall award the grants recommended by the Interagency Committee unless the agency decides not to award the grant due to budgetary or other compelling considerations and publishes its reasons for such a determination in the Federal Register. No grants may be made by any agency from any funds authorized for this paragraph unless such grant award has first been recommended by the Interagency Committee.

(C) Any university or other research institution, or group of universities or research institutions, may apply for a grant for the regional research program established by this paragraph. The applicant must be located in the region, or in a State a part of which is in the region, for which the project is proposed as part of the regional research program. With respect to a group application, the entity or entities which will carry out the substantial portion of the proposed research must be located in the region, or in a State a part of which is in the region, for which the project is proposed as part of the regional research program.

(D) The Interagency Committee shall make recommendations on grants in such a manner as to ensure an appropriate balance within a region among the various aspects of oil pollution research, including prevention, removal, mitigation, and the effects of discharged oil on regional environments. In addition, the Interagency Committee shall make recommendations for grants based on the following criteria:

(i) There is available to the applicant for carrying out this paragraph demonstrated research resources.

(ii) The applicant demonstrates the capability of making a significant contribution to regional research needs.

(iii) The projects which the applicant proposes to carry out under the grant are consistent with the research plan under subsection (d) and would further the objectives of the research and development program established in this section.

(E) Grants provided under this paragraph shall be for a period up to 3 years, subject to annual review by the granting agency, and provide not more than 80 percent of the costs of the research activities carried out in connection with the grant.

(F) No funds made available to carry out this subsection may be used for the acquisition of real property (including buildings) or construction of any building.

(G) Nothing in this paragraph is intended to alter or abridge the authority under existing law of any Federal agency to make grants, or enter into contracts or cooperative agreements, using funds other than those authorized in this Act for the purposes of carrying out this paragraph.

(9) FUNDING.— For each of the fiscal years 1991, 1992, 1993, 1994, and 1995, \$6,000,000 of amounts in the Fund shall be available to carry out the regional research program in paragraph (8), such amounts to be available in equal amounts for the regional research program in each region; except that if the agencies represented on the Interagency Committee determine that regional research needs exist which cannot be addressed within such funding limits, such agencies may use their authority under paragraph (10) to make additional grants to meet such needs. For the purposes of this paragraph, the research program carried out by the Prince William Sound Oil Spill Recovery Institute established under section 5001, shall not be eligible to receive grants under this paragraph until the authorization for funding under section 5006(b) expires.

(10) GRANTS.— In carrying out the research and development program established under paragraph (1), the Under Secretary may enter into contracts and cooperative agreements and make grants to universities, research institutions, and other persons, and States and Indian tribes. Such contracts, cooperative agreements, and grants shall address research and technology priorities set forth in the oil pollution research plan under subsection (d).

(11) In carrying out research under this section, the Department of Transportation shall continue to utilize the resources of the Pipeline and Hazardous Materials Safety Administration of the Department of Transportation, to the

maximum extent practicable.

(f) INTERNATIONAL COOPERATION.— In accordance with the research plan submitted under subsection (d), the Interagency Committee shall coordinate and cooperate with other nations and foreign research entities in conducting oil pollution research, development, and demonstration activities, including controlled field tests of oil discharges.

(g) BIENNIAL REPORTS.— The Chair shall submit to Congress every 2 years on October 30 a report on the activities carried out under this section in the preceding 2 fiscal years, and on activities proposed to be carried out under this section in the current 2 fiscal year period.

(h) FUNDING.—Not to exceed $22,000,000[8] of amounts in the Fund shall be available annually to carry out this section except for subsection (e)(8). Of such sums—

[8] Section 2002(2) of P.L. 101–537 and section 4002(2) of P.L. 101–646 made almost identical amendments to section 7001(f). The amendments made by P.L. 101–537 have been executed.

(1) funds authorized to be appropriated to carry out the activities under subsection (c)(4) shall not exceed $5,000,000 for fiscal year 1991 or $3,500,000 for any subsequent fiscal year; and

(2) not less than $3,000,000[8] shall be available for carrying out the activities in subsection (c)(6) for fiscal years 1992, 1993, 1994, and 1995.

All activities authorized in this section, including subsection (e)(8), are subject to appropriations.

[33 U.S.C. 2761]

SEC. 7002. SUBMERGED OIL PROGRAM.

(a) PROGRAM.—

(1) ESTABLISHMENT.—The Under Secretary of Commerce for Oceans and Atmosphere, in conjunction with the Commandant of the Coast Guard, shall establish a program to detect, monitor, and evaluate the environmental effects of submerged oil in the Delaware River and Bay region. The program shall include the following elements:

(A) The development of methods to remove, disperse, or otherwise diminish the persistence of submerged oil.

(B) The development of improved models and capacities for predicting the environmental fate, transport, and effects of submerged oil.

(C) The development of techniques to detect and monitor submerged oil.

(2) REPORT.— Not later than 3 years after the date of enactment of the Delaware River Protection Act of 2006, the Secretary of Commerce shall submit to the Committee on Commerce, Science, and Transportation of the Senate and the Committee on Transportation and Infrastructure of the House of Representatives a report on the activities carried out under this subsection and activities proposed to be carried out under this subsection.

(b) DEMONSTRATION PROJECT.—

(1) REMOVAL OF SUBMERGED OIL.— The Commandant of the Coast Guard, in conjunction with the Under Secretary of Commerce for Oceans and Atmosphere, shall conduct a demonstration project for the purpose of developing and demonstrating technologies and management practices to remove submerged oil from the Delaware River and other navigable waters.

(2) FUNDING.— There is authorized to be appropriated to the Commandant of the Coast Guard $2,000,000 for each of fiscal years 2006 through 2010 to carry out this subsection.

[33 U.S.C. 2762]

TITLE VII—TRANS-ALASKA PIPELINE SYSTEM

TITLE VIII—TRANS-ALASKA PIPELINE SYSTEM

SEC. 8001. SHORT TITLE.

This title may be cited as the "Trans-Alaska Pipeline System Reform Act of 1990".

Subtitle A—Improvements to Trans-Alaska Pipeline System

* * * * * * *

SEC. 8102. TRANS-ALASKA PIPELINE LIABILITY FUND.

(a) Termination of Certain Provisions.—

(1) * * *

(2) Disposition of fund balance.—

(A) Reservation of amounts.—The trustees of the Trans-Alaska Pipeline Liability Fund (hereafter in this subsection referred to as the TAPS Fund) shall reserve the following amounts in the TAPS Fund—

(i) necessary to pay claims arising under section 204(c) of the Trans-Alaska Pipeline Authorization Act (43 U.S.C. 1653(c)); and

(ii) administrative expenses reasonably necessary for and incidental to the implementation of section 204(c) of that Act.

(B) Disposition of the balance.—After the Comptroller General of the United States certifies that the requirements of subparagraph (A) have been met, the trustees of the TAPS Fund shall dispose of the balance in the TAPS Fund after the reservation of amounts are made under subparagraph (A) by—

(i) rebating the pro rata share of the balance to the State of Alaska for its contributions as an owner of oil, which, except as otherwise provided under article IX, section 15, of the Alaska Constitution, shall be used for the remediation of above-ground storage tanks; and then

(ii) transferring and depositing the remainder of the balance into the Oil Spill Liability Trust Fund established under section 9509 of the Internal Revenue Code of 1986 (26 U.S.C. 9509).

(C) Disposition of the reserved amounts.— After payment of all claims arising from an incident for which funds are reserved under subparagraph (A) and certification by the Comptroller General of the United States that the claims arising from that incident have been paid, the excess amounts, if any, for that incident shall be disposed of as set forth under subparagraphs (A) and (B).

(D) Authorization.— The amounts transferred and deposited in the Fund shall be available for the purposes of section 1012 of the Oil Pollution Act of 1990 after funding sections 5001 and 8103 to the extent that funds have not otherwise been provided for the purposes of such sections.

(3) SAVINGS CLAUSE.— The repeal made by paragraph (1) shall have no effect on any right to recover or responsibility that arises from incidents subject to section 204(c) of the Trans-Alaska Pipeline Authorization Act (43 U.S.C. 1653(c)) occurring prior to the date of enactment of this Act.

(4) * * *

(5) EFFECTIVE DATE.—(A) The repeal by paragraph (1) shall be effective 60 days after the date on which the Comptroller General of the United States certifies to the Congress that—

(i) all claims arising under section 204(c) of the Trans-Alaska Pipeline Authorization Act (43 U.S.C. 1653(c)) have been resolved,

(ii) all actions for the recovery of amounts subject to section 204(c) of the Trans-Alaska Pipeline Authorization Act have been resolved, and

(iii) all administrative expenses reasonably necessary for and incidental to the implementation of section 204(c) of the Trans-Alaska Pipeline Authorization Act have been paid.

(B) Upon the effective date of the repeal pursuant to subparagraph (A), the trustees of the TAPS Fund shall be relieved of all responsibilities under section 204(c) of the Trans-Alaska Pipeline Authorization Act, but not any existing legal liability.

(6) TUCKER ACT.— This subsection is intended expressly to preserve any and all rights and remedies of contributors to the TAPS Fund under section 1491 of title 28, United States Code (commonly referred to as the Tucker Act).

* * * * * * *

SEC. 8103. PRESIDENTIAL TASK FORCE.

(a) ESTABLISHMENT OF TASK FORCE.—

(1) ESTABLISHMENT AND MEMBERS.—(A) There is hereby established a Presidential Task Force on the Trans-Alaska Pipeline System (hereinafter referred to as the Task Force) composed of the following members appointed by the President:

(i) Three members, one of whom shall be nominated by the Secretary of the Interior, one by the Administrator of the Environmental Protection Agency, and one by the Secretary of Transportation.

(ii) Three members nominated by the Governor of the State of Alaska, one of whom shall be an employee of the Alaska Department of Natural Resources and one of whom shall be an employee of the Alaska Department of Environmental Conservation.

(iii) One member nominated by the Office of Technology Assessment.

(B) Any member appointed to fill a vacancy occurring before the expiration of the term for which his or her predecessor was appointed shall be appointed only for the remainder of such term. A member may serve after the expiration of his or her term until a successor, if applicable, has taken office.

(2) COCHAIRMEN.— The President shall appoint a Federal cochairman from

among the Federal members of the Task Force appointed pursuant to paragraph (1)(A) and the Governor shall designate a State cochairman from among the State members of the Task Force appointed pursuant to paragraph (1)(B).

(3) COMPENSATION.— Members shall, to the extent approved in appropriations Acts, receive the daily equivalent of the minimum annual rate of basic pay in effect for grade GS–15 of the General Schedule for each day (including travel time) during which they are engaged in the actual performance of duties vested in the Task Force, except that members who are State, Federal, or other governmental employees shall receive no compensation under this paragraph in addition to the salaries they receive as such employees.

(4) STAFF.— The cochairman of the Task Force shall appoint a Director to carry out administrative duties. The Director may hire such staff and incur such expenses on behalf of the Task Force for which funds are available.

(5) RULE.— Employees of the Task Force shall not, by reason of such employment, be considered to be employees of the Federal Government for any purpose.

(b) DUTIES OF THE TASK FORCE.—

(1) AUDIT.— The Task Force shall conduct an audit of the Trans-Alaska Pipeline System (hereinafter referred to as TAPS) including the terminal at Valdez, Alaska, and other related onshore facilities, make recommendations to the President, the Congress, and the Governor of Alaska.

(2) COMPREHENSIVE REVIEW.—As part of such audit, the Task Force shall conduct a comprehensive review of the TAPS in order to specifically advise the President, the Congress, and the Governor of Alaska concerning whether—

(A) the holder of the Federal and State right-of-way is, and has been, in full compliance with applicable laws, regulations, and agreements;

(B) the laws, regulations, and agreements are sufficient to prevent the release of oil from TAPS and prevent other damage or degradation to the environment and public health;

(C) improvements are necessary to TAPS to prevent release of oil from TAPS and to prevent other damage or degradation to the environment and public health;

(D) improvements are necessary in the onshore oil spill response capabilities for the TAPS; and

(E) improvements are necessary in security for TAPS.

(3) CONSULTANTS.—(A) The Task Force shall retain at least one independent consulting firm with technical expertise in engineering, transportation, safety, the environment, and other applicable areas to assist the Task Force in carrying out this subsection.

(B) Contracts with any such firm shall be entered into on a nationally competitive basis, and the Task Force shall not select any firm with respect to which there may be a conflict of interest in assisting the Task Force in carrying out the audit and review. All work performed by such firm shall be under the direct and immediate supervision of a registered engineer.

(4) PUBLIC COMMENT.—The Task Force shall provide an opportunity for public comment on its activities including at a minimum the following:

(A) Before it begins its audit and review, the Task Force shall review reports prepared by other Government entities conducting reviews of TAPS and shall consult with those Government entities that are conducting ongoing investigations including the General Accounting Office. It shall also hold at least 2 public hearings, at least 1 of which shall be held in a community affected by the Exxon Valdez oil spill. Members of the public shall be given an opportunity to present both oral and written testimony.

(B) The Task Force shall provide a mechanism for the confidential receipt of information concerning TAPS, which may include a designated telephone hotline.

(5) TASK FORCE REPORT.— The Task Force shall publish a draft report which it shall make available to the public. The public will have at least 30 days to provide comments on the draft report. Based on its draft report and the public comments thereon, the Task Force shall prepare a final report which shall include its findings, conclusions, and recommendations made as a result of carrying out such audit. The Task Force shall transmit (and make available to the public), no later than 2 years after the date on which funding is made available under paragraph (7), its final report to the President, the Congress, and the Governor of Alaska.

(6) PRESIDENTIAL REPORT.— The President shall, within 90 days after receiving the Task Force's report, transmit a report to the Congress and the Governor of Alaska outlining what measures have been taken or will be taken to implement the Task Force's recommendations. The President's report shall include recommended changes, if any, in Federal and State law to enhance the safety and operation of TAPS.

(7) EARMARK.— Of amounts in the Fund, $5,000,000 shall be available, subject to appropriations, annually without fiscal year limitation to carry out the requirements of this section.

(c) GENERAL ADMINISTRATION AND POWERS OF THE TASK FORCE.—

(1) AUDIT ACCESS.— The Comptroller General of the United States, and any of his or her duly appointed representatives, shall have access, for purposes of audit and examination, to any books, documents, papers, and records of the Task Force that are pertinent to the funds received and expended by the Task Force.

(2) TERMINATION.— The Task Force shall cease to exist on the date on which the final report is provided pursuant to subsection (b)(5).

(3) FUNCTIONS LIMITATION.— With respect to safety, operations, and other matters related to the pipeline facilities (as such term is defined in section 202(4) of the Hazardous Liquid Pipeline Safety Act of 1979) of the TAPS, the Task Force shall not perform any functions which are the responsibility of the Secretary of Transportation under the Hazardous Liquid Pipeline Safety Act of 1979, as amended. The Secretary may use the information gathered by and reports issued by the Task Force in carrying out the Secretary's responsibilities under that Act.

(4) POWERS.— The Task Force may, to the extent necessary to carry out its responsibilities, conduct investigations, make reports, issue subpoenas, require the production of relevant documents and records, take depositions, and conduct directly or, by contract, or otherwise, research, testing, and demonstration activities.

(5) EXAMINATION OF RECORDS AND PROPERTIES.— The Task Force, and the employees and agents it so designates, are authorized, upon presenting appropriate credentials to the person in charge, to enter upon, inspect, and examine, at reasonable times and in a reasonable manner, the records and properties of persons to the extent such records and properties are relevant to determining whether such persons have acted or are acting in compliance with applicable laws and agreements.

(6) FOIA.— The information gathered by the Task Force pursuant to subsection (b) shall not be subject to section 552 of title 5, United States Code (commonly referred to as the Freedom of Information Act), until its final report is issued pursuant to subsection (b)(6).

[43 U.S.C. 1651 note]

★

www.ingramcontent.com/pod-product-compliance
Lightning Source LLC
Chambersburg PA
CBHW061023220326
41597CB00019BB/3023